The Birthmark Memoirs of a Balinese Prince

The Birthmark. Memoirs of a Balinese Prince

Dr. A.A.M. Djelantik

PERIPLUS
EDITIONS

Published by Periplus Editions (HK) Ltd.

ISBN 962-593-165-1

Publisher: Eric M. Oey
Editor: Kim Inglis

Distributors

Indonesia
PT Wira Mandala Pustaka
(Java Books, Indonesia)
Jl. Kelapa Gading Kirana
Blok A-14 No. 17, Jakarta 14240

Australia
Bookwise International
54 Crittenden Rd., Findon, SA 5023

Singapore & Malaysia
Berkeley Books Pte Ltd
5 Little Road #08-01, Singapore 536983

USA
Charles E. Tuttle Co., Inc.
RRI Box 231-5, North Clarendon
VT 05759-9700

Printed in the Republic of Singapore

Contents

Preface and Acknowledgements

"You must write your biography!"

That advice has been given to me often since the early 1960s by wife whenever I would talk about Bali and changes on the island over the course of half a century.

"But how?" I asked myself. I had never written anything other than medical and technical reports. Moreover, during my years as Bali's Chief Medical Officer I had had no time for anything else apart from my professional duties. Then, in 1963, Mount Agung—the biggest and holiest mountain on Bali—erupted and I was in charge of disaster relief operations. Two years later, the political upheaval in the country in the wake of the abortive Communist coup, and the struggle for survival of the newly created Medical Faculty at Udayana University in Denpasar, demanded all of my time.

In 1968, our friends Len and Polly Doyle from Walnut Creek, California, proposed visiting Bali for three months with a tape-recorder in order to make up a book of my stories. It came to nothing, because at the end of the year I received permission from my Government to join the World Health Organization. For the next 11 years I worked as a WHO malariologist in the Philippines, Iraq, Somalia and Afghanistan, and was unavailable to work on the project.

Once I retired in the 1980s and was back in Bali, I was very soon involved in many social and cultural activities, and nor for one moment did I think about writing anything—and certainly not a biography. Then, the Oxford University Press asked me to write about Balinese paintings. Under pressure from my wife I reluctantly conceded. While working on the book, I found I enjoyed the writing process, and when the book was published in 1986, I felt that I might attempt the biography.

I asked advice from Len and Polly Doyle who 18 years earlier had taken the initiative to approach a publisher on my behalf. Their reaction was enthusiastic and Polly, herself a writer, volunteered to help me with my English. Since then, she has looked over every finished chapter and returned it to me with her corrections. It is therefore appropriate to acknowledge my deep gratitude to her for all the hours she spent correcting my spelling and usage of English, for all the efforts she—at the age of 80—took to mail the chapters, and last but not least, for her continuous encouragement which was of tremendous help and imbued me with the love of writing.

Due to circumstances, progress was very slow. I had to make use of any spare time to write, in between patients' consultations and other priorities. Often weeks passed without any writing and the postal service between Denpasar and Walnut Creek, was not always as fast as we wished. During the slow process, other friends supported me with their comments after reading chapters that I randomly referred to them—Andy Toth, ethnomusicologist, at present Consul for the USA in Denpasar; the writer Stuart Wilber, and painter John Breitweiser, frequent visitors to Bali, and especially to our Puri in Karangasem; and Dr Adrian Vickers, author of *Bali: A Paradise Created* (Periplus Editions, Singapore, 1989). To them I feel deeply indebted for their thoughtfulness and sympathy and for showing to me nuances in style so important in expressing what one wants to tell to the reader.

Suzanne Charlé, who devoted an article on me in her *Illustrated Guide to Bali* (The Guidebook Company Ltd, Hongkong, 1990) and later also from Idanna Pucci, author of the book about the Royal Court House in Klungkung, *The Epic of Life, the Balinese Journey of the Soul* (Alfred van der Marck Editions, New York, 1985) also gave me much encouragement. Very special thanks to Idanna, who helped me with the problem of how to end my book. Her suggestion was that I should try to remember a scene that had taken place after at the same spot as where I started my stories. Such a scene had indeed happened and it came at one moment unexpectedly as a flash into my mind. On that inspiration I wrote the epilogue.

I am also immensely indebted for the technical assistance given by my friend Prof. Hedi Hinzier of Leiden University, Holland, who spent hours and hours before her computer, transcribing my manuscript. I am also indebted to Dr. Jacob Vredenbrecht, the University's Representative for Asia in Jakarta, for facilitating the transfer of the manuscript to and fro between Denpasar and Leiden.

Last but not least, my thanks go to my dear wife Astri, who read each chapter carefully and pointed to me those passages where she felt that my storytelling did not flow smoothly or put a strain to the reader's imagination. Many times I had to rewrite sections of the text before submitting it to Polly Doyle.

That was how this book came into being.

Dr A. A. M. Djelantik, 1997

Foresight

Early in the 1920s soccer was already popular in Bali. The "Dayaks" in the Badung area were the most famous among the various soccer clubs. Enthusiasm for the game quickly spilled over to the smaller towns.

The game fascinated the youth also. As small children we were filled with delight when we obtained a rubber ball—still a rare commodity—to play with. When we did not have this luxury, we used to make our own footballs from paper crumpled together and held in shape with strings. The other alternative was to steal a young unripe grapefruit from a tree. We played barefoot, as we always were, and our playgrounds were not on lawns or grass fields, but the barren and dusty open spaces found in one of the compounds of our Puri.

What is a Puri? In Bali it is a princely court which is divided into a number of compounds depending on the size of the family, more specifically on the number of wives of the Prince. A separate compound is assigned to each of the wives where each will live with her own children and servants. In addition, there are specific yards for the living quarters of the Prince, his reception buildings, courtyards for ceremonies, lodgings for guests and, most important, the sacred grounds of the family temple. Wives of higher caste usually have their compounds closer to those of the Prince. In our case, the compounds at the lower areas to the South were assigned to lower caste wives, the Sudras, to which my eldest brother Gedé's mother, Mekelé Trena; my younger brother Ketut's mother, Mekelé Wiraga; and my own mother, Mekelé Selaga belonged.

One day during vacation time in Karangasem we were playing in the highest of spirits with a new rubber ball on a small yard between three buildings of Mekelé. Trena's compound. Because the place was too small for a real game we were just kicking the ball in turns towards a goalkeeper who had his goal marked between two trees. At an unfortunate moment the ball bounced against one of the trees and flew onto the lower porch of the central main building of the compound. Father was sitting on the floor within, conversing with a very impressive looking visitor clad in white, perhaps a priest or a famous *balian* (believed to possess magic powers). In the enthusiasm of our play none of us had noticed that Father had arrived. Tossing a football, which had been played with and thus had been in contact with the lowest parts of our bodies, over the heads of Father and his guest was of course against all rules of court etiquette. I was panicking because I felt guilty for being the offender. This was unmistakably expressed by the looks of Father's attendants who were seated nearby.

I felt responsible for getting the ball back, so gathering all my courage I managed to come near to the porch and saw that the ball had landed in the corner behind the guest's back. Stammering a few words of apology, I asked permission to retrieve the ball, which Father gave immediately without even looking up at me. He was occupied with some texts of the *lontar*, a traditional Balinese palm leaves book. Being trained in courtly etiquette, I crawled on hands and feet to retrieve the ball. It was considered improper to walk erectly nearby a sitting person of higher rank. Having at last retrieved the ball I sat down and put it on my lap, made with both hands the appropriate *sembah* or gesture of reverence, and tried to get away as quickly as possible. But suddenly the wise old man grabbed my arm, looked into my eyes most ominously—it seemed to me—and touched my father's knee with his hand, saying: "Wait, look here, is this a son of yours?" I saw Father look up at me who was trembling with fear and heard him saying half laughingly: "Yes!". But then, impressed by the man's intense look, he curiously asked: "What is the matter?"

The *balian* pulled me closer to Father and said: "I feel as if there is something peculiar about this boy. It seems to me that he is destined to meet many dangers in his life, and to live through many adventures, but he will not be harmed, he will always survive unscathed. Don't be afraid!" My father looked most unbelievingly and asked: "How do you know?" Then the *balian* pulled me still closer and pointed at a black spot on my skin, a birthmark which was located exactly in between my clavicles. Puzzled, my father looked at it for a while but kept silent. Perhaps out of politeness, he did not want to show his disbelief, and he went on reading the *lontar* texts. That cut short the agonizing session, and very much relieved I ran away with the precious rubber ball.

I was then just seven years old and the incident was soon forgotten. For many many years, at first during the primary school years in Denpasar, then during the four years in Malang and later for three years in Yogyakarta, I had never for one moment thought of it. It was actually when as a medical student in Holland, I met with my first real adventure involving life and death in World War II during the German occupation, that I remembered the scene. Many other extraordinary experiences would follow later, both in Indonesia as well as in other parts of the world. And, as a matter of fact, I have more than once looked in the mirror to see if the black spot was still there...

BOOK I

Childhood in Karangasem and Denpasar

CHAPTER 1

Crows

No photograph of my mother exists so I do not know what she looked like. She died when I was still too young to be able to retain any memory from that period, but I must have been three years old when I had my first extraordinary experience. The remarkable story, related to me later by several witnesses, indicated that I was at the time already able to speak words and short sentences sensibly. That story was about a sort of hallucination which I must have had at the precise moment when my mother died.

Infant mortality and maternal death at childbirth were still very high in those days in Bali. My younger brother, Nengah, died before his first *odalan* (the 210th day after birth). The tragic event occurred after craftsmen had just finished applying *prada*, thin gold leaf to beautiful ornamental drawings on a new cloth, which was to be used at that *odalan* ceremony. A Western-educated Ambonese doctor, Dr Latumeten, who had attended the childbirth, advised my father that he should prevent my mother from having another baby because of the risk of excessive haemorrhage. Methods of birth control as we know of today were not yet known. Most probably, traditional Balinese methods had been applied, but without success. In any case very soon after Nengah's death my mother was pregnant again and eventually another boy was born. This time no medical doctor was at hand. Only several *balians* and traditional midwives, some of whom were permanently attached to our Puri, attended. As usual on such occasions, the presence of so many "experts" only increased the confusion if something abnormal occurred.

My elder sister, Ayu Manik, who later told me the story, was then already six years old. She remembered having seen an immense crowd on our porch and many servants running to and fro with water and pots. Out of curiosity she managed to thrust herself through the crowd and into the bedroom where the delivery took place. She was just in time to see that Mother was squatting on the floor in the traditional way of giving birth, holding with both hands a thick rope which was hanging from the ceiling. She was supported in the back by two women attendants. A man, the traditional midwife (even today traditional midwives in Bali are men) was kneeling in front of her, apparently working on the placenta. She could hear a baby crying somewhere. While she was standing there overwhelmed by the confusion, she saw Mother suddenly letting loose the rope, gasping for breath, as life ebbed away. When she told me this years later, she realized that she had been too confused at the time to be impressed by what she saw. She had no chance to realize what happened, since people hushed her away out of the room and she fled to where I was with my nanny.

At that late night hour, I had been carried away by our nanny, Dadong Madé, my mother's aunt, who tried to get me to sleep in her arms by walking up and down on the verandah of the kitchen building opposite our house, humming nursery rhymes while curiously looking at the nervous crowd. There, suddenly I cried out while pointing with both my arms to the roof of our house: "Eee, eke, ...eee..., *goak*... *goaak*... *goaaak*, liu *goakéé*, ...*Mek pelaibangé*.... *Mek pelaibangé*...!". ("Look, look, crows, crows...many crows, they are carrying Mother away...!".

According to Dadong Madé, I was all the time crying, pointing to the roof and crying out the same words again and again. All the people around were amazed and became frightened, because, no matter how carefully they looked and looked there was nothing to be seen, nothing on the roof nor anything in the sky above the house. Their first suspicion was that I was under the power of some evil spirit and hastily one of the *balians* was called to attend to me with *tirta* (holy or blessed water) and mantras (magic formulas).

Soon, some of them had already dismissed the scene as a small child's fit of temperament. How great was their astonishment when moments later word passed around that my mother had just died because of excessive blood loss. Our *balians* and midwives nursed the baby, but he was born premature and was very weak. They managed to keep him alive for twelve days only.

It was decided by Father that my elder sister and myself were to be adopted by Mekelé Trena, the mother of Father's eldest son, Gedé Djelantik, and taken into her house. She had just a few months before lost her second son in very extraordinary circumstances and to console her she was given another younger brother for Gedé. Although in theory each mother was assigned her own compound, my mother had been given only a separate house and had had to share the compound of Mekelé Trena whom Father had married five years earlier. There with Mekelé Trena I was to stay as a faithful younger brother and follower of Gedé to whom I became wholly devoted. With him I was to go everywhere, at first to school in Denpasar, later to Malang and to Yogyakarta. My adventurous nature, however, later led to our paths diverging...

CHAPTER 2

A Loyalty Test

In those olden days all kinds of people came to the Puris to offer their services, both temporary and on a more or less permanent basis. Those who were lucky enough to be accepted on the latter terms found in the Puri a safe home, a loose sort of employment and, in the eyes of their own people in their village, they gained a certain prestige. The degree of prestige conformed to the status the noble family enjoyed in the eyes of the community.

In our Puri, the Puri Kanginan of Karangasem, a whole range of deliberations preceded acceptance to service. These deliberations involved assessment of their caste, their skills, earlier relationship to the Puri and village of origin. Only when these considerations were met satisfactorily would they be assigned to one of our mothers, who had to provide them with food and housing. When necessary and if space was available, a new house would be built for them. There was no specific scheme by which certain numbers of certain kinds of personnel were employed. All took place in a casual manner, without any contract or written agreement. They were also free to leave at any time, but this was a rare occurence. Once they were accepted, they became part of the extended Puri family although they remained subordinates from whom first of all loyalty was expected. Thus, in the course of time, a community established itself consisting of an assortment of *parekans* in the Puri, ranging from gardeners, bodyguards, cooks, errand boys and girls, but also craftsmen and craftswomen such as weavers, painters, architects, dance teachers and musicians, and—most respected of all—a couple of *balians*, traditional medicine men and women.

Among these *balians*, one who was respected most by all of us, young and old alike, was a middle-aged *dalang* (a puppeteer, who usually performs the shadow play, the *wayang*). He was a Brahman, Ida Bagus Ketut Bergah from Gria Pidada, and he occupied a house on the southwest corner of the compound of Mekelé Wiraga. Because of his profession, Wa-tut—as we called him—knew all the ancient stories of the *Ramayana* and the *Mahabharata* and he became our most beloved story-teller. He was called upon to perform the *wayang* on all religious occasions in the Puri at which such a performance was required. Of course we never missed those occasions. Since such performances usually lasted for the whole night we watched them sitting or hanging in the arms of our nannies or lying on their laps. During the performances we were either intermittently awake, half asleep or in a deep sound sleep, while the sounds of the *genders* (metallophonic instruments accompanying the *wayang*) and the recitations by the *dalang* were constantly penetrating into our subconscious. The next morning, we usually found ourselves awakening on our mats in our bedrooms. Our fantasies were still filled with the adventures—good deeds of gods and semi-gods, awkward behaviour of demons, curses by saints, fierce battles and intriguing miracles—all seen as flickering shadows on the screen the night before. But, at least in my case, the images evoked in my mind were more lively due to the vivid way in which Wa-tut related the stories.

Every evening we went to his quarters at Mekelé Wiraga's compound, where we formed an odd circle around him. The younger ones climbed on his thighs and knees, the older ones either sitting by themselves on the floor or on the laps of servants, or lying on the floor in a scattered manner, trying to be as close as possible to Wa-tut. (Those days we had no chairs in the house, the men sat on the floor cross-legged, the women with both legs astride.) Our servants' children who were also our playmates used to form the perimeter of the circle. And there, in the half dark, under the light of a flickering oil lamp with such an attentive audience around him, night after night the *dalang* told, the stories from the epics, carrying us all away into those regions of magic wonder and delight. As if performing the *wayang*, but then using only his hands instead of puppets, gesticulating and mimicking, he aroused our imagination with such intensity that all the characters of the Pandawas, the Korawas, of Rama, Sita and Laksmana, Hanuman, Sugriwa and Subali and all the others, came alive, became for us real and palpable. It was no wonder then that some of us gradually arrived at the point of identifying ourselves with one or other of the *wayang* characters. That happened beyond doubt with my elder brother, Gedé, and myself.

As was expected from a younger brother, I became a devoted follower of Gedé, his servant brother and errand boy, who was always standing by, and did everything he ordered. On his part, he was and still is a good, gentle, kind and truly loving elder brother, who from those early years already had an unfailing confidence in me. We were most impressed by the noble character of Rama, who was the personification of goodness, mercy and *dharma*, and by the loyalty of his younger brother Laksmana who was the personification of truth, faith, honesty and chivalry. As young as we still were, we wanted to behave and to be in daily life as Rama and Laksmana. We were always together, inseparably attached to each other. In his role as Rama, Gedé was always and everywhere in front, the first, immediately followed by Laksmana, myself. This was in itself nothing unusual, and was in accordance with puri etiquette.

But it meant for us much more than that. Gedé *was* always gentle, kind, soft-spoken. And I was always the faithful servant, vigilant and ready to help with everything, ready even for combat if needed. Indeed, I did my best to be dependable at all times. We slept together, which meant Gedé at the upper end of the bed, I at the lower end, and if there was the luxury of a mattress, I took care that Gedé slept on it and I on the mat at the side, so that he was on the higher and I on the lower level. Hierarchy and etiquette were so well ingrained in us that such kind of differences were not felt as discrimination but as something entirely natural. When we ate together it meant that Gedé had to eat first to satisfaction, and when he stopped eating he would take care that there was some food left on his plate which was then handed over to me to finish. The plate would be replenished for me to eat to satisfaction. Leaving a leftover, a *lungsuran* on one's plate after eating was a meaningful act. It created a bond between the first and the next consumer, and it often happened that a *lungsuran* of somebody who was considered holy or possessing magic powers, had the effect of medicine. The passing on of a *lungsuran* should, of course, conform to the existing hierarchical order.

The whole Puri community were very pleased seeing us assuming the roles of Rama and Laksmana. I was old enough to draw this conclusion from the encouraging remarks they made every time they saw us together. Gedé's mother was happy to see that Gedé was always accompanied and protected by a faithful younger brother and that Gedé was indeed developing into a personification of *dharma*, emanating kindness and patience everywhere all the time. He became an idol to everybody, not in the least to Father. But I don't think that anybody realized the intensity of our spiritual bond. On my part, that feeling was so intense that it often came to the point of being ridiculous. It was in my character to assume that our togetherness was an absolute must and I came to demand from him togetherness all the time. I could not tolerate Gedé's getting up early in the morning while I was still too sleepy to move; he had to go back to bed and wait for me. On ceremonial occasions when we had to be presented to the public in full princely ceremonial dress I demanded to have the same clothes as Gedé. Later in my life I had to hear many of these stories about my egotism, presented to me by elder people in a humorous fashion.

One can imagine the shock when one day I learned that Gedé had to leave Karangasem to enter the "Hollands Inlandse School" (Dutch Indonesian Primary School) in Denpasar, which would bring an end to our bond. At that time Father was already running his own "school" in the Puri, where we were instructed in the basics of reading and writing in the Latin script and the Malay language. I was still too young to have any interest in the school, but because Gedé was attending, I joined the class without participating in the lessons, only to be near Gedé. Our tutor was a Brahman from Selat, who had finished at a teachers' college after the Primary Malay School in Karangasem. I hated him secretly because I felt how much he resented my sitting there just looking and playing and often disturbing the other children. He could not send me away because of Gedé, the Crown Prince, who was three years older than I, and was a diligent pupil who made good progress. One day, the *Controleur* (the official representing the Dutch Government) of Karangasem advised my father that if Gedé was to become Father's successor as *Stedehouder* of Karangasem, he should attend a regular school with an officially recognized curriculum including the Dutch language, which would open possibilities for further study later on. Father, who was very responsive to such suggestions, decided that Gedé had to go to the H. I. S. in Denpasar. Somehow as a result of earlier advice by the Resident (the Dutch official superior to the *Controleur*) our elder sister, Ayu Djelantik, daughter of Mekelé Wiraga, was already at the "Europese Lagere School" (Dutch Primary School) in Singaraja. At the E.L.S., only the Dutch language was instructed; at the H.I.S. the Malay and Balinese languages were also taught. This was considered more appropriate for Gedé's future career.

I felt that our bond, the bond between Rama and Laksmana, was in danger. When I asked my stepmother Mekelé Trena if I could also go to Denpasar, I was rebuffed forthwith because I was still too young. To put the same question to Father was too great an endeavour which was unthinkable for me. I was just too afraid. I felt, however, that if Gedé would ask on my behalf, Father would perhaps give his approval. A request from his Crown Prince might be difficult for him to refuse. Thus I asked Gedé if I would be allowed to go with him to Denpasar since Laksmana could not be separated from Rama.

"And do you intend to go also to school with me?" Gedé asked with some doubt in his voice.

"Of course!", was my answer, although in my heart I was afraid that the teacher in Denpasar would send me right away out of the classroom.

"Are you really sure?"

"Yes, sure", I replied, and added seriously: "I will do anything you demand to prove that I am sincere."

After some hesitation Gedé said: "All right then, I, Rama, will put you to a test, which will prove your loyalty!"

"All right, do as you like!" I was mentally prepared to endure anything.

"Well, I will urinate on your head, and you will not move, nor cry a bit," Gedé pronounced solemnly.

"As you like, my brother Rama!" I replied.

We chose as the appropriate place for this solemn ritual a big stone under an old frangipani tree near the Balé Malang, an elevated empty building, vacated after the death of Father's elder sister who had been living there before. The edge of its high verandah was conveniently right above that big stone. That stone is still there now. It was actually a tomb. Underneath was buried a black *petu* (long-armed monkey) who had been domesticated. One day about five years before somehow the monkey grabbed Gedé's little six-month-old baby brother Rai out of his cradle which was standing in the front porch of Mekelé Trena's house. He climbed with the little baby in his arms high up in the frangipani tree. Instead of quietly calling the monkey back to the grounds the people in the Puri panicked and chased after him, shouting and threatening with sticks and stones. Frightened, the monkey dropped the baby from the highest top of the tree. Eventually the *petu* was captured.

Since this special monkey for some unknown reason was considered a "holy" animal, an ad-hoc council of wise men was formed. After long deliberations a death sentence was pronounced. The poor monkey was executed with the kris and buried at the spot where he had dropped the baby. A huge stone was placed on his grave. The big tombstone was awe-inspiring in itself, as if fraught with magic power. Its sacredness was evident to everyone since offerings were laid on it every *kliwon* day of the five-day week. On special occasions we saw special small ceremonies being performed around it. Physically it was an effort for a five-year-old child to climb on top of the slippery stone, but some bold courage was also needed for such action. Somehow I managed to position myself standing on top of the sanctuary and facing the verandah where Gedé was already standing and preparing himself for his part in this performance. I brought both my hands in the proper *mustika* gesture (a gesture of meditation and concentration, which consists of holding the right hand as a fist with the thumb upwards against the middle of the chest, while the left hand, also with the thumb upwards encircles the right hand, so that the two thumbs together form a peak standing in the middle.)

With bowed head I waited for things to come. When I felt Gedé's urine splashing on my head I was exalted, nearly in a kind of ecstasy. I still clearly remember the sour salty taste of the liquid when I curiously ran my tongue over my lips. I felt as if Gedé had produced litres of liquid, because my shirt and pants were thoroughly wet. When the ceremony was over Gedé praised me and hugged me tenderly. He promised to ask Father for me to accompany him to Denpasar. My happiness was indescribable.

The immediate sequence of that ceremony was however very hard for me to swallow. Gedé's mother was furious with me for dirtying my clothes, and despite Gedé's explanations I got a number of nasty and painful *iluts* (a strong and twisting pinch in the thigh which was as painful or even more painful than a beating. As it was not customary to give a child, especially one of high rank, a slap or a beating as punishment *iluts* were given instead).

Father on the contrary was very impressed by the story of the ceremony and agreed with Gedé's request that I would go with Gedé to Denpasar and also enter the H.I.S. with him. I had withstood the test and was extremely happy.

CHAPTER 3

The Perils of Princehood

Whether my father in his earlier years of service had fully realized the limita-tions which Dutch rule imposed on his sovereignty as Raja of Karangasem must remain a matter of conjecture. The advisory role of the Dutch Govern-ment's representative on the spot, the so-called *Controleur*, was executed in a most tactful manner. To all appearances Father could regard himself as a Raja, ruling over the Kingdom of Karangasem, and what was more relevant, the people of the Region, unaware of politics, saw him as the traditional monarch.

Fortunately he was by nature a man of great intelligence and humour, and never had the inclination to accumulate personal power or riches for himself. The Dutch Government found in him the ideal personality to put into effect the then newly introduced "ethical policy" of its colonial administration.

The benefits of this policy for the population were soon apparent and resulted in the enhancement of Father's prestige. His honesty and modest attitude created a paternal relationship of love between him and his people. This spiritual bond was skillfully exploited by the Dutch to introduce modern administration in public affairs, such as tax regulations, building of roads, irrigation works, schools and hospitals. Later, Father told me that he regarded those initial years as his school years, since he had never had the opportunity to pursue formal education in any school. Gradually he took over the initiatives from his Dutch advisor. Service to his land and people was his maxim. He soon found recognition even among the rival courts and the formerly politically involved noble families of Karangasem.

The shrewd political manoeuvres of his late uncle and predecessor Gedé Djelantik, which resulted in the temporary exile of potential claimants to the throne, receded into oblivion due to the spectacular progress in the Region.

Our Puri became not only the centre of political power but also of the arts and literature and was honoured by frequent visits of priests and spiritual lead-ers from all over Bali and later also from Java. Even the Indian philosopher

Rabindranath Tagore spent a few weeks in the early 1920s in the Puri to enjoy its literature and poetry.

Lineage has always been an important occupation in the minds of the Balinese nobility. It is decisive in the hierarchical ranking of persons, and for any ruling Raja the continuity of his own lineage was paramount.

It has never been disclosed why my father had not married a girl from one of the many noble families in Karangasem or elsewhere in Bali, where there was plenty of choice and ample opportunities presented themselves. Instead he chose as his first wife a *Sudra* (lower caste) girl who died before she had her first baby. His second wife was also a *Sudra* girl. She came from the village of Asak, a village with a strong pre-Hinduistic Bali tradition.

In deviation from the prevailing Hindu Javanese court tradition, which decreed that only a son born from a noblewoman could become a Crown Prince, Father vowed that any first son of his would be his successor, without regard for the mother's caste. Unfortunately Mekelé Wiraga gave birth to four girls in succession. (Mekelé is the title given to a nobleman's wife of lower caste). That was of course very disappointing, not only for Father, but also for the village of Asak.

It was of great importance for a village in Bali if one of its beauties was chosen by a Raja to be his wife, even though many wives might have been chosen before her. The existence of a family tie with the Palace used to enhance the prestige of the village. It brought many advantages, such as privileges in land use or other special treatment. More advantages were bestowed to the village if the girl happened to become the mother of the Crown Prince. It was there-fore no wonder that on great occasions like temple festivals where the Raja was invit-ed, care was taken that the most beautiful maidens were mobilized to serve as attendants to bring food and drinks to the guests in order to be seen.

This was however not always the case. There were horrible stories from ear-lier times regarding the Kingdom of Bangli, where the Raja was notoriously cruel and unpopular. The villagers used to hide their girls on such occasions, and often the beautiful girls had their earlobes sliced through in order to become imperfect and thus escape the danger of being chosen.

Father, who was not only kindhearted but also a very handsome young man, must have often had a difficult time making up his mind. There were just too many choices for him! When Mekelé Wiraga had her fourth daughter great pressure was put on him from all sides to marry a third wife who might bear him a son and thus secure the continuity of the Dynasty. His choice fell on a beau-tiful girl from Butus, a very poor hamlet at the foot of Mount Agung. She was brought to the Puri and became Mekelé Trena.

For six consecutive years traditional medicine and magic had been applied without success to Mekelé Wiraga in efforts to change the course of nature. One after another a succession of famous *balians* and magicians, coming from all over the Karangasem region, were temporarily housed in Mekelé Wiraga's compound. Unfortunately the fifth baby was another girl. At about the same time Mekelé Trena gave birth to a son, named Wayan. The baby died after six days, despite all the efforts of the *balians* in the Puri to save him. There was no medical doctor attending, so that the cause of his death was not known. There was, of course, much gossip about black magic, and suspicion was naturally directed towards the mysterious people who were active in the compound of Mekelé Wiraga.

One year later Mekelé Trena gave birth to another son, Gedé Djelantik. The Butus clan rejoiced. Father took no chances and invited a renowned *balian*, a healer priest from Sidemen, associated with the famous *balian* clan of Sanur near Denpasar, to become his court physician. He resided in Mekelé Trena's compound, where a special *balé pawedan* (building for daily prayers) was erected for him. In order to be close to Gedé at night his bed was placed on Mekelé Trena's front porch.

My memories about him dated from several years later, when he was already a permanent staff member of our puri. The healer priest did not have that impressive and mysterious appearance as his reputation would suggest. His short and stout figure was crowned by a strikingly big round head with grey hair, a short moustache and a thin white beard. What I remember of him as most striking were his eyes, which were grey, not black like all of us have, and which looked so friendly and absorbing that everybody felt comfortable in his presence. The sick felt better as soon as he entered the room. At least that was the case with me each time when he was consulted on my behalf. I can't remember why among us, princely children, he received the nickname of "Kacang" (which meant "peanut"), but most probably it was just the small children's poor pronunciation of the word "Kakiyang" (meaning "Grand Uncle") by which we were told to address him. However, "Kacang" found it funny and encouraged us to stick to it.

Gedé Djelantik, the Crown Prince, was entrusted to his personal care throughout the years. There were many stories of alarming illnesses and of miraculous healings during that time. Gedé was of frail health indeed and was very often sick. The Butus clan which was represented in great numbers in the Puri naturally blamed the Asak people of wrongdoings. But Kacang would never show any indication of suspicion. Years later, he explained to me his theory: if there was any evil intention in people, it should be understood as workings of evil forces from outside, from somewhere in the cosmos. The duty of the *balian* was to fight those evil forces, not the people who were supposed to be bad, for they were themselves the victims of those forces.

Kacang's wisdom, however, could not alleviate the tenacious superstition prevailing among the Puri population. Suspicions, particularly entertained by Mekelé Trena and her Butus clan towards certain occupants of the adjacent compound of Mekelé Wiraga, remained very strong. One day a stray cat jumped over the wall between the two compounds onto the roof of Mekelé Trena's house. A boy of the Butus family happened to see the cat jumping and was struck by that extraordinary event. Considering the great distance between the wall and the roof it was indeed a remarkable feat. As regularly happens in Bali at the sight of something unusual, the boy was so frightened that he saw the cat having powerful wings. He became hysterical. Alarmed, the men from Butus went after the cat with sticks, lances and swords. Bapa Badung, Mekelé Trena's younger brother who had participated in the hunt, later told me his version of the story.

According to him, the cat was soon cornered and two of the men hit the animal several times with their lances. He could not believe what he saw: the cat's skin just yielded to the sharp steel like elastic, there was no wound, and there was no blood to be seen. And suddenly the cat disappeared, it was just no more there.

Later, Bapa Badung revealed to us more about the origin of the mysterious cats. One of the magicians who was applying magic on Mekelé Wiraga to make her bear a son, was a female priest from Lombok, Pedanda Istri Gianyar. She was especially powerful, exercising white as well as black magic, depending on the purpose for which her power was sought. She had also the task to take care of Mekelé Wiraga's fourth daughter, Ayu Madé. One day somebody heard by chance Ayu Madé, who was then about four years old, laughing and asking Pedanda Istri Gianyar: "Biyang, how is it that these cats are coming in and out from under your skirt, where do they come from? Look, look, there they are, look, look,... hey, where are they...they have gone... How did you do it?"

Innocently the boy told other people what he had heard. So the Butus people came to know the story. A boy was sent to spy on the woman. He followed the Pedanda Istri walking at dusk to the far southwest corner of the compound. There she sat down on the ground with her knees far apart, she stroked gently over her lower belly and as if out of her womb a dozen of cats emerged from under her skirt into the dim light. They dispersed in all directions, silently, without a *meow*. Early at dawn the woman returned to the same spot, and soon the cats came from all sides to her. She sat down, lifted her skirt and one by one the cats reentered her womb.

When Kacang heard the story he tried to reassure the people that the priestess had perhaps just been playing a game with the child. He could not believe that a *pedanda*, a priest, would engage herself in black magic.

Some time later Gedé was again very sick. This time he had an immensely swollen belly and he was very short of breath. Everybody in the compound was tense and nervous. One evening Mekelé Trena was sitting in her room with sick Gedé lying on her lap. Outside the room on the porch, just near the door, Kacang sat on the edge of his bed, anxiously watching the breathing of the child. Out of the dark emerged Pedanda Istri Gianyar and placed herself squarely in the door opening. Kacang found it strange that she passed near him without paying the customary reverence. She remained for a long time standing in the doorway with both hands reaching up holding onto the door posts, while staring ominously at Mekelé Trena and her child. Then, still without saying a word, she moved slowly forward and reached out to take the baby in her arms. It was then that Kacang realized that the woman was in a state of trance, for him a sure sign that she was exercising black magic. He sprang up, grabbed her with both arms from behind, just in time to prevent her from touching the baby. He held her fast, and strangely enough, there was no struggle, but Kacang suddenly felt his arms falling limp. Pedanda Istri Gianyar turned round and, still in a state of somnambulance, walked slowly out of the room and disappeared into the darkness. Kacang dragged himself to his bed on the porch.

Some minutes later Father came along to inquire after Gedé's condition and found to his surprise Kacang lying on his bed. That was quite contrary to what he had expected, because it was still very early in the evening. Kacang should still be attending Gedé at such an hour. He stepped closer to the bed and tried to awaken the priest, but something unusual struck him: the priest WAS AWAKE! He seemed to recognize Father, wanted to say something, but despite all his efforts he could not utter one syllable. He made efforts to move, but could not. Father tried to help him but the priest seemed paralyzed. When Father was near panic, he saw that one of fingers of the priest's right hand had started to move a little bit, then another finger and soon afterwards his hand. Moments later the priest came to and sat up. He looked around, as if awakening out of a strong hypnosis.

Meanwhile, a number of servants, having noticed Father's arrival, were waiting nearby. Some of them came closer and customarily started to massage the priest's arms and legs. When fully recovered, Kacang took Father by the arm and led him into the room, telling him what had happened. Mekelé Trena was still sitting there with Gedé on her lap gasping for breath. The priest healer now saw that it was necessary to take action against his female colleague. He recommended that Pedanda Istri Gianyar should be removed from the Puri.

Father was shocked. It was against all ethical principles to send a priestly woman away on sheer circumstantial evidence. A suitable formula for her temporary exile from the Puri was worked out. This was conveniently provided by the six months ceremony after Gedé's birth, which was to be held in two weeks time. It was arranged that Father would give Pedanda Istri, as a professional priestess, the honour of preparing the elaborate offerings for that occasion. By tradition this work could only be done in the *gria* (Brahman priestly compounds) of Bungaya, ten miles away from the Puri. Thus any apprehension on the part of Mekelé Wiraga was prevented. The female priest complied and everybody thought that evil had been averted.

However, every night strange apparitions were reported hovering around Mekelé Trena's house. Some were sure of having seen flaming tongues floating in the air, others saw human legs rotating in circles above the roof. Ominous noises like the flapping of wings and the screeching of windmills were heard.

Gedé's condition deteriorated badly. His abdomen was grossly extended and he could hardly breathe. Kacang, in his last attempt to save the infant, asked for a special kind of onion. He sat himself at the side of Gedé's cot and went into meditation with his hands in the *mustika* gesture, holding the onion between his thumbs. After meditating for a while he muttered a series of mantras. Father and a number of attendants were anxiously watching. Another series of magic formulas followed and suddenly a number of *cecaks* (house lizards) fell from the ceiling and smoke went up from the mattress under Gedé's legs. Somehow a fire had ignited itself in Gedé's mattress. In panic Mekelé Trena snatched Gedé away, the servants grabbed the mattress and put out the fire. To everybody's astonishment a roll of *sirih* leaves that had apparently been hidden under the mattress fell on the floor. Kacang picked it up and examined the object. The leaves were neatly bound with a bundle of human hair. When unfolded they showed symbolic inscriptions which Kacang immediately recognized as formulas of black magic. He ordered a *pasepan* (earthenware bowl used for burning incense) to be brought, put the roll of leaves in it, and set it on fire while muttering a series of mantras.

This accomplished, he felt relieved and smiled to Father, assuring him that from that moment Gedé would recover without any medication. Indeed, according to the stories, the next day the swelling of his belly was already much reduced and he could breathe normally again. He was completely healed two days before the six-month ceremonies were to be held.

Pedanda Istri Gianyar was escorted back to Lombok, unfortunately by force, by the District Police Officer of Karangasem.

The Puri rejoiced, and Father turned the six-month ceremonies for his Crown Prince into a week-long festival officiated by seven priests, with daily dance and music performances, attended by hundreds of guests.

CHAPTER 4

First Journey to Denpasar

Preparations for the big journey to Denpasar and the long absence from home had to be elaborate for reasons of security and the mental well-being of the persons involved. In order to set a propitious date for the travel, the traditional Balinese calendar and various horoscopes had to be consulted. There are usually a number of options available for such occasions, out of which one may choose the one most convenient for one's case. In this case we had to conform with the starting date of the coming school year which was July 1, 1925. The departure date also had to allow us enough time to adapt ourselves to the new environment which was expected to be quite different from that of the Puri in Karangasem.

When the date of our journey was fixed, the necessary offerings were prepared for the series of *mepamitans* (prayers for asking permission to leave and for our well-being in future). These were to be held at our family temple in the Puri and at about seven other temples in the Karangasem District, considered relevant for our well-being during the trip and the long stay far from home. This pilgrimage to the various temples extended over three days, with the farthest temples to be visited first. On the last day we had a big ceremony at our family temple, the *merajan*, attended by the whole Puri community. Two extra sets of offerings were prepared for the temples at Candidasa and Goa Lawah on the road to Denpasar where we would stop to perform our prayers.

On the morning of the departure itself, offerings were laid on the road outside the gate of our Puri in front of the four motor cars which would comprise our caravan to Denpasar. Special prayers were held for our drivers and all of us sat down on the road with our faces to the east, dutifully praying for our own and the drivers' well-being. When we moved, it was a picturesque caravan with Father's old Minerva at the front and the beautiful offerings still decorating our vehicles. Our Belgian-made Minerva pre-dated World War I and was one of the first motor cars introduced in Bali. It was a grand-style stately affair, high on its wheels and with shining brass on all sides: a gracefully designed brass frame around the radiator at the front, flanked by two beautiful brass reflector lamps. The windscreen was set in a solid brass framework and a long brake handle of massive brass glittered at the outside on the right hand side of the driver's seat. A huge brass trumpet horn was fixed on either side of the hood, extending to the rear as a ringed tapering body having a black rubber balloon at its end. Beautiful brass lanterns were placed high up on either side of the closed cabin. All this sparkling brass was magnificently set against the black roof, the black elegant mudguards, and the massive black window frames. Strangely enough the body was painted chrome yellow. I was later told that originally it had been green, until Father found the yellow colour more appropriate for a *Stedehouder*, a functionary of the Dutch Queen. (In Dutch, Queen is *koningin*; yellow is *kuning* in Balinese, so the Balinese associated Queen with the colour yellow. The yellow pennant seen always with the red, white and blue Dutch flag those days put emphasis on the position of the House of Oranje.)

The inside of the closed cabin was still dark green, as were the thick velvet seat covers, the satin curtains and the silk ceiling. In front of the large back seat were two folding chairs, which could be folded up against the front wall. This was provided with a glass window which gave a good view to the front. The wooden window sill which covered the whole width of the cabin had a couple of holes in which fitted beautiful crystal bottles containing *eau de cologne* and other perfumes and there was one crystal vase with roses made of silk. The open front part of the vehicle had two seats, one for the driver and one for his assistant, and had only a simple folding canvas roof on top, which unfortunately did not give sufficient protection against the tropical rains.

There were three devices on the car which were for me especially attractive. A massive brass toy aeroplane was fixed on top of the radiator frame. It had a wooden propeller which turned with the wind as soon as the car was moving. The second device was a brass air pump which was fixed on the floor next to the co-driver. It had to be hand operated from time to time during the trip in order to help the flow of the fuel to the carburettor. Last, but not least, there was the carbide lighting unit, the central part of which consisted of a black box with a brass lid, fixed on the plank at the side of the car. As soon it became dark the car had to stop. The black box would be opened and water would be poured carefully over its contents. Gas with a sharp smell would then escape from the box which had to be closed quickly. The reflector lamps in front, the high lanterns at the sides, and one lantern at the back, which were connected with the black box by tiny hollow wires, could then be lit with fire from a match. My greatest delight was when I got the chance to participate in one or another stage of this miraculous operation.

The three other vehicles which followed our Minerva were far less impressive. They were of later make and were already equipped with electric lights, and were a Dodge and a Chevrolet, both purchased by Father in the early 1920s, and a Ford car belonging to the Javanese chief of the Public Works Department. Those cars were of the open touring type, with folding canvas roofs and standing high on their wheels. They were also already equipped with claxons instead of trumpet horns, but the claxon of the Ford had still to be hand-operated by turning a handle several times clockwise. It produced a funny sound like that of a turkey being caught.

We left Karangasem early in the morning because the ride over the 80-km gravel road would take at least five hours, and with the stops it would be late in the afternoon before we entered the town of Denpasar. The maximum speed of our Minerva was theoretically 40 km per hour, but even on the best parts of the road our driver could not reach a speed of more than 30 km per hour, and over the winding roads uphill it was easy for a rider on horseback to overtake us. There were of course huge crowds in every village to see our caravan pass by. In the larger villages we had to stop at the house of the village head, which we found decorated for the occasion, to take refreshments which people had prepared for us, consisting usually of coconut "cocktails" and cakes.

I was all excitement and enjoyed the trip immensely. With Gedé, however, it was quite different. The poor boy was miserable during the ascent of the hills of Sanghyang Ambu, where the road made a great many hairpin turns. He looked very pale and started vomiting. Every time he had to throw up, Father ordered the car to be stopped, and we had to wait until he felt somewhat better. I felt helpless, having to stand by and just to look on, not knowing what to do, while Father, the priest and Mekelé Trena were attending to him, applying all sorts of oils and ointments over his belly and forehead.

The prayer ceremonies at Candidasa and at Goa Lawah were very helpful for Gedé. We had our lunch after the prayers at Goa Lawah and stayed there for a while. I was deeply impressed by the thousands of bats flying in and out of the huge opening in the stony hill and hanging with their sharp claws from the rocks at the ceiling of the cave. Father told us that if you followed the tunnel of the cave all the way up you would arrive at the top of the Gunung Agung, the holy mountain. The cave was regarded as a holy place, where people from all of Bali would come for special prayer ceremonies. I learned later that actually nobody had ever ventured to climb to the top of the Gunung Agung through the tunnel. On another visit to the place some years later, Father showed me the spot where, according to witnesses, before gathering of all the kings of Bali convened by the Dewa Agung of Klungkung some time before the invasion by the Dutch army, his uncle, Gusti Gedé Djelantik (the late Stedehouder of Karangasem), had smashed an egg against the rock stone to show the assembly the futility of engaging in an armed confrontation with the Dutch, and that it would be better for them to negotiate an honourable solution with the enemy.

Eventually, we arrived late in the afternoon at our destination and we started to accommodate ourselves in the evacuated compound of the Pegeg family in Kayumas. In order to meet certain requirements, Father would have preferred to build a new Puri of his own in Denpasar, but because there was much time involved with the purchase of a piece of land near the school this had to wait until the following year. At that time, it was not considered proper for us as—as princes of Karangasem—to live as paying guests with other people. Moreover, our entourage was far too large for such an arrangement, as it included several kinds of functionaries believed to be indispensable. These included a priest, several servants, Gedé's mother, and an older man, Mekelé Trena's uncle, who acted as supervisor over the servants. Later, when Father had built our own Puri in Denpasar, several young boys—sons and relatives of functionaries in the Puri of Karangasem—joined us. At Father's recommendation and expense, they were admitted to our school. After classes, they served as our playmates and as errand boys in our household.

For this first year, however, Father had been able to arrange temporary housing for us through friends, who found in the neighbourhood or *banjar* of Kayumas, a family willing to evacuate and to put their whole compound at our disposal. Fortunately, this compound was large enough to house our troupe. Plenty of food had been prepared already for us by the family, so that our cooks could rest after their very exhausting trip. This they needed very much. For most members of our company it was the first time that they travelled in a motor car, and many of them had been suffering from motion sickness. Thus, half of the company was busy attending the other half with oils, ointments, and all kinds of herbs. These were either applied as *boreh*, in the form of a watery paste rubbed over the skin, or as *simbuh*, where the herb was chewed until very fine by the attending person who then, after mixing the mass in his mouth with enough saliva, blew the thin liquid as a spray over the relevant parts of the body.

Gedé had been sleeping in the car after Goa Lawah and had recovered by the time we arrived in Denpasar. I felt hungry, but as court etiquette required that nobody have their food before Father had eaten, we had to wait. Father himself was tired too. He was resting on a divan, and two boys were massaging him, one on either side, working unprofessionally at his limbs, calfs, arms and shoulders. During this lengthy ritual, hot water with lemon leaves in it was being prepared for his bath and carried to the fenced part of the back yard near the well, which served as our bathroom. Only after Father had finished his bath was food brought in. As was customary those days, all of us were seated on the floor watching while Father had his meal, sitting on a chair at the only table available at the compound. While he was eating, nobody was supposed to speak unless addressed by him, or to chat with each other. Gedé and myself, sat cross-legged at some distance from the table, myself automatically close behind Gedé's back. The servants poured water out of a big Chinese brass pot above a bowl for him to wash his hands, then resupplied his plate with rice or other dishes and at the final stage had to bring him the *caratan* with drinking water. (This *caratan*, now out of use since the introduction of drinking glasses, was a flattened round pot of earthenware with a conical nipple at one side. It had a long neck as its upper part through which the water was poured and which served also as a grip. One was not, however, allowed to touch the nipple with the lips, so that one had to hold the pot at some distance a little above the level of one's head and while pouring a small jet of water from the nipple by tilting the pot, drink by steering the water jet exactly into one's mouth. There was of course some practice needed before one could master the technique. It was undoubtedly a hygienic way of drinking since many people could drink from the same vessel without contaminating each other.)

Only after Father had finished his meal were we served food, and after we had finished it was the turn for the servants. Gedé and myself were eating together from a *dulang*, a communal platter in the form of a small round wooden table of about one foot high with a single heavy leg in the middle. As was also the custom, we ate with our hands. Being the younger of the two I had to take care that nothing which had been in my hands would land back upon the *dulang*. A second precaution to be observed by the younger person or by anyone being lower in the hierarchy, was never to be the first to stop, but to wait until the older person had finished. These rules were observed naturally without any feelings of stress. To be patient while waiting for one's turn had become so ingrained in us that it was never a problem, even when it involved enduring hunger for a considerable stretch of time.

Our "bed" was a traditional Balinese structure: it was a wooden platform built between four pillars at either side of the room. The walls of the room were erected around these eight inner pillars of the house, leaving a third row of four pillars outside to function as supports for the roof above the open verandah at the front of the house. There was a small door leading from the verandah into the room and a small window opening at each side of the room.

When we could no longer keep awake, we asked permission to go to bed. Being the youngest I was assigned the farthest corner of the platform and since there was no mattress Gedé laid himself next to me on the mat, taking care that his pillow was a little bit further up to the upper end of the bed than mine. He fell asleep immediately, but I was too excited and was still awake when Father came later that night to perform his nightly self-imposed duty as he used to do with all his children. This nightly ritual started with a very tender touch of his hands on our heads after which he made the *mustika* gesture of concentration, and bending himself close over our heads he pronounced with a whispering voice a series of mantras, sacred Sanskrit formulas believed to contain powerful white magic, thus protecting us against possible evil forces during the night. Only after this familiar performance, was I relaxed—and I fell asleep.

CHAPTER 5

Primary School Years (1925–1931)

The next morning we were dressed up in our new white "Western" clothes for our first visit to the Dutch Headmaster of the H.I.S. (Hollands Inlandse School—Dutch Indonesian Primary School). We wore short pants and a closed jacket with long sleeves and an upright collar, all stiffened with starch and neatly ironed. At the front from the collar downwards we had a row of gold buttons which were actually American half-dollar coins provided with a metal loop at the back side. These loops were inserted through small holes at the rim of the jacket corresponding with the buttonholes at the opposite side. Safety pins, spiralled metal rings, or just a sturdy cotton string held the buttons in place. The stiff collar was held closed by two small golden knobs with a flat base at the inside. We were barefooted, and we wore no hats. Our heads had just been clean shaven, a once monthly operation for which the old fashioned barber's knife was used. It was only when we reached the fifth grade that we were allowed to let our hair grow and to be cut by a hairdresser. Father had put on his official white *Stedehouder's* uniform, with several medals on his breast.

When we arrived at the Headmaster's office many parents were already waiting on the verandah with their children, submitting their entrance applications. As a matter of course Father, the Raja of Karangasem, was received by the Dutch Headmaster, Mr Van der Hem, with special honours. After the usual formalities Gedé and I were led to one of the classrooms to undergo a preliminary test in writing, reading and arithmetic. Gedé passed the test for the third grade. Since I had never followed classes seriously before, and with the arm test over the head I could not reach my ear with my hand, they found me even too young to enter school. Father was advised to take me back to Karangasem, but that was out of the question. He had promised his eldest son that I, Laksmana, would accompany him, Rama. Out of respect for the Raja of Karangasem the school committee decided favourably on my admission. I was most happy that day when I was told about the decision.

However, what happened the next day came as a great shock! Gedé was placed at the third, while I was put at the first grade, in another classroom together with totally strange boys. After sitting there for a while I was overcome with panic, ran out of the classroom, crying loudly, running from one classroom to the other, calling all the time: "Atudek..., Atudek..." as was my brother's nickname. When I at last found him I clinched myself to him on his desk, and refused to be separated.

The teachers tried in vain to persuade me to return to my classroom. At last they pulled me forcibly from Gedé and brought me back to where I was supposed to be, but as soon as I felt myself free, I ran away to Gedé's class. When they tried to separate us again, I cried and fought wildly.

I must have caused a considerable upheaval at school that morning. In the end I was allowed to stay with Gedé for the rest of the day. Meanwhile the teachers had consulted with Father and they came to the conclusion that it was not possible to separate us from each other. They made a compromise that would not have been possible elsewhere outside Bali: Gedé had to shift back one grade and I had to go up one grade, so that we would be together in the second grade. In order to enable me to follow class I would get extra lessons in the afternoons. There was already being organized an extra class in the afternoons for a number of children from different grades who were not making sufficient progress or who had specific problems. A young Dutch lady teacher was in charge of this class. Perhaps it was because of Father's position that Mr van der Hem, the Headmaster himself, came to teach me in the afternoon class. However, many years later, older friends of mine told me that the special interest of the Headmaster had more to do with the pretty lady teacher than with my special case. My friends made me understand why, after only a few weeks, the lady teacher was nowhere to be seen. She had been replaced by the Headmaster's wife, a qualified teacher herself who had become suspicious when too often her husband came home very late from the afternoon classes.

As was expected, I did not make much progress despite the special treatment. Enthusiasm on the part of the teachers began to wane and I dropped out of the afternoon class without much fuss. However the teaching staff managed to keep me together with Gedé in his class from year to year despite my extremely low marks for nearly all subjects. They found it too embarrassing for the Raja of Karangasem to have a son of his staying behind with every exam. Never having been at any school himself my father perhaps did not realize the "workings" of the written school records, perhaps his mind was only focused on Gedé's excellent progress. Perhaps the teachers themselves did not want to create any more scenes at school. In any case, extraordinary provisions were made: each year I was passed to the following grade, and every time when the Inspector of Education from Headquarters came to visit the school on his quarterly inspection tour I was told by the teachers to go home and I had a nice day off!

Gedé made good progress at school, but it had never occurred to me to ask him to help me with my school work. It would have been of no effect either, since I was just not interested in what the teachers were teaching. On their part they were never cross at me, as if for them it was completely irrelevant whether I did my work or not. They had given up any hope.

Due to my complete lack of interest in learning during that time, it is impossible for me now to recall for sure everything about the H.I.S. curriculum. During the first few years my mind was occupied for most of the time with a host of conditions which I found very perplexing, since they were different from those in Karangasem. Being used to courtly language I found the boys and girls very rude and uncivilized in their behaviour and especially in their language. In the beginning I was very much taken aback and was afraid to offend anybody, not in the least because all of them were much bigger than I was. It took some time before I was able to communicate with my classmates. And then there was that awful experience with the older girls of the higher grades. It seemed that they found me such a cute little baby, something that brought to life their early motherhood instincts. Playing with dolls was not at all common among our girls in Bali at the time, as manufactured dolls were a rare commodity. At home they carried their younger sisters and brothers on their hips and nursed them as soon as they were physically fit for the task. Most of them loved to do this, and of course it was at the same time a great help for their mothers. It happened that one of these older girls thought of me as her baby doll and soon she was joined by her friends. In the beginning I found it nice to be hugged, kissed and passed around from one girl to another. Soon, however, the fun became an agony... I tried to run away, but with five girls chasing after me it was not possible to escape. Crying was always of great help because it attracted the attention of the teachers. However, it took them quite a while before they succeeded in getting the girls to stop chasing after me. I wondered later whether those agonizing experiences had something to do with my insurmountable shyness with girls for a long time during my later life.

My first experiences with our Dutch teachers were no less perplexing. The first shock took place soon after the pretty lady teacher in the afternoon class was replaced by Mrs Van der Hem, the Headmaster's wife. She also took over from her husband the "special tutorship" which was bestowed on me. At one time when she saw how clumsily I started to write, she wanted to show me how to hold the pencil correctly and plopped down next to me at my desk, taking my hand in hers. I was struck with nausea from the totally strange odour emanating from her fat body. I was able to avoid vomiting by turning my head away and by starting to cry. Mrs Van der Hem was very surprised and when I did not stop crying she became a bit frightened. She wriggled herself out of the chair and took out of her bag some sweets which she offered me for consolation. That helped my nausea. For many days thereafter I had been wondering what had caused my feeling of disgust until I discovered that she had been breastfeeding her baby. It was the smell of Dutch human milk!

Hygiene practices were in Bali still almost unknown. As far as cleanliness was concerned it was mainly limited to our bodies and our clothes. At school we were taught to keep our nails clean and short, to bathe twice daily and to wash our hair with soap every day. If we were caught with dirty nails we would get a hard rap on our fingers with a rattan stick. With hindsight I now wonder if our teachers themselves really knew what hygiene was. One of them certainly did not! For Balinese language and script we had a Javanese teacher who always came to school in his neat Javanese dress, a batik *kain* and a batik closed *blankon* on his head. He did not understand Dutch, so every time the Headmaster had to tell him something, another teacher had to translate the message. He was the common terror among us pupils, because he had the unsavoury habit of punishing one who failed for three times to read out a certain word by having him open his mouth in front of him and... ("yes, really!")... spitting in it.

Toilets were as yet unknown. In Karangasem there was plenty of running water in streams and gutters, which served as public toilets. Where possible people directed the water into ditches running through their compounds and a part of it would be fenced off to serve as private toilets. In Denpasar there was to our embarrassment no such running water system. Every compound had a part of its backyard surrounded by a mud wall of about four feet high where the pigs were kept in the open. There were ditches in the pigsty serving as toilets and the pigs cleaned up everything. We had to use the pigsty of our neighbours whose pigs seemed to never have had enough food because they were very thin and aggressive. The sows were especially ferocious when they had sucking piglets. They came up screaming and running at great speed as soon as one entered the pigsty to relieve oneself. It was not surprising that we children were frightened to enter the yard and preferred to defecate squatting on the high mud wall with our backs towards the hungry animals.

Naive ignorance still prevailed in our community regarding all other natural processes involving discharge of superfluous bodily material. As long as one did not offend somebody else by doing things right in front of him, any ditch, bush or corner was considered a suitable place to pass urine, to spit or to empty one's nose or throat. One can imagine my sincere curiosity when one day our Headmaster, whose height in itself was already so awe-inspiring (he was a giant of over six feet from Friesland), came to school with a bad cold, coughing and sneezing all the time. From time to time he took out of his pocket a big white handkerchief in which he blew his huge red nose. That interested me much more than his arithmetic lessons. Every time the handkerchief came out of his pocket I figured out how much mucus he had already collected. Most intriguing for me was however the problem *why* he should collect all this material and bring it home and what he would do with it. My classmates did not know the answer. They dismissed my question as something very trivial and said that such was only a matter of habit. Some of them had even heard from older people at home that it was the custom of the *raksasas* and that the Dutch people were so extremely big because they were descendants of *raksasas* like Rawana and especially Kumbakarna from the Ramayana stories. All kinds of the most fantastic stories circulated those days. We knew from the *wayang* stories that not all *raksasa* were bad creatures. Wibisana, the brother of Rawana, was good, wise and kindhearted. One story related that Queen Wilhelmina of the Netherlands was a direct descendant of Wibisana, and that was the reason why we should pay respect to the Dutch and their Queen.

If I had a very faint idea of what the lessons were about, it was due to my frustration later in the fourth grade where I had been promoted automatically and where only the Dutch language was used. At that time I was still at the second grade level mentally. The requirement to speak Dutch was a very good measure actually for learning well the foreign language. We did learn Dutch, but in many aspects the entirely Dutch orientation of the education led to ridiculous paradoxes.

There was for, example, our booklet, used for step-by-step training in beautiful handwriting, in which the characters were neatly captured between two horizontal lines running from left to right. Our first book (at least the one I saw first when at the second grade) had on its first page the sentence: "Met de hoed in de hand komt men door het ganse land". Literally translated, this was: "With the hat in the hand one comes through the whole country", which meant that when one is polite (with one's hat in one's hand!) one would be welcomed by everybody everywhere. However, no explanation about this was given, and since nobody in Bali wore a hat except farmers or labourers working in the hot sun, walking with your hat in your hand did not have any meaning for us.

In singing especially we were conditioned to recite words and sentences which were totally unintelligible to us, or totally irrelevant to our way of life. Thus, we sang beautifully the song:

"*Slaap met open ramen want de frisse lucht,*
jaagt dan allerhande kwalen op de vlucht".

This translates as "Sleep with your windows open because the fresh air will chase away all sorts of ailments". However, most of us never slept in a bedroom with windows, but on an open verandah. Moreover, none of us had ever seen a mattress well made up with sheets and blankets. Nevertheless, we sang cheerfully the rest of the song:

"*In je frisse bedje, lekker toegedekt,*
zal je heerlijk dromen tot de zon je wekt".

This means "Tucked up nicely in your clean bed, you will dream lovely dreams until the sun awakes you". The only thing we knew was that we woke every morning with the first crow of the fighting cocks long before sunrise.

It seemed that even our Dutch teachers were not aware of these odd paradoxes. We bravely ploughed through the classical Dutch book of songs "Kun Je
Nog Zingen, Zing Dan Mee!" and some of us became so apt in memorizing that
they nowadays still 60 years later are still able to sing those songs which are no
longer known to the young generation in Holland today.

Being part of the Dutch colonial system, the schools in Bali were required
to celebrate the Queen's birthday on the 31st of August each year. For many
weeks, in anticipation of the celebrations, the four upper classes of the H. I. S.
rehearsed the Dutch national anthem, the "Wilhelmus", and several other
Dutch patriotic songs for the "aubade" at the residence of the highest Dutch
official of South Bali, which was at that time the Assistant Resident. In charge
of the rehearsals was a handsome young Balinese teacher "Mijnheer" Patra. All
of our teachers at school were to be addressed by this title, the Dutch equivalent of "Master", which pleased them very much. By the time that we reached
the higher grades most of us were already able to read and write simple sentences in Dutch. Those anthems were however written in "Old Dutch" which
was even for Dutch children difficult to understand. That did not pose any
serious problems with us. We just sang the notes and pronounced the words
perfectly. It sounded very good indeed, and "Mijnheer" Patra earned the most
enthusiastic approval of our Headmaster. For the parade each of us was required
to make a Dutch national flag of red, white and blue paper with an orange
streamer at the top of the flagstaff. We competed eagerly amongst ourselves
and did our best to outdo each other.

On the festival day we were all dressed in immaculate white and marched
with our flags and pennants in military fashion to the Assistant Resident's
house on the north side of the big square, the *alun-alun*. We were drawn up
neatly on the grounds in front of the mansion, the smaller children more to the
front, closest to the assembled civilian and military officers who were standing
on the porch in full gala dress. After a few short speeches which were completely beyond our understanding "Mijnheer" Patra made a bow to the
Assistant Resident and took his place on a small wooden platform in front of
the choir. We had been especially told to sing at the top of our voices and to
articulate the Dutch words as flawlessly as possible. Starting with the
"Wilhelmus van Nasaue", one after the other of a series of Dutch patriotic
songs sounded full blast in the open air for about three-quarters of an hour.
Thereafter, we marched back to the school where we were allowed to disperse.
It was by then nearly noon time and very hot, but that did not stop us from
running wildly to the *alun-alun* where for the Queen's birthday celebrations a
great many folk games were in progress. There was pole climbing to grab attractive prizes like shirts, umbrellas, towels, and so on, from horizontal bamboo
sticks at the top of the slippery greased pole. There was jute sack racing, ball
throwing, rattan fighting and many other games. Later in the afternoon there

were folk performances: *topeng*, *barong landung*, and *gamelan* gong competitions. Huge crowds came from all over South Bali and there were of course hundreds of food and drink stalls and there were many Madurese sweetsellers drumming with their fingers nice melodies on their tin sweet-boxes.

At night, there were processions organized by the Chinese community with a beautiful parade of the most fantastic Chinese lanterns in the shapes of fish, crocodiles, smoking steamboats, castles, motor cars, demons and dragons. Usually there were fireworks at the end of the nightly celebrations watched by thousands of people on the big square.

It happened that Father was present as an official guest at one of the celebrations during the "aubade" in front of the Assistant Resident's house. It turned out he was not happy to see his two sons marching as members of the crowd. For the following year he had a Chinese tailor make gala suits for us of thick green velvet, essentially replicas of the Dutch military officers' gala uniform. Except for the short pants in place of long ones, it was a complete gala dress with golden waistband, golden braids, a golden cord with golden tassel over the shoulder and a stiff high officer's cap with a big knob in front above the peak.

Gedé found it a marvellous dress, but for me it was a torture. Nevertheless, to remain the obedient servant to Gedé, I put on the dress whenever required, although reluctantly. The most literally painful items were the shoes and socks which for such a grand occasion as the Queen's birthday we had to wear for the first time in our lives. At the celebrations the following year we had to march, of course at the head of the column, moving from our school to the Assistant Resident's house. One can easily imagine what a terrible exercise that was for me. The thick green velvet allowed the heat of the sun to penetrate but did not allow body heat to escape, and my feet suffered from blisters with every step. Only the sight of the gasping spectators along the road watching our spectacular show prevented me from bursting into tears. Gedé seemed to enjoy the performance, and he was eager to put on the gala dress whenever Father requested it. Father was genuinely proud of his novelty and had us put on that uniform on many other occasions, even at religious ceremonies at home.

Peak occasions which I still remember were the visits of important guests such as the King of Siam, the Governor General of the Dutch East Indies, and the French Governor of Cochin China. At all those events, six of us—the eldest sons of Father, children between six and twelve years—had to parade in our gala uniforms, with Dutch flags in our hands, before the honoured guests and their retinue. Father was visibly moved when the guests applauded enthusiastically. I myself dreaded most the moment when one of them would come forward and, with the loveliest intentions in the world, pinch my cheeks.

In the course of years, I did indeed learn something at school.... even if it was in a remarkably selective way. From the fourth grade onwards I got good marks for drawing and for beautiful handwriting. In the seventh grade I was much interested in the simple experiments which the teacher demonstrated in front of the class with weights and balances and metal cylinders submerged in water, to show us the working of the Law of Archimedes. I marvelled at the emergence of seedlings from the peanuts which the teacher left on the window-sill on a wet cloth. For the first time I sensed that there was something myste-rious which I vaguely understood as Life itself. So there appeared in my record book another mark not written in red ink. It was for "Natuurkennis" as Natural Sciences were called at that time. By then we were already nearing the end of the seventh grade, the last school year. A new problem arose.

There were in the early 1930s still no secondary schools in Bali. For further study those who passed the final test at the H.I.S. in Denpasar had to go to a H.B.S. or a M.U.L.O. in one of the bigger towns in Java: Malang, Surabaya, Semarang, Yogyakarta, Bandung or Jakarta. The H.B.S. (Hogere Burger School) was a five year course, completely Dutch-oriented and supposed to be more suitable for the brighter students. The M.U.L.O. (Meer Uitgebreid Lager Onderwijs) was in fact an extension of the Primary School, with a course of three years, and had as its follow-up the A.M.S. (Algemene Middelbare School) also of three years duration, functioning as a bridge towards higher education. The less bright pupils and those who were having more trouble with the Dutch language could in this way have six years time at the secondary school before entering the University. With Gedé there were no problems for the teachers. He passed the exams very well. They had more problems with me. I did not pass any test. This resulted in much lobbying between the teachers, my father and high Government officials. They found a suitable compromise in the fact that the M.U.L.O. in Malang (East Java) had at that time also a *voorklasse*, a preliminary grade in which problem students could follow lessons for one year before entering the first grade. My school records were "doctored" so that I became just good enough to qualify for entrance in this preliminary grade.

This time it was Gedé himself who spontaneously volunteered to be put back from the first grade to the *voorklasse*. Even though our fantasies about Rama and Laksmana had withered considerably, our conscious personal attach-ment had grown. Although in the classroom I was considered dumb, I was by nature and, perhaps because of the assumed role of Laksmana for so many years, more dynamic than Gedé, vigilant and practical. In fact I continued to take care of Gedé in practical matters of daily life. As far as Gedé was concerned I remained a companion as essential as during our Ramayana fantasies. He felt it would be unfair to his faithful younger brother to pass over him to the first grade and felt more comfortable to be together with me in the lower grade. As for myself I did not feel as before that compelling urge to be with Gedé all the time, although I still loved him deeply. And thus somehow our teachers suc-ceeded in arranging with the Headmaster of the M.U.L.O. in Malang that Gedé and Madé Djelantik would enter together its preliminary class.

CHAPTER 6

Kayumas

Outside school, our life was subordinate to the position of Gedé Djelantik, Crown Prince of Karangasem. He found himself willy nilly in the centre of the stage, with attention focused on him all the time. All our behaviour was a continuous confirmation of his role as the principal actor in a play, even though it was mainly a passive role. By nature he never had any inclination to take up any opportunity to assert himself. Any other boy at the age of nine years would have been spoiled easily and would have quickly turned into a tyrant. Perhaps it was the strong influence of his earlier self-imposed identification with Rama that prevented him from becoming a despot. His ideal was to pursue authority by good deeds, kindness and forgiveness; in short, by becoming the personification of *dharma* such as King Rama who was believed to be the reincarnation of God Wisnu. We were at that young age already imbued with a strong feeling of respect for someone who showed those noble principles in his attitudes and behaviour.

In public we formed a group solidly united behind Gedé with a tendency of showing off our reverence towards him, and emphasizing the hierarchical order between ourselves. In general, this was displayed quite naturally not only among Gedé's younger brothers and sisters, but also among the children of the dignitaries of our Puri and among the servants who were at the same time our playmates. This showing-off of proper behaviour to the "outside world" stemmed partly from a kind of chauvinism, in our strong belief that the Puri of Karangasem was the highest and therefore the most important among the princely courts of Bali. Infusion with courtly etiquette did not disturb the general pattern of behaviour normally characteristic for school age youths. It established a remarkable blend of seemingly contradictory forms of conduct, in which we learned instinctively the boundaries of what could still be tolerated.

We played ball games like other children, but we succeeded in observing strictly the hierarchical etiquette: no one would ever touch the body of a playmate who was of higher caste or an older one of the same caste anywhere above the waist or throw a ball towards his head. We reserved also the honour of doing the first kick or throw of the ball for our Crown Prince. He himself did not excel in any of the games except in marbles; he could hit marbles precisely from a distance as far as six yards away. In our games a marble is held in the left hand between thumb and two fingers. The middle finger of the right hand is then inserted under the left hand's thumb upon the marble. By pressing with the left thumb on the back of this middle finger and at the same time bending it backwards a strong tension of this finger behind the marble is created. After aiming at the target marble, the middle finger is then released suddenly, thereby shooting the marble with force towards the target. How Gedé acquired this remarkable dexterity, a result of his self-identification with Rama, the sharp shooter, remains anyone's guess. In any case, in our fantasies it provided a living proof for our vague notion of reincarnation, and it gave more meaning to our established concept of proper conduct towards him.

It was in the context of the atmosphere of the time not surprising that our behaviour developed also in conformity with what we witnessed in the classical drama and dance performances such as *topeng*, *gambuh*, and *arja*. The true heroic leader in those plays was usually portrayed as a refined and noble character and the *penasars* or "servants" usually fulfilled the roles of the actual managers of the play, directing the course of events.

So we became the *penasars*, those who in fact decided what would be done. If we wanted to go and see a soccer match at the *alun-alun*, we only had to persuade Gedé, that *he* wanted to go and see the match. Usually his wish would find immediate approval with the elders in the Puri. We would then proceed to the place in a sort of procession with our priest at its head, followed by Gedé. I would walk close behind Gedé, followed by our retinue of servants and playmates from the Puri. Here again strict etiquette was observed, with those of higher caste in front and those of lower caste more to the rear. This hierarchical order was also maintained on the spectators' area at the soccer field. Usually the public on seeing such a disciplined hierarchical structure would by itself pay due respect to our group and would make space free for us. We would then set ourselves properly on the grass. It just did not occur to anybody to rush forward and get ahead of somebody else.

One day, during a soccer match, an accident occurred which we had not anticipated. We should have known that Gedé, sitting right at the front, would be the one of us most likely to be hit by a stray ball. That is exactly what happened. The ball hit him right in the face and he fell back screaming. We sprang up in shock and pulled him to the edge of the square where we took water from the stream to cool his face with wet towels. Together we carried him on our shoulders to Kayumas.

Fortunately, there was no damage inflicted to his eyes, nose or mouth. It was of course a very painful affair. By the time we reached the Pegeg compound in Kayumas his face and eyes were very red, but Gedé could already smile and told us that the pain was nearly gone. We felt most relieved.

Our sense of relief was however of very short duration. Gedé's mother, Mekelé Trena, was furious and wanted to find out who were the culprits who took the initiative for going to watch the soccer match. None of us knew of course, as it was a general spontaneous impulse. Since none of us said anything she became more furious and summoned all of us one by one to appear before her to undergo our punishment. And we bravely faced our fate. The routine punishment consisted of a series of *iluts* on one's thigh. She did it obviously with uncontrolled fanaticism. I was of course the first to receive this piercing sharp and painful treatment, which left several deep blue marks on my thigh. And so all our playmates lined up dutifully after me. One of the older boys, Ida Bagus Pidade, then already at the sixth grade at school, saw what was going to happen. He silently slipped away and found an old discarded rubber tire which Father's driver had left in a shed that served as a garage, cut a one foot long piece out of it and slid it as a sleeve over his thigh under his *kain* (skirt-like cloth most of us wore at that time instead of pants). It turned out to be a very effective and protective measure. When his turn came he "endured" the *iluts* laughingly. The more he was laughing the more furious Mekelé Trena became. She went on and on fiercely pinching and twisting until her fingers were aching most painfully. Then she discovered the thick rubber protection under the *kain*. In a rage of anger she took a piece of wood and started to beat the boy on his bottom. Pidade sprang up in panic and ran away before the second blow struck him. We burst in a roar of laughter and we forgot all the pain in our legs. "Sampun! Sampun! Sampun!" ("Enough, enough!") shouted some of the elder women in the compound who came to the scene, trying to stop Mekelé Trena. "Sampun.... Sampun!" and they led her away , sobbing, to the main building.

Later, as a medical doctor, I could identify the cause of the unrestrained violent reactions of Mekelé Trena to any event which upset her. She must have been suffering—even then—from hyperthyroid disease.

The scene was for a long time thereafter a source of great fun for us, and Pidade was afterwards regarded as a kind of hero among our playmate-servants.

To the east, separated by a narrow lane from Pegeg's compound, there was a large plot of land available, which Father wanted to have for his new Puri 'in Denpasar. After the ritual ceremonies customarily required before starting the construction of any new building in Bali, a host of diggers, masons and other workers moved in on the new plot, headed by *undagis* (traditional architects) from Karangasem. A five-foot high mud wall was erected around the new compound, with a one-foot layer of rice straw on top which served as protection against erosion by the rains. A narrow opening was left on the west side as a back door, and a large one on the east side later became the main entrance gate. To the south our new compound bordered on a Government plot of land, which was already provided with a barbed wire fence, so that a wall was not needed on that side. A modern European-style house of brick was later built there for a Dutch official, the "Aspirant Controleur" (equivalent to "District Chief in Training") of Badung.

In our compound, first of all, a section at the northeast corner was prepared to build the *pawedaan*, a high, open pavilion with a wooden platform, where our priest would perform his daily prayers in the early mornings. Only after the completion of this structure was the construction of the other buildings of the *puri* started. A large kitchen with a store-room was built near the back door, a deep open well was dug, and not far from it an open bathroom took shape. All along the western mud wall became a "long-house" containing a number of rooms, which were to serve as living quarters for our servants and playmates.

In the centre of the compound the large main building was to be erected, a smaller-sized replica of the "Maskerdam", the main building in the Puri of Karangasem, containing a front porch to the south, two bedrooms on each side and a broad corridor between the four bedrooms. The construction did not proceed any further than the foundations.

Meanwhile, another house was being set up on the southern part, an L-shaped structure with brick walls, a covered verandah in the middle and at lower level an open porch running along the whole length of the building. The house had three rooms, one of which was separated from the other two by the covered verandah, and was assigned for our priest, Pedanda Gedé from Selat.

As soon as this smaller building was completed we vacated Pegeg's compound and moved into this brick house. We learned later that the construction of the central main building was stopped because of lack of funds. Father had never been able to make up for that shortage, as other priorities had to be attended to.

When we left Denpasar at the end of our school term in 1931, the planned mini-Maskerdam still consisted only of its foundations. All those years the abandoned sub-structure had provided us with a most interesting playing ground which stimulated our fantasies. The spot served as hide and seek fields, as battle grounds in the hot sun, as mysterious labyrinths in the dark, as flower gardens and experimental seed beds, as racing circuits for toy motor cars for which any piece of wood or ceramics with a conical shape could serve. Our imagination did the rest. Later Father found it no longer worthwhile to continue the project: he had previously anticipated that our younger brothers and sisters would also come to Denpasar to attend school. In the meantime, however, he had, with other prominent Balinese citizens, taken the initiative in building a private Hollands Inlandse School in Klungkung. This plan materialized much faster than he had expected. Klungkung, being half way between

Karangasem and Denpasar was much more convenient for our family. Thus, Father's children who came after us, starting with Madé Karang, went to the H.I.S. "Siladarma" in Klungkung, which had a curriculum of the same level as the school in Denpasar. It was more attractive to Balinese parents because of its emphasis on a number of specific traditional Balinese values.

As result of the efforts of our teachers at school we gradually learned new ways of life which were more consistent with hygiene and modern standards. The use of soap and brushing our teeth twice daily with a real toothbrush were two of the earliest habits we took over from the boys of the higher grades. It gave us a certain feeling of being superior to others who had not yet adopted such tokens from Western civilization. Our motivation to adopt such new habits was more often the wish to appear more "Western" or modern, than the actual purpose of the action itself. Our heads were no longer clean shaven every month. Instead we had a haircut by a barber, who came to the Puri in Kayumas once a month and worked on all of us one after another, using the same tools without any cleaning or disinfection during the whole process. It was not considered fitting for us to have our haircut somewhere on the road-side under a tree, which was then common practice since barber shops did not yet exist.

Later we preferred wearing pants rather than *kains* because it conformed with Western habits. It signified "progress". By the time the girls entered the fifth grade they were shy to appear at school in *kain* and *kabaya*, and wore instead ill-fitting European dresses.

By wearing pants we boys could no more just stop anywhere for a moment to urinate by only lifting the *kain* a little bit to the front. The procedure of opening buttons required us to look for a secluded spot to avoid embarrassment. At school we learned to use the toilets provided for the purpose.

There were no such toilets in Pegeg's compound, nor had any been built in our Puri. Father did not think to build one and for our traditional *undagis* such provisions were beyond their imagination. For our natural needs we used to go outside the Puri about 200 yards away to the *teba*, an open garden with ditches where bamboo stools and various fruit-bearing trees provided plenty of shade and spots for hiding. Stray dogs and sometimes stray pigs took care of the cleaning up. Among ourselves these conditions did not pose any problems nor did it create feelings of discomfort, even if as was often the case there happened to be several people at the place together at one time. Our attitude to these natural processes remained completely natural, innocent and uncomplicated. However, it became different when alien elements would come into the scene, such as at school where we knew that we were being watched by our teachers, especially our Dutch Headmaster. In such an environment it was shameful to display one's backwardness by not conforming to the rules of modern conduct.

Once, we accompanied Father who was asked by the Assistant Resident and his wife to join them for a cup of tea in the afternoon in their garden. We were nicely dressed in newly made shirts, a novelty, instead of the stiff closed jackets, and new sarongs (a closed *kain* folded like a skirt reaching to the ankles). Father had over his *kain* his official jacket with only one of his medals on his breast and had as he did more often later put on a pair of shoes which had been over-zealously rubbed shiny by one of the servants. As we descended from our big Fiat limousine on the driveway in front of the official residence, Mr and Mrs Jansen walked down the steps of their verandah to meet us. While I was looking with awe at the nearing couple they suddenly stopped and turned their backs on us, as if we did not exist any more. For one moment I was puzzled, but found immediately the answer: coming out of the car Father had taken a few steps to the rear side, lifted his kain and squirted his urine neatly on the wheel of the shining limousine. It could not have lasted more than ten seconds, but for me it seemed an endless ordeal of the deepest humiliation. I felt as if I was sinking through the ground into a deep well.

Quite unerringly Father walked up to our hosts who were very polite and friendly and acted as if they had not seen anything wrong. The tea (with milk) and the cakes tasted very strange in my mouth. But I was too shaken with shame to take much notice of it. I was so deeply shocked that I failed to give answers to Mrs Jansen's simple questions, even after Gedé translated them from Dutch into Balinese to help me. Father apologized on my behalf, saying that I was still too shy. Yes! It was shyness, but of a very different quality!

Under the huge *waringin* tree on the north-western corner of the square, the Denpasar Tennis Club—which included only members of the European community—had built a cemented tennis court, secluded from the public by a three-metre high wire fence. We never questioned why only Europeans should be able to play tennis. We took for granted the existence of another way of life for the whites in contrast to ours. We used to sit crosslegged on the grass very close to the fence to watch the game, with our noses pressed against the metal wire in order not to miss anything of the most interesting scenes. We liked to be at the place very early in the afternoon before the club members arrived so that we could see the servants of the club preparing the place, setting up the table and the chairs for the members to drink their tea in between the games. I was particularly fascinated by the setting up and the stretching of the tennis net between the iron poles in the middle of the court. Every time, I felt delight in seeing this mechanism at work. Then the ball boys would come. While waiting for the *tuans* (gentlemen) and the *nyonyahs* (ladies) to arrive, they would play on the court with old discarded tennis balls and makeshift "racquets" cut out of wooden planks, not unlike the present ping-pong racquets but of course much coarser and heavier. We secretly envied those boys for the privilege of being allowed to enter the sanctuary and out of curiosity we made friends with them. Soon we learned from them the rules of the game, and it was not long before we also had made our tennis "racquets" out of wood and marked our own "tennis court" outside the compound on the bare and dusty grounds in front of the main gate. The ball boys provided us with old discarded tennis balls.

We were very much intrigued by the costumes the Dutch ladies were wearing those days. It was said that they had *guwungans* (bamboo baskets used for keeping fighting cocks in Bali) under their dresses. Most of the boys believed the story to be true, because some of the ladies had hips which looked unbelievably broad to our eyes. But some of us, myself included , did not believe the rumour at face value and thought that things should be verified. The tennis court was found to be the most appropriate place to check the truth. So we all went there together one day. The Dutch ladies however felt most embarrassed to see a large number of small boys along the fence, lying on their backs on the grass with their heads pressed against the wire, eagerly trying to have a good look under their skirts every time when they happened to pass nearby. There was some tumult among the players and suddenly one of the gentlemen ran out of the court and chased us away, furiously threatening us with his racquet.

When, with throbbing hearts, we gathered again far away from the square and checked each other on our observations, I was satisfied to have verified that the stories were not true. None of us had seen a fighting cock's basket hidden under a lady's dress. The only peculiar thing that I had seen was that some of the ladies, especially the fatter ones, showed around their middle a few thick vertical lines in their dresses, caused by what was later to be identified as corsets.

During the later years of our stay in the new "Puri Karangasem" in Kayumas, Father came to visit us in Denpasar only now and then since he had his duties as Rajah in Karangasem. Also Mekelé Trena spent most of her time in Karangasem. The daily household business was entrusted to Gusti Ayu Karang, a middle-aged lady from Puri Kaler Kauh, Karangasem, our grand-mother's Puri of origin. "Ayu" as we called her, was even more devoted to Gedé than Mekelé Trena herself and prepared for him the best dishes, the nicest clothes and would do everything for him to show her sincerity in the discharge of her duties. She had, however, the peculiar habit of saving as much as possible from the household budget, which Father handed to her at the beginning of each month when he came to Denpasar. This habit resulted in a gradual deterioration of the food that we all, except for Gedé, got to eat. Gedé himself, unaware of this situation, enjoyed the special care he got, and out of love for his follower Laksmana would usually pass over to me part of his portion. However Ayu would watch sharply and guarded that I would not get too much of the nice dishes she had prepared for him. Sometimes she even snatched back pieces of meat from my plate.

In order to get enough protein for himself and his family, our priest had to go out fishing at a nearby river every afternoon. He became later such a fishing maniac that among the people in Denpasar he was jokingly known as "The Priest with the Fishing Rod".

None of us knew what Ayu was saving the money for, but our servants heard her every month complaining to Father that the money was not enough to run the household. They knew also that Father had several times dutifully increased the allocation. Although our servants and playmates felt the effect of Ayu's scrimping badly, they never complained. But there was a gradual loss of respect among the inmates of "Puri Karangasem" in Kayumas towards our Lady of Housekeeping. It was very depressing.

About that time in the early 1920s, an exciting novelty was introduced in Bali: the bicycle.

The year we entered school, there were only a few of these remarkable vehicles in Denpasar, but during the following years their numbers increased rapidly. Father found that new product of Western civilization too dangerous a tool for Gedé to have, so there was no chance for us to enjoy the excitements of riding such a vehicle which, we felt, would have been a great asset in our Puri. One of our older playmates found out later that there was a shop in town where bicycles could be hired at the rate of ten cents per hour. That was big money at the time, when a portion of *tahu* (tofu—a popular snack) cost only two kepengs, the equivalent of two fifths of a cent. The problem was how to get that much money. We immediately sensed that we should somehow "work" through Gedé Djelantik. If we only could get him excited about our plans the attainment of our goal would be only a matter of time.

From the beginning of our stay in Denpasar we had learned to save our monthly pocket money in an earthenware pot which was made in the shape of a pig. This pig had a slit in its back through which to insert the coin. Since the pig was made in one piece, the money could not be taken out unless the pot was smashed into pieces. It was made that way on purpose.

Among the population in Bali, pig raising is a practice that easily increases low incomes. Pigs eat everything and grow fast and can easily be sold for much more money in a short time. That is why the *celengan* (traditional Balinese saving pot) is made in the shape of a pig. (Pig is *celeng* in Balinese.)

Gedé got one silver guilder every month and I got a silver half-guilder. Thus Gedé's pig was twice as big as mine. (A guilder was one hundred cents.) The *celengans* were kept in a locked cupboard, so that we actually never had access to our pocket money.

It occurred to me that we could use our pocket money in order to hire a bicycle. We knew for sure that Ayu would never allow us to spend anything, so we should do it without her permission. With the help of Gedé who under some pretext got her one day to open the cupboard, I was able to snatch my *celengan* away and to hide it in Pidade's room. Being the son of our priest he had the privilege to share with his father a separate room in the main building in which he occupied the farthest corner, an excellent hiding place. Since we did not want our beautiful *celengans* to be smashed into pieces we widened the slit by carefully abrading its edges with a piece of iron, to allow the silver coins to escape through it by tumbling the *celengan* upside down. Later Gedé's pig also was exploited, and thus we had plenty of money and enough opportunity to practise riding on hired bicycles. In order not to arouse Ayu's displeasure or suspicion, we took care that the vehicles were never seen inside the Puri compound. Ayu hardly ever came outside the Puri walls.

During the six years that we attended school in Denpasar, modern and more democratic ideas started to have their impact on many areas of daily life. We grew older and found ourselves mature enough to venture beyond the Puri walls all by ourselves. Only on special occasions—such as going to a crowded temple festival—was it considered necessary to be chaperoned by our priest. We got used to the fact that in Denpasar, unlike in Karangasem, people in the *warungs* (food stalls) on the roadside would remain seated on their benches when we passed even at a very near distance from them. In Karangasem the people would come down and squat on the ground, paying due respect to us. Among ourselves, the rigid court etiquette became gradually more relaxed. Outside the Puri walls it became more important to conform to the behaviour of our schoolmates than to adhere to strict conservative court rules. By this time, nobody would take offence when, for instance, "by force of circumstances" during our riding practices, a servant playmate would be sitting high on the bicycle while we, princes, would be stepping beside him, holding his saddle to prevent him from falling.

Before long we had all mastered the bicycle. Only Gedé, who as Crown Prince had always been protected and taken care of too cautiously, took more time to acquire the skill. For the same reason he was also always slower in his reactions to sudden events. Very much to our shame and regret, once during practise on the main road in Klandis, he panicked at the sudden signal coming from a nearing motor car, lost control of his steering wheel, and fell just in front of the vehicle. It was sheer luck that the car could stop in time. Gedé was thrown from the bicycle and landed in the middle of the road. He was deeply shaken, but completely unhurt. The bicycle, however, had come under the wheels of the car. We were speechless when we saw the gruesome and distorted convolution of metal which the minute before had been the shining bicycle for which we felt so much affection and (somehow) respect. We felt guilty for not having watched over Gedé more carefully, certain that if we had not allowed Gedé's bicycle to get so far ahead of us, we could have prevented the accident.

This time, we were lucky that Mekelé Trena was not in Denpasar. It was agreed that Ayu should be kept ignorant of the catastrophe. We could easily organize to extract from Gedé's *celengan* enough money to pay the shop compensation for the damaged bicycle. The older servants and even the priest, who welcomed every opportunity to do something nasty to Ayu, approved of the plot.

Unavoidably, the "theft" out of our piggy-banks was soon discovered and also the purpose for which the money had been used. Not being able to punish anybody, Ayu was torn between fury and grief. We had successfully misused Gedé's position, had made him volunteer to be our accomplice! He had no choice but to surrender. When she complained to Father later, it turned out that Father's wisdom and sense of humour had prevailed. He understood the making of our plot and he forgave us all our misdeeds. He even promised to buy a bicycle for Gedé and one for me.

Since by that time we were already nearly at the end of the seventh grade, plans were in the making for us to leave Denpasar and continue our studies in Java. These bicycles were given to us when we entered the school in Malang, East Java, at the start of the school year.

CHAPTER 7

Early Perceptions

Dutch colonial rule established itself on the island as recently as 1908 after the conquest of South Bali, which culminated in the spectacular event known in Indonesian history as the "Puputan Badung". This was a massacre in which the Raja of Badung with hundreds of his followers, dressed in white and magnificent ceremonial ornaments of silver and gold, charged the approaching Dutch colonial army with bare krises (swords) and lances and let themselves be mowed down by Dutch bullets. The Dutch Government noted this Balinese determination, and applied from the beginning a mild and beneficial colonial policy on the island. They pledged to leave the social and political structure of Bali as much as possible in its traditional form as long as it it did not contradict Dutch interests.

The following year, my father, Bagus Djelantik, succeeded his uncle Gedé Djelantik as Raja over the autonomous region of East Bali, Karangasem, bearing the Dutch title of *Stedehouder*. A descendant of the former King of Gianyar, the region east of Badung, was appointed by the Dutch as "Regent" of Gianyar, which became a semi-autonomous region. In both Regions Dutch administrators were placed as advisors. The remaining six regions of Bali were directly administered by Dutch civil servants, so-called *Controleurs*. All those Dutch administrators and advisors were supervised by the "Resident of Bali and Lombok" stationed in Singaraja. He was assisted by "Assistant-Residents" stationed in Denpasar and Mataram.

Under this administrative umbrella, a durable peace, unknown in the past, was established on the island and the Balinese communities continued their traditional life patterns, which included besides the daily business of agriculture and commerce, a regular schedule of recurring temple festivals and many other religious ceremonies. Meanwhile, modernization penetrated into the island, at first slowly and uneventfully, but soon with increasing speed and intensity, starting with the establishment of schools, followed by road building, the introduction of modern means of transport, and the advent of telephones and electricity.

Being schoolchildren, we were at the time not consciously aware of the profound changes which were occurring around us. Life, as we perceived it evolving in our Puris, consisted of a series of familiar happenings within a secure enclave. The events which were of concern to us were predictable, and we knew at any time our place and role, and we acted accordingly. We knew the sequence of affairs during the day from early morning until the evening. We knew when and where dangers were likely to be met, such as the workings of evil spirits at midday when one is bound to step on one's own shadow while walking in the sun. For our safety it was better to stay inside the house under the roof. Dusk was another hour preferred by those evil spirits to roam around. Woe to those who happened to be in their way!

Outside the Puri, our life was occupied by school, by sport events on the town square, outings to nearby river streams for fishing and swimming, and at nights by various forms of folk entertainment in the neighbourhoods, such as *gandrung*, *janger*, and other dance drama or *gamelan* music performances.

Janger

Squeezed between Gedé and Mekelé Trena, sitting on the outer earthen wall of Pegeg's compound, I looked with fascination down upon the busy crowd on the wide open space between us and the main road. Around us it was already dark. Under the bright light of two "Stormkings" (kerosene pressure lamps) which hung from bamboo poles on opposite sides of the open yard, men of the Banjar Kayumas were preparing the stage for a *janger* performance, a novelty which those days became a very popular folk entertainment. Lontar palm leaf mats were spread out on the ground between the lamp posts, forming the boundaries of a large quadrangle, and one mat was placed right in the centre. In the meantime a group of musicians arrived. The small ensemble consisted of a flute, a pair of cymbals, a *kenong* (small gong), and two *terbanas* (flat drums, probably of Turkish origin), a small one producing a high pitch and a large one giving a low bass tone at percussion. The musicians sat down at one of the corners of the stage and the flute player started to play melodies of newly composed folk songs while the other instruments served to accentuate the rhythm.

Out of the dark, two rows of dancing girls emerged, stepping along the mats on two sides of the rectangle. They were arranged by height: the smallest marched in front, each followed by nine increasingly taller girls. They were beautifully dressed in colourful woven *kains*, held by ornately gilded *sabuks* (3-5 metre-long strips of cloth), tightly bound around their bodies. They had, neatly fitting around their foreheads, circular flower headdresses with three to four tiers of sparkling spikes to which colourful artificial flowers were attached, all quivering at the quick little sideways jerking movements of their heads at the rhythm of the music. I looked with awe at this glittering spectacle, but my excitement was aroused much more when I saw the boys marching in two rows into the light, stepping along the remaining two rows of mats. They were dressed in costumes which appeared to me at first grotesque, but at the same time fascinating. They wore blue shorts and long-sleeved white shirts decorated with bright red epaulettes with silver embroidery and fringes on their shoulders. Over their breasts they wore enlarged bibs reaching down to their waists. The bibs were made of dark velvet, fringed with silver tassels and ornately embroidered with pairs of silver *nagas*—mythical snakes—facing each other with opened jaws and flaming tongues. The boys put on hard, unsmiling faces, their fierce looks enhanced by enormous black false moustaches, which turned upwards at the ends. Their loose hair flashed in the bright lamp light.

The girls sat down upon the mats with their knees bended, and their back-sides on their heels, forming two rows facing each other, while the boys moved to the middle of the rectangle. Here they gave a short performance of a chore-ographed parade, a display of various formations, frantically gesticulating with their arms and hands, all the time rhythmically jerking their shoulders and their heads. These movements caused the ferocious *nagas* to seemingly to come to life. At rhythmical intervals they barked out bursts of yells, sounds without any meaning, "Chippeu'eu', chippeu'eu', Chippeu'eu', Chippeu'eu'..." while the rhythm and the music from the ensemble grew louder and faster.

I was thrilled and felt the rhythm getting hold of me to the tips of my fingers. Suddenly, the boys broke into two groups and sat down crosslegged on the remaining two rows of mats, facing each other. While we were wholly absorbed by the show, people had hung curtains around the bamboo structure which had been erected at one side of the yard. Suddenly, I saw the front cur-tain being wildly shaken and its two halves brusquely torn apart. Out of the mysterious enclosure emerged a most impressive figure, dancing his way with jerking movements to the centre of the stage where he seated himself and con-tinued dancing crosslegged on the mat. His costume was traditional, but his false black moustache was exaggerated and his headdress much more elaborate. He was the so called *daag*, functioning as the foreman of the whole group.

Suddenly, a mighty loud and sharp yell burst out of his throat: "Chaaaaaq!" This was instantly followed from the two rows of boys by a multitude of echoes ringing: "Chaaaq!" followed by a frenzy in quick tempo: "Chak echechaki che chak chaaqk!". This continued in a rhythmical play of sounds and yells, accompanied by brisk movements of heads, arms and bodies, swaying and shuddering. In quick succession there were movements which I recognized as parts of the *pencak*, the Malay art of hand-fighting, movements from tradi-tional Balinese martial dances, from ancient rituals, all mixed together and interspersed with grotesque gesticulations, entirely incomprehensible but nevertheless fascinating. Their performance ended abruptly with a thundering "Daaag!" from the foreman's throat.

The man with the flute began to play a sweet and slow melody, which after the first strophe was joined by the girls, singing with their high voices. Quite different from the soothing and reassuring traditional folk songs the melody and rhythm of these (at that time) modern songs were very stimulating. They aroused interest and excitement and had an immediate appeal for us, inciting us to move hands, arms and legs and shake with our necks and heads, imitating the boys and girls in step with the overwhelming rhythm. The boys, called *kechaks*, joined the song by filling up the passages, interlocking the rhythm of the melodies by their "Kecha a pung, kechak apung" or "Sagsig-sigya sig ya sig byong!" and a host of other similarly meaningless sounds which only served to enhance the quickly varying rhythms.

Each piece followed a distinct pattern, starting with a strophe by the flute and ending with a thundering yell from the *daag*.

After a number of songs the *kechaks*, as if by some invisible sign from nowhere, sprang as one man to their feet and started to demonstrate a series of fancy acrobatic exercises, climbing and balancing upon each other's shoulders, forming bridges and pagodas, while continuously dancing to the rhythm of the music, occasionally yelling a burst of sounds which emphasized the visual effect of their movements. I was too much thrilled by the show to notice the reactions of the spectators, which by then had swollen to a huge crowd around the stage. The rhythm must have brought me in a kind of hypnosis because, although I was being poked in my side, it took some time before I woke up and heard Mekelé Trena calling: "*Ngiring mantuk!*" ("Let us go home"). She was apparently bored, and thought it had become too late in the night, since we had to attend classes early the following morning. I felt very disappointed and looked hopefully at Gedé, but I saw him letting himself slide down from the wall. I had no other choice but to follow him reluctantly.

That night in bed the songs of the *janger* girls and the staccato sounds of the *kechaks* continued to reverberate my head. It was a thrilling experience, shared by all of us, except perhaps Mekelé Trena for whom the sounds and appearances were too unfamiliar. I noticed later that Father profoundly despised the *janger* play, classifying it as a barbaric manifestation.

Nearly every week there was a *janger* performance in one or another Banjar in Denpasar or in a nearby village outside the town. Each time when we wanted to see the performance, we had to persuade Gedé to come with us, because without him we would not be allowed to go out at night. On such nightly excursions we had still to be accompanied by our priest or at least one elder person from our Puri. Almost always Gedé was easily persuaded. He was by then already a teenager and was, unlike myself, much more fascinated by the *janger* girls than by the *kechak* boys. We had only to mention the name of one of his favourite dancers who might perhaps appear on the stage that night and he would announce his wish to our priest and the elders in the Puri.

At school everyone was in a frenzy about *janger,* and often during the class intervals a number of boys and girls grouped themselves spontaneously around somebody who happened to hum or whistle a *janger* melody. Everybody seemed to find his proper role in the group quite naturally, the biggest boy as the *daag,* other boys as *kechaks* and the girls sang their *janger* songs entirely uninhibited. Time was, of course, never of any concern to us and often the teachers had to chase us back into our classrooms. Our Balinese teachers were also excited by the *janger* and allowed us many times to continue singing and dancing long after due time, but eventually the Dutch Headmaster forbade us to sing any more of *janger* during the intervals. Perhaps he was afraid that our attention would become too much distracted from the Dutch book of songs "Kun Je Je Zingen Zing Dan Mee"!

Sanghyang

Mekelé Trena's uncle, Bapa Badung, was particularly interested in the *sanghyang* dances which were performed once every 35 days at *Tumpek* evenings in the nearby temple of Banjar Bun. These dances were actually religious rituals in which girls were brought into trance by letting them inhale incense, while monotonous chants were sung by a chorus of several men and women. As soon as they were deep enough in trance they would start swaying with their heads and making dance movements with their hands. Then they would raise themselves on their feet and start dancing to the rhythm of the chorus and eventually they would dance with their bare feet through burning cinders of coconut shells.

Gedé was not very interested, but it was not necessary for us to persuade him, because we could join Bapa Badung, our elder guardian, whenever he wanted to go. He did, however, not bother to explain anything to us about the ritual, assuming that we would understand all by ourselves. I never got any satisfactory answer from him to my questions, so soon I stopped asking. When I asked our priest what the *sanghyang* was about, I received the reply that I was still too young to be able to understand anything about it. Thus, I remained puzzled...

Many other questions which came into my mind resulted in similar disappointments when I asked elder people in the Puri for explanations. The typical answer was: "*Mula sapunika*", which meant that it has always been like that. When I asked our priest why we had to pray with our faces to the east, he explained: "We are praying to Batara Surya, the Sun God, who comes up in the east every morning". But when I remarked that we could also pray to Batara Surya with our faces to the west in the afternoon, the answer was: "One does not pray in the afternoon to the Sun God". "Why not?" I asked. "Well, because we only pray to Him in the morning". That answer was not quite satisfactory to me, but Gedé, feeling that I was unhappy, consoled me and advised that I should not ask such silly disturbing questions, in order not to arouse the anger of our elders. So I remained still very puzzled....

At the same time, I remained fascinated by what I saw at the *sanghyang* performances: the monotonous singing of the men and women; the gradual coming into trance of the girl; the devotion by which the attendants paid homage to the girls as soon as they came into the state of somnambulance, addressing them in the highest language; the mysterious gestures of the temple priests and the similarly mysterious whisperings which sounded in the atmosphere, saturated with the smell of smoke, incense and human sweat. All these perceptions and sensations remained with me, because of the frequent repetition of deeply engraved experience. However, they would remain as only images without any meaning for me, until twenty years later when, as a medical student in Holland during my studies in psychiatry, I read articles in psychiatric magazines dealing with trance as a phenomenon of religious practices.

Gandrung and Kebyar

Late one night, we heard the roaring of people in the community building of Banjar Kayumas. They were going wild and hilarious because of the inept odd movements of the unlucky men who had fallen victim to the uncompromising touch of the *gandrung* dancer's fan. This old folk entertainment called *gandrung*, which is nearly extinct nowadays, was still very popular in the 1920s. It was performed by a group of artists who wandered from village to village and could be hired for a night's entertainment for a small sum of money.

The group consisted of a few musicians playing on bamboo xylophones (*tingkliks*) and one drum (*kendang*) and two, three or more young boys who danced solo dances to the attractive music of the small ensemble. They were dressed as girls and performed appealing flirtatious dances in the course of which they would invite men from among the audience for a duet dance by touching them by surprise with their fans. Usually these dancing boys were effeminate with fine features. Some were very talented dancers. They whirled graciously around the stage, flirting with the spectators by their looks and gestures throughout their improvised dances, meanwhile figuring out with whom they might be able to dance a beautiful duet, and who were likely not at all to be adept in dancing and thus could be ridiculed on the stage. A good *gandrung* could in that way provide superb entertainment by alternating magnificent dances, which drew admiration from the public, with caricaturesque performances, teasing and making a fool of his poor partner, inciting wild hilarity.

We went many times to see the *gandrung* at the Banjar but mostly we came home disappointed. We could not see much of it, because of the public standing packed several metres thick around the stage. Sometimes I was lucky when

Uncle Badung was in a good mood and allowed me to sit on his shoulders.

I was old enough to enjoy the music and the dance, but I was still too young to grasp the meaning of the rumours that the *gandrung* dancing boys were sometimes used by men from the Banjar.

When more and more tourists came to visit Bali, the management of the Bali Hotel in Denpasar (which was built by the K. P. M., the Royal Dutch Shipping Company), organized weekly presentations of Balinese *gamelan* music, performed by the "Sekehe Gong" (Music Club) of the nearby Banjar Belaluan. Spurred on by the generous payments, the club rehearsed diligently and soon became one of the best *gamelan* orchestras of the island. In accordance with the fashion of the time, the club used to play modern *kebyar* music, which was much more exciting than the traditional classical genre.

We were, of course, curious to see those performances of which we heard enthusiastic stories from our schoolmates. But since they were held within the premises of the Bali Hotel where the general Balinese public was not admitted, our priest advised us first to send Bapa Badung to find out if and how we could best attend the show. Badung reported that we should try to come very early before the start of the performance to secure a proper place for our group on the street in front of the hotel, just outside the walls which were fortunately less than three feet high.

Thus we went from home while it was still daylight, but even then there was already a large crowd on the street in front of the Bali Hotel, strolling leisurely and excitedly chatting in anticipation of the performance of that evening. We occupied an open space near the gate. Soon other children joined us there, some of whom ventured to sit on the wall, eliciting my envy until I saw that malignant-looking guardians of the hotel chase them off their seats. Sitting on the ground was out of question. That would be considered too humiliating for our princely status, since everybody passing by would have their bodies in a position higher than our heads. Moreover we would then not be able to see much of the show. So we had to remain standing on our feet all the time, leaning with our chests against the wall. We followed with fascination the activities taking place before our eyes. Hotel boys in neat white uniforms were placing rattan chairs in a wide circle on the front yard, leaving an open space in the middle, where mats were spread on the ground. It was getting dark and no fewer than eight Stormking pressure lamps were placed high on tripods outside the ring of chairs, flooding the area with a brightness which I perceived as brighter than daylight.

One after the other the *gamelan* instruments were brought in by the members of the Banjar Belaluan, who arranged them in a special order on the mat-covered square inside the ring of chairs, leaving open a quadrangle in the middle. It was the positioning of the then "modern" *kebyar*, whereby a boy would perform the *kebyar* dance in the middle of the orchestra. It was going to be a very special performance that evening. I overheard people telling each other that for tonight's show, Mario, a famous dancer from Tabanan, had been rehearsing for one week with the Belaluan club. I heard also that a large group of tourists had arrived by boat that morning in Singaraja on the North coast and made the trip in not fewer than twenty touring cars via Kintamani to Denpasar in the afternoon.

The *gamelan* players took their seats on the mats behind their instruments. They were dressed in uniforms, consisting of batik *kains* and bright yellow silken *saputs* (over *kains*) around their middle, leaving their bodies bare. They wore beautiful *udengs*, headdresses of embroidered cloth, folded and bound elegantly around their heads.

After a while the guests emerged out of the hotel building and seated themselves on the chairs. Apparently the sight of that many white people together was so impressive that the noisy crowd around us fell silent for a few minutes. Everybody was staring curiously at the behaviour of the guests, some of whom were moving from one chair to another several times before they seemed to be satisfied. When all the chairs were occupied we smaller boys could not see much of the orchestra inside the ring and soon we were sitting on the wall from where we had a better view. This time the guardians did not bother us as they had already their whole attention focused on the show which was about to start.

Suddenly a powerful "BANGNGNG...." reverberated from the *gamelan*, the sensational start of the *kebyar* music, followed by a few exciting passages in crescendo, which ended abruptly, to make place for a beautiful melody, which sounded like crystal from the group of smaller *genders* (metallic xylophones), lingering in the air at first, soon gaining momentum and ending in a dynamic explosion, at which the whole orchestra joined in. I was immensely thrilled by the music which sounded fresh and new, so different from what I was used to. I found it not only beautiful but also invigorating and animating.

New to me also was that after the end of each piece the guests applauded; this practice had not yet been adopted by the Balinese public at that time.

I could not see much of Mario's dancing because most of the time he danced sitting on the ground or hopping around in the squatting position. I could only see brief glimpses of his head and his face making coquettish flirting grimaces to the tourists. I saw much more of his large gilded fan which fluttered swiftly and erratically in the air like a big golden butterfly above the heads of the guests. The dance did not much attract me. Somehow I found his flirtatious grimaces even a bit repulsive, but the music completely overwhelmed me.

Now and then the Balinese public on the street roared enthusiastically, which I could not understand at first. From my sitting position on the wall I could not see what caused the excitement. So I stood up on the wall as the other boys had, and saw Mario performing flirtatious dances with the *gamelan* players, at turns with the drummers and with the main xylophonist. Of course these players could not abandon their instruments and, thus handicapped, they could only dance with the upper parts of their bodies and with their heads, thereby producing something helplessly odd, which the public found most amusing. The flirtation and the roaring of the public reminded me immediately of the *gandrung* evenings at the Banjar Kajumas.

In the course of the following years the *kebyar* genre of *gamelan* music conquered Bali and, due to Mario's genius, the *kebyar* dance developed into a magnificent spectacle. Soon the dance was described by many foreign observers in books and magazines as the most intricate and fascinating of Balinese dances. Mario became the most celebrated dancer of Bali and his name well known abroad. Many talented young dancers became his pupils, but none of them ever reached the artistic level of the master.

Although I found extreme delight in the *kebyar* music, I could not yet appreciate the qualities of the *kebyar* dance at that time. It did not evoke any perceivable world in my imagination. I missed the stories which were usually attached to the Balinese dance drama. Thirty years later, through my involvement with the dance and *gamelan* group of Peliatan, I started to comprehend the meaning and the aesthetics of Mario's creation. That was due to Mario himself who, already in his mid sixties, came to participate in the composition of new dances and to help in the training of young dancers in the group, among whom was my talented eldest daughter. There I found the opportunity to observe his style and to interview the jolly old master.

He told me that he had been originally a *gandrung* dancer in the early 1920s. To make a living his small *gandrung* band wandered from village to village. Once they happened to be In the village of Busungbiyu in North Bali, where a famous *gamelan* orchestra was rehearsing the *kebyar* music. One of the drummers of the orchestra spotted the *gandrung* ensemble among the crowd of onlookers. He stopped playing and went to the group which he had seen performing in the nearby village the night before. He addressed the leader, asking: "Where is your best dancer of last night?" and, recognizing Mario, "Hey, you dear boy, could you dance the *gandrung* to my *kebyar* music?"

Mario, already stirred by the music from the beginning, immediately responded: "Sorry, I have never done it, but if you allow me, let me try!" Out of eagerness he allowed himself no time to put on the required female *gandrung* dress and went with the drummer to the middle of the orchestra. Completely absorbed by the music he danced and danced seemingly automatically, improvising during those moments of ecstasy a modification of the *gandrung* which he later developed into a most intricate and exciting male flirtation dance, the *kebyar duduk*, or the crouching *kebyar* dance. It is a physically demanding dance, and the technique can only be mastered after a very long and rigorous training.

When I asked Mario why he chose to hop all the time in the kneeling position, which is extremely difficult, he laughed: "When I danced the *gandrung*, I used to invite somebody from the public to dance with me. But that night in Busungbiyu I was inside the ring of the Kebyar orchestra from where I could not get out. Since I could not resist the compelling need to *ngibing* (do the flirtation dance) I was, by lack of a normal audience around me, forced to dance with the *gamelan* players. They were sitting on the ground and were unable to leave their instruments. Therefore it was I that had to kneel and to come down dancing."

And he went on laughing: "Ha ha ha..., hee he hee..., ha ha ha..." as if he again experienced the great fun which he must have had during those very historical moments for the development of the dance in Bali.

BOOK II
Java

CHAPTER 8

Journey to Java

Our previous headmaster in Denpasar and other Dutch officials had been eager to help Father find a good boarding-house in Malang for us. They advised him to have his sons stay with a Dutch teacher's family. That would ensure proper supervision and health care, and would offer the best chances for good progress at school. Dutch education outside school was also highly valued and pursued by many Indonesians at considerable cost. Father was happy that he could afford the expense for his two eldest sons.

The art teacher of the M.U.L.O., Mr Bolland, was willing to take us as boarders at the rate of 100 guilders a month. We were not aware of this high remuneration. Even later when we learned that our schoolmates from Bali had to pay only fifteen guilders a month for their boarding with Javanese families, we were not bothered by the existence of such a gross difference. We were accustomed to take for granted that we were of higher class. Two years later the ambitious Regent of Gianyar, who always tried to equal Father in all respects also brought his son to Malang to enter the M.U.L.O. school. He did not content himself with having his son stay with one of the teachers, but succeeded in boarding him with the Headmaster himself.

In 1931, travel by car was already quite common in Bali and accordingly the preparations for our journey from Karangasem to Singaraja, where we would take the boat to Surabaya, were not as elaborate as six years earlier when we first travelled to Denpasar. Of course, we still went for prayers to the seven temples in and around Karangasem, which were closely associated with our family. Three sets of offerings were prepared for prayers at three temples on the way: the first one at Candidasa, then at the Goa Lawah, and lastly at the temple of Penelokan on the rim of the Batur caldera.

The seven of us were: Father with an attendant; the principal priest of Karangasem, Pedanda Gedé Putu with his attendant; Gedé Djelantik; myself; and our guardian Bapa Badung, who had been with us in Denpasar before and would stay with us in Malang. We had grown much older and were already used to travelling by car so that even for Gedé the six-hour journey from Karangasem to Singaraja did not cause any trouble. A Chinese friend of Father's in Singaraja, shopkeeper, An Tong, treated us to a delicious lunch, lavishly enjoyed by all of us except the Brahman priest for whom pork was taboo. We had to ask our host to prepare special food for him, and to my embarrassment, to provide even brand new tableware, since for a Brahman priest it was taboo to eat from a plate which has been used before by non-priests. Our host could not be expected to know these rules, and Father, realizing this, bought a whole new set of plates, cups, glasses and pots for exclusive use by the Priest and which had to be carried along during the whole journey.

Our eminent escort had another moment of discomfort that afternoon when we went on board the ship. Except for Father and his attendant this was the first time that the rest of us had boarded a big steamer. The K.P.M. vessel was anchored about one mile off the coast. We took off by launch from a shaky wooden pier in front of the K.P.M. office building. The outboard motor pushed our launch swiftly over the water. The nearer we came to the "Valentijn", the bigger and mightier the vessel seemed to appear to us. I was thrilled by the ride and even Gedé enjoyed the boat trip. Pedanda Gedé Putu, however, looked up in anguished disdain as the motorboat went very close to the side of the ship underneath the stairway in order to secure an easy hold on the ramp for the crew. He felt his priesthood being challenged by the unavoidability of his head coming underneath the stairs on which people had been stepping with their feet. He called to Father who was sitting at the opposite side of the boat: "Sorry, Dwagung! This is impossible! What shall we do now?"

Father had anticipated the trouble and was already figuring out how to appease the mind of the High Priest. He also noticed the various decks on the ship, one above the other, promising more trouble. Unless he could find an agreeable formula, all these decks would spell total sacrilege to his beloved priest.

"Well," he said, "there are circumstances in which anybody, without being at fault himself, can be overcome by something which is inconsistent with his status in one or another specific hierarchy. Fortunately, certain measures are at hand by which one can be rehabilitated following such a condition. I think that in your case we have to be realistic and to accept the fact that by force of circumstances you will be desecrated for a while. This would not matter much since you will not be required to function as a High Priest during our journey. We can arrange a *pelukatan* (consecration ceremony) later, after which you will be again entitled to resume your priestly functions." His Eminence stared at Father with wide eyes, but was visibly relieved. The embarkation went smoothly.

Father had bought first-class tickets for the four of us and three third-class tickets for Bapa Badung and the two attendants. To my consternation, Father insisted that the attendants should bring their mats into the two first-class cabins and sleep there on the floor. I could not brush off my feeling that the ship's crew regarded us as uncivilized passengers who did not know the rules.

Respect for Father and tradition withheld me from expressing my feelings. We knew that both Father and the High Priest were fond of *pepaosan*, a celebrated entertainment, and since we knew that the Priest's attendant was a good singer, we anticipated that Father was planning to have a *pepaosan* that evening.

That evening, however, we were not particularly interested in attending. Instead, out of curiosity, I took Gedé and Bapa Badung on a sightseeing tour through the ship. It was fantastic! We saw beautiful salons, splendid dining rooms and glorious promenade decks with many Dutch passengers, who (as I later found out) were travelling to Java from Ambon and Makassar. We were even allowed to peep through large round windows into the engine room. Bapa Badung wanted us to see the third- and fourth-class decks where he hoped to find some acquaintances from Denpasar whom he had seen when boarding the ship. However, those quarters were too crowded with people, sitting or lying on their mats, eating, chatting or playing cards. Many of them were obviously having trouble with seasickness. Gedé could not stand the sight of those people in distress and the mixture of sickening odours in the air. So we hastily made our way over and between bodies back to our quarters. When we reached our cabin we were quite exhausted and fell down on our berths.

Coming to rest on our beds we heard the *pepaosan* reverberating animatedly in Father's cabin next door. *Mebebasan* or *pepaosan* is an age-old and still celebrated entertainment among the Balinese literate. In such meetings, a singer loudly recites verses from the ancient classical epics, such as the Ramayana and the Mahabharata, reading from the *lontar* before a group of listeners. The text is in the Kawi language (Old Javanese) and thus incomprehensible for the common public. After each strophe or part of it, a narrator translates the content of the text in colloquial Balinese language. The participants and attendants enjoy the music of the recitation and find delight in the style and language of the narrator and his intonations, while at the same time they critically assess the accuracy of the translation. Everybody is entitled to throw in his comments after the translation of each stanza. Usually, lively discussions result from differences of interpretation between the participants. It was one of Father's greatest hobbies to call together such *pepaosan* groups, to stimulate among the members literary and philosophical discussions and to act both as resource person and as mediator between opponents. It was quite common that such meetings extended until deep in the night, or even until the next morning, if the participants were carried away by their enthusiasm.

I recognized the voice of the Priest's attendant who was reciting, now and then interrupted by the Priest, asking him to stop or to repeat some words. Then we heard the Priest translating, now and then interrupted by Father, who either found a better translation or a more beautiful phrase for the same thing.

We could not understand the Kawi songs, but from the translated recitation we understood that they were reading the "Arjuna Wiwaha", the story in which beautiful nymphs try to seduce the meditating Arjuna, the second of the Pandawas. We knew the story very well from our *dalangs* or puppeteers and were therefore not so much listening to the story itself as to the melody of the recitation and the beautiful language used by the translator and his particularly musical intonations.

Perhaps in my subconscious I was anticipating radical changes to happen in my life, or perhaps the excitement of travelling to an unknown world made me that evening sensitive to the beauty of the *pepaosan*. While I was listening, I suddenly heard the rhythm of the stanzas beautifully stressed by the singer with his fine voice. Somehow I found it harmonizing with the rhythmical dash of the waves outside and with the throbbing of the engines far below. I found myself enjoying the cadences of the translation by the High Priest, who seemed to sing the narrative in the same way as he would recite the religious incantations during his daily morning prayers. And indeed, I started to feel delight when I heard Father coming out with new phrases and sang his interpretation, fashioning a musical duet with his priestly friend.

On many occasions, in later years, I have deeply regretted not having been obliged to learn the Kawi language. This lack of knowledge was made more apparent to me especially in the 1960s when I was much involved in Balinese arts and culture. Unfortunately, professional and other activities did not allow me the time to start a new discipline.

Bapa Badung who had stretched himself on the floor between our berths started to snore peacefully. His regular breathing and the rhythmical sounds of the recitations next door gradually had a kind of hypnotic effect on us and soon we also were in a sound sleep.

In the midst of the night I was suddenly awakened by loud voices and heavy footsteps in the corridor along our cabins and there was a hard and frightening knock on Father's door. Terrified, I violently woke Bapa Badung and Gedé, hiding myself behind Bapa Badung's broad shoulders. We heard Father's door being opened and there was for a short time a cacophony of many voices, partly in Dutch and partly in Indonesian, which because of my bewilderment I could not comprehend. Bapa Badung seemed petrified. He did not dare to open the door until a long time after the people had left. It became very quiet. Obviously the *pepaosan* had stopped. Badung slipped out of our cabin and we heard him whispering with the Priest through the blinds of Father's cabin door. Slipping back quickly he informed us that the Captain had asked Father to stop the meeting which had kept the other passengers awake. Father had found the request quite reasonable and had sent the attendants back to the third-class decks.

We disembarked the next day in Surabaya in great confusion not being used to coolies aggressively grabbing our luggage and running away far ahead of us.

Father's friend, Raden Mas Haryono, who waited for us at the harbour with his two big limousines, tried to reassure us. Only on arrival at his house in the town did we verify that none of our luggage was missing.

We were to stay and have a rest at the Haryonos for one day before continuing our journey early the next morning to Malang, 80 km south of Surabaya. I found Surabaya extremely hot and when asked to join Father and Gedé that night in their common bed which was provided with a mosquito net, I declined and asked permission to sleep with Bapa Badung outside on the floor of the verandah where it was much cooler. There I had a sound and refreshing sleep, but on awakening, everybody had great fun and laughed at me because I had hundreds of small red dots all over my body from mosquito bites.

Mr and Mrs Bolland looked a bit confused when our assorted band of ten arrived at their door the following afternoon. They certainly had never seen a Balinese High Priest before and could not make out which one was the Raja of Karangasem who was respectfully and laudably mentioned in so many letters. Fortunately Mr Haryono, who in his European dress looked as a high official, quickly introduced all of us in Dutch to the family. I noticed that it took Mr Bolland some effort to pay the required honours to the barefooted tiny figure, clad in a *kain* and a simple white jacket, and to the High Priest, who looked so strangely dignified. I noticed also that behind Mrs Bolland two very blond children were giggling all the time at the unusual sight of our odd company.

This visibly annoyed Mrs Bolland very much. Suddenly her hand struck and to my dismay the girl with the blond curls ran away, screaming, and disappeared in one of the rooms, followed by her little brother. I was both impressed and alarmed by such an exhibition of displeasure in front of strangers!

The host of new impressions made me incapable of following the conversation. I can only remember that it was Mr Haryono who did most of the talking and that Father was listening thoughtfully, now and then nodding with approval.

A teenage Javanese boy, Soenyoto, son of the Regent of Blitar, who had been with the Bollands for the past two years, was introduced to us. He had just passed to the third grade of the M.U.L.O. To me he looked a complete adult "man". I was most impressed by his neatly ironed long trousers. We were happy to find someone with whom we could communicate freely, and from whom we expected to get more information about school and about what life with a Dutch family was like.

Father was deeply moved when he had to leave us alone with Bapa Badung, as there was no place for him and his retinue to stay at the Bollands. The Haryonos brought them back to his bungalow in Lawang. Father came to visit us every day during the week before he returned to his duties in Karangasem.

On his last visit he brought with him the two gleaming new bicycles which he had promised us some time before in Denpasar.

CHAPTER 9

Transformations

We were housed in the Bollands' backyard in a high building which consisted of only two rooms one above the other. These rooms were connected with the main house by a long open corridor running along the garage, the kitchen, two bathrooms, two toilets, two rooms for servants, and the godown. Soenyoto occupied the ground floor from where a wooden staircase led to our bed- and sitting room. Living on an upper floor was in itself an exciting experience for me and the wooden balcony attached to the back of the room was an additional delight.

Before entering school we had one week to adapt ourselves to the new circumstances, especially to the new lifestyle with the Bolland family. Soenyoto was of great help; we had only to do exactly the same as he did. Even that first night we had our first shock when Mr Bolland ordered Bapa Badung out of our room. He could not approve of our having a servant guardian sleeping with us during the night. Although we did not understand the reason, we were too shy to protest and we complied. Of course we did not sleep well that night. Superstition was still very much with us and we were deadly scared. In our large iron bed, provided with sheets and a mosquito net which was incredibly clean to our senses, we held each other tight, listening apprehensively at every sound, expecting all the time something unusual to happen with every unfamiliar noise.

The next morning Mr Bolland discovered that we had been sleeping in our daily clothes. We did not know about *pajamas*! The first thing that Father had to do when he came to visit us was to buy each of us two sets of pajamas. Before going to bed that night we had to go to the family and show that we had changed into our new night gear. Mr and Mrs Bolland looked satisfied and we learned to say neatly "Wel te rusten!" ("Sleep well!") before we retired. This "Wel te rusten!" before going to bed did not mean anything to us, but was to become a daily ceremony for which we prepared ourselves with great care.

The following night, Mr Bolland, making his evening rounds, woke us out of our dreams and told us to put off the lights. We understood that we had to sleep in the dark. We looked at each other, frightened, but since Father had told us that we should obey our teachers, we hesitantly switched off our lamp. It was with a kind of fatality that we went to sleep again that night. However, we soon got used to sleeping in pajamas with the lights off and without a guardian on the floor under our bed.

In the beginning, food was a great problem. We had Indonesian food only at midday after school. For breakfast we had bread and butter with cheese, brown palm sugar or chocolate granules, which I found delicious at once. Soenyoto had to demonstrate how to smear the butter on the slice of bread and how to eat with knife and fork. It was all very interesting. We had some difficulty with the butter and the cheese which were just too alien to our taste. At our first breakfast our appetite vanished after the first couple of bites. When we started to leave the table Mrs Bolland told us that it was impolite to leave anything on our plates. With great effort we managed to finish our second slice of bread. In the evenings there was always soup or a light snack before the bread meal. After three months we got used to European food and we even started to like many items such as ham, sausages, cauliflower and Brussels sprouts.

We were not allowed to have food in our quarters and had to have our meals together with the family. Since we were already used to court etiquette in Bali, it was not difficult for us to observe rules, especially where restraint was essential. Adaptation was however most difficult where things contrary to Balinese customs were required. This happened when the Bollands encouraged us to engage in conversation during meals. In the beginning the problem was compounded by our still poor command of the Dutch language. When, after finishing the soup, Mr Bolland asked: "Why don't you say anything?", we looked totally blank. What to say? "Do you like the soup?" Oh, my! Shall I tell him that the onions nauseated me? That would be a great offense in Bali. Moreover, I did not know how to say it in Dutch. Fortunately, Gedé liked onions and answered politely: "Yes, Sir!" but he did not go much further. We learned later that it was good manners to comment on what one had eaten, something considered very rude at home. And to mention that one likes it, would be like asking for more and that would be most offensive.

It took quite a long time before we had overcome our inhibitions. But even after we learned to speak Dutch better, Mr or Mrs Bolland usually had to take the initiative to start any conversation. We had been too strictly trained to wait with talking until asked by elder people. I noticed that Soenyoto after having been with the Bollands for two years still had the same difficulty.

Mr Bolland very seriously took on the task of coaching us through the preliminary class. He examined our homework every day and meticulously corrected our mistakes. With great patience he explained every difficulty. He was most helpful especially in guiding us through the perplexities of Dutch grammar. Dutch language was the most important item for admission to the first grade. Arithmetic came second. As expected, Gedé made good progress, as he had already been at first grade standard when we finished school in Bali. Mr Bolland had much more trouble with me, since actually I was two grades behind. Somehow he succeeded teaching me enough because at the end of the year my marks were just sufficient to enter the first grade of the M.U.L.O. school. Gedé was most happy that I could remain with him in the same class.

The harsh guttural voice of Mr Elenbaas, our maths teacher, crackled through the classroom: "This, my boys, this is what we call an axiom, a plain fact, a truth, that neither you nor I nor anybody in the world can deny!" Leaning with his left hand on his inseparable rattan walking stick he turned himself away from the blackboard and pointing with the chalk between his thumb and forefinger to a boy with curly black hair far back in the classroom he thundered: "Hey there, what did I say?"

Matulesi, the Ambonese boy, rudely awakened from his daydream, looked up in bewilderment. I could not help laughing. This rescued the poor chap because immediately the teacher's anger was diverted towards me. With a red menacing face he came so near to me that my heart stood still. He repeated in a bass tone: "What did I say?"

I pulled myself together and succeeded in stuttering: "An ax...ax..axiom! That it is an axiom, Sir". He continued: "And why?", coming still nearer, and looking at me with his penetrating eyes.

I murmured: "A true fact, undeniable".

"But why? I was not asking 'what', but 'WHY', why is it an axiom?"

I felt the class becoming tense, as was always the case with this fearsome teacher. I happened to look in his eyes and saw something odd: while his face looked so ominous, his eyes appeared to be laughing, like joking! I felt reassured and answered: "Because if those lines were meeting each other in more than one point, at least one of them should not be a straight line." I expected another thundering, but to my astonishment his face relaxed. I was overcome with great relief. I felt that everybody was looking at me as if I was a strange creature. Mr Elenbaas took my arm and led me to the front bench, saying: "Boy, from now on you will sit here, I will have more talks with you!"

I was puzzled, guessing at the meaning of that pronouncement and wondering why I should be sitting so close to him all the time. What could I have done wrong to earn such punishment? Only a little bit of laughing?

Mr Elenbaas went back to the blackboard and started to draw. I saw two straight lines again, crossing each other at an angle and then the teacher drew a bow between the lines close to the crossing point, indicating the smaller angle.

Then, Bang! All of a sudden I knew what he was going to tell us: the opposing angles *were equal*!

Somehow I had a strange feeling that everything around me had suddenly become so bright and clear. All colours around me in the classroom seemed to be more intense. It was a most beautiful sensation. I became restless. As if he sensed my excitement Mr Elenbaas turned to me and asked: "What is it? Do you want to say anything?" I told him what I thought about those opposing angles. "So? And why?" he asked with wide open unbelieving eyes. I stepped out of my bench, took up one of the chalks lying on the table, went to the blackboard and showed that the opposing angles had the same angle as its supplement to cover a straight line. I was too much filled with triumphant excitement to notice the teacher's reaction. I rushed back to my bench.

That very moment during the second lesson in geometry with Mr Elenbaas turned out to be an important milestone in my school years and for the rest of my life. It was as if by a magic wand something dormant was loosed or brought to life in my brains. From that on I started to have interest in learning. Knowledge became attractive, exciting and enjoyable. Especially the logic in geometry and mathematics revealed itself in all its beauty. Almost every time when Mr Elenbaas entered the classroom and started to draw something on the blackboard, I sensed what he was going to tell us. No wonder that with the routine tests I always scored the 10 mark without even having to learn my lessons at home. As if triggered by maths, other faculties of my mind started to function remarkably. The other subjects such as geography, physics, biology, chemistry, so cumbersome to my friends, became to me most interesting. It was for me sufficient just to listen, actually just to enjoy listening, during the lessons in the classroom. My classmates who had been with me in the preliminary class the previous year were astonished to see that I scored also in these subjects the highest marks. They often asked me how I did it. Of course I could not give the answer, it all came by itself. Because it came all by itself I never felt the ambition to be better than my classmates. On the contrary, I always helped any one of them who came and often even did their homework for them, without realizing that it was no solution for their real problem.

What did not come that easily were the languages. Already in the first grade we had begun to learn English, French and German. Rules of grammar and words had to be memorized, pronunciation had to be practised. However, I liked the logic of German grammar, and to chant the manifold groups of words with specific grammatical features, which lent itself to be learned by heart like musical rhymes.

Before long I was the top student at school and won all the school prizes in competitions over the whole country each year. It was a strange phenomenon which remained with me during all those school years, first at the M.U.L.O. in Malang, later at the A.M.S. in Yogyakarta. Also at the University in Holland I never had any difficulties with my studies. Because of the ease that I had with learning I always had plenty of time for a wide range of extracurricular activities. Not less than my professional training, the experiences during these activities became very essential and decisive elements in my further development.

CHAPTER 10

Inclinations

Beginning with our second year in Malang Gedé lagged more and more behind me in our studies. After we received our second quarterly reports Mr Bolland found it no longer necessary to supervise my school work. Gedé, however, continued to need his help until the very end of the school term. He especially had trouble with mathematics, but was quite good in languages. His strong sense of duty compelled him to do his utmost. By studying very hard, often until late at night, he made reasonable progress. All that time he was marvelling at his younger brother whom he saw always playing around, hardly ever looking into his textbooks, and still getting the highest marks. Despite my much younger age Gedé never had any feeling of jealousy towards me. On the contrary he was very proud of me, telling everybody about his clever brother. He also marvelled at my complete indifference to my achievements of which he was so proud.

I remained very much attached to Gedé as his faithful younger brother throughout the years. Indeed, I helped him not only with his homework, but also arranged practical matters for him, continuing my role of Laksmana as Rama's servant brother, now in a modernized version. I did this instinctively, out of duty, maybe also out of love, not realizing that I was contributing to the circumstances which prevented Gedé from overcoming his weakness of character. This became apparent later, when as Father's successor, strong leadership was demanded from him.

Despite our strong attachment, we inevitably grew apart from each other. Our interests became different. Freed from the binding conformities of traditional life in Bali we followed more and more our individual inclinations.

Our school was one of the about sixty M.U.L.O. ("Meer Uitgebreid Lager Onderwijs" or Expanded Elementary Education) schools spread over the Indonesian archipelago. By Government regulation Balinese students had to enroll themselves in one of the two M.U.L.O. schools nearest to Bali, in Malang or Surabaya. There were about twenty of us in our school and quite naturally we had a small club of Balinese students, called "Bali Dharma Laksana" (Bali Social Activities). It was basically a community welfare organization dealing with family and socio-cultural matters such as the celebration of our traditional Balinese days of worship, and had only a very slight touch of Indonesian nationalism. Most of us were not at all interested in politics. Nationalism was something still very far away from us. From what we learned in history classes about the three centuries of Dutch colonial rule in Java we could not in the least imagine its oppressiveness. When we learned about wars with the Dutch in Sumatra and Celebes at the end of the 19th century, those events remained completely outside our concern. It was not only because we were still too young to be able to grasp the true meaning of colonialism. In Bali our generation had actually never felt any oppression by the white rulers, due to the fact that the Dutch conquest of the island took place years after the adoption of Van Deventer's so called "Ethical Policy" for their colonies which were then renamed "Overseas territories". Moreover, at the H.I.S. we had been effectively indoctrinated about the beneficial effects of Dutch administration in our country.

In Java, national consciousness grew steadily in the wake of the founding of the "Budi Utomo" in 1918, a mainly cultural movement aiming at the promotion of Indonesian nationalism through social and cultural activities. Soon radical groups of nationalists became more and more involved in politics. Political parties came into being, varying in their aims from gradually increasing participation in government to the immediate and complete independence of the Indonesian Nation. For us Balinese students in Malang the cultural aims of "Budi Utomo" had more appeal than the politics. The Balinese students' clubs in the bigger cities such as Surabaya and Jakarta were more affected.

Our small club in Malang had no strong leader. My classmate Ngurah Rai who later became the leader of the guerillas in Bali fighting against the re-establishment of Dutch rule after the Japanese occupation, had had to leave school in his second year, to return home because of the death of his father.

After two years our club lost for me most of its magnetism. It remained in existence only because we Balinese felt the need to be together regularly, to make trips together by train or on bicycles to places of interest around Malang. Gedé clung happily to the club. Although I enjoyed the trips outside the town I found the other members' company at times most boring. Instinctively, I looked for new and more exciting experiences.

These were provided by other groups in our school, which had special appeal for me because of their exciting initiatives and their constant display of activity. These groups existed mainly of Eurasians, while some of them were totoks (of pure Dutch blood). They numbered about one third of our schoolmates. Their frankness, their uninhibited way of expressing their views, often cross and impolite, which was strongly resented by our Javanese and Balinese friends, attracted me. They accepted me and I joined their swimming club. Not all of them were bright at school and of course I was always ready to help anyone with their schoolwork. In this matter it struck me that these boys and girls were nowhere near as ambitious as our Indonesian or Chinese schoolmates. I found them at times incredibly indifferent about their schoolwork. In my naivete I ascribed this to the fact that since they belonged ethnically to the "rulers", they enjoyed the privilege to be careless and that the teachers would make concessions if and when needed.

No hostility whatsoever existed between the Dutch-Eurasian groups and their Indonesian schoolmates. There just did not exist that feeling of coherence or the need for normal casual communication with them. The Javanese students were too shy and too polite to actively seek their company. Perhaps they unconsciously felt in them their colonial oppressors. Our small group of Balinese students had no such feelings. Their attitude was plain indifference, regarding them as belonging to another world and not to be bothered with. Thus, the members of the various ethnic groups stuck comfortably to their own worlds, showing no inclination to get better acquainted with others. It was like a kind of benign apartheid defined by nature and socio-cultural conditions.

Although I spent most of my time with the Eurasians I felt myself at ease with all the groups. Perhaps it was due to my special position in my class. Since I had no trouble with learning the teachers entrusted to me various tasks such as the ringing of the schoolbell between classes, for which every time I had to walk all the way down passing all the classrooms. I had also the task to maintain the daily register of homework given to our class by the teachers, thereby seeing to it that we were given no more homework than can be done within three hours. From experience, I knew approximately what this meant.

During our years in Malang, the Bollands wanted to give us the best possible education. Mr Bolland, the art teacher, was a painter in the naturalist style, doing mostly still life paintings. I learned from him to see the real colours of objects and shades, and he taught me the technique of aquarelle painting and the classical method of drawing. He also wanted to acquaint us with the other European arts. He played the violin and the piano, and the *pauk* (a type of kettledrum) in the Malang Amateur Symphony Orchestra. He took us to regular performances of the orchestra and there we learned to listen to Mozart, Beethoven and other composers. I loved the music. Mr Bolland was also very active in the Theatre Club, and we saw performances of plays by a whole range of Dutch, European and English dramatists all in Dutch translation. It was excellent for our training in the Dutch language.

Daily association with Eurasian and Dutch friends did not fail to influence my behaviour, my preferences and even my way of moving around. Once when I entered the room where Gedé was doing his homework, he remarked:

"I knew that you were coming..."

"How?" I replied in surprise.

"From your footsteps. Different from Bagus Oka, who will be coming in a moment, and from the others."

"What difference?" I laughed unbelievingly.

"Much quicker, louder and firm, you behave yourself un-Balinese, like Europeans!" he explained.

Later, when I was cycling to the swimming pool for water-polo training, I found myself thinking about Gedé's remark. It was the first time that somebody had told me that I had become different. Or was I already different from Gedé and our Balinese friends from before? Educated to conformity and to nurture that sense of belonging to one's community, the thought of becoming a stranger, an alien, was quite disturbing. But perhaps Gedé was right! I did walk much faster than any of my Balinese friends who used to stroll leisurely along. My footsteps were indeed firm and purposeful. I had no patience at all when shopping with Gedé and Bagus Oka, who could bargain endlessly with the shopkeeper and could return to the same shop several times before deciding on a purchase. I realized that we had become different also in taste. In going to the cinema I preferred to see Tarzan films, while Gedé and the others went to pictures with sweet songs and romantic love stories.

Our paths would have separated after finishing the M.U.L.O. in Malang, were it not that Father wanted us to remain together. Gedé should not be left without my assistance. Because of my high marks at leaving the M.U.L.O., I was entitled to enter the fourth grade of the H.B.S. ("Hogere Burgerlijke School" or the Dutch College) in Malang. This would enable me to enter university after two years. Gedé's destiny, however, was to succeed Father as ruler of Karangasem and the Dutch officials had advised Father that Gedé should study law at the university in Batavia (now Jakarta). To this end he should first complete three years' study at the A.M.S.–A, the literary and socio-cultural department of the higher secondary school, in Yogyakarta. In the same town, as a separate school, was also an A.M.S.–B, the mathematics and natural sciences department, which was considered suitable for me, since at that time, I wanted to become an engineer. It was therefore decided that we would go together to study in Yogyakarta.

Our first boarding-house in Jogyakarta was with the French language teacher of the A.M.S. –A. and his wife. The Lunenburghs were a young Dutch couple, fresh from Holland, with two-year-old twin daughters. What struck me most about the family when I met them for the first time was that they were so unnaturally white! They appeared to me much whiter than the Dutch people I knew, who had been in the tropics for a couple of years. Another difference I later noticed was their approach to us and the Indonesian students. They spoke to us as friends, on an equal footing, which puzzled us at the beginning. Could we just drop that polite reverence which had always been with us by tradition?

So, for the first time, Gedé and I found ourselves at separate schools, each with its own curriculum. The schools were about three km apart from each other, so that there was little contact between the A and B students, except during the regular sports competitions. Gedé had different books, no more mathematics, and a token of chemistry and biology. Except for these subjects I was of little help for him with his homework. He had to work very hard and as the years proceeded, and as the material of learning increased, he had to study more often until deep at night. He found the help and attention he needed from his chemistry teacher, Mr Wechgelaar, a very friendly and kind-hearted elderly man, who had been in Java for a long time and was very interested in Eastern culture. When the following year Mr Lunenburgh was transferred to another duty station, Gedé took the initiative to ask Mr Wechgelaar if he could take us as boarders. I was very surprised because it was one of the very few times that Gedé ever took an initiative on his own. The Wechgelaars appeared to be willing. I was happy because their house was close to my school and also close to the swimming pool where my club was in training.

At the Wechgelaars we found our boarding as pleasant as if it were our second home. The Lunenburghs were fresh from Holland and still very Dutch. They had not yet adapted to Indonesian life and apparently did not much care for it. We had Dutch food six days a week and only on Sundays was there a rice meal modified to European taste. At the Wechgelaars, only breakfast was Dutch, consisting of bread, butter, ham and eggs, and sweets. They had rice at midday and in the evening. European food was served occasionally on Sundays and on special days.

Mr Wechgelaar was a wonderful man who revealed so much of understanding, wisdom, patience and love in his day-to-day life. His family life was that of complete harmony, and there was never a hard or unfriendly word to his wife and his children. His discipline was that of persuasion. For Gedé especially he had great compassion. Seeing that the studies were very hard for Gedé, he constantly assured and encouraged him. We loved him and regarded him as our second father. Gedé sensed in him that kind of *dharma* which remained his true ideal and became very close to him.

Mrs Wechgelaar was German-born. She had two daughters from her late husband and a baby boy of six months by Mr Wechgelaar. She was much closer to me, being typically German—romantic and sentimental. Having the custody of two "royal princes" in her house (later three, since our younger brother Madé Karang joined us the following year) was for her a limitless source of excitement, pride and satisfaction. When she learned that I was the top student of the school I became her idol. Later when she discovered that I had never known my own mother she wept and hugged me affectionately and ever since she bestowed upon me her genuine motherly love. Although at times I found it smothering, I was deeply moved, as I had never experienced this before.

Paradoxically, while Mrs Wechgelaar made me really happy, her sincerity evoked in me a feeling of sadness: I came to realize that I had been missing my mother. I wondered how life would have been with her. Eventually, at Mr Wechgelaar's suggestion, I decided to accept life as it was. However, there came a period that often at night I awoke from a dream in which I saw what I imagined as my mother, and on approaching and touching her, discovered with a shock that it was a cold stone statue of the Madonna, with myself kneeling in a Catholic church. Always it was exactly like the church where the Bollands took me in Malang several years before. Out of fear to be laughed at for being sentimental I never told anybody about those recurring dreams.

The two daughters of the family, twelve year old Nienke and nine-year-old Janny, were having lessons on the violin with a Chinese musician. Out of curiosity I occasionally took one of their instruments and tried to strike some notes. When Mrs Wechgelaar heard my efforts, she urged me to have lessons too. I knew that it was expensive and I was not sure if Father would agree to the extra cost. But Mrs Wechgelaar who was convinced that her idol must be a "Wunderkind", and thus must also be a musical talent, would not listen and wanted to pay all the expenses. Mr Tan, the music teacher, who had taken great pains in teaching the girls the art of playing the violin without achieving much progress, was delighted after my first lesson. There was apparently enough musical talent in me. I mastered the technique quite easily and found great fun in the exercises, turning them into musical experiences. Soon I was able to participate in simple string quartets. Mr Tan was so moved by my progress that later when I left for Holland for further studies he awarded me for my musical achievement one of his two violins, a concerto instrument with a beautiful sound, made and signed by a Swiss craftsman, George Uhlmann.

It was eventually Mrs Wechgelaar who unknowingly by circumstances diverged my initial intention to become an engineer. She was fat and liked good food. One night she got an acute attack of gallstones. She vomited continuously and was suffering terribly. From the pain she could not lay still in bed and was throwing herself to all sides, crying. I could not stand the sight of this suffering. There was no way to get her into a taxi and there was no telephone in the house, so I offered to get the doctor, sprang on my bicycle and raced to the doctor's house three miles away. Overcoming my fright of the barking shepherd dog, I managed to find the bell in the dark, rang and waited. It seemed an endlessly long wait. I rang again and again. At last, the door opened and a sleepy Dr Liem, the Chinese doctor, appeared in his pajamas in the doorway. He was not very friendly. I explained the emergency of the situation with Mrs Wechgelaar. He yawned and promised to come immediately. When I told him that I wanted to wait and go with him and pick up my bicycle later, he declined and wanted me to go first. I gave him the address because I believed him, which I regretted later. I returned to the sickbed and attended to Mrs Wechgelaar who continued vomiting and crying from pain. I could not do much except support her in the back and under the forehead every time she started to belch. From biology class I knew the function of the gallbladder but I had no idea of what to do to relieve the pain.

And there we were waiting and waiting—and no doctor was coming. I was getting impatient and angry and looked at Mr Wechgelaar. He was praying. After one hour I could not stand waiting any longer and vowed that if I were a doctor I would not let people wait and suffer like this. I took my bike and rushed back to the doctor's house. It was four o'clock in the morning and the sky in the East had become a little lighter. This time I rang the bell much more vigorously. It was an old-fashioned bell that had to be pulled at by a steel wire. I must have behaved myself not too politely, because the doctor was angry. He cursed me and chased me away, but told me at the same time that he was really coming. This time I did not believe him and waited on my bike in the dark behind a tree at the corner of the street, planning to make a hell of a noise with a stick on his door if he was not coming in a few minutes. In those minutes, I pondered about the medical profession, the duties of a doctor, about humanity, morality, human suffering and about the loss of my mother for lack of medical assistance. Perhaps that was the moment that I gave up my intention to become an engineer and wanted to become a doctor instead.

The lights of Dr Liem's motor car when it turned around brought me back to reality and with a sense of relief and great happiness I raced after the car and arrived completely out of breath at the Wechgelaars at the same moment as the doctor. I followed sharply all the doctor's movements while he examined the patient and when he gave her an injection later. He left a number of tablets for Mrs Wechgelaar to be taken every hour until the pain abated and placed a rubber sac with hot water on the site of her gallbladder.

I looked at the doctor's face and saw how tired he was. He apologized to Mr Wechgelaar for not having come sooner, and explained that he had overslept his alarm clock which he had set for fifteen minutes after I had called on him the first time. He badly needed a little rest after returning from a long and exhausting delivery of a baby that night. Mr Wechgelaar thanked him and accompanied him to the gate. He was greatly relieved seeing that his wife was no longer in distress after the injection and was becoming quieter. I waited for a while, assuring myself that she was sleeping already, before I went to bed myself.

That morning I told Mr. Wechgelaar that the medical profession seemed to me more exciting and more rewarding than that of engineering. He agreed and brought for me that afternoon a fine book from the library to read: *Albert Schweitzer of Lambarene*. I was thrilled by the story of this Swiss doctor working among the natives in Africa and read the book three times. At Christmas the Wechgelaars gave me another delightful book: *Microbe Hunters* by Paul de Kruif. My future destination was then decided!

CHAPTER 11

Javanese Connections

Origins

Conditions in Bali before 1925 were still very primitive compared with Java. Manufactured goods such as paper, books, textiles, metalware and household items like soap, lamps and glassware had to be imported from or through Java. For the common people in Bali the word "Jawi" (which means "Java") was identical with "abroad". Any item which was of superior quality to locally produced goods was respectfully referred to as "*saking Jawi*" meaning "coming from Java". The Balinese nobility loved to regard themselves as originating from Java. This claim was basically correct, particularly for those among them who were able to trace their genealogy to the rulers of Majapahit. They claimed to belong to the upper echelons of the Balinese nobility, because it was the King of Majapahit who conquered Bali in the fourteenth century and thereafter consolidated the Hindu-Javanese culture on the island.

Once Father told us that we should not feel ourselves inferior to the descendants of Majapahit, since our ancestry could claim to be of a much older dynasty, going back to King Erlangga of Kediri, who ruled 250 years before Majapahit.

Erlangga was born a Balinese prince. His father, King Udayana, ruled over Bali at the end of the 10th century. By marriage to the Princess of Kediri of East Java, Prince Erlangga became King of Kediri. Because of a revolt he had to take refuge for a short period in a monastery, but was later returned to power. Before long, he defeated his many rivals and became ruler over the whole of East-Java and Bali. Due to his education at the monastery King Erlangga was a great man of literature and the arts. He brought his kingdom to glory and prosperity.

He always wanted to be just and fair, and when he retired he divided his vast kingdom into two equal parts between his two sons, who—alas—soon after his death waged war against each other. Eventually, after a long period of unrest, the eastern kingdom prevailed and Kediri became once again the capital of East Java.

Peace did not last long. One of Kediri's vassals, the Prince of Singasari, was assasinated by an adventurer, named Ken Arok, who proclaimed Singasari as his kingdom and whose step-grandson, Raden Wijaya, later seized the throne of Kediri. After assasinating most of the Chinese army who had helped him to defeat Kediri, Wijaya founded his capital, Majapahit, more to the north.

Two generations later, under the leadership of its able prime minister Gajah Mada, who reigned on behalf of Wijaya's under-age grandson, Hayam Wuruk, the kingdom of majapahit expanded over the whole Indonesian archipelago. Thus, it was Gajah Mada who brought Bali again under Javanese rule. Kediri had long since become a vassal state under Majapahit. Its subdued nobility had to provide courtiers for the king and officers for Majapahit's army. Many came in Gajah Mada's expeditionary force to Bali and among them, according to Father, were our direct ancestors.

Father told us about Erlangga before we had history classes at school in Denpasar. I was not yet able to place the story in any historical perspective. If I had any concept of Erlangga at that time, it was shaped by the masked *topeng* dance-drama, that was regularly performed in our Puri as entertainment at religious festivals and many other family celebrations. I was fond of the *topeng*, of its masks, its characters, the fascinating dance movements full of life and dramatic expression, and the exciting accompaniment by drums and the *gamelan*. In those dances Erlangga was always portrayed as a most elegant and handsome king, with a beautiful white mask, gracefully moving over the stage, a personification of justice, wisdom and compassion. The music which accompanies this "dance of the *Dalem*", still being performed to this day, is of a serene crystalline beauty, and creates a special atmosphere of divine purity. Thus, when Father told us that King Erlangga was our direct ancestor, it created in my mind the ideal of a "super-ego", a lifestyle to aim for, a style of beauty, sincerity and honesty.

The Mangku Negara

It was not possible for me to trace in what way Father formed a lasting friendship with Prince Mangku Negara VII of Solo, Central Java. One source mentioned that the Mangku Negara also claimed to be a descendant of King Erlangga. In any case, the two men shared the same ideas concerning cultural, political and many other matters. The Mangku Negara, being far more educated than Father, who had never attended any school, found it his most pleasant duty to give Father all kinds of advice and to extend to him all the help he could think of. Their friendship had already existed for some time when we went to Malang to school. The Mangku Negara asked his cousin, Mr Haryono in Surabaya, to assist us in our journey to Malang. Later, when our younger brothers finished their H.I.S. in Bali, four of them went to the M.U.L.O. in Solo and were housed in the palace of the Mangku Negara.

When we first visited the palace, we were immeasurably impressed by what we saw. It was a real palace! The huge buildings, the vast *pendopos* (open quadrangle structures under a roof) with their spotless gleaming white marble floors and golden ceilings, from which hung enormous crystal chandeliers, made our image of our Puri in Karangasem fade away in rustic obscurity. It was just overwhelming, at least in the beginning. I was also struck by the atmosphere of refined discipline, created by the silent measured movements of the extremely well-dressed servants, in contrast to whom our servants at home seemed noisy, gaudy and untidy.

I felt overcome by a feeling of uncivilized barbarity, when during our first conversation after our arrival at the palace, I happened to let my eyes wander over the white marble floor from Father's bare feet covered with dust, sticking out from under his loosely wrapped kain, to the shiny leather sandals under the neat folds of the finest batik the Mangku Negara had around his legs. I had the feeling that the Mangku must regard us as paupers, an underdeveloped and impoverished branch of an antique family, who needed to be taken care of.

That gnawing feeling of barbarity became worse when, on a later occasion, Father, at the Mangku's request came to Solo with several Balinese dance groups and musicians to perform at his palace. The erudite Mangku Negara had a genuine interest in our dances and music. He engaged in long philosophical discussions with Father about Balinese and Javanese art, all beyond my comprehension at that time. What shocked me immensely was the outspoken difference in the appearances between the Mangkunegaran dancers and ours. Headdresses, costumes and dance movements of our *wayang wong* seemed to me clumsy and untidy compared with those of their Javanese counterparts. I looked shyly at Father's face, but could not see any sign of that disturbed feeling of mine. He looked completely happy, unconcerned and relaxed, and seemed to enjoy both the performances by his groups as well as those by the Javanese. I was too timid to ask questions, moreover we had been drilled to behave ourselves as guests, especially in the presence of persons of high rank. Thus, I was left pondering about my feelings all by myself. I looked at my brothers Gedé and Ketut Djelantik, who were speechless and wholly absorbed by the exquisite beauty of the Javanese dance and *gamelan* music.

Although I was impressed by its beauty, its discipline and its refinement, I did not feel stirred as with Balinese *gamelan* or our dance-drama. To me, all remained far away, an object of beauty in which I did not participate. I found myself just an observer. The language was alien, and the tempo was too slow for my taste. Was it that my responsiveness was blocked? Or was it perhaps the unconscious longing for that spontaneity in Balinese dance that I felt missing?

The Mangku Negara suggested that Father should develop new crafts in our Puri other than our ancient traditional weaving and embroidery, like he did in his palace. He provided Father with modern weaving looms and with batik-making equipment. Before long, a number of buildings in the Puri were transformed into small factories, where simple cotton cloth and batik were produced at high cost and with great effort. Balinese enthusiasm for these activities waned quickly when the novelty of the projects was over. There was just not enough demand in the local community for those products which people could easily buy much cheaper at the market.

Some time later, Father requested the Mangku Negara to send instructors to teach our boys and servants in the Puri another novelty which he saw in the Palace in Solo: scouting! Soon, the Puri of Karangasem was proud to have the first Boy Scouts in Bali. Except for their uniforms and the standard paraphernalia there was not much of Baden Powell about our assemblage of youngsters. Besides undergoing the obviously useful drill in marching and gymnastics, their main function was to parade and perform as guards of honour when Father was receiving high guests in our Puri.

Mystery and Spiritism

Soenyoto, the son of the Bupati (Head of a Regency in Java) of Blitar, was already boarding with the Bollands in Malang when we arrived there. Blitar is situated southwest of Malang at the foot of Mount Kelut, notorious for its big eruption in 1917. As result of many previous eruptions the crater has become an enormous lake. At the latest event, this huge amount of water, mixed with lava, was thrown over the crumbling southwest rim, flooding the plains of Blitar with hot mud, which caused tremendous devastation and loss of thousands of lives.

We went many times with Soenyoto to Blitar for long weekends. In his father's *kabupaten* (residence of a *bupati*) I never failed to approach the large round marble table standing in the middle of the *pendopo*. Except for the large size of the one-piece marble plate measuring about eight feet in diameter, there was nothing remarkable about the table. It was believed, however, to be sacred. According to the legend the Bupati told us, his grandfather who was Bupati more than fifty years earlier, had taken refuge with his family upon this miraculous table when the town was flooded by lava from Mount Kelut. To everybody's astonishment the table expanded by itself in all directions when other people, fleeing the lava stream, climbed on it. A great number of people were rescued in that way and when the lava had cooled off and all returned to their homes, the table shrank to its original size.

Although I had my doubts about the story, the sheer dimensions of the massive table always impressed me. Every time I touched the rim of the table I imagined being gently pushed back by the expanding marble and being invited to climb upon it. Of course, I did not dare do so, since there was always somebody around.

There was another mystery hidden in the Kabupaten. At one time our faithful guardian Bapa Badung, who remained with us in Malang for a long time, was required to be in his village in Butus. He was temporarily replaced by one of the traditional healers belonging to our permanent staff of guardians in our Puri, 'Wa Deruma, a renowned magician. We were very happy because 'Wa Deruma was also a *dalang*, a puppeteer for the *wayang* shadow play. He knew all the stories of the ancient epics and could narrate all the mysterious adventures of gods, saints, demons and princes in great detail. Father was happy too, being reassured that 'Wa Deruma would be most useful in case one of us got sick.

Like all Javanese, particularly those of the aristocracy, the Bupati of Blitar had a keen interest in mystics and occultism. He was very strict in observing the ceremonies with offerings and prayers, required on certain days considered sacred according to the Javanese calendar. When Soenyoto told his father about 'Wa Deruma, we received an invitation to bring him for a weekend to Blitar. The weekend was selected to fall on a special sacred day.

The Bupati was much impressed by our guardian. 'Wa Deruma was indeed an imposing figure, tall and robust, with long hair worn in a knot, a heavy black beard, moustache and greying whiskers. His very small black eyes were at the same time twinkling and penetrating, in lively contrast to his low speech and his deep bass voice. His task was to make an assessment of the esoteric situation of the Kabupaten.

At dusk in the afternoon we all gathered at the northeast corner of the compound and sat down on the grass. 'Wa Deruma, clad in white, sat cross-legged in deep meditation before a *pasepan*, (an earthenware pot with a pedestal and a long handle) in which incense was burning on a charcoal fire, filling the air with smoke and a penetrating fragrance. His hands were in the *mustika* gesture above his lap. Now and then, he muttered a few incomprehensible syllables. It was a long session. I became restless and it was getting dark. Nothing happened and I was losing interest, but out of respect for our host and other elder guests who looked very taken in by the ceremony, I remained on the spot. At last, 'Wa Deruma awoke from his meditation and looked around as if he was trying to find out where he was. It seemed as if he came to his senses only after he had recognized Gedé and I among the group of people. His eyes then moved to the Bupati, and greeting him with a faint smile on his face, he apologized. He made a gesture indicating that all was over and we all moved silently to the *pendopo*. There 'Wa Deruma told us the story.

He spoke in Balinese because he could not speak the Indonesian language well enough. Gedé had to translate, now and then joined by me. 'Wa Deruma revealed that he just returned from the unseen world. He recommended that the piece of ground where we had been sitting should be left undisturbed, because it was actually the dwelling of the guardians of the Kabupaten compound. They formed a small family consisting of a frail old couple with two daughters. He had met them and he had a long conversation with the old man.

They were clad in yellow robes, and the old woman was moving around wearily with a stick. The two daughters looked healthy and vigorous. They were working hard in the fields and at their weaving looms.

The Bupati was struck with astonishment. For some minutes he was speechless, but soon he started to ask many questions, which 'Wa Deruma dutifully answered. I was actually not very interested, regarding the whole show as superstition, and soon left Gedé alone with doing the translating. I missed most of the conversation.

My interest was awakened when the Bupati excitedly spoke to us expressing his amazement about 'Wa Deruma's revelations. Some time ago he had arranged a similar session with a Javanese healer-magician on the same spot. The description of the guardian family by 'Wa Deruma tallied with that given by the Javanese to the minutest details. He elaborated at great length about the holiness of the place where we were, about the sacred marble table, about extraordinary apparitions in the Kabupaten, about voices and about dreams. The Bupati spoke with great conviction. Despite my scepticism, I felt some shivering in my flesh.

Still, however, I was thinking of telepathy, which I had read about in a magazine article at the library. I reminded Gedé of the psychometrist and magnetiser, Mr Bosch, who once visited the Bollands in Malang some time before and demonstrated his occult capacities before a group of intimate friends. Mrs Bolland was immediately hypnotized and followed his instructions blindly. When he tried it with me, he failed. I did not feel anything extraordinary. A few days later he showed us a photograph which he had taken of Gedé and me in the backyard. Indeed the picture showed us being engulfed in the body of a fat *raksasa* (giant demon). According to him it was the unseen inhabitant of the place, but I recognized in the *raksasa* on the picture the huge statue of a guardian at the entrance of the ancient temple of Singosari, 25 km north of Malang. I wondered if it could not have been a double exposure of the film.

Mr Bolland agreed with me. But Gedé, who absolutely believed in the existence of inhabitants of the unseen world warned me that it would be better for my well-being to stop joking about these matters.

CHAPTER 12

Bali Revisited

At the end of the school year and at Christmas, we had vacations which were long enough to make it worthwhile to undertake the journey home. Public air travel did not yet exist, nor were there bus services, between Java and Bali. We had to take the train to Surabaya and try there to get on the boat to Buleleng. The K.P.M. (Koninklijke Paketvaart Maatschappij), or Royal Steam Navigation Company, maintained a regular schedule twice a week to Bali which continued to Lombok, Celebes and the Malukus. From Malang to Surabaya took only three hours and it was easy to board the boat on the afternoon that same day, if there was one. That was not possible from Yogyakarta, so that when we were in the (A.M.S., or middle school) we went home only once a year. During the shorter vacations there were always excursions to interesting places in Java, organized by the school, under the guidance of one or two of our teachers. I was always eager to take part in such excursions, which delighted me, and made all that we learned in geography, history and geology classes more meaningful.

Although the boat trip from Surabaya to Bali became routine after some time, it remained great fun for us. For reasons of prestige we had to travel first or second class in cabins, while our school mates travelled on the so called "Klas Dek" (the open space on deck) on top of the wooden planks covering the cargo room, or in the "Klas Kambing" (goats' department) as the covered space at the rear end of the boat, often used for transport of cattle, pigs and other husbandry, was named. In these cheap classes the passengers had to bring their own mats, pillows and other sleeping gear, and provide for their own food. We found great joy in mixing with our friends in those overcrowded quarters and in listening to their stories about experiences in other parts of Java. There was usually someone with a guitar or a mandolin, providing entertainment for the assembled groups of Balinese students. We shared our longing for Balinese food, for the Balinese environment, for the atmosphere of animated togetherness during temple festivals and other ceremonies, anticipated at home.

Often there were also clusters of students from Lombok, from Celebes or from the Malukus on the boat, travelling home for vacation. We did not mix with them. The sense of Indonesian citizenship, of being Indonesian, had not yet grown in us. We felt only Balinese, or Sasak, or some other ethnic group. Times have changed very much since then.

* * * * *

Since I suffered from chronic trachoma, my eyes hurt terribly every time I tried to follow the brisk movements of the kites displaying a variety of bright colours in the glaring sky. Gedé held the thread, manoeuvring his kite in the air by alternately pulling or loosening his grip, under the expert guidance of Uncle Oka, who with professional skill had crafted the kite for him. Uncle Oka was an unusually gifted artist, a dancer as well as a musician, a craftsman, carving masks for the *topeng* dance-drama, and creating out of his hands anything from dancers' wigs and headdresses, decorations, to birds' cages and all types of kites. The three of us, Gedé, myself and Gedé Oka had arrived home on vacation from Java a few days before and were now standing at the far end of the *rurung*, a lane between two rows of walled compounds, which led to the southern part of our Puri. For the purpose of releasing our kites there was no place more suitable than our *rurung* which functioned as a funnel through which the prevailing south winds of the season blew with force and accelerated speed. A few servant playmates were squatting around us on the ground, following the game with awe and fascination.

I would have loved to take part in the exciting play with the kites itself, but this time my hurting eyes compelled me to be quiet. I consoled myself with the idea that I had made myself useful with one essential part of its preparations. The day before I had prepared the 500 metres of thread for Gedé's kite. The strong cotton sewing yarn had to be made sharp by powdered glass.

To prepare such "glassed" thread, the yarn was first wound radially on a Chinese coin, evenly in all directions. The yarn formed a tight knot like a bullet, from which it would let itself easily be pulled loose. Pieces of carpenter's glue were then heated until liquid in a tin. Then glass, crushed to fine powder, was thoroughly mixed with this liquid, in which the knot of yarn was submerged, one end attached to a pole. By moving the tin from the pole to another pole at some 10 metres away, while supporting the thread with the finger to prevent it from falling on the ground and winding it alternately around both poles, the thread unfolded by itself and, stretched between the two poles, it was then left to dry in the air for a day.

The quality of the glue, the fine size of the glass particles, and the density of the mixture, besides the strength of the cotton yarn, determined the sharpness of the "glassed" thread and its effectiveness in combat. The thickness of the yarn and thus its weight was also to be considered. With thick yarn the manoeuvrability of the kite would be much reduced, so that one had to use the thinnest possible yarn, which should also be strong at the same time.

For the kite fighting game several participants released their kites from different sites, about 50 to 100 metres away from each other. The kites were designed and constructed in such a way that they could be steered in the air by certain manipulations on the leading thread with the finger. On the other hand, the kite had to be stable in the air when one did nothing. The stability and mobility of the kite depended on the craftsmanship of the kitemaker. Less skillful kitemakers would usually achieve stability by providing the kite with a tail, but this would hamper its manoeuvrability. The actual manoeuvring depended on the skill of the person playing the game. He must be able to feel in his fingers how the wind was catching the kite, when and how much to pull at the thread in order to let the kite turn to the left or to the right, how to let it dive or to climb straight upwards.

The sport of the game was to cut the opponent kite's thread with one's own. The player would manoeuvre his kite in such a way that his thread would come above that of his opponent, crossing it at a favourable angle. Then he would suddenly make his kite dive and let the thread veer out with the greatest possible velocity. The kite would be carried further by the wind, making the thread run with great speed over the opponent's yarn, thereby cutting it. The most exciting moment occurred when the opponent's kite was seen suddenly falling limp and swaying in the wind, uncontrolled. Then one started to manoeuvre to the next victim.

The player would also manoeuvre his kite into the most favourable positions. He might be able to avoid being cut down by letting his kite make a sharp dive, followed by a quick ascent on the other side and come up with his thread above that of the attacking kite. It was a truly exciting sport—to know how to choose the best strategy, to anticipate the opponent's intentions, and to manoeuvre at the right moment in the right direction.

Gedé was quite good at the game, but Uncle Oka was the real expert and we were delighted to have him nearby. I was proud when he expressed his satisfaction with the way I had prepared Gedé's thread the previous day.

"Well done", he said, "since you can't look in the sky tomorrow because of your red eyes, will you prepare my thread too? My next kite will be named 'Hanuman' after the famous Ape King in the *Ramayana* and will be a very swift and strong one". It will be able to cut down all his opponents," I promised.

Suddenly two of our servants rushed forward, out of the lane, over the courtyard onto the street, and ran as fast as they could to catch the kite which Gedé had just cut down. I had missed the most exciting moment.

According to the rules, the losing kites belonged to nobody; whoever caught them first would be the owner. The two came back empty-handed—

others were at the spot earlier. We were in the highest of spirits watching the manoeuvring of the three remaining kites in the sky, when Father's messenger came to the scene. He told us that Father had arrived home from his office and wanted to see all his children at lunch. Although we found it a great pity to leave the exciting game, we complied as a matter of course.

It should not be thought that we would have lunch together with Father around a large table. Rather we were required to be present while Father was having his midday meal. Seated crosslegged on the floor Father would be eating from a *dulang* on which the food was served, while we would be sitting at a respectful distance of about six yards in a half circle in front of him, the boys on one side and the girls on the other, all in hierarchic order according to age, the eldest in front and the youngest at the rear. These lunch gatherings did not occur too often, perhaps only once a week, since it depended on Father's available time, his mood, and other unpredictable circumstances. They were held at two different places, either at the "Ekelanga" (a Balinese mispronunciation of "England") by which the compound of Madé Karang's mother was named, or at Ayu Ratih's mother's compound, named "London". These mothers belonged to the second caste and had therefore the privilege of preparing in turn Father's meals, which implied that they should be provided with the means and material to be able to produce the best food out of their kitchens.

Although we had already eaten our early lunch at our own mothers' compounds, the anticipation of enjoying the most delicious dishes, as *lungsuran* always filled us with delight. After Uncle Oka reassured us that he would take care of the two remaining rival kites, we followed Gedé to Mekelé Trena's compound where we quickly washed ourselves and put on clean clothes.

On our way to "Ekelanga," where Father would have his lunch that day, we were joined by Ketut Djelantik, coming out of Mekelé Wiraga's compound and Gedé Agung, son of Uncle Oka who emerged from the opposite side of the *rurung*. Madé Karang and Ketut Karang were already waiting at their mother's compound. When we arrived, some of our elder sisters were already seated on the porch. Father stood up from the top of the stairway where he had been playing with our two-year-old youngest sister on his lap. Meanwhile the maid-servants arrived, one with the *dulang* and the others carrying the trays with the dishes of food balanced on their heads. Father handed the baby to one of our elder sisters and looked with satisfaction at the six of us who were standing below the porch, waiting for his sign that we could ascend the stairway.

According to etiquette we did not say a word while Father was eating. Now and then, I heard our sisters whispering softly something to each other, while our eldest sister was humming a nursery rhyme to keep the baby quiet. From time to time Father commented on the food, asking some technicality about its preparation. We were not supposed to talk except when answering a question from Father. Otherwise we were sitting silently with bent heads because it was considered impolite to look a higher person straight in the face. However, I could not help spying now and then out of the corners of my eyes at moments when I felt that Father was looking at us with some intensity. I felt that he was probing us and perhaps asking himself what would become of us in the future. It must have been very puzzling for him all the time, the more so as we progressed at our schools. Having had no formal schooling himself, he had no clear idea of what we were learning in Java. Curriculum matters were therefore never discussed; he was convinced that everything we learned was good for us and as long as we passed to a higher grade each year, all was well.

Most of his attention was naturally focused on Gedé, his Crown Prince. Learning that Gedé was studying very hard, often until late at night, he was happy in his way. For him it meant that Gedé was a diligent student, and therefore would later become a very learned person after having accumulated a huge amount of knowledge. He was confident that Gedé would be the right man to succeed him.

Second after Gedé, Father's mind was concerned with those sons whose mothers were of higher caste—Madé Karang and Ketut Karang. For some reason, he never felt much affection for Madé Karang, but Ketut Karang was his favourite. Favouritism was (and still is, but much less so) a very common phenomenon in Balinese families. Since there never existed that intimate personal relationship between father and son that we know of in modern families, we children were not much disturbed by the existence of favouritism and accepted it as something quite normal. Moreover, absolute obedience to Father without reserve was dogma. It was never necessary for Father to hide whom of his sons or daughters he loved more than the others. His affections were very genuine and natural and were quite obvious to everybody. That such affections might partly be the result of influences from the mothers was also generally accepted as a matter of course. There were unavoidable jealousies among the mothers and in a lesser degree also among the children.

From early childhood I had accepted my place as younger brother/servant of Gedé, and as stepchild of Mekelé Trena was very happy. I never felt the need for special attention from Father or from any of the mothers. It was therefore natural that I never felt any jealousy towards Gedé or towards any of my younger brothers who in turns became Father's favourites. Having no mother of my own, I knew that nobody would ever plead anything with Father on my behalf and that I would always have to stand on my own.

During those moments when I was looking stealthily at Father I tried to assess what Father was perhaps expecting from each of us. I did not come far with my assessment. At that time, I had no concept about my future. It was much later, during my second year in Yogyakarta, that I decided to become a doctor. My mind was drifting back to the kites and Uncle Oka, wondering whether my glassed thread had been holding. The silence during the session made me sleepy and, not accustomed any more to sitting crosslegged for a long stretch of time, my limbs started to feel uncomfortable.

Patting softly on my knee, Gedé awakened me from my daydreams, indicating that we should form a circle around Father's *dulang* which had been moved over to our side. Father had finished and was now rinsing his mouth above a copper Chinese bowl. We started to savour the *lungsuran*, generously replenished by Mbok Uma, Madé Karang's mother with a great variety of delicacies. While having our meal we were allowed to turn our backs to Father. Eating rice was considered a service to the rice goddess Dewi Sri, which gave exemption from profane worldly formalities. Father remained for a while seated on his mat, and looked with pleasure at his children who were enjoying the food. After chewing his *sirih*, a complex mixture of pepper leaves, betel nut, gambir, lime and tobacco, he retired to his sleeping quarters to have his afternoon siesta. As soon as he was out of sight we burst into animated chattering, laughing and teasing each other, joined in eagerly by our sisters.

We had to wait until Gedé, our eldest, had finished before we could stop eating and leave our places. We ran back to the *rurung*, where we found Uncle Oka already collecting Gedé's kite and thread. He had vanquished the remaining rival kites. Although we had missed the most exciting moments, we were very proud and happy.

As much as we loved our gatherings at Father's lunch hours, we loathed the obligatory visits we had to pay at least once during each vacation to Uncle Gedé Putu in his old Puri, located just opposite ours on the main street in Karangasem. Although Father knew that none of us ever felt any affinity, not to speak of sympathy, for Uncle Gedé Putu, (among us nicknamed "'Wa," from "Iwa," which means "uncle,") Father imposed upon us this formality. Apart from adhering to courtesy, these visits stemmed from Father's feeling of indebtedness towards his nephew and his sincere wish to heal the wounds of the past.

Being the son of Father's eldest brother, the 'Wa Gedé Putu was actually our cousin, but because he was much older than Father himself we called him "Uncle". Our common grandfather's youngest brother Gedé Djelantik was previously ruler over Karangasem as vassal under the Raja of Lombok. In 1896, after the conquest of Lombok by the Dutch, he was reinstated as ruler over Karangasem by the Dutch government for his merit of having been nonaligned during the Lombok war and received the title of *Stedehouder*. He never married and adopted his nephew Bagus Djelantik, as his son. Bagus, who later became our father, was very intelligent and as a young adult already showed much interest in literature, in matters of government and jurisdiction.

When ten years later, because of his advanced age, the question of succession arose, Gedé Djelantik preferred to have his adopted son as his successor, rather than one of the sons of his two elder brothers who, on account of hierarchy, claimed priority. The Dutch government, finding that Gedé Djelantik was making the right choice, and at the same time alarmed by the anti-Dutch attitude of the brothers, feared that a plot was being set up against the *Stedehouder*. This was found good enough reason to put the two brothers with their families into exile to Jembrana in West Bali.

Father succeeded his uncle as *Stedehouder* in 1909. Although the measure taken by the Dutch government was to his advantage, he had always felt the step as an act of injustice. Therefore, in his capacity of *Stedehouder,* he later continuously pursued the approval of the Dutch government for the return of the families to Karangasem. His efforts bore fruit at last after almost 20 years.

Father planned to reunite the families. Soon after the re-establishment of Gedé Putu in his old Puri he made with him and the family an agreement that Gedé Putu's 16-year-old daughter, Ayu Karang, was to become the bride of our eldest brother Gedé Djelantik, who was at that time only eleven years of age.

If courtesy visits to people of high rank were in themselves boring, particularly loathsome were the visits to 'Wa, with whom we felt completely alien. This feeling was obviously recriprocal. Like Father he had never been to school, but unlike Father he had never had any interest in literature, art, or in anything else except cockfighting, gambling, *perkututs* (singing birds) and, in his younger years, according to stories reaching us from older people, in women. Having no interest in, or rather despising developments towards modernization in the world outside the Puri, he refused to send his children to school. Although he had many wives, he had, besides his daughter, only one son who was born before the mother was confirmed as his wife with the required religious ceremonies, so that he became an *astra* (bastard son, without rights of succession or any rank of nobility).

The only pleasure we found in these forced visits to the 'Wa was the opportunity to tease Gedé about his "bride". However, since Gedé never reacted strongly to our teasings, the fun waned quickly.

As we filed behind Gedé down the stairs of our main gate and crossed the street, pedestrians stopped and paid reverence to us by kneeling and making the *mepes* gesture, bringing both hands with the palms closed against each other in front of the breast. Those who happened to be close enough asked the standard question: "Where are my beloved princes going?" We hardly paid any attention to them—only Gedé who walked in front reacted by a slight nod with his head towards the high walls of the Puri Gedé. That was all that was required to maintain communication between us princes and the common people. In the early 1930s this mode of reverence was still strictly observed by the people in Karangasem, even though all the other regions of Bali had discontinued the practice. However, in the course of one decade Karangasem would follow suit.

When we entered the Puri Gedé we were immediately overcome by a feeling of depression. The buildings in the vast compound around us were old and in decay. In sharp contrast to our Puri which was bustling with life, where carpenters were working on furniture, woodcarvers making panels or statues, craftsmen applying gold leaf on doors, windows or music instruments, and people waiting outside Father's office, here in the old Puri Gedé time had stopped. A shrivelled old woman with a broken half broom in her hand appeared from behind a wall and blinked at us as if we came from outer space. A dog barked in the adjacent compound, from where a young man emerged and indicated to us that we should follow him. The 'Wa had just erected in the inner courtyard a high new building whose fresh whitewash conflicted sharply with the moss-grown crumbling structures surrounding it. A steep, cemented stairway led to the front porch, where 'Wa Gedé Putu was seated on a mat on the floor, leaning with his back against the wall. There was no greater contrast thinkable than the contrast between this sagging huge fat body and Father's lean and agile figure.

Before we ascended the stairway I tried to get a glimpse of 'Wa Gedé Putu's face, wondering whether he was sober or still tipsy. Our servants who heard stories from his attendants, told us that 'Wa Gedé Putu liked whisky and gin as well as *tuak* (Balinese palm wine) and often got drunk at night. While drunk he would draw his long sword and—pacing up and down the porch—he would scream the whole night, threatening and thundering curses towards imagined enemies all around.

Perhaps frustration caused by eighteen years of exile and unfulfilled ambitions had driven the man to this condition. The late *Stedehouder* of Karangasem, Gusti Gedé Djelantik, knew his character and, deeming him unfit for government, silently approved of the Dutch authorities' decision to deport him and his father. Understandably there perhaps still remained vengeful feelings against our branch of the family. Father had, intentionally, never told us about the conflicts which happened in the past among our families. I acquired my knowledge about our family history only much later from books I read in Holland.

At the time of our visits, the only thing we knew about him was that he had lived for a long time in Jembrana. Therefore, we did not associate what we saw and heard about 'Wa Gedé Putu (and for that matter also of Uncle Gedé Oka) with past hostilities. Being a schoolboy, thirsty for science and eager to see progress, I evaluated people's behaviour around me in terms of progress and backwardness. I believed in progress and thought 'Wa Gedé Putu's drunkenness was a result of his lack of education, since he had not been "enlightened" by modern schooling. Likewise, I attributed his cockfighting and gambling addictions to the same cause.

'Wa greeted us in a friendly manner. I could not however escape the feeling that it was only a formal gesture and that in actual fact he was annoyed with our visit, knowing perhaps that we loathed the exercise.

We sat down according to hierarchical order behind Gedé, crosslegged, on the opposite side of the porch, and with our heads bent, we waited silently and patiently until he would ask us something. Minute after minute went by without him saying a word to us. I managed to study his sluggish face which looked bored and unhappy. His eyes were glassy, staring meaninglessly over our heads in some far distance, causing me to wonder what he was thinking. Or was he not thinking at all?

About half an hour passed, and there we were still neatly seated, silently waiting for something to happen or for some word to come out of the immobile plump figure before us. Hiding behind Gedé's back I ventured to look around and noticed that 'Wa's huge belly prevented him from sitting crosslegged properly, allowing only his feet to cross at the ankles. He was constantly short of breath and his lips were blueish.

After long minutes of inertia his head moved, and, turning sideways, he wearily waved with his hand to the attendants who were sitting on the ground in the courtyard. One of them crouched on hands and feet up the stairs and stopped in reverence on the last step below the porch. 'Wa wanted to see a trial fight between his favourite cock and his latest acquisition.

Two attendants went to a large shed at the far end of the courtyard, where fighting cocks were kept in several rows of baskets. They returned to the open space in front of the stairway with two roosters, still in their baskets. Here they took out the birds and holding them up in the air, showed them to the 'Wa who nodded approvingly. Facing each other at some distance with the fighting cocks in their hands, they tickled them expertly with their fingers against their necks and behind their wattles, and still holding them fast making them jump against each other several times. That was the standard and effective way to arouse anger and the urge to fight in the birds. The excited cocks looked viciously and menacingly at each other, with their neckfeathers raised, forming frightening manes in a circle behind their heads. They tried to jump at each other, but were prevented by the men who held them fast by their tails. At last they let them loose and a fierce battle ensued, the birds flying up against each other, pecking at each other and striking with their spurs. Since it was only for a trial, this time no sharp metal blades had been fixed to their spurs as would have been done before the real contest. In those cases, the wounded bird would die in a minute because of the poison usually applied on the blade. The fight we witnessed was held to evaluate the vigour, the endurance and the fighting style of the cocks. After a number of furious attacks the roosters were exhausted but neither of the two would give up fighting. Time and again, they rushed at each other, each time more feebly, and ended up by holding each other fast in their necks with their beaks, staggering in circles around each other. 'Wa, who suddenly came to life during the fight, gesticulated wildly and shouting comments, gave the sign to stop. The attendants collected the birds, fondled them, and caressing their heads and feathers affectionately put them back into their cages. After giving some instructions to the attendants 'Wa waddled back to his seat against the wall and returned into his previous absent minded inertia.

None of us liked cockfighting, nor did we know much about its rules and its technicalities. We had remained politely where we were seated. We found the cockfight a welcome time-killer, during which we were able to freely change the position of our aching knees and legs. Now we were looking forward to the end of our ordeal. Gedé was supposed to take the initiative to ask permission to leave, but as usual this did not come fast enough for us. Half an hour later, I felt Madé Karang tickling my back. I understood that he was fed up. So was I, and in turn I tickled Gedé's spine. At last, after several repeated ticklings, Gedé who was waiting for the moment that 'Wa happened to move his eyes slightly in his direction, muttered the prescribed farewell formula. Relieved, we slithered on our bottoms to the edge of the porch and, still with our faces towards 'Wa, steered ourselves backwards down the stairs.

Were it not for his artistic talents, Uncle Gedé Oka (who also had been in exile in Jembrana together with his father, Gedé Djelantik's second elder brother), would have suffered from the same frustrations and resentments as Uncle Gedé Putu. He was also much younger and was at the time of deportation still a small child. Moreover, back in Karangasem he developed into a very handsome young man, later fell in love with our eldest sister and married her. The wedding, which took place in 1922, was a spectacular celebration, with Father himself at the same day marrying a new bride, the sister of his fourth wife, Madé Karang's mother, from a noble family in Lombok. She became later Ayu Ratih's mother.

It was never necessary for Father to oblige us to pay visits to Uncle Gedé Oka, for we all loved him, and not only because of his kites. With pleasure we frequented his Puri, which was actually the southeast part of our Puri, beyond the *rurung*. There we found so many objects of delight: a wide variety of birds in large aviaries, aquariums with beautiful coloured fishes, and we found him always busy with his hands, woodcarving, making masks and headdresses for dances, sometimes embroidering, painting, or producing paraphernalia for our temples or for use in religious rituals. We loved to see him performing the *topeng*, the masked dance drama, in which he usually had the role of the refined noble king. Besides being a good dancer and musician he had great imagination and liked all kinds of novelties. When the *janger* group dance became popular, it was no wonder that he started to organize a *janger* club with the nearby community of the Banjar Kodok, training the members in the dances and composing new songs for them. His artistic genius encompassed both the most classical of Balinese dances, as well as the most modern manifestations.

In the evenings he often held literary meetings with selected people, reading from the ancient epics, the *Mahabharata*, the *Ramayana* and other classics.

We regularly found him attending the *pepaosans* organized by Father in his reception hall called the "Maskerdam" (a mispronounciation of "Amsterdam").

However, Uncle Gedé Oka had one weakness for which he became notorious and which was, for us teenagers, an inexhaustible source of amusement: he could not keep his hands off girls. He seemed to have an insatiable sexual drive, and since he was very handsome and amiable, no maiden was safe near him. We learned time and again about his amorous adventures with new fresh virgins at such amazingly short intervals, and before long Madé Karang had invented for him in our Dutch jargon that we used to keep our secrets from others the grand title of "De Ontmaagder" ("the Deflowerer"). This soon became abbreviated into "De Ont". Such a secretive language greatly heightened the fun in our teenage gossiping. We were so much carried away by the grand title that once during a conversation with the Dutch *Controleur* of Karangasem, one of us found himself making the unfortunate slip of the tongue when referring to our uncle, mentioning "De Ont", which of course elicited the most embarrassing enquiry by the Dutch official!

CHAPTER 13

Maligya

Coming home on vacation in June 1937, we found the whole population of Karangasem frantically busy with preparations for the seven-day-long *maligya* festivals to be held in August in honour of our ancestors, who had been cremated years earlier. After consultation with all the priests of the region, Father had concluded that the proper time had come to perform the *maligya* ceremonies, particularly on behalf of his late uncle and predecessor Gusti Gedé Djelantik. As is customary, there were numerous deceased close relatives whose souls would join the principal spirit in his ascent to the highest of all heavens.

The *maligya*, a sort of follow-up to the cremation, is held to attain a place in heaven for the souls of the cremated ancestors believed to be supreme, more sublime, to that achieved by the cremation ceremony. It is considered the highest duty of anyone who can afford the expenses, in honour of his ancestors. In this highly symbolic ritual the souls are represented by *puspas*, flower effigies consisting of sandalwood, white cloth, certain ingredients, decorated with silver or gold, and each provided with a scribbled palm leaf label for identification.

With great reverence we watched the priests and priestesses making these effigies and listened to their subdued voices while they arranged them, according to hierarchy, in four beautiful white cremation towers, magnificently decorated with gold, erected under a high platform under a huge white ceiling speckled with golden stars. For seven consecutive days elaborate ceremonies were carried out by the priests, priestesses and their assistants: these involved symbolic washings, feedings, and the singing of sacred hymns, while on the grounds before the platform a continuous series of dance-dramas and music performances were held as entertainment for the deified souls. As a grandiose climax to the ceremonies, at the end of the seventh day, the four beautiful ceremonial towers were to be carried together with about twenty similarly elegant but smaller towers in a mile-long colourful procession to the sea at Ujung, three miles from the town.

Immediately after our arrival a wide variety of duties were assigned to us. It was considered useful for us to take part in the preparations of the festival.

It was a huge organization. On the west side of the Puri Gedé a new complex had been built, consisting of the traditional three tiers of courtyards. The lowest outer courtyard was situated at the south end along the main road, and north of it was the middle courtyard, on the west side of which a high-rise beautifully carved building was erected, the Lembu Agung—this would serve as Father's residence during the festivals. On higher ground was the inner courtyard measuring about 200 by 150 metres, where the actual ceremonies were to take place. Here several temporary structures were being set up, open pavilions of bamboo and thatch roofs. On its east side a huge-roofed platform was erected facing west, which had at its front a 30-metre-wide staircase. About 200 men were busy day and night to get the place ready for the ceremonies and performances. About the same number of women were busy in the kitchens and preparing offerings in the *suci* (purified) pavilions at an adjacent court.

During the preparations hundreds of people from all the villages of Karangasem region came in large processions to pay their respects, bringing with them all sorts of produce from their land: coconuts, bananas and banana leaves, sugar cane, firewood, rice, corn, fruits and many other items, such as chickens, pigs and even buffalos. In order to prevent chaos in the town these processions had to be arranged weeks ahead in such a way, that people from no more than three villages were to arrive on the same day. They had to get at least drinks and snacks, those coming on foot from far distances were given food also. People coming from distant villages could not return home the same day and had to be given shelter for the night.

All neighbourhood communities in the town, the *banjars*, were to take turns hosting the hundreds of visitors and they had to be provided with the necessary supplies of food and equipment for serving and shelter.

Our duties were manifold. As officers of our Boy Scout regiment, a novelty which Father was very proud of, we took part in the cutting of sugar cane on the fields near Sekuta and we proudly marched through the streets in our uniforms with the canes on our shoulders, carrying them all the way into the purified kitchen quarters of the *maligya* complex. We had to supervise our Boy Scouts in decorating the various pavilions on the ceremonial grounds. Every day we had to dress up to receive the hundreds of villagers coming in large processions with their gifts to the main Maligya courtyard. As a special attraction on those occasions, Gedé had to fulfil his pleasant duty of spraying eau de cologne at the lovely young girls who were arranged in rows at the front of the seated crowd. We had great fun watching him moving between the girls, putting on his most amiable smile, which invited provocative looks from the older maidens. When the crowd was too big and a second sprayer had to be mobilized, I should have been the one to join Gedé, but I was always too shy and left the task to one of my younger brothers, Ketut Djelantik or Madé Karang who obviously enjoyed the exercise very much.

A special task was assigned to me throughout the whole *maligya* festivals: that of making a filmed documentary of the event. (Due to my reputation of having a propensity for technology, the year before I had had the privilege of trying out the huge His Master's Voice gramophone, purchased by Father at an auction in Singaraja held on behalf of the departing Resident of Bali and Lombok.) A few weeks earlier Mr Fonteyn, the *Controleur* of Karangasem, had acquired a Kodak 8-mm film camera, a truly exciting novelty for the time. Father had been invited to see his first films and was very impressed. He immediately had the idea of making a documentary of the planned *maligya* festival. Mr Fonteyn helped with ordering a camera and projector from Holland with twenty rolls of film, at that time still black-and-white. (Later towards the end of the festival the first colour films were available.) The goods were delivered exactly one week after we arrived from Java and Father appointed me camera man and film operator. I was delighted and proud, and made a thorough study of the accompanying manuals.

The camera was still of the spring-driven type which had to be wound up every time after shooting a few feet of film. Cameras running on batteries did not exist yet. It struck me that it needed quite a force to wind up the spring, which somehow gave me confidence in the strength and durability of the mechanism. As soon as I was familiar with the camera, I proudly demonstrated the inside of the mysterious instrument to Father and my brothers, sisters and attendants in the Puri, showing them the complicated threading of the film. I enjoyed seeing the amused bewilderment in their eyes when I pushed the release button and the film crept like a snake between knobs and cylinders in the compartment.

It was remarkable that none of my brothers showed any inclination to take over my task or to learn from me in order to be able to replace me if necessary. Before long I mastered the technique and used one film as a trial, shooting haphazardly everywhere, everything and everybody coming on my way. The film had to be sent to Surabaya for processing and it took more than two weeks before I could demonstrate the result in the Puri. For some reason Mr Fonteyn forgot to include a silver screen when ordering the equipment. I improvised a primitive one from white cloth, stretched by cords within a wooden frame, modelled after the screen used at the traditional *wayang* play.

The trial show was a great success. The setting-up of the film projector and the screen elicited much excitement among the crowd who gathered on the courtyard of the "Maskerdam" and the atmosphere was charged with expectation. In those days, only very few people of Karangasem had ever been to a cinema, even though there was one was in Denpasar and one in Singaraja, showing mostly silent cowboy films. Those *gambar hidup* (living pictures) were a miracle for them. But to see oneself and people of one's own environment coming to life on the screen was a most thrilling experience! There was enormous excitement with frequent roars of laughter. The film lasted only five minutes and that was of course far too short for them. People wanted to see it again and again. I had to show the film about six times that evening. The rewinding of the film in itself was for those who were lucky to be close to the projector a breathtaking spectacle. I felt myself the embodiment of progress!

In order to systematize my documentary film I tried to figure out the logical course of events in the complexity of the Festival's proceedings, as often so many things were occurring at the same time. I interviewed our priests and administrators to get a clear picture of what was going to happen and when, in order to plan my shootings. I took care that nothing would be especially arranged for me, because I wanted to just record what was actually happening.

I enjoyed my task immensely, even more so later when it came to editing. I had to decide wholly on my own how to compose the course of the documentary. Father's silent confidence in me made me extremely happy. He never commented. From his reactions I concluded that he was satisfied with the outcome. Later, I had the opportunity to show the film many times to high guests in the Puri and even at receptions in the palaces of the Mangku Negara, and the palaces of the Susuhunan Paku Buwono in Solo, Java.

At that time I was not particularly interested in the meaning lying behind all the various symbolic rituals and religious performances. When I asked our priests about them, I was not satisfied by their explanations. Too many things had to be accepted as truth and wisdom, more than could satisfy what my youthful search for reason and logic. The existence of so many unanswered questions, however, did not really disturb my mind. Perhaps it was because we had been conditioned from childhood to conform to community behaviour, to find peace and happiness in doing and thinking what the community expected us to do and think. Thus, I did not bother to argue or to discuss matters with any of my brothers or with Father. The only resource person to whom I occasionally ventured to express my doubts was 'Wa 'Dek, a high priest from Gerya Pidada, who had been very fond of my mother and had attended her the night when she died. The wise old man seemed very worried when he was not able to explain to me why red was the colour of Brahma, black of Wisnu and white of Siwa.

"That is mentioned in the holy scriptures", he told me, and that it was not proper to ask *why* it was so.

On another occasion I asked him: "We are Hindu, aren't we?"

He answered: "Of course we are, otherwise we would not hold a *maligya* like now".

"You are a Hindu *priest*, aren't you?"

"Yes. Of the Siwa sect".

"So you are not Buddhist?"

"No, the priest who sat next to me is Buddhist".

"If we are not Buddhist, why then do we have a Buddhist priest also officiating?" I persisted.

"That is to make our service to God more complete".

"Which god?"

"Ida Sanghyang Widi, the One and Almighty, who can have three appearances to us, Brahma the Creator, Wisnu the Preserver and Siwa the Destroyer, who brings us back to the Almighty".

"So the Buddhist priest is also praying to Brahma, Siwa and Wihnu? Is he then also a Hindu?"

'Wa 'Dek thought for a while and said: "Yes, he is. He belongs to our religion, but his rites are different from our Siwa rites".

I continued: "At school we have been told that the Buddha preached the very simple life, that he was the saviour of the poor. So, why does our Buddhist priest have during the prayers a much richer, more elaborate and magnificent attire than yours?"

There was silence. Suddenly I felt uneasy, sensing that I may have embarrassed him. He looked at me with much compassion, saying: "Sorry, I can't tell you. But don't ask further. You just go on with your studies and you will find out for yourself later".

I was reassured, because I loved him. I would have been very sad if he was displeased with me. Several times in the past he had shown his special compassion for me, by visiting me on the evening before our departure back to school at the end of our vacations. Every time, after praying for my well-being he silently pressed a silver guilder into my trembling hands.

Of course there were ritual duties which we had to perform. All of us had to be present at prayer times and other ceremonial events. Dutifully we did everything that was expected of us. Although we did not bother much about the spiritual meaning or symbolic significance, we were happy to perform our part in the whole process, thereby in the typical mood of adolescents finding ample opportunities for cheerfulness and mirth. Often, however, I was not to be seen with my brothers who most of the time stayed together as a group. I had to be filming events and preferred to wear my Boy Scout uniform for those activities instead of the elaborate Balinese ceremonial dress.

As a matter of courtesy, Father had to invite high Dutch officials to witness the Grand Festival, and for that occasion a special day was arranged. Out of convenience, other foreign visitors were also allowed that same day. Father did not bother to introduce us to those foreigners, nor was there any desire to know more about them on our side. To us they were human beings belonging to another world, whose presence was to be tolerated, and where appropriate (as with high officials), to be respected. In regard to their behaviour we generally assumed that our traditional laws and taboos did not apply to them. Except for some very obvious affronts against sacred principles of hierarchy which unavoidably they unwittingly committed, causing alarm among the elders, but amusement among us teenagers, they were generally left free to move everywhere while Father took great pains to explain the meaning of the *maligya* to his special guests.

At Father's request, our grand-uncle Anak Agung Madé Djelantik Brayawangsa, the son of the late Raja of Lombok, who was still in exile in West Java, got permission from the Dutch authorities to come to Bali to witness the great *maligya* ceremonies. Another highlight was Father taking part in the *gambuh*, one of the many dance-dramas performed in the main court. This most classical of all dances had no appeal at all to me, but because of Father's participation we stayed and watched the dance. I found it boring, too slow-moving, with endless dialogues in Kawi, the old Javanese language which I did not understand. Father wanted to perform the dance in honour of his late mother who loved the *gambuh*. He had been rehearsing with famous dancers especially brought from Klungkung, so we were obliged to watch the performance to its end. I had learned the *baris* dance and was thrilled by it. That was very different, much more vivid, martial, much more imaginative, and of a magnificent intensity. In contrast the *gambuh* was a long poetic drama, enacting at length formal proceedings in the medieval courts in Java many centuries ago, and was good to fall asleep to. That actually happened to me that night!

The apotheosis on the last day of the festival, the great procession of all the towers of white and gold with the huge crowd forming a mass of colours moving over winding roads between green and yellow paddy fields to the sea, was magnificent. I had been able to obtain colour films for the event. One hour before the procession started I had secured for myself a number of points along the road from where I could get good shots, tracing out shortcuts across rice terraces over which I would run from one point to the other in order to be ahead of the column. It was a most thrilling experience. As I was too busy filming and running around the entire time, the spiritual essence of the day—the returning of the purified souls (symbolized by the effigies), to the infinity of the sea—wholly escaped me. However, the filming was a great success!

CHAPTER 14

Frustrated Plans

When we were nearing our final examinations, Father had to decide about our further studies. As in other circumstances where it was difficult for him to gauge the implications of possible alternatives, he consulted Dutch officials all of whom were eager to give him the best advice they could.

In Father's opinion, Gedé, who would succeed him as Raja of Karangasem, should leave school and work as his apprentice, gradually assuming more and more responsibilities of government. He was not quite convinced when he was advised to send Gedé to the Law School at the University of Batavia (now named Jakarta). To his logic, law had to do with courts and not with government in general, not with building roads, bridges, schools and irrigation works, matters he was dealing with day by day. He could not understand that the study of law would prepare his son for dealing with problems of community traditions, of religion, of temples and priests, which constituted a major part of his daily concerns. However, eventually, he took the advice of the "experts".

In my case, the decision was straightforward. The medical profession was easily conceived as a distinct entity. Father was very happy when he was informed that there was also a medical school in Batavia, feeling reassured that I would continue looking after my elder brother. He did not know that I already had my own plans.

For a long time already I had been dreaming of going to Holland, about which I heard many stories from my Dutch friends in the swimming club. Some of them on return from home leave with their parents during the winter told exciting stories about snow and winter sports. One of the school prizes I had won was a beautiful big volume *Amsterdam in Beeld* ("Amsterdam in Pictures") which I enjoyed immensely. Every time I read the book and saw the numerous beautiful photographs of museums and palaces my curiosity was aroused. There had been growing in me an urge for adventure, a great desire to know other worlds.

I knew that travel to Holland was very expensive and that Father would not think of spending a great sum of money for me, while depriving Gedé of his brother servant at the same time. So I kept my yearning all to myself, while secretly looking for some way or other to fulfil my ambitions. For fear that my intentions would become known I never discussed the matter with anybody and certainly not with Gedé.

In those years Dutch civil servants working in tropical countries were entitled to an eight-month home leave after each six years of service. Families with small children enjoyed the additional privilege of bringing with them at the expense of the Government, a servant for domestic help during travel and for the duration of their home leave. So I just had to find out if there was a Dutch family with children going to Holland soon after my examinations. Then I would be able to leave straightaway with the family without having to go home to Karangasem first, avoiding the chance of being forced to go with Gedé to Batavia. Completely ignorant of the hard realities involved, I indulged in my own fantasies, inventing solutions for any problems I could think of.

I wanted to be completely independent of home. My plan was to complete my domestic duties with the family during their home leave and somehow find someone to replace me for their return travel. I was informed that there were in Holland many Javanese waiting for such an opportunity. I would then stay behind and find other work from which I could earn money for my tuition. I fancied that I would be able to do it as a taxi-driver or working in a restaurant.

As if it were preordained, I heard that our English language teacher, Mr Adelaar, was due for home leave and would depart in July, just two weeks after our exams. I knew him well and found him very sympathetic. I did not know his wife, but I knew that they had two children, whom I liked from the times they occasionally came with their father to our school. Thus, I did not anticipate any trouble with my job as a houseboy or a babysitter. Full with hope and expectations I went to visit the family and asked them if they could use me during their home leave. I did however not reveal my plan to quit by the time they would return to Indonesia.

Mr Adelaar liked the idea and seemed very amused. His wife was obviously pleased when she saw that her children were immediately at ease with me. They invited me to their room to see their dolls and other toys. When we were seated again Mr. Adelaar asked about my age.

"Seventeen", I answered, "almost eighteen!"

"Have you discussed your plans with your parents?"

"Well, no", I replied, and hastily, "Not yet".

I felt there was something nasty looming ahead. Mr Adelaar started to look a little worried, and said: "Well, we all would like very much to have you with us, but since you are not yet twenty-one, you have to have written permission from your father. Otherwise we could get into trouble later".

I concluded that I had no other choice than to write to Father about my plans. In my letter I was more straightforward and explained in detail why Father should not be worried about the expenses for travel and how I planned to earn my living and money for my studies.

Father's reply came very quickly. It was very brief and sounded very firm: "Do not put your father and family to shame by working as a servant on a boat. Find enclosed a cheque for 1,000 guilders for your ticket and the first necessities in Holland. Before going abroad you must come home and visit our ancestral temples for your farewell prayers".

Although I sensed with a shock that I had displeased my Father, I was filled with extreme joy. Gedé who had helped me with editing my letter was genuinely happy for me, although he obviously envied me at the same time. He was studying very hard at the time in order to pass his examinations for entry to the University in Batavia, and his efforts were not in vain. He passed his examinations with reasonably good marks and applied for the School of Law. As was anticipated I passed my exams *cum laude*, first in my class, and won another school prize.

Mr Adelaar was sad that I could not travel with his family, but they easily found someone to take over my job. I, in turn, obtained from the travel agent in Yogyakarta a boat ticket on the *Christiaan Huygens* of the Netherlands Steam Navigation Company, leaving Batavia at the end of July.

After receiving our diplomas, we went home on vacation, my last and the shortest one since I had to get on my boat on time. My worry about how to present myself face to face to my Father whom I had caused such displeasure turned out to be without ground. Instead of reprimanding me he affectionately fondled my hair. I was very moved and could not withhold my tears. Father was very proud of me, not only because of my winning the first prize but more so because of having a son going for studies abroad and to the Netherlands for that matter! Gedé and all my brothers and sisters shared his pride.

I dutifully prayed at the traditionally prescribed series of ancestral shrines and took off for Batavia a few weeks earlier than Gedé, to board the big steamship for my grand journey to the unknown.

BOOK III

Holland

CHAPTER 15

On the Boat to Holland

Whilst I was studying, the schools in Indonesia were at the same level as those in Holland, and our certificates entitled us to enroll in any Dutch university. Discrimination between Dutch and Indonesian students was unknown. In the Netherlands East Indies (as Indonesia was then known), however, the prevailing colonial atmosphere created an invisible barrier between colonizers and the colonized in other ways. Although never expressed verbally, it was apparent in many areas of social behaviour. It was very subtle, ranging from suppressed disdain to polite avoidance of intimate personal contact.

My best friends at school were mostly Dutch and "Indos" (Dutch Eurasian) and I had never felt such a barrier. Having little interest in politics and having stayed with Dutch families for so many years had insulated me and made me relatively insensitive to any sign of discrimination. In any case I had never thought of it. However, a boy from Celebes, Wim Kaunang, who occupied a berth in my cabin, suddenly made me aware of my unconcern.

"Do you know that we are the only Indonesians who are travelling to Holland on this ship?" he asked me when he came in.

Wanting to be polite I said: "We don't know each other yet. My name is Madé, and this is Kwie Iet, a former classmate of mine. We are going to study medicine in Amsterdam."

After mentioning his name, he continued: "Do you know that they have put us three together so that we don't mix with the Belandas?" (*Belanda* is the Indonesian word for Dutch.)

He elaborated further about racial segregation and other colonial inhumanities. I found his arguments quite exaggerated and suggested that our being put together in one cabin might well be by sheer chance or even with good intentions. We were of about the same age and perhaps people wanted us to feel more at ease. We started arguing for some time but I failed to get my kind of logic across. Tan Kwie Iet was completely blank. Although he was listening to our argument, his face seemed to express pity, as if he was pitying us for wasting our time. He was not at all interested in politics. His aim was—like most of his ethnic group—to have success in his career and to become rich as soon as possible. I felt annoyed and frustrated because I did not succeed in getting my opponent to be more logical. I was amazed at the tenacity of his belief in the racialist motives of the boat staff. It was most disturbing and puzzled me.

Tan Kwie Iet ended our argument by mentioning that it was almost time for dinner. In the dining room we took our seats together at the end of the long dining table. About fifteen Dutch and Eurasian youth were already seated, noisily discussing the menu of the day. Still in its silver clamp the menu card went from hand to hand during which the boys snatched it from each other several times without giving the others the chance to finish reading it. We were baffled by such behaviour, wondering why it should be so important to know beforehand what we were going to eat. When the noise became unbearable end even one chair fell with a crash to the floor, the head steward rushed into the dining hall and with a thundering voice called the troupe to order. I could not help smiling, because somehow I found the scene amusing. Tan Kwie Iet looked puzzled, but Kaunang shook his head and remarked: "Look how they behave! They are so content with themselves and will not pay any attention to us because we have no white skin."

Since I did not want to enter again into debate as in our cabin, I kept quiet. We had a choice between Indonesian and European food and the three of us opted for Indonesian. I noticed that most of the boys at our table preferred rice above potatoes. The head steward found it wiser to stay and supervise the dinner, so for the rest of the evening all was quiet and orderly.

The following day I forgot about the argument and for the rest of the trip I did not pay much attention to Kaunang. He was not of the talkative type and had perhaps dismissed me already as belonging to the useless colonial "*priyayi*" group (civil servants under the colonial administration).

In Medan in North Sumatra, Kwie Iet went ashore with me for a long sightseeing tour by horsecart through the town where we visited the famous beautiful mosque. Also in Singapore and in Sabang we made trips together to interesting places. At Whiteway Laidlaws, a huge department store in Singapore, I bought myself my first woollen European suit and as expected Kwie Iet did the same, only his was much more expensive and of better quality. Since I did not know what was lying in store for me in Holland, I was careful with the 450 guilders left from the 1,000 Father had sent me. The boat ticket had cost 540 guilders and I had spent 10 guilders in Medan and Sabang.

At the harbour of Suez I enjoyed the sight of the numerous small boats crowding around the stern of the ship and the boys diving from it to recover coins thrown by passengers from our decks into the water. Without realizing that they were driven by poverty, I only imagined how much fun they must have in doing this. Suddenly I was startled by a big flop on the floor behind me. An Arab, carrying a large bag with merchandise over his shoulder, had flung himself from the top of the mast of a passing sailing vessel over the railing of our ship. There was great consternation on deck when the ship's crew rushed to the man, grabbed him and tried to push him back over the railing. During the struggle the purser hit the man's head with a rubber club, the thudding sound of which made me gasp! Nailed to the floor I watched the scene breathlessly. I couldn't believe my eyes when I saw how in one split second the Arab leaped from the floor upon the railing bar and grabbed the vessel's mast that at that right moment swung back to his ship. It reminded me of the trapeze acrobats at a circus I had seen a few times in Malang. He spiralled down the mast with his bag of merchandise still over his shoulder!

In Genoa, most of our troupe disembarked to continue their travel to Holland by train. These arrangements had been made by their parents who knew about the boring monotony of the last ten days on board the ship and the nasty storms in the Gulf of Biscay. The trip over the Alps and through the Rhone Valley was more attractive and the boys would have more time in Holland for their preparations before entering school or university. Actually I would have loved to join them. However, a few days before we arrived at Genoa the captain of the ship called me and showed me a cable which he had received, which read: "On behalf of your father you are advised to take care that when you arrive in Amsterdam you must have a large white card on the left lapel of your jacket with your name clearly written on it. A gentleman by the name of Caron will be waiting for you on the quay at the harbour. The Governor of The Great East".

The cable was not signed by name but only "The Governor". I thought it must be very official and was deeply impressed.

"The Great East" was the name of the large eastern province of the Netherlands East Indies comprising the whole area east of Borneo. The captain did not know the Governor, nor my father, nor myself, and he could not give any information other than what was stated in the cable. I started guessing. The name Caron sounded vaguely familiar to me. It must be an old friend of Father, perhaps a former Dutch civil servant now on pension living in Holland.

When we arrived at the watergates of Ijmuiden entering the North-Sea Canal, the weather was beautiful. While the boat was steaming slowly towards Amsterdam harbour I could not stop marvelling about the waterway that was several metres above the level of the land on both sides. I knew the facts of course from our geography classes, but to experience the real thing was quite different. I enjoyed immensely the panorama of the flat land reaching far away until the horizon, the windmills and the hundreds of cows grazing peacefully on the green fields. It was as if a dream became reality. And that it had indeed. Tears welled up in my eyes.

The sun was still well above the horizon when the boat drew alongside the quay at Amsterdam's harbour, even though it was eight o'clock in the evening. I had my luggage neatly packed waiting for the porters in the corridor and stood at the railing looking at the waiting crowd below. Of course I did not recognize anybody. I ascertained that the white card was visibly attached to my jacket's left lapel and with my violin under my arm I followed the porter who carried my suitcases down the staircase.

Hardly had I put my feet on the quay stones when I was tapped on the shoulder by a tall lean gentleman, saying: "I am Jaap Caron. My father is a good friend of your father, and he asked me to meet you at the boat and bring you to our home in Bussum. Where is your luggage?"

I pointed at the porter and he called a taxi to drive us to the railway station. On the train to Bussum, Jaap told me that tomorrow morning he would bring me the next morning back to Amsterdam where he had already found a small room for me to live for the first month. It was located conveniently between the University and the Students' Club House. Afterwards I could decide for myself if I wanted to move. It all sounded very new, strange, but exciting in my ears. I could hardly wait.

It was already dark when we arrived in Bussum. Jaap's parents welcomed me as if they had known me for a long time. Mr Caron had been in Bali for five years as Resident (the highest Dutch civil servant of a Region) of Bali and Lombok and was later promoted to Governor of The Great Eastern Province, with Makassar (now called Ujung Pandang) as duty station. From there he returned to Holland on retirement. He had been a very close friend of Father and had seen me several times during my school years.

Mr Caron was the prototype of the efficient, enlightened, but authoritarian colonial civil servant, who with genuine idealism and devotion worked for the benefit of the population in the colony. His features and posture displayed his very strong character while his eyes expressed deep sympathy and sincerity. Pointing with his finger to Jaap he explained to me how he had succeeded in getting his son to continue his studies at the Law faculty after years of idleness. At the age of sixty-five, he had enrolled himself as a student at the same Faculty and challenged his son as to who would be the first to finish his studies. A few months previously, they had graduated at the same time.

After dinner, Mr Caron told us stories of old times in Bali. Carried away by sentimental nostalgia, he could not stop telling me of Father's many good deeds and achievements as ruler of Karangasem. He told me about the history of Bali and how Father had become *Stedehouder* instead of those in our family who according to hierarchy should have been given priority but were found unfit for the job. He had only praise for Father's qualities, his integrity and his wit. I felt moved by his words, and happy to be staying with the Carons.

CHAPTER 16

Initiation I

The next morning Mr Caron brought me to the railway station. We went on foot through slightly winding green shady lanes. Looking around, I was impressed by the cleanliness of everything, the neat villas and the beauty of big old trees and colourful gardens. It was like a dream world. Bussum was a place where wealthy businessmen and pensioners had their residences, commuting by train to Amsterdam. The environment breathed an air of dignity and respectability. Jaap Caron stayed behind. He would join us in Amsterdam later that afternoon and bring my luggage.

Old Caron told me that he preferred walking because it kept him fit and healthy. We did not need to hurry since the trains to Amsterdam left every half hour. On the train he said: "You see, Madé, in Indie (Indonesia as it was still called in those colonial days) I would have been in a big car with a driver, keeping up Dutch prestige. Otherwise we would lose respectability in the eyes of the people. But here it is different. There is no difference between me, the ex-Governor, and the people you see around us. Here we are all equal. Even our Minister in The Hague goes by tram to his office". Strange as it sounded to me at first, I found it reasonable and I liked the idea. I looked around and studied the people in the train. Two youngsters were chatting with each other, an elderly lady was knitting, and I noticed that most single men were reading the newspaper. Old Caron chatted away, telling me about the cows in the field, canals we were crossing, about church towers we saw far away, dykes and windmills.

In Amsterdam we went to a huge department store. Mr Caron wanted first of all to buy clothes for me, explaining: "Madé, it is already late in the summer. There is nothing as treacherous as the weather in Holland. It can be suddenly very cold next month, even next week, and especially for you, a person fresh from the tropics, it is most important to be on guard against the cold. Too many students from your country have succumbed here from tuberculosis because they did not take proper precautions. They caught a cold before being aware of it. So don't be surprised that I am going to buy you woollen underwear from Jaeger, the best of its kind. Let it be expensive, you will not regret it later". And raising his voice: "Be sure that you wear them, preferably from now on!" Later two suits were included, shoes and socks, and even two neck ties to match the suits. I was wondering how I would pay for all that material. Noticing my worried looks Old Caron smiled broadly: "Don't worry, my boy, all has been arranged for you by your dear father!" I found it wise to undergo passively the old man's shopping spree. More items followed, a shawl and a pair of leather gloves, and something which later caused me a profound embarrassment in my students' club: a felt hat!

We had lunch in a Chinese restaurant where Jaap was waiting for us. "Good morning, Madé, I have brought your luggage to your room, together with the big trunk which I collected from the harbour. I will bring you up there after lunch". I felt relief, because I had been wondering how I would get my trunk from the harbour. I thanked Jaap for his kindness to take all the trouble.

After lunch Old Caron returned to Bussum. Before leaving he took me aside saying: "Now it is Jaap's turn to take care of you. Listen well to what he has to say. He will brief you about the university, about students' clubs and organizations, especially about the "Amsterdams Studenten Corps" that you must join. This is very important for you. You must become a member, otherwise your time in Holland will be wasted". This pronouncement left me puzzled, and he did not elaborate.

The restaurant was not far from the apartment building where Jaap had taken a room for me to live for the first month. With two large packages in my hands, it took me some effort to keep pace with Jaap's long strides over the pavement. Entering the huge building, Jaap pushed me into a small chamber which looked to me like an iron prison cell. With relish, he explained to me the working of an elevator! After riding up and down a couple of times we landed at the top floor. Jaap produced a key and opened the door to my room. I was baffled. In the tiny cubicle my two suitcases and trunk filled all space which was left around the small round table and a chair which seemed to be the sole furniture of my dwelling. Jaap smiled broadly, and stepping over the suitcases, he reached to the wall and "Flup!" a large built-in wardrobe sprang open before my astonished eyes. I had never seen such a miracle before! There were drawers and a shoe-rack inside. Just when I was going to ask where the bedroom was, Jaap made a juggler's gesture and drew aside a chest-high curtain which ran over the remainder of the wall and pulled down a bed which was already made up with mattress, sheets, pillow and blankets. He had to stop halfway because of the luggage which could not be pushed aside. "Well, Madé, before going to bed you will have to first move things away", he noted.

Jaap had me seated on the only chair and making himself comfortable on the round table, started to brief me. For nearly one hour he talked about the

University, where to register, about the students, the faculties and when to register at the "Societeit", the Clubhouse of the "Amsterdams Studenten Corps", where I would get detailed information about the Club's rules to which I should strictly adhere. "Otherwise?" I ventured to ask. Jaap put up a most solemn face and with a deep bass he pronounced: "Otherwise? Then you might get in great trouble!" I was impressed and kept silent. Jaap ended his briefing.

"Well, I think that is all. I will go now and tell the landlady that you have arrived. She is living one floor just below this room. She certainly will come and see you soon. Farewell!" And suddenly he was gone.

I felt a strange emptiness and there was a lapse of time during which—I don't know for how long—my brain did not function. Perhaps my mind was just over-saturated. When I came to, I found myself sitting on top of my trunk with my elbows on my knees, supporting my chin on both hands.

Slowly I started to take my belongings out of my trunk and suitcases and arrange them in the cupboard. There was room for the emptied suitcases in the trunk, which fitted exactly in the space under the bay window on the street-side of the room. It functioned as an extra table. There was a knock on the door and a plump woman in her forties with curly blond hair entered, greeting me with a friendly smile: "Welcome Sir, are you Mr Maday Dje... how is it? Sorry, it's too difficult for me, Sir!"

I felt disconcerted. For the first time in my life somebody had addressed me as "Sir"—and to my eyes this was a Dutch lady for sure. I decided to behave myself. She instructed me how to handle the folding bed and showed me the bathroom downstairs which I had to share with three other gentlemen. I understood that Jaap had arranged for the rent to include breakfast which would be brought to my room every morning. For lunch and dinner I should go to a restaurant or cafeteria and she gave me addresses of a few nearby. She apologized for not being able to provide meals since she was a widow without help.

She asked me at what time I wanted to have my breakfast brought to my room. With my mind still in the tropical habit I made unwittingly my first blunder: "At six o'clock, please!" She stared at me with wide open eyes: "But Sir, that is impossible! Everybody is still asleep in bed at such time." Meaning to be tolerant I corrected myself and said: "Well, let us make it half past six or at seven." She suggested that half past seven would be the best, although it would be still quite difficult for her to get up so early. I was puzzled.

The next morning I got up at seven, had a bath in the huge bathtub, because there was no shower, and waited for my breakfast. At seven-thirty nothing happened: I waited and waited. There was no way to call the landlady because I did not know which of the rooms downstairs was hers. I was afraid to knock at the doors at random. Another fifteen minutes passed and I decided to leave without having had my breakfast and to complain later, although I did not know exactly how to do that.

I rushed to the University, looking every minute at my watch and checking street names on my map. I was so afraid of being late at the registration office that I did not notice how empty the streets were. Arriving at the place I was very surprised to find the office doors closed. Nobody was to be seen around. Had I been mistaken? I checked the date and address in my notebook and found everything was right. I went back to the corner of the street, checked street names, then to the next corner and found nothing wrong. A man who saw me running to and fro stopped me: "Sir, what are you looking for?" I explained my problem. He looked amused and laughed: "Well, you have to wait for another hour. Did you not know that from to-day we have Winter-Time?"

"What is that?" I asked, and he explained about the time shift taking place twice a year.

How simple! And how stupid one can be! I should have enquired better. Jaap had not told me, perhaps taking it for granted that everybody knew.

Not knowing what to do, I walked to a bookshop nearby and spelled out the titles of books and magazines on display. Glued behind the glass of the door I saw a number of notices with addresses of rooms for rent, with and without breakfast. Some of them were crossed out and marked "Occupied". My mind quickly registered prices which ranged between 15 and 30 guilders. Jaap had told me the day before that my room rent was 35 guilders per month. I decided to move to a cheaper place as soon as possible.

Meanwhile the porch in front of the registration office was gradually filling up with students arriving from all directions. I hastily assured myself a place in the queue. A few minutes later I saw my previous classmate Tan Kwie Iet entering the porch, accompanied by two elder Chinese students who had met him at the harbour on arrival in Amsterdam. They had arranged everything for him. He looked very happy when he saw me and wanted to push himself behind me, but his friends took him to the end of the queue. The registration was smooth and swift, a matter of routine. The last official at the counter gave me a whole set of information booklets and brochures, which I regarded as treasures.

Back home, I was surprised to find my room neatly made up, the bed folded behind the curtain, and my breakfast waiting on the small table. I felt hungry, enjoyed the coffee and Dutch bread and started to study the booklets and brochures carefully one by one. I was glowing with pride! Because now I was a real Medical Student! The humiliating defeat of the early morning was forgotten, also my plan to complain to the landlady, which after all would have been another self-defeating blunder...

CHAPTER 17

Initiation II

There were three days left before the start of the so-called *groentijd*, the traditional initiation period required to become a member of the "Amsterdams Studenten Corps". After having studied the map of Amsterdam carefully, I concluded that crossing the town by tram was the cheapest way to orientate myself. So for three days I chose at random one tramline, rode it until its endpoint and changed on any other connecting line, thus making every time two trips on one ticket, until I had covered the whole city. Among the host of new experiences I found out that there were certain rush hours which were better avoided and the time better spent in one of the many interesting museums. I enjoyed these exciting excursions immensely and learned a great deal.

Although Jaap had been talking to me for nearly one hour about students life in Holland, I realized too late that he actually had told me nothing about the *groentijd* except that I should follow the rules strictly. Thus, I was kept completely in the dark as to what would happen at the initiation. I didn't care too much, however, and with great fervour, I strictly followed the instructions given to me by the Students' Initiation Committee during my first visit to N.I.A. These initials stood for "Nos Iungit Amicitiam" ("Let friendship Unite us") and were marked decoratively at the front of the clubhouse of the Amsterdams Studenten Corps.

On the morning of the great day I bought the long-sleeved white shirt according to specifications with three detachable stiff white collars, a black bow-tie and the prescribed flat grey cap. I was surprised to discover that the shop-keeper was well informed about my necessities. He asked me if I knew where to go to have my hair completely cut off. When I opened my notebook to find addresses, he took me to the door and pointed to the corner of the street. "Take it easy, boy! There it is, and from there it is less than a hundred metres to N.I.A. I would suggest that you wait until late this afternoon before going to the barber—afterwards you can go straight to the clubhouse".

With my Balinese sensitivity to ways of addressing people it came to me as a flash that the man said: "Boy" and not "Sir"! Feebly, I sensed that I had been downgraded somehow. However, I found it sound advice and I went home to try on my new gear. In the mirror the large downward hanging collar-tips, with in between the black bow-tie, looked particularly silly and the obligatory flat grey cap completed the absurdity which I thought perhaps was required to be recognized as a novice.

On the way to the barbershop that afternoon I put a shawl around my neck and held my cap hidden under my coat. When I seated myself on my chair and removed my shawl the barber knew immediately what his job was. "Boy! What have you done with your hair? This is no hair, it is a brush, my razor will get blunt." I had indeed very dense and thick hair, due to having been shaved completely with an old-fashioned barber's straight-edged razor every month during the first ten years of my life. The barber had to change his electric razor twice before he finished. While I found his exaggerated behaviour amusing, I grew apprehensive when I heard a great turmoil on the street outside as if a riot had broken out. There was shouting and running and great excitement. Suddenly, the door burst open with a crash and four angry men stormed inside, shouting and gesticulating, and with ominously threatening sounds they pointed at me. Two of them tried to pull me out of my chair, but the barber stopped them saying: "Let me finish my work first!" He had hardly completed his job with the razor and removed the white napkin from my neck, when I felt myself lifted in the air and carried away onto the street. I could not see anything because my overcoat was thrown over my head and wrapped tightly. Then I felt myself being turned around several times and pushed forward. The noise of shouting, scuffling, commanding and threatening increased. After some minutes when my coat was taken off my head, it slowly dawned on me that this must be part of the *groentijd* and the noisy, angry-looking crowd must be students having fun scaring the newcomers. My panic evaporated when I saw the street full of other groups of shouting students around other novices. I saw some horrified faces grimacing painfully.

Realizing the harmlessness of the spectacle I let myself be pushed along by the current of tumultuous hordes of students. In the half dark I recognized the front of the N.I.A. building where we were noisily encouraged to enter through the wide open door. That turned out not to be easy, since a throng of heavy muscular students barred the way. The first batch of novices was thrown back onto the street immediately, only to be pushed forward again by the howling crowd outside. A wild and intense pushing game ensued. I saw that it was useless for me to try to fight my way through. Being lithe and much smaller than the Dutch boys, I succeeded easily to free myself from their grips and to slip through quickly by diving between their legs and I was the first novice to enter the big hall. There I was greeted with a deafening cry from half-drunken elder students who were sitting in groups around low round tables behind huge glasses of beer. They commanded me roughly to take off my shoes and to crawl to them on hands and knees. I was made to understand that during the three-week initiation period, that was the only way novices were allowed to move around within the clubhouse.

The atmosphere in the hall was thick with cigarette smoke and smelled profusely of spilled beer, but inside was not as tumultuous and confusing as outside. Any novice who successfully managed to come through the human barricade was called immediately to crawl to one of the groups to introduce himself and be interviewed. This interview soon assumed the character of an interrogation, in which the novice by means of questions, scoffing, scolding, commands and counter-commands was severely tested in regard to his character, his strength of will, his sincerely, honesty and integrity.

The arguing game between one novice and at least three or four older students was, of course, an unfair matter. The inequality was moreover enhanced by the novice's position, being nailed to the floor with the older students menacingly hovering above his head. It was easy for the novice to follow orders when he was asked to climb on the table and sing a song, even when during the singing he was scorned and ridiculed. When, however, the order was to take off his clothes, problems arose.

With most of the novices, it resulted in a tense argument and a fight, which of course was only mockery because it was not at all intended that the novice should follow such a ridiculous order. At last, however, he would be so scared and intimidated that he reluctantly would obey. But when he was halfway he would be rudely rebuked and be asked to account for his indecent behaviour. That would lead to new and long arguments.

I was completely ignorant of the mock character of the show at the time and believed that all was in earnest. Apparently my reactions on the circumstances were quite different from what the students expected. I was not at all scared or intimidated, and when I was asked to remove my clothes, I started forthwith without any concern. Being accustomed in Bali to bathe naked together with other people in the river, I found nothing indecent in the performance. But when after having removed my shirt, I started to remove my pants, I was angrily rebuked: "G.V.D. (Dutch term of abuse) what are you doing? How do you dare to perform such obscenity here?"

I looked very surprised and asked innocently: "What is wrong with being naked? This is a very natural thing!"

The students were taken by surprise, as if it was very new to them. I told them that we in Bali were not ashamed of each other's nakedness when bathing together in the river. The crowd obviously enjoyed my story; they forgot their role of superiority and became suddenly very friendly. They asked if there were also girls and women in the river.

"Yes! but they are usually bathing at some distance from us".

One asked further: "Are they also naked?"

"Yes", I said.

"And can you see them?"

"Of course we see them", I answered.

They looked at each other, completely perplexed. They helped me to put on my clothes. From my side, I was puzzled by such ignorance, but I was not given the chance to reflect.

The novices were then summoned to circulate from one group to another. In each group they were subjected to similar interrogations and insults, against which they had to defend themselves.

I found myself being singled out for a different kind of discourse. The students found it very interesting to hear from me about the part of the world that I came from, about my past, about history and cultural aspects of Bali and Indonesia. I did not have to defend myself against insults or abusive language. I found their curiosity remarkable, but at the same time I discovered how little I actually knew about my own country, its many different cultures and, shamefully, about my own religion. On many questions I could not give any answer and just shrugged my shoulders, and I felt very disturbed when they laughed hilariously. I controlled myself, but inside I nearly wept.

It was nearly midnight when we were told roughly that we could go home. Our joy was, however, severely tempered when we found our shoes stacked in a large heap in the corner of the corridor. They were tightly strung together in batches of three to five unmatching pairs. It took more than half an hour to sort things out.

We were exhausted when we plodded our way home in little groups through the deserted streets.

CHAPTER 18

Initiation III

The following day, the initiation activities started to assume a certain pattern. The mornings were for singing lessons: club songs, yells, declamations of all sorts. Most of the songs were extremely vulgar, some of them so obscene they could have been invented only by a sick brain or by a genius. Coming from well-to-do and respectable families, many of my novice mates felt offended and some even became rebellious. They were easily persuaded. I naively believed in the value of everything that was related to the life of the Amsterdams Studenten Corps. I accepted all of it eagerly and participated with fervour and sincerity. After all there was also much fun to enjoy during the singing exercises.

In the afternoons we were herded together to visit one of the various sport and entertainment clubs belonging to the Amsterdams Studenten Corps such as the swimming club, the boxing and fencing club, the music club and the equestrian club. Favourite among these was Nereus, the rowing club whose Team of Eight had won at all Varsities for the past few years. There was no bridge club since playing bridge was considered "bourgeois". At the clubs our abilities in the various branches of sport were tested. During these exercises many kinds of obstacles and hindrances were rudely put before us. While very nasty for us novices, it produced fun, laughter and hilarity among the students, many times bordering on sheer sadism. I was frightened when I was forced to climb one of the horses at the equestrian club. The animals were so much bigger and higher than our ponies I had learned to ride on in Java, but after succeeding to hoist myself in the saddle I found the animal very cooperative and riding it relatively easy and enjoyable, despite the bombardment of rotten tomatoes and the terrible noise made by the students. I passed the test triumphantly. At a later occasion when I was asked to join the club I sadly declined because I could not afford to pay the high cost of its membership and the other expenses associated with the sport of the elite. I chose swimming and fencing instead.

At our visit to Nereus, I was immediately assigned as pilot of the famous eight because of my small size and light weight. I felt it as a great honour. My team won easily. A thundering applause burst from the excited crowd. There came however a sudden end to my enthusiasm. Before I realized what was happening I found myself swimming in the icy water of the Amstel River still with my clothes and shoes on. I was shivering terribly from the cold when at last I reached the boathouse and a bunch of cheerful students lifted me on the platform. They got a towel for me. By tradition the pilot of the winning team was thrown in the water. Silently I vowed not to get involved in the rowing sport if I could help it.

During the evenings we were divided into 11 groups, each assigned to visit one of the 11 "Dispuutgezelschappen" ("Debating Clubs"), abbreviated to "Dispuuts", which together constituted the Amsterdams Studenten Corps.

While at the other universities in Holland the student associations were composed of "year clubs", groups of students belonging to the same year of enrollment, the Corps in Amsterdam was formed in 1851 as a conglomerate of the then already existing "Dispuuts". In the 1850s they were genuine debating clubs where the members by turns had to present a thesis around which debates were held in Latin. Within these clubs friendships were born. Gradually the purpose of the clubs changed from scientific to social, putting more and more emphasis on character development of the students. Each club shaped its own life-style and character and had in the course of time built up its own traditions and mores. After inauguration in a "Dispuut" one remains a member for life; the first four years one joins as a "working member", afterwards as an "honorary member". The longevity of the Dispuuts depended on the enthusiasm and the tenacity of the members to uphold their ideals and traditions and also on their ability to attract each year from the novices new candidates consistent with the character of the "Dispuut". With the exception of the UNICA, all the Dispuuts existing before 1851 had died out—and ten new groupings had emerged since then. Novices were not allowed to apply for membership themselves. At the and of the initiation period, each novice was officially informed which "Dispuut" he had been asked to join.

Thus, for eleven evenings we were subjected to the same kind of interrogations and harassments, but not as harsh as those we had received at N.I.A., the students' clubhouse. These visits were meant for the Debating Clubs to acquaint themselves with the novices in order to enable them to select suitable candidates for membership. On occasion, the novice was treated with obvious care, when for some reason or other a Club hoped to have him as its member. At these meetings much older members also participated, people who were no longer students, but established citizens such as doctors, lawyers, professors, artists, writers and businessmen. They were honorary members. We soon found out that the "Dispuuts" were indeed trying their best to select suitable candidates and many times they were competing with other "Dispuuts" for the same potential candidates.

Some among us who happened to have a brother or relative as a Corps member, already had some knowledge about the various "Dispuuts" and they became valuable sources of information. For me, however, all information they could give was almost meaningless since I had still no idea at all of its relevance or of differences in the historical and social backgrounds of the clubs. The only information which made sense to me was that most of the members of the Dispuut VIATOR were sons of former Dutch officials who had been in the East Indies for many years, like Jaap Caron. As expected, I was sought out by VIATOR, and Jaap Caron advised me to accept the offer. It was obviously the most natural choice. On the other hand, I had not been much impressed by their members during our visits to their Clubhouse, nor from what I saw from them at N.I.A. and on other occasions. I found them very superficial and easy-going. There was nothing of the fighting spirit, the intellectuality and the sincerity which I felt among the members of UNICA. There, I was impressed by what seemed to me at that time their highly intellectual conversations.

When VIATOR asked me to join, I sensed that they were too eager to embrace me in their midst, while UNICA offered me their membership with the warning that to become a true UNICIST I would have to work very hard and that I had to be prepared to put aside my personal interests on behalf of UNICA. Otherwise I would find myself being expelled from the club in a very short time. There was a choice to be made between having a pleasant time or meeting a challenge. Without hesitation I opted for the latter.

At the conclusion of the initiation period the traditional inauguration ceremony for membership of the Amsterdams Studenten Corps was held in the Aula of the University, attended by various officials and families of the novices. For this occasion our black bow-ties were replaced by white ones. When entering the hall I was taken by surprise seeing that the left half of the Aula was occupied by girls. It was then that I heard for the first time of the existence of the female Amsterdams Studenten Corps, which had finished their initiation at the same time. At the sight of the large assemblage of girls, many of my year mates became excited, some of them trying to recognize former classmates or dates among them. I had never been much interested in girls and I found the sight of the pale, exhausted and somewhat dishevelled damsels quite disappointing. I learned that their Corps also consisted of "Dispuut-gezelschappen". My year-mates mentioned the name EOOS, the oldest of them, with particular reverence. Like the three of us UNICA candidates, the five EOOS candidates had the honour to occupy the front row of chairs. I found the honour that was accorded to seniority quite natural, since it was similar to what we practised in the East. Much later I came to realize that it was only an empty formality, intentionally maintained to fool the students.

The inauguration ceremony in UNICA which took place two weeks later after a very different kind of probation period was much more impressive than the public ceremony in the Aula of the University. It was exclusively intimate and had more the character of a ritualistic initiation into a Brotherhood. The ceremony was performed by the "High Priest" of UNICA, using mysterious symbols and the various sacred paraphernalia of the "Dispuut". There was the thick parchment volume called the "Rarekiek", which was UNICA's "bible", read from a high and beautifully carved lectern; also, the large rectangular red woollen plaid bordered with white tufts; and no less impressive was the staff with the real Capricorn horn.

The ceremony was held in the dark attic of the UNICA clubhouse, ghostly illuminated by a few floor lights shining through red transparencies. We entered the sanctuary via a heavy wooden trap door which squeaked melancholically when we pushed it open and again when it dropped slowly back as soon as we were inside.

Although I was already at the age when I no longer believed in ghosts or mystic appearances, I found the shamanistic performance, which reminded me of the practices of our seers and witch doctors back home, very attractive. I was impressed by its earnestness, but at the same time I was confused. How could this be happening in a modern Western literary debating club? The apparent contradiction became more puzzling by the hilarious cries of disdain from the crowd of UNICA members every time I managed to give an honest and serious response to the High Priest's very personal questions. Were they possibly making fun of me? Were my answers that stupid?

"Now, my son, my last and most crucial question," the shrill voice of the High Priest sounded as a recitative, "have you prepared your Life Slogan? And what will it be?"

"Yes Sir," I murmured, "it is 'ik dien'". (I serve).

The High Priest screamed: "Whwhaatt?" Immediately his shrill scream was joined by a deafening cacophony of shrieks, roars, whistling and cries of contempt from the two dozen or so UNICA members attending: "Impossible!" "Hey, look at that!" "Hey listen, who do you think you are? A saint?" "Death, death, bury him!" Some of them took off their shoes to drum vehemently on the bare planks of the floor. "Woooh, bury him quickly, we don't want to see him!"

Trying to come to the defence of my well-prepared slogan was out of question. There was no debate possible in that wild tumult. That seemed to me as a final refusal. I was hustled into a small cubicle where it was pitch dark and told to starve there. I was very miserable, all hope was gone and for the first time during the whole of the initiation period I felt depressed.

The other two candidates underwent the same interrogations and were refuted with the same tumult. The last one did not have to join the two of us in the dark cubicle, instead we were taken out and ordered to stand up.

Suddenly all lights went on and we found ourselves surrounded by the whole troupe of UNICA members, cheerfully raising their glasses of red wine in the air, yelling the UNICA yell:

"UNICA, UNICA, IS A FRIEND OF MINE,

"UNICA, UNICA, IS A FRIEND OF MINE,

"HOLD YOUR TONGUE!"

followed by the slow and dignified Anthem, which ended with

"UNICAM   BIBAMUS,   U-U-N-I-I-CAM   BI-BA-A-MUUUUUS! MUUUUS!"

At the second strophe of "Bibamus", full glasses of red wine were pushed in our hands and we were ordered to work down the sour liquid in one gulp: "AD FUNDUM!" they yelled.

"Proficiat, proficiat!"

There followed a lot of hand-shaking and shoulder clappings. Cautiously, I took notice of the various sacred paraphernalia. Some of the older honorary members of UNICA took me aside and we had a family-like get together, as if they had known me for a long time. When they asked how I invented my Life Slogan, I told them that it was not my invention, but that I had been inspired by my reading about Albert Schweitzer. I felt encouraged by their appreciation.

I ventured to ask: "But why then that outburst of scorn and contempt? Was it serious?"

They laughed wholeheartedly: "Of course it was! And of course it was not! It can be both ways. So it is with UNICA!".

I was left puzzling.

But one thing that I vaguely sensed was that perhaps I was destined to become a "Unicist".

CHAPTER 19

Coming of Age in
UNICA

The first weekend after the inauguration I went to Bussum and told Mr Caron that I had joined UNICA instead of VIATOR. Contrary to what I expected Mr Caron did not comment at length, he congratulated me. But from his eyes I sensed disappointment, even a little bit of apprehension. Of course I attributed this to my failing to heed his son's advice. Years later, however, when I knew more about politics in Holland, I found a better explanation for his reaction. Among conservative circles at that time, UNICA was believed to be much under the influence of left-leaning intellectuals. It happened that that year a fourth-year Unicist was fighting in the Republican Army against Franco in Spain. Mr Caron did not mention anything about politics, but gave more practical advice on how to organize my life in the big city. He strongly warned me never to economize on food and assured me that I was very welcome to spend the weekends in Bussum, even if only to enjoy good meals. Apart from that, he indulged in nostalgic memories of his years in the East. He advised me not to waste time with visits to Indonesians in Holland from whom I would not learn much, but that I should try to learn as much as possible about Western culture from close contact with Dutch families, for which membership of the Amsterdams Students Corps would give ample opportunities.

The N. I. A. Clubhouse Committee had completed its one-year term of office about two weeks after the inauguration of new members in all of the eleven "Dispuuts". A new team of five fourth-year students was composed after consultations with the Senate, the Governing Board of the Amsterdams Students Corps, itself traditionally consisting of five fifth-year students. It was never difficult to find suitable candidates for the various functions in the N. I. A. Committee as well as for the Senate. Academic rules at the universities were at that time much more liberal than they are nowadays. Attendance at the lectures was not obligatory, one had only to pass the examinations. For that purpose the students customarily went into seclusion for two or three months to catch up with the material. The timing of the examinations was not strictly according to semesters, it depended entirely on when the Professor was available, and willing, to test the candidate. Money also did not pose a problem for the usually well-to-do Corps members. Although these time-consuming jobs were wholly voluntary and cost a lot of extra money for the students involved, the prestige which they gained and the public relations which they acquired during their term of office, besides experience in organization and management, were enough motivation to sacrifice one year of study.

Each year the installation of a new N.I.A. Committee was a great event. Traditionally, the new dignitaries were on that occasion put to a painful test by the grand assembly of Corps members, asking painful questions concerning policy, work programmes and other issues, mostly absurdities, with the intention of ridiculing the new team.

As on that first occasion after our inauguration, I was not yet familiar with that kind of theatre. The large hall was packed with old and new members, all eager to see the performance of the new Committee under harassment from the floor. At the far end of the hall the outgoing and the new N.I.A. Committee members were seated at a long green table, ready to perform the ceremony, presided by the Chairman of the Senate. All of them were officially clad in frock-coat and tails, adorned, according to rank, with stars and ribbons glittering around their necks. In conformity with tradition, UNICA occupied the chairs at the corner nearest to the green table, common ordinary chairs for the new and younger members, large comfortable armchairs for the older ones. As expected, the gathering became immediately tumultuous with a great many members from all sides trying to be the first to speak. With great effort the Chairman succeeded only partially to obtain a semblance of a meeting, but very soon the noise became nearly unbearable and the Chairman's periodic vehement hammering on his table only increased the turmoil. Most of the time there was yelling, shouting, shrieking and only now and then a timid applause from small groups giving support, out of loyalty, to the new Committee member under attack.

I was not able to follow the debates, because of the noise and because I did not fully understand the issues.

Suddenly it occurred to me that something was missing at N.I.A. and I would like to ask for it. I became very excited by the idea and before I had realized it, I had stood on my chair and raised my hand. Then the crowd fell silent and I felt a hundred pairs of startled eyes staring at me. That was something extraordinary! It had never occurred in history that a first-year student, fresh from the *groentijd* and still without hair on his skull, had the guts to raise a voice at such an important meeting! Somehow I overcame my panic, and raising my voice as loud as possible I asked: "Would the N.I.A. Committee be willing to consider providing a ping-pong table at the clubhouse?"

Instantly a tremendous and deafening roar burst from the crowd, followed by whistling, screaming and howling and an enthusiastic loud applause from the entire hall. I felt myself being lifted up from my chair and carried on shoulders around and above the heads of the cheering crowd in the hall. At the end I was put down before the green table. Confused and not understanding what was happening, I did not know whether I should laugh or cry, nor did I know what to say. Shyly, I retreated as quickly as possible to safety in the UNICA corner. There the elder Unicists explained to me why I was hailed as a hero: unlike nowadays ping-pong was then considered as a game only fit for children and teenagers. It would be very denigrating for the respectable N.I.A. Committee to even consider such a play-toy for the Clubhouse. Therefore, that request was considered a magnificent joke aimed at ridiculing the Committee, especially coming from a newborn member. It took me some time to realize that my sincere request had been misunderstood.

In Holland the 5th of December is traditionally Saint Nicholas' Day. Old and young celebrate that day by giving each other small gifts, usually with a humorous flavour. Children are made to believe that Saint Nicholas arrives each year from Spain in a boat and goes around on a white horse, accompanied by his black servant, "Zwarte Piet" (Black Peter). Black Peter is reputed to spank naughty children with his broom, and give the sweet ones nice presents which he carries in a huge bag over his shoulder.

By tradition, a visit to our Clubhouse N.I.A. was included in the itinerary of Saint Nicholas' tour through Amsterdam. On account of my brown skin and black hair—and because the memory of my performance at its installation was still fresh—the N.I.A. Committee asked me to act as "Zwarte Piet". I felt it as a special honour and agreed eagerly. I was told that Saint Nicholas would arrive at our clubhouse in a very special way which was kept secret. An older Corps member who had apparently played the role of St Nicholas a few times before took me on the evening of the 5th of December to a secret place where we clad ourselves in impressive costumes. I had a grey velvet jacket with a broad collar of white lace, with long sleeves ending in a ruffle of white lace, and wide short strangely blown-up pants of black velvet, all decorated and lined with gold. Under my pants I had only a pair of long black stockings and on my feet a sort of thin black ballet shoes with golden buckles. A beret with a large white plume completed my transformation.

St Nicholas was clad in a beautiful red bishop's robe, a high mitre in red and gold and was provided with a long bishop's stave. A long white beard and abundant curly hair added to his dignity and respectability. I found it great fun and I became more excited when we climbed on top of a crane carrier, a very unconventional vehicle for our tour to the Clubhouse. The fun was, however, of a short duration because soon after the vehicle started to move the small wooden platform on which we were standing was lifted up by the crane and we were dangling high in the air during the whole ride through the town. The cold winter wind which blew through my jacket and thin pants greatly dampened my enthusiasm and my urge to respond to the cheers and applause of the crowds on the streets. My friend who could keep his own clothes under the bishop's robe was undisturbed by the sharp cold and performed his duties on our wildly swinging platform as best as he could, holding on to two of the four ropes by which our platform was fastened to the hook of the crane. I was not able to keep the wind out of my jacket which blew open all the time, because I had to hold the other two ropes fast in my hands. The ride became as much ridiculous as it was hazardous, and the fun of it was entirely on the side of the spectators. In the end I was happy to feel solid ground again under my feet when the crane manoeuvred our platform perfectly on the balcony at the second floor of our clubhouse, high above the jubilant crowd of students.

The Committee received us with ceremonial dignity and the traditional St Nicholas songs resounded through the house when we entered the great hall. It was a cheerful party with a great many jokes and much fun, and of course great quantities of beer and wine. There were no children around to be spanked and out of my bag Saint Nicholas produced the traditional mock presents for the members of the N.I.A. Committee. Otherwise, we as St Nicholas and Zwarte Piet functioned only as background decoration.

During the ride to the Clubhouse I had been thoroughly chilled by the cold. The prospect of a repetition of the ordeal horrified me. Fortunately a taxi was provided to take us back to our secret dressing room.

* * * * * *

My two year-mates in UNICA, Tamme Tjebbes and Merijn de Jong, and later all the other Unicists, invited me to spend weekends with them at home with their families. I was more than happy to accept their invitations. Tamme's parents lived at the then famous farmstead Oud-Bussem, a few miles from Mr Caron's house. Tamme's mother, whose husband had died a few years earlier, was married to the manager of the farmstead, Floris Vos, a staunch Socialist and quite a character, who made headlines in the newspapers. The 140 cows in the most modern farm (at that time) were milked electrically, which was a novelty attracting hundreds of visitors to the place. The beautiful buildings were kept strictly traditional on the outside, but were hyper-modern and impeccably clean on the inside. The most stringent hygienic measures were applied at the farmstead because out of principle Oud-Bussem brought pure milk on the market, unboiled and unpasteurized, claiming that it contained essential life substances which otherwise would be destroyed. This claim was disputed by the official medical world, where public health doctors considered it superstition and were more concerned with the risks involved in the handling and transportation of unboiled milk. Because of the painstaking measures taken during

the production process, the operational cost of the farm was very high. It resulted in the paradox that the Socialist was producing milk which was only obtain-
able by the rich.

I was very much impressed by the cleanliness of the farm and the animals,
and the discipline observed by the workers. I found it odd to learn from them
that each cow had her own name—Mary, Betsy, and so on—and to see that
they indeed listened to the name when called. All that at first seemed strange
to me became enjoyable: the smell of the hay, of the cows and even that of cow
dung. The mooing of the cows became familiar and in the house I learned to
like the taste of raw milk and the various kinds of cheese.

The wanderings I made with Tamme over the green meadows with speck-
les of white daisies or yellow buttercups, and over the lovely stretches of heath-
land filled me with delight. During these rambles our friendship grew.

Tamme was often too serious for my taste. He could argue endlessly about
trivial things I found unworthy of discussion and wished to discard lighthreart-
edly. I admired nevertheless his perseverance, straightforwardness and sincerity, sensing that I could learn a great deal from him in this respect.

Of course, we talked much about UNICA. Having been brought up in a
family of Socialist principles, Tamme could not entirely agree with many
aspects of UNICA's life-style. As a student of economics he found literature
and philosophy which often dominated our discussions extremely boring. Most
of all, he resented our being "out of touch with the working class". This resentment remained with him for many years, but he realized also that there was
nothing one person could do about it unless one could change the whole
system on which the Amsterdams Studenten Corps was founded. The logical
consequence would be to quit, but because of the prestige that UNICA
enjoyed in the student world, that would be a distinct disadvantage.

My other year-mate in UNICA, Merijn de Jong, was a sweet character,
friendly and soft-spoken. His friendship did not have that intensity which I
felt radiating from Tamme. Because he was also a medical student and we
were always together in classes, he actually could have been much closer to
me. His mind was, however, most of the time occupied with his girlfriend
from his school years, who still lived in his hometown, The Hague. When he
brought me to his home on weekends I was mostly stuck with his parents
while he was with Helga somewhere else. For some reason Merijn broke off
with Helga later and immediately found another girl to take her place,
Tineke, a medical student in our class. Being too much occupied with his girlfriend, he could not find the time to participate in all of UNICA's activities.
Gradually the UNICA members, myself included, lost interest in him and
Merijn eclipsed into oblivion.

* * * * * *

The selection of new candidates for membership in the "Dispuut" towards the end of the initiation period was a major event, which each year enhanced a sense of maturity among the younger members. There were endless and serious discussions concerning the evaluation of candidates and their potential for nurturing the ideals of the "Dispuut". At the same time these discussions served the members to know and appreciate each other better, and thus to cement our friendships. It was then that I learned to appreciate something which before I had learned to avoid: straightforward criticism.

In Bali we had been trained either to suppress our criticism or to present it indirectly in order not to evoke confrontation. Even during our stay with European families in Java we had not been encouraged to voice opposing views. But here I found that confrontation was being sought as a means to identify our deepest self. True friendship was believed to be possible only after having been exposed completely to each other. Since alcohol helped to overcome one's fears and inhibitions, drinking beer, wine or gin was considered a "must" among the students. This was a big problem for me because I did not like the sight of drunken people. I had seen older students forcing younger ones to drink until they were completely drunk and I just could not share the fun of it. I reasoned that the best way to avoid being stowed away under the table like a dirty floorswab, would be *not to drink* at all.

To the dismay of the Unicists, I refused to drink alcohol, sticking to tea and soft drinks. There were long arguments in which I found it very difficult to present a valid reason for my abstinence, while at the same time I found the idea of the attainment of friendship through uninhibited openness a good thing. Was my abstinence out of principle? Religion? Not at all. At last I improvised a motive to justify myself: I wanted to challenge the wisdom that uninhibited openness could only be reached by alcohol. According to me it should be possible to do it by will without the help of any drug. I challenged my friends that my abstinence was to show them just that, and that I would start to drink alcohol after receiving my baccalaureate in three years time.

That indeed happened. While taking it for granted that I had passed my examination, I prided myself on having withstood for three years all challenges and temptations to step over my self-imposed alcohol barrier. To emphasize the act of turnabout I treated my Dispuut-mates to two rounds of champagne. The party was superb as usual, all of us soon in the highest of spirits, some bursting with fun and wits, others resigned in deep philosophical discourse. Although I felt somewhat light in my head and strangely euphoric after many glasses of wine, I stopped short of getting drunk. I was silently hoping that at least someone would make remarks praising me for having successfully completed my three years of prohibitionist exercise. Nothing happened. In the end I had to admit to myself that my self-imposed abstinence might have been nothing more than vanity.

CHAPTER 20

Challenges

During my first months in Holland, Tan Kwie Iet and the other Indonesian students visited me frequently. They felt a compelling need to visit each other as much as possible. They were sincere and eager to help me with any problem which might arise. Since I found it fascinating to find out things on my own, they were often disappointed. Moreover, the more I got involved in the many activities of the Amsterdams Students Corps and UNICA the more often they found my door locked and their enthusiasm waned gradually.

I took full advantage of every occasion to know more about Holland and its people. From their side the Dutch were no less curious about me and in every family which I visited I had to answer the same questions time and again. At last it became so boring that I decided to attach on my shirt under my jacket a sheet of paper on which I wrote a few lines in calligraphic script, with the words:

"I come from Bali."

"I have no trouble with your climate. I like the cold weather."

"I eat potatoes and I like cheese."

When I came to know the families better and also participated in their family lives I was fascinated by the succession of new horizons which opened before me. Many times there were night-long discussions after which I got the impression that facets of life were taken up with intensity and depth by the Dutch, in particular by my friends in UNICA. It seemed that there was nothing as distasteful as superficiality, a trait which to my dismay I often discovered in myself. This discovery spurred me to study hard, not only medicine. I started to look more deeply into everything which I experienced as new and alluring.

Thus I became a devoted visitor of libraries and spent hours reading there. I visited all kinds of exhibitions and went to concerts, plays and operas, of which Amsterdam had so much to offer. All these events formed a great part of our discussions in UNICA. Of course my taste in these matters started to conform to that of the Unicists. I shared their aesthetic delights at the annual performances of Bach's *Matthaeus Passion* in the old Church of Naarden on Good Fridays, at listening to Beethoven's symphonies in the Amsterdams Concert Gebouw, or seeing Mozart's operas in the Stadsschouwburg. The films which we went to see on Friday nights after our weekly dinner at the Tram-House opposite the Central Railway Station were always carefully selected on merits of substance and artistic form. Among others, Jean Gabin and Lawrence Olivier were our favourite filmstars.

Through my friends in UNICA I became acquainted with Western litera-ture. Their discussions roused my interest in books by Dostoevsky, Tolstoy, Stefan Zweig, Oscar Wilde, Kafka, Aldous Huxley, D.H. Lawrence, and many others, while on the light side *Winnie-the-Pooh* and *Alice in Wonderland* were considered as required reading in our "Dispuut".

Unmistakably there was in UNICA a tendency towards arrogance, stem-ming from a desire to be "different" and "exclusive". Besides aiming at high intellectuality this tendency had led to the emergence of various absurd taboos and prejudices. Hats and waistcoats were regarded as symbols of mediocrity, belonging to the inferior citizenry. Once one of our new members ventured to enter our clubhouse with a hat on. It was immediately snatched away and he had to witness it going up in flames in what looked like a solemn cremation ceremony. Contact with girls was condemned since it would easily distract our members from the cult of true friendship in our Brotherhood. In all our behav-iour we prided ourselves to be above the law, different, and against the mores of the Establishment. When in the beginning I once questioned an elder Unicist about his way of life, which according to my newly acquired wisdom did not conform with our exclusive principles, he remarked laughingly:

"Boy, don't you know yet our golden principle? It says: The Unicist is INCONSEQUENT." And that was that! For one moment I was puzzled and then, oddly enough, I found myself bursting with laughter. I got it!

My extra-curricular reading required much time. The liberal principle, underlying the system of study at the universities in Holland, could not be fully applied at the Medical Faculties. We could not miss the practical training courses held in the laboratories for the various disciplines, such as anatomy, physiology, chemistry, histology and others. Many of the lectures, however, given by the Professors in large auditoriums, were often boring and their sub-stance could better be learned from textbooks. In due course, each of us knew to select for himself the minimum of lectures to be attended.

As a result of my reading, I was more attracted by those Professors whose lectures contained humanitarian and philosophical thought as well as medical material. There was in particular Professor Heringa, who during his lectures in histology made us wonder every time about the mysteries of life and creation, by unfolding before our eyes, under the microscope, the structural manifesta-tions of growth, multiplication, regeneration, decay and death. He imbued our hearts with a deep respect for that inscrutable phenomenon which is Life. Professor Van Rijnberk excited us with his speculations about the meaning behind the biologically determined reactions of man and animal. I was deeply moved when he made a passionate appeal to the students, in which he emphasized that to become a good doctor, one should first of all be a good human being. The medical student should make good use of his time during his years of study to develop his personality, for we should never forget that the medical profession was not only science but also an art. He therefore encouraged us to study not only medicine, but also the fine arts and philosophy.

With the intensive exchange of views and opinions as cultivated in UNICA and among Corps students in general, it was no wonder that more than once the subject of Bali came to the fore. To my great shame I discovered that I knew very little about my island, its history, its arts and culture, and its religion. I searched frantically for literature in the libraries and scanned second-hand book shops. Fortunately there was plenty of literature about Bali in Holland and a great part of my visits to libraries was devoted to "Balinese Studies". What I *knew* about Bali until then was actually only a series of experiences, from childhood and later during vacations from school in Java, and I had never felt any need to go deeper into the meaning of our activities. Our participation in religious events was mainly passive, we did what was expected from us, in conformity with the elders and the community. There was of course the concomitant experience of *feeling* Balinese, the secure feeling of togetherness and communality. The factual knowledge which I gradually accumulated from the wide variety of Dutch literature about Bali seemed to blend smoothly with that inner experience and gave me a deeper insight in Bali and its people.

One time when I was leafing through the pages of a heavy volume in an antique bookshop my eyes were struck by a portrait of a handsome young man and was surprised when I saw the caption above the beautiful drawing, reading: "I Goesti Bagoes Djilantik van Karangasem".

It was my father in his adolescent years! I began to read page after page and was fascinated by the description of Bali as it was in the first decade of the 20th century. The writer's eyewitness account of Denpasar immediately after the massacre of the Raja of Badung and his followers by the Dutch in 1906 and of his travels on foot from Denpasar to Singaraja in the north could not fail to impress me deeply. I did not know how long I had been reading when I heard the voice of the shopkeeper: "Young man, this is not a library. Will you put the book back in its place or do you want to buy it? It is late and I am closing now".

His warning startled me. I dearly wanted to possess the volume, but I had looked at the price and I knew that I could not afford the expense. I understood also that the book was already for a long time out of print and I was afraid that somebody else would buy it. So I had to make my decision while the man was closing the door, inviting me to leave. I made a quick calculation and resolved not to take hot meals in restaurants for a whole month. I paid for the book and in a jubilant mood I cycled home with W. O. J. Nieuwenkamp's *Zwerftochten op Bali* (*Wanderings over the Island of Bali*) under my arm.

Nieuwenkamp's observations made during his travels in Bali impressed me by their accuracy and—above all—with the love that shone out throughout the text. It made me feel that there must be something special about an island which could so fascinate a stranger. Was it because he was an artist himself? Some time later, I found in another second-hand bookshop two more books by the same author: *Bouwkunst van Bali* (*Architecture of Bali*) and *Beeldhouwkunst van Bali* (*Sculpture of Bali*), both profusely and beautifully illustrated with his drawings and photographs, published in 1926 and 1928 respectively. That was the beginning of a modest library of old books about Bali which I collected in the course of the following years.

Looking for sources to remedy my incompetence in answering questions about Balinese religion, I found great help from a book written by Father Kerstens, a Catholic priest who worked in Bali in the 1930s. Although it did not describe Balinese religious texts, it did reveal to me much about our religious practices and the fundamental differences with Christianity. Matching the Christian point of view with my inner experiences during religious events in the past, it started to dawn upon me that there was a distinction between the Balinese religion as a creed and as a body of religious practices. I understood that we in Bali do believe in one God the Almighty, denoted as "Ida Sanghyang Widi Wasa" and, at the same time, we believe in the eternal spiritual existence of our ancestors, our "Leluhur" to whom we often extend our prayers.

Time and again however my friends challenged me: "Well enough, but what is *your* position? *You*, at this moment, Madé Djelantik, medical student and member of the Brotherhood of UNICA. What do *you* believe?"

I had to admit that I could not give a satisfactory answer. On the one hand, I found it inappropriate to contradict my family and to disclaim my ancestry; on the other hand, I could not convince myself where the truth was, in Christianity or in what my people were practising in Bali. I preferred to be honest and my answer was always a timid: "I don't know".

While I, myself, was not satisfied, strangely enough, that answer seemed to satisfy my friends. Later, I realized that they were in the same position, they also did not know. I learned from them that it would be wrong to believe in God just out of convenience or because everybody else in one's environment did. None of them ever went to any church for prayers.

Still not satisfied with my position I did not stop looking for answers. At that time many older Dutch people were influenced by Annie Bessant and shared her admiration for Indian philosophy and culture. One of them advised me to read the *Bhagavad Gita* and the works of Rabindranath Tagore, since according to her the Balinese religion was Hindu.

Starting with Tagore, I struggled through all eleven volumes of his works in German translation, but found all of it too vague, too lyrical and sentimental, and boringly repetitive. In the *Bagavad Gita* I recognized much of what I knew from the *pepaosans* back home in my younger years, but I found many of the pronouncements which it contained too dogmatic, leaving little room for reasoning. Looking for logic everywhere I was more excited when reading Kant's *Kritik de Reinen Vernunft* (*Critique of Pure Reason*).

In the window of a bookshop near the University, I saw by chance the name of Albert Schweitzer on the unimpressive cover of a small book *Die Weltanschauung der Indischen Denker: Mystik and Ethik* (*The Philisophy of the Indian Thinkers: Mysticism and Ethics*) (München, 1935). Perhaps because of my earlier affection to Albert Schweitzer, it excited me and without hesitation I bought the book. I was thrilled by his philosophical work. There I found what I missed in Tagore: logic, reasoning and critical reflection. Although it did not provide the ultimate answer, which was certainly not the aim of the treatise, it made clear to me the limitations of man in his quest for the absolute truth. His critical analysis of the Upanishads, the *Bagavad Gita* and of Tagore's philosophy led me to my own kind of dualistic concept: firstly, that in terms of reaching the ultimate goal of one's life, it should not matter if one does or does not belong to an organized religion; secondly, that the fulfillment of one's own personal mystique and the unselfish practice of ethics should be the crucial points which matter.

Such thoughts, which have gradually ripened in a person as result of a great many challenges during the most sensitive period of one's life, tend to leave a lasting stamp in one's personality—and I think that has happened with me indeed.

CHAPTER 21

Uncertainties

A small wooden partition of the draughty attic of the UNICA House at 34 Reguliers Gracht in Amsterdam served as my bedroom, where I used to sleep under a wide open window throughout the year. One night I woke up because I felt wet around my ear and on my neck, and found my bed and blanket covered under four inches of snow.

Four months later, a strange noise, coming through the window out of the clear sunny blue sky, awakened me very early in the morning of that memorable day of May 10, 1940. It sounded from far away like a siren at a high pitch which suddenly became low and mixed with a series of thuds. It repeated itself again and again. For a long time I wondered what it could be. It seemed to come from above the house and out of curiosity I jumped out of bed, put on a coat and climbed up on the roof. I saw that many of my neighbours were also standing on their rooftops, pointing at the horizon in the West. Some-one shouted: "It's war! Those damned Germans! They are bombing our airfield!"

Then I saw them: the notorious *Stukas* (dive-bombers) as tiny dragonflies in the far distance, one after another, screaming down and lifting up again after discharging their deadly load. Behind the skyline of buildings, some smoke was vaguely visible. I was perplexed. I had read about the *Stukas* when they were being tested during the Spanish war. Meanwhile the other occupants of the UNICA House had joined me on the narrow ridge. They were as stunned as I was. We were speechless and just looked at each other. We felt the same. We heard a man shouting: "Look out, they are coming nearer! Boys, we better go down! Quick!" While we were scrambling down I, an Indonesian, a citizen of a Dutch colony, felt an emotion of genuine Dutch patriotism welling up in me.

Everywhere on the streets and on the bridges, groups of people were agitatedly discussing the situation. At several points people were clustered before an open window, where the owner of the house had placed his radio. Joining one of the groups we heard the latest news:

"In the Eastern provinces, the Dutch army has blown up all the bridges while retreating before the advancing German tanks and infantry. In many places large contingents of German paratroopers have landed behind the Dutch defences". The situation seemed chaotic and hopeless. We were warned to look out for parachutists and to report any suspect objects to the nearest police station or army post. The atmosphere was tense.

My friends wanted to go home and see their parents. I did not object. There was not much for them to do in our UNICA house or on the streets. Since I was a medical student, I had my own plans already. I took my bicycle and rode to the Wilhelmina Gasthuis, or University Hospital, in Amsterdam to volunteer for the Red Cross.

* * * * * *

There were, of course, too many volunteers for the Hospital management to cope with. I felt disappointed when I was told that I could not be assigned in the medical section, because my study was not yet advanced enough. I was still at the pre-clinical level. Instead I could join the Fire Brigade.

Each of the hospital wards would be under the care of a number of fire squads which in turns would stand guard on the roof to watch for fire-bombs dropped from the air and for German parachutists. Each of us was equipped with an overall made of asbestos cloth, presumed to be fireproof, and a big shovel and a pail of sand. We received clear instructions as to how to handle a fire-bomb, but none of us, our squad chiefs included, knew what to do if a German with an automatic weapon in his hands would land in our midst.

"Hit him hard with your shovel!" bragged one of them. Others however found it more practical to raise our hands and surrender. Then we should keep talking with the intruder, while one of us should slip away and warn the military. Fortunately nothing like that happened during the five days of the war.

On my first night of duty I was really scared. We placed ourselves about 20 yards from each other on the roof. I chose a spot close to a twin chimney, to make sure that if the need arose, I could take cover quickly. There were no *Stukas* or other planes in the air. Behind the skyline of buildings the western sky lightened up continuously and now and then the sound of artillery was faintly heard. We were told that there was fierce fighting going on around Schiphol airfield.

When I was again on duty on the third night I did not feel scared at all. The same happened to my friends. Although we were vigilant all the time, the long hours became boring. Some of us started to make jokes, until another squad relieved us after midnight.

To my great joy, the medical students among the fire fighters were given an intensive training in First Aid during the idle hours between duty shifts. The various techniques of bandaging and transportation of casualties, which I learned in those days, proved to be very useful later, especially during work in remote jungle areas in Indonesia. That kind of work had always been regarded as the duty of nurses and was therefore missing in the normal medical curriculum at the universities in Holland.

The Dutch army, outnumbered and poorly equipped, fought bravely. It surrendered only when the Germans, while negotiations about their ultimatum were still going on, ruthlessly bombarded a large section of Rotterdam, reducing the town to rubble and killing thousands of people. The war was over in five days and the horrible period of the German occupation began.

* * * * * *

There was great confusion during the first days after the capitulation. The hospital staff did not know what to do with the large number of volunteers. Since there was nothing for us to do, we were sent home. There were enough personnel to take care of the normal patients and of the casualties of the war, since not too many had been referred to the main hospital in Amsterdam. Most of them were treated in the many excellent hospitals in the provinces.

The *Blitzkrieg* and capitulation had taken the Dutch completely by surprise, for they were accustomed to living in freedom and had taken their liberty for granted. My friends just could not believe what had happened. Nobody had any idea what it would be like to live under foreign occupation. The Germans made use of the confusion, numbness and the general prostration to impress the people with a gigantic show of force. A few days after the surrender of the Dutch army the German war machine rolled into Amsterdam.

We stood on a high bridge over the Amstel river to have a good view of the miles-long cavalcade, consisting alternately of motorists, tanks, various types of canons, trucks with ammunition, and armoured cars with soldiers. There were no soldiers marching on foot. It was obviously calculated to impress by machinery and speed. We were filled with awe by the display of discipline and perfection. All equipment was impeccably clean and shiny, their rifles, their helmets and boots. The Dutch had always been contemptuous of militarism. Up to the last day before the war they had been making fun of their army. The conscripts had never taken their duty seriously. Compared with what we saw that day their army looked more like a band of Boy Scouts. They made, however, superb fighters during the real war, defending their country as lions, but their leaders did not have the experience of modern warfare.

Witnessing such a parade for the first time in my life, I was overwhelmed by the sheer numbers of soldiers on machines, rolling with a thunderous noise before my eyes. I found most fascinating the columns of motorists, five in a row, steering their vehicles in a perfectly straight line. We had been standing on the spot for nearly one hour, when suddenly I no longer saw soldiers of flesh and blood under those gleaming helmets on the motorbikes. They seemed to me one with their machines, to be part of them, and to be made of steel.

"No wonder that they have won the war, they are not human, they are machines, invulnerable, superior to human beings", so I thought! (Was the word "robot" already invented at that time?)

Looking at my friends, I saw that they were not as fascinated as I was. Although they were visibly impressed by the show of force, I sensed their anger and frustration and my fascination faded away. I was overcome with a feeling of uncertainty and hoped that the course of events would not in any way affect our friendships. We did not wait until the end of the parade. Struggling our way through the crowd we walked listlessly to N.I.A., the Clubhouse of the Amsterdams Students Corps.

At N.I.A. the mood was very different from what it was before. There was no cheerfulness, no merry-making and no fun. Everyone was depressed and spoke softly. As if the situation had made us forget our differences, we did not seek company with our "Dispuuts" as usual. Automatically, groups formed themselves consisting of members of several "Dispuuts". The younger students were listening, while the older ones were discussing. Most of the talk concerned recent history, about what had happened in Czechoslovakia and in Poland after the Germans had overrun those countries. We tried to get some idea of what might lie ahead of us. Of course we did not arrive at any conclusion, nor at any decision for action. The situation was still too confusing, too uncertain.

CHAPTER 22

The Fateful Ration Card

During the first months of the occupation, the Germans were very cautious and tried to avoid any interference in public affairs, except where military operations were involved. Their propaganda insisted that they were in Holland not to conquer the country, but only to push their way westwards to bring the British to their knees.

Life soon returned soon to normal. There was of course a curfew and the rationing of certain food items. The people found these things acceptable under the circumstances. The schools and universities were allowed to function as usual. While the battle front moved more and more to the South, into Belgium and France, life in Holland became quiet and uneventful. Many among the older generation started to believe that the occupation was not at all bad. In many families where I was a regular visitor, there was often disagreement between the older and the younger generation.

Roland Kalff, a medical student, who joined UNICA a year after me, was a very sensitive and outspoken character. His father, a senior teacher and a highly erudite scholar, refused to believe that the Germans could have committed those crimes against humanity that the papers had reported in the past. We were perplexed by his naïvety. The bombardment of Rotterdam was reasoned away to conform to the official propaganda, and alleged to be the result of a tragic misunderstanding. Once, when the argument between Roland and his father became too excited and even bitter, I came in between and said: "Roland, better stop arguing! I think that it is not possible to convince your father or elder people in general. Not that they are in favour of the Germans. They themselves are just too good and humane and cannot imagine that people can be so bad and cruel".

Roland looked angrily at me as if I was a fool. "What do you know, Madé! Goodness is different. This is stupidity, criminal stupidity, because it makes Nazi propaganda more effective!"

He was right of course, but I found that I was right too. Not wanting to upset him more, I did not say anything. Fortunately, Roland stopped talking; he had apparently blown off his steam.

Roland's mother, attracted by the excited voices, emerged from the kitchen, her friendly face a question mark. She was used to arguments between her husband and her eldest son. She came near to my side and said: "I am glad that you are here, otherwise they would have continued quarrelling".

Later in the evening two of our friends came, both with their violins under their arms. Roland, who also played the violin, cheered up immediately. Mr Kalff, who had retired to his study upstairs, heard the instruments being tuned and came down with his cello. Mrs Kalff served tea and cakes and until shortly before curfew time, when our friends and myself had to leave, we enjoyed string quartets by Schubert and Beethoven and forgot the war.

Mrs Kalff was a lovely lady. She once confided to me, that since Roland and I had become friends, her son was much less nervous. He had become much more reasonable, as if he had found a purpose in life. She treated me also as her son. That evening she sat next to me on an antique easy chair and during the performance she said compassionately: "Madé, let us only hope and pray that this war and all this killing will be over soon, and you can again hear news from home."

I was always moved by her sympathy, but actually I did not often think of Bali or my family at home those days. My mind was too much occupied with the daily occurrences around me, by uncertainties regarding my financial situation, by events in the student world, by rumours about pending conscription of young men for labour in German factories, rumours about groups of students starting to organize nuclei of resistance against the occupation. Vaguely I anticipated danger and that things would become worse.

There was blackout in the city, and on my way home the dark abandoned streets and the sight of only a few pedestrians, who sped silently to their homes, enhanced my anxiety and uneasiness.

* * * * * *

In the course of the following year, things turned worse indeed. Analysts attributed the deterioration to the many setbacks which the Germans suffered in what they initially claimed to be their glorious war. The Battle of Britain did not come out as they expected. The invasion of the British Islands did not take place and seemed to be postponed indefinitely. The British Air Force had not been eliminated; on the contrary, they carried out bombing raids on German soil and even reached Berlin soon afterwards. The Germans became more and more nervous. In the East they wanted to punish the Russians with a shattering *Blitzkrieg* but after reaching the outskirts of Moscow, they were driven back with heavy losses in men and material. After the conquest of

France in the South and brilliant advances in North Africa they failed to push further into Egypt and had to retreat later completely.

In Holland, resentment against the occupational forces grew steadily.

Clandestine information through radio from the B.B.C. and the Free Dutch "Radio Oranje" became more and more widespread and acts of sabotage increased. The occupation authorities became more and more ruthless in their repressive actions.

Public disgust was deepest when the Nazis started to discriminate against the Jews, at first by obliging them to wear the Star of Bethlehem as their mark on their coats. This apparently innocent regulation was only the first step in a refined scheme toward other more severe restrictions, harassment and later mass arrests and deportations to extermination camps.

These harsh measures were not restricted to Jews. Everyone suspected of helping or hiding Jews ran the risk of persecution, deportation and extermination. At the slightest act of discontent, such as the breaking of a window of a German vehicle, the severest measures were applied: the whole block of buildings would be searched and all males between twenty and thirty rounded up and driven away in trucks. There was terror all over the country.

While measures were taken against acts of sabotage, schools and universities were still allowed to function normally. However, we did not believe that the German Intelligence Services were ignorant of the many student organizations which were already active underground.

* * * * * *

For the first two hours on Saturdays we had lectures in Public Health by Professor Charlotte Ruys, which were particularly boring. She was a renowned scientist and she was always nice and helpful to the students, and thus loved by everybody. However, the unimaginative presentation of her material which consisted of Health Regulations and endless statistical data, made listening to her a dreary and tedious exercise. Because she often treated subjects which were not to be found in any of the textbooks, we felt obliged to attend classes and endure the strain. Fortunately there was always a short pause between the two hours, which brought us great relief.

Once during such a pause I discovered with a shock that I had not yet collected my new ration card at the municipality and since it was Saturday, the office would close at noon. At first, I considered waiting until the end of the second hour but changed my mind immediately. I did not want to miss Professor Swellengrebel's brilliant lecture in Parasitology, which was usually full of humorous remarks and philosophical thought. His demonstrations of the life cycles of tropical parasites were also most engaging.

Thus, I sneaked away, telling my friends to keep a seat open for me at the third hour. It was early spring 1942, the weather fresh and sunny, and I greatly enjoyed the bicycle ride through the town. The rationing office in downtown Amsterdam was crowded with latecomers and I had to stand in queue for quite a while. Afterwards, I raced back to the auditorium of the Tropical Institute, anxious to be on time. Just before I mounted the last bridge about 300 yards before the Institute, I was stopped by somebody whom I did not know by name but recognized as an elder medical student. He told me not to go further. Although he spoke very casually, I saw from his face that something was wrong. I asked: "Why? What is the matter?"

He signaled me to come nearer and when I was close enough, he continued softly, nodding in the direction of the Institute: "The Gestapo is rounding up our friends. They have been loading all the boys into trucks. Look there! I think that is the last batch of them being driven away!"

I was dumbfounded. We saw the vehicle disappearing around the corner, but could not see the people inside as the canvas covers had been brought down.

I asked innocently: "Why? What have they done?"

He replied: "Nothing of course! You are lucky that you were not there. Perhaps the Gestapo was after Professor Charlotte Ruys". (Years later, I heard that she was one of the earliest organizers of the underground resistance.)

Entirely puzzled I asked him what would happen to our friends. He said: "Nobody knows. Probably forced labour, somewhere in Germany or Poland. I wonder how many of them will ever come home alive".

I felt fear and alarm overwhelming me. Meanwhile, other students, eager to attend Swellengrebel's lecture, joined us. All were caught by bewilderment.

We asked the senior: "What shall we do?"

"There is nothing that you can do for the moment. Shhh, come here, closer. Listen all of you. Please tell all your friends not to attend any more lectures. Perhaps there will be no lectures as from today, except by those traitors who sympathize with the Nazis. Last night some of our Professors were taken away. So perhaps they were looking for Charlotte Ruys this morning in her class. And now, don't ask any more questions. Get away from here quickly! Don't go in groups. Be careful with what you tell others, especially by telephone. And you have not seen or spoken to anybody on this bridge today, do you understand?"

I did not. I caught up with one of the older students, who explained everything to me. What he said made me feel uneasy. He advised me to go to my room and take a rest. I turned my bicycle and pedalled slowly home.

* * * * * *

In order to have more time for my medical studies than was possible in my room at the UNICA house, I had moved three months previously to a quiet residential area in Southern Amsterdam. There I had found a small furnished room in the Paulus Potter Street in a house of an old widow, who apparently had known better times in the past. The house was stately, had a heavy oak front door which was ornamented with elegant ironwork and opened into a wide hall with marble floor and walls. The wide carpeted marble staircase led straight to a square landing on the first floor, where my room was located. The room was comfortable, and provided with central heating, which was a great luxury compared with the old iron stove in my room at the UNICA house.

On the day of the encounter on the bridge, I found it wiser to have my lunch in the city instead of at the Students Clubhouse, and arrived late at home. The landlady met me at the door and handed me a closed envelope, saying: "This has just been brought for you by a friend of yours".

She could not tell me who it was and from her description I could not make out the boy's identity. More bewilderment overcame me when I read the message: "You are advised not to sleep here tonight. Destroy this letter immediately!"

The letter was not signed and I could not recognize the handwriting as that of any of my friends. I said nothing, but asked my landlady for a match and lit the piece of paper and envelope before her astonished eyes. She did not ask anything, perhaps guessing that it was strictly personal and none of her business.

In my room I sat down on the bed, pondering what to do next. It must have some connection with what happened that morning and the student on the bridge. That was clear. But how could they know my address? Why me? No, it could not be only me, they must have warned other students too.

"Well," I thought, "let me get out of here first of all!" I gathered some clothes, toilet necessities and a book, put them all in a rucksack and went out. On the street I realized that I had not yet figured out where to go. Instinctively my steps led me to the UNICA house. While walking, I pondered further about the puzzling events of the day. I came to the conclusion that there must be already a well-organized underground system working among the students. It must be essential for all of us to be very careful with any information in order not to jeopardize their system. They must have a list of all the students of my class supposed to be present at Professor Ruys's lecture. The raid must also be associated with the refusal of all the students to sign the "Declaration of Loyalty" to the Germans, which had been imposed on us recently.

At the UNICA house, my friends confirmed that they also had been notified of an impending raid that night and everybody had already chosen his secret address. It was no problem for them. The old charwoman who came daily to clean the UNICA house, offered me an empty room in her house for the night. So I went with our *Mevrouwtje* as we called her and felt myself protected and safe. That night I slept soundly in her guestroom at the Hobbema Kade.

When I wanted to go back to my own room at the Paulus Potter Street the next morning, *Mevrouwtje* protested and warned me that it was not safe yet. But I was stubborn and went with the promise that I would come back for the night. That good woman must have had the right premonition.

I was shocked by what I saw when I entered my room. Everything had been turned upside down, my bed, table, cupboard, the chair, while my books were scattered all over the place. My old landlady came after me, crying and shaking all over. "Oh, Mr. Djelantik, how terrible! Last night they came, they forced me to open your room and they searched all over! I was not allowed to move, they put me on a chair in the corridor and later they searched the other rooms and asked me if I had more students in the house. I am scared!"

At seeing her distress I found to my surprise that I was calm, but realized that it was serious business now. My mind started to make guesses again. Could there perhaps be some misunderstanding somewhere? What were they looking for? Secret documents? I had never been involved in any illegal activity. Had somebody purposely misled the Gestapo? Was my name on the list perhaps too strange for them and thus caused suspicion? But how could "the organization" know that the Gestapo would come and search *my* room in *this* house?

For the poor old lady I could not do anything. I consoled her that it was very unlikely that "they" would come back again and that, if so, they would not do any harm to her, an old lady in her sixties, that they were only after young men, needed to work in their factories. She kept sobbing.

After putting my room in order I told her that I had better look for another place to live. I felt very sad to leave her alone. She promised me that she would look after my belongings until I could move them away. I packed as much as possible in my rucksack and returned to the Hobbema Kade. *Mevrouwtje* was very happy to see me back and insisted that I should have lunch with her. I complied and she treated me as if I were her own son. She told me that I could stay with her indefinitely. However, that afternoon something happened which made her offer unnecessary.

CHAPTER 23

A Hiding Game

In the afternoon, my friend Was ter Kuile, one year my junior in UNICA, came to see me at *Mevrouwtje*'s and told me that we had to bring Henk, a Jewish student, to safety. There were rumours that the Nazis were intensifying their raids on Jews. It had already been decided that Henk should be brought to Tamme's home at the Oud-Bussem farm first. I would remain in hiding there for some time, while Was would travel the next day with Henk further to the East. His hiding place could not be disclosed, not even to us.

On the train to Bussum that evening we instinctively had Henk seated between us, as if we could have protected him if a Nazi agent would grab him. We had chosen an empty compartment and were soon chatting cheerfully.

At the first stop, many commuters boarded the train and our carriage filled up. As if the devil wanted to play us a trick, two men in brown uniforms took their seats on the empty bench facing us. We immediately identified them as the notorious Gestapo. Seeing my friends' faces turning pale, I was scared to death and felt my knees shaking. Henk, whose features were unmistakably Jewish, hid his face behind his newspaper, pretending to read the bottom lines. I tried to resume our conversation but my throat was blocked. Was seemed to have the same trouble, and was very tense. I tried to look as relaxed as possible, but did not dare to look at the faces of the two men, not even stealthily. I saw only their uniforms and boots.

The ten minutes ride until the next stop seemed endless. When the train slowed down, Was called loudly: "Boys, here we are. We have to get out. Quick, otherwise we'll miss the connecting bus!" He was already on his feet and made for the aisle. I was startled and thought: "He is crazy!". Were there not two more stops before Bussum? Henk and I looked puzzled at each other for one second, but then we saw Was gesticulating to us from the aisle, winking with one eye and twisting his head towards the two Gestapo agents. We understood, collected our luggage and followed him to the end of the carriage. Before the train came to a complete halt we jumped out and quickly crossed the platform. Behind the corner of the station building we fell down on the grass. We were out of breath. There we waited. When the train whistled and took off we saw with great relief that the two uniforms were still on their seats. We had a good laugh and gave Was a heartfelt spanking.

We treated ourselves to a cup of coffee and boarded the next train which came through 20 minutes later.

* * * * * *

When Tamme's stepfather Floris Vos, the Director of the Farmstead Oud Bussem died, Mrs Vos needed her son to assist her in the management of the dairy farm. He quit his studies while still in his third year and was no longer registered as a student at the University. Therefore his home in Bussem was considered safe, with little chance of a visit by the Gestapo. He had just married and the young couple moved into a lovely little house in the middle of the farm.

It was nearly curfew time when we arrived, so nobody saw us entering his house. Tamme and Bellie had been informed of our arrival. They were happy to get the chance to help friends, while at the same time, like all of us, they found it most exciting to do something illegal. They had prepared a nice hiding place for us in the attic above their storage room, accessible through a camouflaged opening in the ceiling by use of a ladder which could be pulled up and taken into the attic. Food had to be hauled up by a rope. We would allow ourselves to come down only twice a day for washing and use of the toilet. We found it great fun and complied seriously, at least in the beginning.

The following day in the afternoon Henk and Was continued their journey and I was left in my confinement on my own. As a matter of course Tamme and Bellie came to visit me in turns as many times as their work permitted them. When I heard the UNICA whistle I opened the ceiling and let the ladder down. They had great fun seeing me lying there wholly content and relaxed upon my mattress. The attic was too low for even a chair to sit on, but it was no problem for me. I was completely happy. "That must be your Eastern blood," they said, shaking their heads, as if they could not understand my placid attitude. Like most of the Dutch they were charged with revolt caused by powerless anger. That pain and anger spurred the people to undertake actions which might serve to obstruct the intentions of the German occupational authorities, no matter how great or little its effect. Giving shelter to Jews or students was very common.

Nevertheless, one had to be very careful and all the time be on guard for Nazi sympathizers. This was not too difficult since these few persons were generally known. It was more difficult to keep things from being mentioned unintentionally by loose-lipped chatterers.

When after a few days nothing happened, our vigilance slackened. I came down for breakfast, lunch and dinner and soon spent only the nights in my cage. When after a week nothing happened, we regarded the danger to be over and I moved freely everywhere. I went even by train to Amsterdam to get my bicycle. We thought that if the need arose, moving away on bicycle following small paths would be safer than by public transport.

On my ride back to Bussem I saw a ragman pushing laboriously his two-wheel hand carriage over a high bridge. I stepped off my bicycle to give the poor man a hand. Great was my astonishment when I recognized the ragman as one of the older members of the Amsterdams Studenten Corps, a jolly fellow who used to fill our clubhouse with cheerfulness and jokes. I gathered that he was doing something clandestine and when we were past the highest point of the bridge, I asked curiously what his disguise meant. He said nothing, laughed heartily and lifted one corner of the canvas cover of his carriage. I saw a heap of worn out clothes, but when he pushed some of them aside, parts of rifles and sten guns were visible underneath. I was thrilled but felt scared for him at the same time. Quietly he covered up everything again and from his looks I understood that no questions should be asked any more. I wished him good luck and continued my ride.

At Tamme's, my hiding became a farce. We made fun of it all the time. However, when a visitor came, I had to take cover quickly, and emerged only at the sound of the UNICA whistle. I spent most of the time catching up with my medical studies.

* * * * * *

A week later a letter came from Mrs Van der Waals, who had moved earlier than planned to her summerhouse in the country at Boeschoten, where she owned a piece of farmland. Her lovely wooden cottage stood near the farmhouse, where Melis, the farmer, who tended the land, lived with his family. Her son Joan, who was one year my senior in UNICA, had already taken refuge there since the closing of the universities after the student raids by the Gestapo. Mrs Van der Waals asked me to stay with her and Joan in Boeschoten, to enjoy the country life while studying and doing some errand jobs at the farm. Tamme and Bellie agreed, considering that the tiny hamlet Boeschoten was much more secluded than the Farmstead Oud Bussem, and therefore safer.

The day before my departure rumours abounded that the Germans were setting up checkposts on all bridges on highways and roads. Tamme knew of an abandoned path leading to small country roads to Boeschoten, which was about 70 km to the east from Bussem. To reach that path I should avoid the military camp behind the village by crossing some pieces of grassland. It was an excellent plan.

In order not to be stopped by the owners of the meadows, I left soon after midnight. Between the plots of grassland I had to wade through small canals or ditches and to creep under barbed wire fences with my bicycle and backpack. It was not as easy as I had imagined. I proceeded very slowly. While I was pedalling quietly over the last bumpy meadow, just about 20 metres from the last fence, I was startled by a stamping noise behind me. Looking back, to my horror, I saw a huge bull running after me! I dashed forward in panic, and shoved my bicycle quickly under the barbed wire. Seeing that the wires were very closely spanned, and that it would take a long time to wriggle myself through, I threw with all my might my backpack over the fence, climbed over the wires and hurled myself to the other side. In the process I slipped at the last moment, my leg got entangled and hooked at the barbed wire behind my knee and I fell on my shoulders to the ground. The bull stood still behind the fence, looking at me, sniffed noisily and nodded with his enormous head, as if he was satisfied with his accomplishment.

Carefully I recovered my bicycle from under the fence, happy that the bull had not trampled on it. I did not feel the pain in my leg until I was 500 metres away on the abandoned footpath. I stopped to examine the damage. It was very little, only the skin was torn over 3 inches, but it was bleeding profusely. Fortunately I had my first aid kit in my rucksack and could stop the bleeding with a bandage.

The ride over the countryside in the early morning was most enjoyable. Several times I had to overcome my fear of ferociously barking dogs, when I entered a farm to ask for the way to Boeschoten. All the people were very friendly and helpful, and in some houses I had to drink a cup of coffee together with the family. I arrived at noon at the farm in Boeschoten. Since I had not been able to announce my arrival in advance, Joan and his mother were very surprised, but happy that I had come so soon.

The month long stay in Boeschoten was pleasant and peaceful. Mrs Van der Waals treated me as if I was her son and automatically I felt part of the family, sharing with them the delights of primitive country life. There was no electricity and no running water. Light was by butane gas from glass cylinders, cooking and heating was by firewood. There was a beautiful antique stove in the living room. I volunteered to take care of the firewood with Joan. Every morning after two hours of study we spent one hour sawing and chopping wood. Joan and I shared one room in a separate small wooden hut near the farm. In the afternoons we took long walks in the vast woods all around. Often Mrs Van der Waals, who knew very much about trees and forestry, joined us and told us many interesting observations during our wanderings.

Joan was a very serious student. He had an exceptionally high I.Q. and passed all his examinations Summa Cum Laude. He was not very talkative, being more of the thinking type. In conversation, he was always inquisitive and always exploring. It became clear to me why my other friends were never intimate friends with him. Perhaps fear of being "analyzed" kept them at a distance, and Joan remained to some extent a solitary figure. His inquisitiveness did not disturb me at all. On the contrary it spurred me to think and be critical. During those weeks that I got to know Joan much better, we found great happiness in our growing friendship.

* * * * * *

One morning while I was chopping wood, a man on a bicycle rode up the farmyard and talked for a while with Melis, the farmer. I saw Melis pointing at me. The man put his bicycle against a tree and stepped over the pieces of wood towards me. "Good morning, Sir. This is for you", he said, lifting his cap from his head and producing out of it a sealed envelope which he handed to me.

I took the envelope, but seeing that it was blank, I shook my head in disbelief. The man laughed: "It's all right, it is for you, I am sure. Don't be afraid!" and before I could say anything, the man was already on his bike and off he went with great speed.

Astonished, I turned the envelope several times before opening it. It was a typewritten letter, and signed Hans R. After guessing for a while I thought that it must be Hans Rhodius, a wealthy lawyer in North Holland. Before the German invasion I had spent some weekends with him in Heemstede, where he lived with his parents in a large estate. Their house was a huge three-storey building like a castle, constructed in the late 19th-century Romantic style, with a dome-shaped roof and turrets protruding at the corners. There was a vast garden with well-kept lawns, beautiful old oak trees, a swimming pool, a tennis court and stables.

Hans had been in Java and Bali just before the war and had fallen in love with the beautiful country, especially with Bali, where he was enchanted by the paintings of the German painter, Walter Spies. He was so enthralled by his experiences that immediately after his return to Holland he started organizing cultural evenings at home, inviting artists and scholars who had been working in Indonesia, as speakers or performers. He learned from one of them that there was a Balinese studying medicine in Amsterdam. Somehow, he got my address and one day I received an invitation to give a talk about Bali at one of his cultural evenings. I did my best and it was a great success.

Since he was ten years my senior and already an established citizen, we had not become close friends, but we maintained a good relationship and occasional contacts. After the outbreak of the war in Holland we lost contact. It was therefore a great surprise to receiv this letter from him, and especially that it was delivered at the right address! I was extremely puzzled. How did he know? The content of the typed letter was even more surprising: "Madé, I have been looking for a better place for you, where you can work in line with your studies. It will be useful and perhaps may shorten the time of internship later. Go to the General Hospital in Almelo and see my friend Dr Rethmeyer, the

Roentgenologist. I have informed him, he will recognize you and will tell you further what to do. Important: destroy this letter after reading. Hans R".

I went to my room, wrote "Rethmeyer" in my notebook and tore the letter in a hundred pieces. I discussed the case with Joan and his mother. They were excited. Although they did not want me to leave, they found the prospect of study an opportunity which I should not miss.

Thus, I got my bicycle ready, packed my rucksack again and went off early the next morning. At the last moment Mrs Van der Waals stacked a bunch of sandwiches on top of my backpack. "You will need them," she said, "it will take at least five hours on the bike to Almelo". I felt really sad to leave the idyllic place and the family.

In the countryside the atmosphere was much more relaxed than in the towns. There were no German soldiers to be seen except near their camps. I was told that it was safe just to follow the bicycle paths along the main roads. There were indeed no hold-ups, no check posts for identity cards. Since I had always loved cycling I enjoyed the ride. There was also that exciting anticipation of new experiences, a new environment and making new acquaintances.

Halfway, I stopped on the bank of a canal to eat my sandwiches and enjoy the sight of the farmers working in the fields. It was so peaceful all around as if there was no war. I lay down on the grass and tried to figure out how I should present myself to Dr Rethmeyer. Vaguely I remembered having heard his name at one of the meetings in Heemstede long ago. I told myself not to worry, that the man would certainly recognize me. I felt assured and mused for some time. When I looked on my watch I realized that I had been idling too long, but it was a pity to leave that beautiful spot. Reluctantly I climbed my bicycle again.

* * * * * *

On the outskirts of Almelo suddenly the war showed its face. There were German soldiers marching and singing their martial songs, and soldiers on guard at the bridges over the canals. Military vehicles rumbled over the streets. When I arrived at the hospital in the afternoon the duty nurse told me that Dr Rethmeyer had just gone home. She explained to me how to get there.

Dr Rethmeyer recognized me immediately. He was friendly, but not very talkative. He told me only to be back at the hospital the next morning. He would introduce me to the Hospital Director, the internist, who actually would be my supervisor. Five minutes later I was again on the street. First of all I had to find a room to spend the night and if possible to stay for a longer period. I went to the main street where I had seen a bookshop displaying announcements hanging behind its window, and I tried my luck. Indeed, there were advertisements of rooms for rent, with breakfast or full pension. I jotted down a few addresses which looked suitable and started my search.

When I rang the bell at the first address, I heard men's voices behind the door in what seemed to me a heated discussion. After a while I rang again. The door was opened briskly and I heard a harsh voice: "What do you want?"

If I was startled already by the sudden opening of the door, I was shocked by what I saw: there were three men in the corridor, all of them in the despised black uniforms of the N.S.B. (Dutch Nazis). That was the last thing I had expected! Somehow I recovered from my shock and stammered: "Oh, pardon, is perhaps Mr Boon living here?" I knew it was risky. What if there was one Mr Boon there?

"No, my boy! You are at the wrong address!"

"Oh, well, excuse me, Sir!"

Relieved, I jumped on my bicycle and, with my knees still trembling, I raced away as fast as I could. As if by instinct I rode in the direction of the hospital. I stopped at the gate, where I saw the doorkeeper and showed him my piece of paper with the addresses.

"Good afternoon, Sir. Could you please tell me which of these addresses is the nearest from here?"

He put his finger on No. 5 on the list, saying: "This is just here around the corner. Follow this street until the canal and turn to the right. The first door is that of the Vermeulens".

I did what was told, and it was easy to find. I arrived at an old building with a high and heavy wooden door. I pulled at the old fashioned bell. A small square window (behind iron bars in the door) was pulled open from inside and was closed immediately. In that one second I saw through the bars a pale girl's face looking horrified at me. I was puzzled and amused at the same time, and while I was wondering what to do, I heard footsteps behind the door and the spying window was pulled open again. This time the face of an elderly man looked at me for a long time, examining my appearance curiously. Fearing that he would close the window again, I did not wait and asked if there was still a room free.

The old man's face became very friendly, he nodded, opened the door and said: "Come in! There is a room free upstairs. I think, you must be a student from far away. You are welcome!" His daughter, standing behind him, looked amazed at me still. I must have been the first brown person with black hair she had seen in her life. I gave her a broad smile, but it had no effect.

"You can bring in your bicycle", and pulling the door wide open, he called: "Arie, come here, help and bring this bicycle of our new guest in the backyard".

A red-haired young man emerged from the end of the corridor and took my bike. Mr Vermeulen took me to his desk in the shop. I looked around, studying the merchandise which looked strange to me. The racks along the walls and the furniture looked very old and old-fashioned. There were piles of canvas cloth, ropes of all sizes, pulleys, paint, ironware and other necessities for boats and sailing ships. The old man was very pleased when he heard that I was a medical student who was going to work at the General Hospital. I told him briefly about Indonesia and Bali, my time in Amsterdam, and how I came to Almelo. I gathered that he must be very kind and goodhearted, and what impressed me most were his eyes. They looked so reassuring and trustworthy, but there were moments when they looked very sad and absent. I learned later that he had lost his wife recently.

He called his daughter. "This is Tille. What is your name again? Madé? Oh yes, Madé. Tille, show Madé his room, but come down quickly to prepare the supper". I took up my rucksack and followed the tiny skinny girl up the stairs to the third floor. The room was larger than I was used to in Amsterdam. The over-sized bed and other old-fashioned furniture looked somehow funny to my eyes. There was no running water upstairs, but I saw a table with a wash basin and jug. I wanted to wash my dirty hands, but the jug was empty.

"I'll bring water later," Tille said, "better wash your hands downstairs where the tap is," and she ran down the steps. I started to unpack, the cupboard was much too spacious for the few things I had with me. Tille came back, out of breath, with a new jug of water and replaced the empty one. I gathered that she was already at ease with this brown foreigner, because she smiled and told me to come down for supper. I was ready.

At the large dining table I met the other boarder in the house, a tall Southerner, who worked with a firm in town. I noticed that he was the only one in the group who made a cross before starting his meal. Mr Vermeulen continued with interviewing me. His curiosity was genuine, as he had heard much about the Dutch colony, but had never spoken to a real Indonesian. I felt completely at ease and also told him about the situation in Amsterdam and the students, about Bussem and my time in Boeschoten. He told me that there was still enough to eat in Almelo. Although food had begun to become scarce, here in East Holland it was still much better than in the west. Arie went often to the countryside to get extra butter, rye, eggs and even bacon or ham occasionally.

The Vermeulens were a close-knit family of plain, simple people. I immediately liked them. Although the food and other provisions in the house were very modest, the eight months that I lived with them were among the happiest times of my stay in Holland.

It was also there that a completely unexpected turn took place in my life.

CHAPTER 24

At a Crossroads

Dr Pannekoek, the Director of the General Hospital, received me with a warmth and cordiality which contrasted strikingly with the detached reception from Dr Rethmeyer the day before. His small dark eyes twinkled with joviality under his prematurely balding head. After having assessed my capabilities from my account of past examinations, lectures and readings, he told me that the most suitable work for me was at the clinical laboratory.

"The most common shortcoming I have seen with young doctors is that they have too little experience in laboratory work," he said, "they either neglect the laboratory because they don't know enough about it, or believe too much in it and ask the lab to do too many tests which are not relevant. In order to get the right attitude, you should master as many laboratory techniques as possible yourself."

He looked approvingly at my hands and said: "You have the right hands for laboratory work and, by the way, for a doctor too!"

I blushed shyly, because I saw that the Head Nurse who was present, had her eyes also fixed on my hands.

Dr Pannekoek stood up from his chair: "Come, let us bring you to introduce you to the Sister Dokter!"

When the Head Nurse saw my puzzled look, she laughed in a friendly manner, and said: "Well, it is odd indeed, but 'Dokter' is the family name of the Sister who is in charge of the laboratory."

A tall blond nurse with thick eyeglasses received me with the same curiosity as I felt in the looks of all the personnel we passed in the corridors. Dr Pannekoek explained to her that I was to be her new assistant and that her task was to teach me all laboratory procedures, beginning with the simplest and gradually proceeding to the more complicated ones later. He stressed further that to the patients and the public in general I was to be identified as a Laboratory Technician and not as a medical student.

Some underground organization, unknown to me, must have been at work, because I received a new identity card on which my profession was mentioned as "Medical Analyst" and a set of new ration cards. Also the monthly payments of my stipend via the Bank continued as before.

I was an enthusiastic apprentice and liked the work from the beginning. There were so many new things to learn. I found it interesting to do the manual work as perfectly as possible. From Sister Dokter I learned to aim for perfection in everything, like cleanliness of instruments and glass-work, and to be precise in reading the results. I was as proud as a child when she was satisfied. No work was too much for me, and I never looked at the clock. Dr Pannekoek was very pleased with my progress. In the end he had enough confidence in me to have me taking part in his clinical research and experiments.

* * * * * *

Meanwhile my stay at the Vermeulens continued to be very pleasant. One morning after breakfast when I was leaving the house Mr Vermeulen stopped me at the door and said: "Madé, since you are going to the hospital, I would like to ask you to do me a favour. Can I?"

"Of course," I said, "with all pleasure!"

"A good friend of ours, Sister Zwart, is a nurse at the hospital. She is ill with scarlet fever and has already spent three days in the sick room for nurses," and giving me a glass jar, he asked: "Will you be so kind to bring this to her?"

"What is it, if I may ask?"

"Home-made cherry jam, made by my wife. She used to make all kinds of jam and this is one of the last of our stock".

At the hospital I asked the Head Nurse if the jar should be taken to Sister Zwart by a messenger or if it would be better if I took it myself.

"Sorry, Mr Djelantik, we are all too busy today. You had better go yourself. Follow this corridor all the way and at the end you will find the stairs. Go up until you can't go further and knock at the door".

I was out of breath when I reached the door at the fourth floor. For one moment I was taken aback by the "do not disturb" sign and hesitated. Finding it too ridiculous to just put the jar down before the door, I knocked, and when I heard a weak "Ja!", I opened the door.

My heart that was pounding after the climb, stood still when I saw the sick nurse sitting on the single bed in the room. What I saw was a congested red face above a thick collar of cotton wool. But what struck me was the loveliness of that face and the penetrating eyes that looked at me in amused amazement. I was nailed to the floor, totally confused and excited at the same time. In the flurry I managed to approach the bed, but instead of handing the jar to her I put it awkwardly next to her bed on a table which was already overladen with bowls, dishes, pots and plates, saying: "This is from Pa Vermeulen". At the same moment, it flashed to my mind that I had not told her who I was and had forgotten to introduce myself properly.

The discovery of that failure and fear that it was too late for it by now, made me extra nervous. In an attempt to improve my stature, I pretended to be an assistant of Dr Pannekoek and asked: "Well, how do you feel this morning, Sister?" while reaching with my hand to the foot end of the bed, to have a professional look at the temperature card. Oh, dear, that device was not hanging there! (Old-style nursing tradition did not allow patients, especially if they were nurses, to see temperature cards or any other medical records.)

I realized that I had completely out-manoeuvred myself and stammered: "Oh sorry, it is not there. I hope that you will be better soon", and I disappeared as quickly as possible. Whatever kind of impression Sister Zwart might have had of me on that visit, it was certainly not flattering.

That was the strangest experience I had had in my life. I was silent for the rest of the day, wondering why I was so nervous and had behaved so awkwardly without any reason. And all the time the image of that lovely face above the cotton wool collar remained in my mind. For the next few days I did my work at the lab silently, concentrating my mind on the job only, but I was absent-minded in regard of my environment. Sister Dokter tried several times in vain to start some small talk with me. She must have had her own suspicions. When after a few days she came to know that I had been upstairs with cherries for Sister Zwart, she told me jokingly: "Ha, I know why you have changed so suddenly: you are *in love!*"

Was I? I did not know. I answered her: "No, that is not the case. It is something else. It is strange, I don't know!"

* * * * * *

During the weeks that followed, I experienced a whole range of emotions. I did not visit Sister Zwart—or Astri, as that was her name—again in the sick room. An unknown fear prevented me. But I knew that after some weeks she recovered and took a few days off. She went out of town, and, although I had not spoken to her since my first visit, I could not restrain myself and at her departure I asked her to send me a postcard. I did not receive anything, of course. Thereafter, I did not want to see her and hardly saw her. She didn't come very often to the Vermeulens and when she did come I did not know how to behave.

Those were agonizing days. I could not discern in her the slightest indication of any feelings towards me, neither affection nor dislike. I was only afraid that, like everyone else, she found me too strange. We seemed to shun each other all the time. When by chance it could not be avoided that we met each other at the Vermeulens, I felt a lump in my throat and was unable to say anything. If I managed to overcome my shyness, I went to the other extreme and bragged or launched belittling remarks about nurses. Later she came less and less to the Vermeulens. I got nervous and was overcome with despair. I felt that I could not sustain my indifference for long, without going mad. If only I could have a faint idea that there was some regard for me on her side! I desperately needed a bit of certainty.

Perhaps it is normal that under such circumstances one tries to escape by looking for other relationships. I paid more attention to Sister Dokter of the laboratory, and made friends with the laboratory assistant at the Catholic Hospital, a pretty red-haired girl, who owned a sailing boat. Many Saturdays we spent sailing on the Twente Rhine Canal. I realized that there was falsehood in it, but I honestly wanted to involve myself with others to get rid of my obsession for Astri. I went also more often to the Rethmeyers and the Pannekoeks. But all was in vain, it did not distract me enough and did not stop the turbulence within me. At night I was plagued by violent dreams and in the hospital I was day-dreaming. I found it difficult to concentrate on my work.

This torment lasted for about three months. My excitement reached its climax on the 21st of July, when Sister Dokter and Astri came to wish me a "Happy Birthday" with a huge bouquet of flowers. Shaking with emotion I thought: "This is the end!" But of what? I did not know.

Fortunately, however, a few days later, Astri asked me if I wanted a ride on a tandem. We discovered there was no tandem bicycle available in Almelo, so the overture resulted in an enchanting day trip on bicycle to Ootmarsum, a village nearby. In the early morning we felt already the hot breath of the day. The heat of the asphalt hit our cheeks. Astri was radiant. To my disappointment she had more attention for the beautiful countryside than for her companion. The sun was casting its golden rays over the sloping hills, the birch trees, oaks and the high standing wheat. It was beautiful indeed. All the time I kept wondering if she did not feel a bit of what was boiling within me. Somewhere we swam in a small lake, where I picked some lilies which withered long before we reached Almelo. In Ootmarsum we visited the archeological museum, where the most interesting specimen was the curator of the institute: an atrophic small gentleman with a head like a coconut, who in an emotional speech juggled with millions of years. Later we somehow came to lie side by side on the grass slope of a dyke from where we could see only the silver blue sky behind high stalks of grass undulating in the wind. While we rode back to the town with the purple sky before us, Beethoven's "Romance" was singing in my head.

Our own romance developed at a whirl-wind speed. More escapades to the countryside followed, on bicycle or hiking. Astri revived in me my love for my own country, because she had imbued me with her love. Such a love, great and infinite, was emanating from her. As if by magic my whole body was impregnated with new vitality. I felt capable of doing anything.

We were on the top of the Holter Hill, enjoying the scenery around us, when Astri for the first time asked me: "What actually are your plans with me?"

I answered: "Nothing", but at the same time I knew that it was a lie. I knew that there was something of a "plan" inside me, but I did not know yet exactly what it was. I had never thought fully about the social side of our relationship. I had been entirely engaged by the turmoil of my inner self. The deeper I went into the many socio-cultural questions, the more difficult it seemed to become. Nevertheless, it did not bring me into despair as it had before, when I was still in doubt about myself and Astri's response to my feelings. Now, I felt strengthened by her love, which infused in me the confidence and the courage to meet any challenge.

The time came when Astri had to go to Rotterdam for her training at the School for Midwives. Since she was already a registered Nurse, her midwifery training would only require two more years. We spent the evening before her departure for Rotterdam amidst purple heath shrubs on the top of a hill, enjoying the beauty of the setting sun. It was unbelievably peaceful around us despite the war. That was the moment when for the first time we confessed to each other our infinite love. The thought that we would perhaps not see each other in two long years depressed us. On the ride back our immense happiness was tinged with sadness.

Mr Vermeulen and I saw her off at the railway station. After her departure, my sadness subsided and I realized that I was at a crossroads. I could make an end to all of it, saying that it had been just one period in our lives, a beautiful experience, to be left to history. Astri had said that she would accept such a decision on my part, as I had touched something beautiful in her, for which she would be grateful to me forever. She said that she would never with anybody else find such a genuine, deep love, but it would, however, not destroy her life. She had her ideals, her vocation in her profession, and plenty of confidence.

Within me the question arose as to whether she would be strong enough to be with me forever—to meet the hundreds of challenges of the East: there was the climate, the huge social and cultural problems she would experience as a Western-educated person in the East. How could I judge, if I had the right or if it was fair, to bring her into such arduous situations. Day and night I fought my inner struggle.

In the end it was my belief in her idealism, her absolute love, and her strong personality, that generated my determination: I knew with absolute certainty that Astri, and Astri only, would be capable to live, to endure and to enjoy the difficult life at my side forever.

CHAPTER 25

Between Heaven
and Hell

When Astri's train disappeared around the corner, I was overcome by a strange mixture of fulfilment and emptiness. For a few moments Mr Vermeulen and I remained standing on the platform looking in the same direction, as if expecting the train to return. Then we walked slowly home together. We were silent, each of us lost in our own thoughts. On arrival at our doorstep the old man, obviously sensing my feelings, remarked: "Well, Madé, at least you can see her once in two weeks on your free weekends. I can't leave the place because of the shop. I will be missing her, such a good girl!"

His words triggered off emotions which suddenly welled up from deep inside me. With great effort I held back my tears and without saying anything I fled upstairs to my room. There I took up my violin, but laid it down again. I just could not play. Instead I started my first love letter, asking Astri when she would have her first free weekend. It turned out that the Rotterdam Midwifery School had a very tight schedule. The students were employed at the same time as regular nursing staff of the Maternity Hospital and one could not know beforehand when they would have a day off. They were housed in a dormitory on the top floor of the hospital and were not allowed to receive male visitors.

My longing to see her became so strong that I decided to take a chance and on my first free weekend I took the train to Rotterdam. The doorkeeper at the Hospital was a very kind man and showed compassion with me. He told me several times that I was entering forbidden terrain, but he promised to help me to meet Zuster Zwart. "Oh, yes, you mean one of the new students, that very petite girl?" I nodded and his eyes glistened. But since he was risking his job, I had to promise him that I would not come for a second time.

He led me through what seemed to me a labyrinth of cellars and narrow corridors until we arrived at an iron fire escape at the back of a three-storey building. There was nobody to be seen at that late afternoon hour. I followed him climbing stealthily up the stairs to a landing on the third floor. There was a green iron door in the wall. He took a bunch of keys out of his pocket, opened the door and pushed me inside. I found myself in a dark corridor where three uniformed girls abruptly stopped their chatter and gazed at me curiously. The man whispered over my shoulder: "A messenger for Sister Zwart! Is she here?"

The girls got excited, rushed giggling down the corridor and brought Astri out of one of the rooms. I understood that I was in the students' dormitory. Forbidden territory! It was great fun! Astri was greatly surprised. The meeting was very brief, but I felt as if in heaven. Much too soon the doorkeeper looked at his watch and indicated that we should make an end to our meeting. As practical as ever Astri proposed that the next time we should meet when both of us would have a free weekend. With some preparation it could be arranged and she would like to bring me to her father's house in Wassenaar.

Four weeks later I found myself seated at a square dining table at her father's home in Wassenaar, with Astri, her father Piet Zwart, his second wife Nel and their four children, all much younger than Astri. Her parents had divorced when she was just seven years old. The children remained with the mother, who except for a short period of marriage with a wealthy engineer, had always had a hard time to make ends meet. She was incredibly energetic and took up all kinds of work for her livelihood in order to take care of her three daughters. To support the family Astri had to start working at a very early age at a bookstore. As soon as her age permitted she worked as a nurse in a mental hospital and went later to Almelo for further training at the General Hospital, where I eventually met her. There seemed to have been from her earliest years a special bond between Astri and her father. Unlike her two sisters she was not influenced by the bitterness her mother felt towards her former husband. Astri continued her relationship with Piet Zwart, even after his marriage with Nel.

At that first visit I tried very hard not to show how confused I was. It was immediately obvious to Piet how deeply in love we were with each other. For my part, I did not know exactly how to behave. Should I regard him as my potential father-in-law? On his part, I guessed Piet must have been trying hard to assess me, which made me a bit nervous. I kept wondering how much Astri had told her father about me. My uneasiness soon faded away. I felt very much attracted by his sense of humour and I was impressed by his knowledge.

It was a delightful weekend. I slept on a canvas camping bed in a sort of lumber room in the far back of the house. Very early in the morning Astri came down with a cup of coffee. When I awoke I found her bending over me to give me a kiss. Thereby the front of her kimono fell open a bit and I could not withhold my hands to reach out and feel the delicious softness of her breasts. We delighted in the stillness of the house and savoured our togetherness in the splendid snugness of the lumber room.

* * * * * *

On another Saturday Astri met me at the railway station in Hertogenbosch where I had arrived from Almelo ten minutes earlier. From there we boarded the train to Oisterwijk, a small village 20 km to the south, beautifully situated between sloping heath-covered hills, dotted with stretches of forest. It was a superb area for hiking, with numerous footpaths, carefully laid out for sightseeing and well kept by the Netherlands Tourist Association. We delighted in our hike and, as is common with young lovers, we forgot about time and wandered at random, assuming that at the right moment we would certainly come across some sign indicating which way to follow. However, on that late October afternoon it became dark much sooner than we expected. We found it quite strange that for a long time during our ramble we had not seen any of the so called *paddestoelen*, the low, mushroom-shaped sign posts usually to be found at every intersection of foot or bicycle paths. When darkness fell we were not sure where we were. We had nothing like a compass to orientate ourselves. There was nothing but to rely upon the sense of direction that Astri had developed during her Girl Scout years. We walked on and on, tightly closed in each other arms and, being extremely happy, could not have cared less. We felt full of energy and we could have walked for the whole night.

All of a sudden, a sharp demanding call in German split the air: "WERDA?" Heavy bootsteps on asphalt followed. Startled we held our breath and I felt my heartbeat galloping wildly. We realized that we were going to cross an asphalt road near a sentinel where a sentry was standing guard. We retreated quickly and turned into the first side path.

Another "WERDA!" and we heard two soldiers shouting at each other and *clickclackclickolackclickclack*, one of them running swiftly on the road, fortunately away from us. A sigh of relief escaped us. But what to do now? Which way to go? I was deadly scared. There must be a military camp nearby. The last thing we wanted was to be caught by the Germans. While I was tense, Astri was surprisingly calm.

"Let us go this way", she said, turning into another path, "we must leave the asphalt road as far as possible behind us". I followed her, groping in the half-dark. Astri's calm gave me confidence. My fear ebbed away and I started to like the adventure. At a small open space in the woods we saw the silhouette of a low roof against the sky. Without hesitation Astri crossed the open space and I followed. We landed in an open shed with a concrete wall at one side and a wooden bench against it. We sat down with our backs against the wall and felt safe because we could not be seen from the outside. In front of us we saw all kinds of rubbish, in the midst of which the remainders of an open fire with some pieces of wood still glowing. The fire was too small to give any heat. We held each other tightly and made ourselves as comfortable as possible. With my jacket wrapped around our shoulders we were still shivering from the cold. Perhaps we were exhausted because of emotion. We had no idea of time, and we did not dare to light a match to look at our watch. It must have been past midnight and we decided to wait there until morning. Despite the cold it was a sweet silent night. I began to feel my legs becoming heavy and several times I dozed off into the sweetest of dreams. And every time I awoke I felt Astri's cheek against my lips, fresh, firm, healthy and astonishingly desirable.

Before dawn we stood up and relying on Astri's intuition we followed a narrow road in the direction of a few farmhouses which we could see in the far distance. At one of the farms we met an old couple coming out of the house in their finest Sunday attire, obviously going to church. We stopped and asked them the way to the nearest railway station. They looked at us with scrutinizing eyes and smiled.

"Where do you come from?" the old man asked.

Astri explained: "We have been walking yesterday from Oisterwijk and lost our way," and pointing with her finger, "There, beyond those trees, we fortunately found a shed there, where we have spent the night. We were afraid to go anywhere further, because there were voices of German soldiers. Have we been close to a German military camp perhaps?"

"Yes, you're right, the shed is just on its border."

"But there were no signs, how could we know?"

"Sure, they don't want people to know! They have removed all the *paddestoelen* and there are only no-entry signs, which you might not have seen in the dark. The Oosterwijk railway station is that way, one hour's walk from here. But wait, you look very tired, both of you. You need some sleep first. Please, come in!"

Before we could say anything he opened the door and pushed us inside. He led us straight to their bedroom on the ground floor, saying: "We will be back at noon. You can sleep in our bed. Go ahead! Sleep well!" and off he went.

We were speechless, stunned, but found the prospect of a few hours sleep very attractive. We quickly slipped under the sheets. The bed was still warm, most gratifying to our chilled bones. We slept a heavenly sleep in each other's arms.

When the old couple returned from church, we had already washed ourselves and made up their bed. They insisted that we stayed for lunch. We complied thankfully. They were very interested in our plans and we told about our ideals. In talking about them with the old couple we felt strengthened in our idealism. It made a wonderful ending after the frightful night's experience.

* * * * * *

On other free weekends I often went by bicycle to Enschede, where two of our younger members of UNICA lived. The town was situated near the German border about 20 miles east of Almelo and had earned fame before the war due to its flourishing textile industry. My friends' parents owned large textile factories and lived in stately mansions, surrounded by beautiful gardens with big trees and well-kept lawns. Their hospitality and easy lifestyle made a sojourn in Enschede most enjoyable and relaxing.

One Sunday morning while we were playing croquet on the lawn behind the villa of the Ter Kuiles, the beautiful spectacle of the silver birds high in the sky distracted us from our game. My friends were elated. "Look, Madé, what a wonderful sight! Let the wretched Germans feel what they have done to us".

We did not know which German towns would be the target for that day. The great number of planes suggested that a large area would be bombarded. There were three waves of plane formations and it lasted for more than half an hour before the last of the planes disappeared in the eastern sky. When they returned later in the afternoon or at night on their way back to England, we could calculate and plot on the map where they had been bombing.

That afternoon on the ride back to Almelo, while passing through the main street of Hengelo, another town with textile factories, I heard the familiar thundering sound again, and looking up I saw high in the sky behind me a few formations of bombers flying West, apparently belonging to the large contingent of that morning, now home bound. More formations followed. Being used already to such events I did not pay much attention to it, nor did the people on the street. Suddenly the noise became much louder. Looking up I saw planes flying very low over the apartment blocks which lined the street on both sides. I noticed something like sticks or rods falling out of their bellies. While I was wondering what those objects could be, the planes crossed over and within seconds the roofs of the buildings caught fire and the asphalt on the street went up in flames, making a six metres high wall of raging fire less than 100 metres in front of me. Frightened, I swiftly turned my bicycle to get away.

The spectacle I saw before me was unforgettable. Fifty metres away another wall of flames rose high from the street and fires were everywhere on the roofs on all sides. People were screaming and running in all directions to safety, and strangly enough, not far from me I saw a woman squatting in the middle of the street: she was vomiting. It could not have been for more than two seconds that I was witnessing the jumble, because suddenly the deafening noise of an approaching aircraft filled the air. As a reflex I jumped from my bicycle and flung myself across the pavement into the portico of a building where three men were huddling for shelter. At the same moment the whole building block above us came down with a thundering and prolonged crash. I felt the earth trembling under my feet and the wall against which my back was crushed was shaking vehemently. The next moment the world around me turned pitch dark. I could not see anything before me and for an instant I was terrified, thinking that I had been struck blind. Since there was no pain I felt all right again. When the noise of the crumbling building faded away I heard screaming and people crying for help all around me. It lasted some minutes before the dust settled down and things around me became gradually more visible. I was surprised to find myself still standing with my back and my hands against the side wall of the building. The portico was intact, so was the arc above it. It was a miracle! Where the door had been there was now a wide opening and beyond it I saw a fallen staircase under an immense heap of rubble. The three men were no longer there. Had they left already, or had they been hurled inside and buried under the staircase and the rubble? The thought made me shudder. I could not muster the courage to try to find them under the rubble and reasoned to myself that it would be of no use anyway.

Stepping up the street I found my bicycle still lying there, unharmed, but its handlebars had been twisted by the fall. I saw bodies on the street and on the pavement between rubble and debris, and people attending to the wounded. Still numb I just stood there, not knowing what to do until one of them shouted at me to get an ambulance from the hospital. I felt happy to be of some use, picked up my bicycle and raced between broken pieces of pavement and burning asphalt. On the way I met a number of ambulances speeding in the direction of the disaster. Numbness struck me again. What should I do now? Then I realized that I could very well help the doctors at the hospital. There must be many casualties to be attended to.

I was not mistaken. When I arrived at the hospital there were already many casualities on stretchers waiting in the overcrowded waiting room. I reported to the Chief Surgeon and was immediately put to work in the operating room. Since I had already had some training during operations in Almelo, the procedures of washing and aseptics were not new to me. Except for brief pauses for coffee and some sandwiches I was standing at the operating table for more than 16 hours, assisting several shifts of surgeons. To me the work was most interesting and seeing at close range a wide variety of operations was a great learning experience.

When at ten in the morning I mounted my bicycle and pedalled to Almelo, I did not feel tired at all. Instead, I felt energetic and very happy, but also I started to feel a sharp aching pain in my left eye. The ophthalmologist in Almelo diagnosed a bad keratitis, caused by the dust at the bombardment. My friends congratulated me that I had come out of the disaster with that slight injury only, it could have been much worse. And a disaster it was! According to analysts the bombing had been a grave error, carried out by British pilots who thought they were still above Germany. "War is war," they said, "it has its consequences and errors cannot entirely be eliminated".

CHAPTER 26

War and its Casualties

By the end of 1943, active faculty members at the University of Amsterdam had finalized preparations for conducting underground courses for medical students. With the universities closed down, concern had been growing that if nothing was done, there would be a great gap in the ranks of the medical profession later. Because of the risk involved, the selection of students had to be careful. Dr Pannekoek was informed that I was among those who had been selected for the first batch of students and he advised me to join forthwith.

In Amsterdam I found *Mevrouwtje*'s apartment free and I moved back in. She was glad to see me back, healthy and well, because she had been very worried about me. I too was happy for her, since she could use the room rent very well. For the past year she had had great difficulty in making ends meet. She could not afford to buy extra food on the black market. There was just not enough to eat, she had grown older and weaker, and could not take up much work. I was lucky also to find a lady nearby who received a few customers for evening meals, much cheaper and of better quality than in the restaurants. It was considered better for us, clandestine students, not to be seen in public places everyday. Thus all in all, I was well taken care of.

My time as a medical analyst in the laboratory with Dr Pannekoek proved to be very useful in my theoretical studies. I followed all the courses with ease, passed my examinations smoothly and got my "Doctoraal" (the equivalent of M.A.) well ahead of my friends in the group. Soon afterwards I was assigned to the Catholic Hospital in Nijmegen, one of the many hospitals all over the country which had cooperated in the secret undertaking. There I was to start the series of ten student internships in the various branches of the medical profession, required to qualify for the final examinations to become a physician.

I found a room with a family called Jansen on the main street near the Keizer Karel Plein—the spot where the Emperor Charlemagne build his fortress more than 11 centuries ago—just ten minutes walking distance from the hospital. A few weeks later Roland Kalff passed his "Doctoral" and joined me in Nijmegen. Out of convenience he shared my room. We had a marvellous time working and learning and taking long walks on free afternoons along the banks of the river.

However, the pleasant and relaxing atmosphere of the town did not last long. That summer the Allied Forces launched their big offensive from France and Belgium to the north, liberated Nijmegen and were bogged down in the hills just east of the city. The battle to push the Germans out of Nijmegen had been very fierce. The Keizer Karel Plein near the bridge over the Waal and the place where I lived had changed hands between the German army and the Allied Forces three times. Only after the third time were we liberated. The beautiful bridge was conquered intact due to underground forces who had prevented the Germans from blowing it up by removing the explosives during the night. Winter came and it was another two months before the Germans were driven out of the hills east of the town and further back into Germany. During these months Nijmegen was constantly under artillery fire. Day and night German shells and bombs fell haphazardly in the town, causing many casualties among the civilian population.

Roland and I had to walk twice daily and often at night from our boarding house to our work. The house had a cellar which was considered a safe shelter. Once we spent agonizing hours there with the landlord's family, while shooting and hand-to-hand fighting took place between Germans and Canadians in the streets and inside the house just above our heads. Sometimes if there was not enough room in the cellar, we often spent sleepless nights in our room on the second floor, taking cover under our beds, hoping at each whistle that the shell would land somewhere else.

Many casualties of the war had to be dealt with in our hospital daily. Despite the extra work for which our assistance was needed, our training continued to conform to the curriculum. In the course of the following weeks more students were taken in, increasing our group to about ten. Besides our formal training we learned a great deal from working at emergencies and assisting in the operation rooms.

In Almelo I had developed a special dexterity in giving intravenous injections. No matter how difficult the circumstances, I always got the needle into the vein. Due to this ability and my experience in laboratory work I was always sought after to take care of the blood transfusion in cases of emergency. Sometimes the great number of emergencies kept me running with flasks of blood between the wards for most of the day. During my work with the blood transfusion service I had a number of unforgettable experiences.

One day I had to attend to a patient in shock on the second floor. I had just succeeded in inserting the needle into his collapsed vein and was counting the falling drips in the flask above my head, when with a thundering crash a grenade hit the concrete floor under our feet and the whole window with a part of the wall next to us fell down outside. I must have been struck numb by the tremendous shock of the blast, because I was only aware of the event when I suddenly saw the wards on the opposite side of the hospital yard through the gaping hole next to me. The patient was too far gone to move. I felt my arms and legs shaking, but I still held the patient's arm with the splint, the needle and the tube in my trembling hands. I assured myself that the blood was still dripping in the wildly dangling flask. The next moment I saw two nurses running towards me. One of them took over the patient, the other lifted me up from my stool and led me down to the underground shelter. She gave me a glass of milk to drink and told me that I should have a rest.

There were not only civilian casualties in the wards. The day after the Germans had been pushed out of the town we had to treat German soldiers, left behind by their retreating comrades and picked up by the Americans or Canadians. We did not question why they should be treated in our hospital and not by the military. Perhaps their field hospitals were at times too full.

A few days later I was assigned to give a blood transfusion to a wounded German soldier, a member of the notorious "Waffen S.S." corps. I guessed the boy could not be over 20 years of age. His leg had to be amputated, and the doctors had decided that he should first get some blood. I could speak German very well in those days and had no trouble talking with him. While I was checking his blood group he was quite talkative. He came from Lubeck and was homesick. Several times he asked me why the people who had found him lying in a ditch just outside the town had not killed him. He had been told that the Dutch would kill every German they could lay their hands on. I tried to convince him of the contrary. He was wondering where I came from and I was amazed to hear that he had never heard of Indonesia. He knew only of Japan in the East. I tried to explain the geography of my country, leaving him with a rough sketch of it, when I went to the laboratory with his blood sample.

When I returned with a flask of blood, he looked very frightened.

"What is that?" he asked.

"Blood, good for you!"

Suddenly he started shouting: "No, no, no, I don't want it! That can be Jewish blood, I would rather die than have my blood contaminated with that of a Jew. Take away that stuff."

I was perplexed. I had not expected a European to be so superstitious. When I looked at his face and eyes I was convinced that his fear was real. He was really frightened, as if I was going to inject him with poison or deadly bacteria. I took the flask of blood and went to the Chief Surgeon who was in his office, discussing matters with his staff. When they heard my story the younger doctors broke out in laughter: "There you are! *Das Herrenvolk*! Ha, ha, ha, let him go to hell!"

The Chief Surgeon however looked very concerned.

"Please, stop joking, Gentlemen! Don't forget that we are responsible for his life. We have to keep our morals". With bent head he thought for a moment and said: "Djelantik, go to our pharmacy, ask if there are still a few bottles of plasma left from the stock that we got from the Americans some days ago when they were here".

He scribbled on a small note block, tore the piece of paper, handed it to me, saying: "Give the soldier two bottles of plasma. If he asks, tell him that it is a protein solution, made in Germany, don't tell him that it is plasma, he might know that plasma comes from blood. Make sure that you have removed all labels from the bottle first of all."

I did as was told and succeeded in reassuring the soldier. He withstood the operation very well. Thereafter I didn't see him again. I was told later that he had been taken away as a prisoner-of-war for further treatment in the Canadian Military Hospital.

I had a different kind of experience when I had to deal for the first time with an American soldier. It was on the evening of the liberation of the town. That morning we saw to our great surprise a number of GIs, in full combat gear with their guns ready, walking between the patients in the ground floor ward. Nobody had seen them entering the hospital. There had been no bombing, no shooting. They had entered the hospital from all sides stealthily and noiselessly on their rubber boots. Seeing our startled faces they smiled only, pointing out of the windows to the main street. We looked and saw their fellow GIs, in single file on both sides of the street, proceeding slowly towards the city centre. With their guns at the ready, they looked sharply to the left and to the right, down the street and up to the rooftops. Suddenly, a small open vehicle with three soldiers passed at high speed going towards the city. We had never seen a jeep before. There was the cracking sound of machine-gun fire in the distance, followed by the screeching of brakes and tires, and the same odd vehicle sped back past the soldiers. There was shouting of commands and suddenly they were all gone. As we looked more closely, we saw that they had taken cover in ditches, behind trees and buildings. We found the spectacle most exciting, but the GIs in the room told us to clear the windows and to lie down behind the walls. They took position at the windows. Nothing happened, except that we heard from time to time the steps of soldiers, running for cover from tree to tree. Then we heard more vehicles—armoured cars or tanks—passing by, and about 15 minutes later the GIs left the ward, some of them jumping out of the windows, calling to us with wide grins on their faces: "Ladies and gentlemen, the show is over, now back to work!"

For the rest of the day we heard shooting and bursts of machine-gun fire in the far distance, with a series of explosions in between. They were fighting in the city. Towards the afternoon the shooting died down.

That evening a military ambulance unloaded a few wounded GIs at our hospital, cases for urgent treatment. Two of them had to receive blood transfusions. I was in charge and did my utmost to deliver good work. They were lying in two adjacent rooms, but had to get their transfusion simultaneously. I put up the transfusion on the first soldier, waited a while to make sure that the blood was flowing well and left him alone. Then I went to the next room and quickly put up the set on the second patient. After assuring myself that all was fixed properly I rushed back to check the condition of the first GI. Entering the room I was shocked to find the air thick with smoke. Two visiting GIs and our patient were cheerfully smoking their cigarettes, all of them sitting on the one bed. That was completely against the rules of our Dutch hospitals. I was too shy to stop the GIs and went to report to the Chief Nurse. On my way I met the American Medical Officer in charge and told him about the embarrassing situation. He looked both surprised and amused, and said:

"Come, let us have a look!"

I followed him back to the ward. He looked at the three GIs who were still joking with the patient on the bed and told me laughingly: "Boy, as long as our guys can smoke and have fun, leave them. It is all right? Okay?"

It was the first time I heard the term "okay". It sounded funny in my ears, and although I didn't know what it meant, I murmured: "Thank you very much!" and shrugged my shoulders. I did not report to the Chief Nurse.

Another night, when I was on duty, the bombardment of the town by German artillery was very heavy. I was asked to check on the surgical patients on the ground floor, lying there in a row in the corridor which had been converted into an emergency ward. It was considered safe since, except for the windows, it was provided with a double layer of sandbags from the outside. A man with a traction splint on his broken arm was moaning from pain. When he saw me he moaned much louder and asked me to come nearer.

"Please, Doctor, the pain is terrible. I can't bear it any longer. Can you please take off the traction for a while. Also my back starts aching terribly in this sitting position. I need to lie down."

He started to cry. I felt great compassion, but I knew that giving in to his request would, medically speaking, be a great mistake. His bones which were aligning themselves by the traction would fall back in the wrong position. The surgeon would curse me severely. Seeing his tears and his suffering face I could not help looking around me to see if there were any nurses or other medical staff in the ward. There were none. I checked the weights hanging from the pulley and felt a shock: 5 kg!

"The fellow must be suffering a lot," I thought, and I did what I was not supposed to do. I took off the weights and loosened the cords. The man gave a sigh of relief: "Oh, oh, thank you very much, doctor. You are very kind. Thank you!"

I went over to the head end of the bed, pulled down the support and adjusted the cushions. The man laid himself down carefully and made himself comfortable. I ran back to the foot end of the bed. Standing there and looking anxiously around I applied manually some light traction on the splint, hoping to minimize the damage I was doing. Meanwhile I was frightened, not so much because of the bombing, but fearing that any moment the Surgeon or Chief Nurse might enter the ward.

After some minutes I could not bear my anxiety any longer and asked the man: "How do you feel?"

"Oh, thank you. Much better".

"Well, sorry, I can't leave you for long in this way. I have to put the traction back in its place".

"Don't do it, Doctor, please don't. I cannot bear the pain. I beg you".

"Sorry, I have to", I said, and just when I got the pulley straight up again, there was a deafening blast outside. Pieces of wood and broken glass flew around and fell clattering on the floor under the patient's bed. As a reflex I ducked for cover and instantly the room was darkened by dust. When the air cleared again I saw that the bed was entirely covered with debris and a large chunk of metal was stuck in the wall beside the patient just one foot above his chest. It was an irregularly shaped piece of a grenade that had smashed through the window, measuring about 5 inches, half of it buried in the concrete by the impact of the blast.

It was not difficult to imagine what would have happened, had the man still been in the sitting position.

CHAPTER 27

An Extraordinary Wedding Party

At last, in the spring of 1945, the hills east of Nijmegen were captured and the Germans were pushed further to the east. Life in the city returned to normal. There was suddenly plenty of food and no longer fear of bombardment. Soon thereafter the German army retreated from Belgium and the Netherlands. At our hospital in Nijmegen we celebrated the liberation of the country jubilantly.

Communication with Rotterdam was restored. Travel was still restricted in the beginning, but Astri's letters came through very quickly. The gates of heaven opened again! In Rotterdam people had suffered badly from hunger during the winter. There were rumours that out of despair mothers had smothered their newborn children in the hospital. Astri had managed to study well and was now preparing for her final examinations. However, she did not have to travel to Nijmegen, because the universities reopened and students emerged out of their hiding places from all over the country. I moved back to Amsterdam to complete my four remaining internships at the University Hospital.

In my old flat at the Hobbemakade *Mevrouwtje* had taken care of my furniture and books which I had left with her. I enrolled at the University and was assigned as co-assistant at the surgical department of the Hospital. A few weeks later Astri passed her examinations in Rotterdam and became a Registered Midwife. She took up a temporary job in a village south of Amsterdam, to replace the local midwife who had gone on a long vacation. This gave us the opportunity to be together quite often. Meanwhile I had to study hard, since I did not want to fail another test as had happened to me in Nijmegen on Neurology, where I had been over-confident.

Perhaps because we took things for granted, we did not plan anything for the future. We decided just to let life develop by itself, knowing for sure that we would never part. Early in the morning of the 15th of April a very fortunate event happened to me. When I entered the lecture room, the Professor had just started. Feeling guilty for being late I sneaked to the nearest empty seat near the door, but before I could sit down, he spotted me and called me to the podium. With my heart throbbing in my throat I walked down the steps to the platform where a patient was on a sickbed. I understood that this was a particularly interesting and difficult case to be demonstrated to his assistants and the students.

"What is your name?"

"Djelantik, Sir!"

"When is your examination due?"

"Next month, Sir!"

"Hmmm ...! Can you find out what is wrong with this patient?"

I was asked to examine the patient, and to report my findings loudly so that everybody could hear me. When I hesitated the Professor looked amused and said: "Come on!" I did what was asked and examined the patient as meticulously as I could. Afterwards I had to answer a host of nasty questions relating to the case for more than half an hour. I was tense, knowing that the audience was listening critically. The Professor appeared very pleased, however, and at the end he shook my hand and said: "Congratulations! You don't have to come back. You have passed your examination!"

At first I could not believe my ears, but the applause of the audience made it clear to me. The next moment I was very happy, realizing that I did not have to go through all the textbooks again. When I told Astri, she was most delighted.

Two weeks later we decided that we should register ourselves for marriage at the Registrar's Office. On the way to the Municipality we saw that the whole town was decorated with flags. It looked as if the town were celebrating our happiness. We were moved and looked at each other amazed. When we asked someone why the flags were out, we were reminded that it was Princess Juliana's birthday, her first in the liberated fatherland! We left the Registrar's office in a jubilant mood and celebrated the day with a long walk in the Vondel Park among the festive crowd. That evening we concluded our celebration by going to see Mozart's "Figaro's Hochzeit" at the Opera House.

* * * * * *

I don't remember how we came to fix our wedding day on the 31st of May, another day of fortune. In Bali a number of priests would have been consulted and they would have scrutinized the traditional horoscopes. But at that time no contact with my family was possible. The Netherlands East Indies were still under Japanese occupation. Even if the facility had been there, I would probably not have sought any advice from home. We were somehow very determined and self-confident. My friends in UNICA shared our happiness. Tamme and Bellie offered to hold the wedding lunch in their house at the Farmstead Oud-Bussum. I was not aware until the morning of the wedding itself, that my friends in UNICA had other great things in mind. Roland's mother, Mrs Kalff, knowing that Astri's mother had died during the war, insisted that Astri together with her younger sister, Futri, should spend the night before the wedding in her house. She wanted to help Astri with her wedding dress. She and Futri would be delighted to sign the book as witnesses at the Municipality. We could not afford to buy a traditional wedding dress, and in fact Astri found it unnecessary. She found a dark-blue dress which had once belonged to her mother, took thread and needle and remade it to fit herself. On advice of my friends I put on my frock coat, inherited from a retired Unicist, which I had worn during examinations at the University, as was required in those days. It was certainly more than 30 years old and impressively antique, but made of first-class material. A top-hat and a dark-blue cloak completed my attire.

On the way from my flat to Mrs Kalff's house I stopped at the florist on the corner, where I bought a huge bouquet of white asters which I took on the crowded tram, ignoring the people who gleefully grinned at me and gesticulated to each other in benevolent amusement.

At the Kalffs, a radiant Astri awaited me. Mrs Kalff expressed her amazement at Astri's imagination and skill in transforming the old-fashioned gown into a lovely suit. Astri plucked one of the white flowers from my bouquet and put it in the Balinese way in her hair. She looked exquisite!

As we were waiting for the taxi to bring us to the Municipality—so we thought—we suddenly heard shouting on the street and the clattering sound of hoofs on the pavement. Looking out of the window we saw our UNICA "brik", a stately open carriage on four high wheels, drawn by four horses, two white and two red-brown (to conform to our UNICA colours), driven by two coachmen in bright-blue liveries, with long colourful whips in their hands. Behind the "brik" we saw Tamme, in frock coat and top-hat, indicating to us with a deep bow to come down and mount the carriage. What a wonderful surprise!

Driving in that grandiose vehicle through Amsterdam was like a dream. Everywhere the people in the streets were smiling, waving and applauding cheerfully at the sight of the unusual spectacle.

In front of the municipality building we were noisily welcomed by a jolly troupe of Unicists, all in frock coats and top-hats. Our Chairman had the large red-and-white UNICA plaid over his shoulder and was swaying with the Unicorn staff. Our Secretary announced our arrival by blowing with all his might on a brass trumpet, splitting the air between the stately buildings with the ugliest false tones possible. Other friends and Piet Zwart with Nel and their children were waiting at the entrance of the building. Piet confessed to me later: "When I saw your stately carriage with the four horses and all those people in frock coats and top-hats, I went inside to check the location of the ceremony and discovered that they had prepared the cheap fourth-class room which you had ordered. With a few cigars and a cheque they were willing to transfer the protocol to the first-class.'

At the ceremony itself the large hall was filled with Unicists, friends and relatives. Unaware of the transfer that Piet had manipulated, we were very impressed by the stateliness of the hall and chairs. Nervously, we nearly put our signatures on the wrong places in the book. Then the Registrar took up his hammer, but before this awesome attribute could strike the green table, the air suddenly burst with the thundering UNICA yell:

"UNICE! UNICE! IS A FRIEND OF MINE! IS A FRIEND OF MINE! UNICE! UNICE! IS A FRIEND OF MINE! HOLD YOUR TONGUE!"

I felt as if I were in trance, but could not help smiling when I saw the Registrar's hammer stopping in mid-air, waiting for the noise to stop. Then it came down forcibly as if asserting its authority and thereby convincingly confirming our bond.

The ride on the UNICA "brik" from the Municipality to the train station was another Cinderella-like experience. Another surprise befell us when we entered the building: the hall and the platforms were fully adorned with flags and confetti. Station personnel were hastily unrolling a red carpet and a brass band in uniforms started to play patriotic march music. The alarmed station master rushed down from his office onto the platform. He soon discovered the error and immediately stopped the band.

By sheer coincidence it was the inauguration day of the first electric train to run from Amsterdam to Hilversum. At the sight of so many frock coats and top-hats the railway personnel thought that the Mayor and other officials had arrived. Jubilantly our crowd boarded the train which stood ready along the platform. The first real electric train was to depart ten minutes later. When we approached the next stop at Weesp we saw the decorations from afar and all of us leaned out of the window. Again, surprised personnel mistook our party for officials, hurriedly unrolling the red carpet as the merry sounds of a brass band filled the air. The train stopped and we waved our hats triumphantly and roared with laughter when the band, realizing their mistake stopped playing. The same fun we had at Naarden-Bussum, our destination. All in all it was an exhilarating journey.

Bellie, who had stayed in Oud-Bussum to prepare our lunch party, provided us with another astonishing surprise. Coming out of the railway station we saw two huge farm carts, their solid wooden frames and wheels fully decorated with pink rhododendrons. Coachmen in colourful traditional costumes held the enormous Brabant horses in check with their reins. The twenty-minute ride on those carts through the countryside to Oud-Busum was fantastic.

Fully in style, the lunch took place in one of the stables, decorated with rhododendrons for the occasion. There were speeches, toasts and wines as usual. When late in the afternoon all the guests had left, Tamme, Bellie and the two of us sat down in the garden, happily reflecting on the wonderful events of the day.

CHAPTER 28

Political Interlude

After our idyllic six-week honeymoon on the island of Vlieland, I was fresh and ready to take on my new position as assistant to Dr Pannekoek, at the very modern hospital in Deventer. I worked long hours without feeling any fatigue. In the beginning my small stature and boyish appearance often aroused misgivings among the patients, most of whom were farmers from the countryside. They were suspicious of being used as guinea pigs for the training of a young medical student, always requiring Dr Pannekoek to reassure them that I was a real doctor. But soon confidence in me grew on all sides, among patients and nurses, among my colleagues and most rewarding of all, among the specialists, the chiefs of the various departments at the hospital.

After a few weeks I put aside my shyness and talked to Dr Pannekoek and the Department Chiefs about my long-time dream. I wanted to be able to work on my own in remote parts of Indonesia, to bring medical help to the forgotten population. I asked if the hospital staff would be willing to help me to acquire that ability in the shortest time possible. Dr Pannekoek and his staff were enthusiastic, and they decided to organize an intensive crash programme for me, in three stages: one year internal medicine, one year surgery and six months rontgenology. They warned me that it would be hard work, I would have to learn in each period about three times as much as in the normal training of specialists. I was delighted and studied very hard. The rigorous practical training and the guidance given to me by the staff proved later to be invaluable.

Meanwhile far-reaching political developments were taking place in the Indonesian Archipelago. After the atomic bombing of Hiroshima and Nagasaki in August 1945, the Japanese surrendered. The reoccupation of Southeast Asia by the Allied Forces took too long. Before the British and Australian armies landed in Jakarta in December 1945, more than five months had passed. During that period of great confusion the Japanese hesitated about whether or not to hand over political authority to the Indonesians. On 17th August 1945, yielding to pressure from young political leaders, Sukarno and Hatta proclaimed the Independent Nation of Indonesia in Jakarta. The political parties in Java succeeded in creating a preliminary Government and an Indonesian army, consisting of various groups of freedom fighters. There were also the thousands of Dutch citizens to be evacuated after their terrible ordeal in Japanese camps. Confusion and tensions increased after the the Netherlands Indies Government returned to Jakarta from exile in Australia, and subsequently rebuilt the Royal Netherlands Indies Army. Clashes between this colonial army and the Indonesian freedom fighters broke out, at first around Jakarta and later, in 1946, spread to the outer islands, including Bali.

Fully occupied with my training and studies, I did not follow the news from Indonesia too well at that time. Communications were still bad due to the confused political situation. News about Indonesia was scarce and heavily censored. At the first opportunity I sent a message home through the Red Cross, using the standard form for family news. For a long time I did not receive any answer, so I thought that either my message had not gone through or there was still no possibility for the people at home to send messages abroad. I forgot about it, until one day in September I received a letter from the Ministry of Overseas Territories (as the Colonial Office had been renamed), asking me to come to The Hague for an urgent interview.

At the Ministry I was met by a senior official who, after reassuring me that he was not going to interrogate me, said:

"We have received a request from your father, the Raja of Karangasem, to bring you home. He has received your message and would be delighted to see you back alive and well".

Although I was happy with the news, I was not too happy with the prospect of going home to Bali while I was still preparing myself to become an all-round medical doctor. I felt myself not yet ready for my future task. I told the officer that I had married a Dutch girl and that I would not be happy to leave her alone in Holland.

"Yes, we know and we have anticipated this problem. Everything can be arranged. We are very pleased to meet your father's request. If you want to continue your training, we can arrange for you and your wife to have a round trip travel to Bali, say for instance for six weeks".

I thanked him for the wonderful surprise and said: "I'm sorry, but I can't decide yet. I must discuss the matter with my wife first, and I have to get permission from my boss to leave my job for such a long period. They have just started a crash programme especially for me!"

"We can give you a letter of recommendation, if necessary. It is very important. Let me be frank. It will not be only for your father's pleasure. We want something in return from you".

I became alert, by instinct feeling that there must be something like politics in the air. I asked: "And what would that be?"

"Yes, it is politics! Bali is in great trouble. You know that your father was very much loved by his people. It is still so, but only by the older generation. There is trouble with the youngsters, the *Pemudas*. Many of the young generation have joined the Republican Army, they proclaim themselves freedom fighters and are waging a guerrilla war against the Dutch, using hit-and-run tactics. We fully appreciate their ideals, their longing for a free nation, but we should be able to talk to each other and not fight. We don't want to kill them, because among them there are many bright people who can be very useful for your country. We need somebody to communicate with them, somebody whom they trust, to convince them that we have not come back to colonize, but to help them to build a new, free Indonesia".

While listening to his speech, I felt my brains working very hard. His ideas tallied with those expressed by the liberal left of the political spectrum in Holland. He had not mentioned the hardliners in the old colonial army and among the politicians who were still much in control at the Ministry of Overseas Territories. Nevertheless I felt that he was sincere himself.

I said: "I am only a medical doctor and I have no political authority. Nobody will listen to me".

"You are wrong. We know that you have good friends among the guerrillas who are now hiding in the mountains in Bali. They know you well and we know that they trust you. We are sure that you will be able to convince them that it is better for all of us to stop fighting and start to talking with each other."

A whirlwind of thoughts went through my mind, mixed with doubts and suspicion. How did they know that much about me? What did they know about my political stance or ideas? I did not want to start a political debate with the man. When I remained silent, he continued: "Well, think it over, if you think of accepting our offer, come back to this office, the sooner the better".

Back in Deventer I told Astri about the meeting. She was excited about the prospect of having a round trip to Bali and thought that I should accept, but under the condition that I should be free to express my own opinions.

Leaving our apartment was no problem. By coincidence a young doctor who just finished his internist training, applied for a temporary job at the hospital to have more practical experience while preparing his Ph.D. thesis. Dr Pannekoek, assured me that if I decided to go, he would keep my job open.

On my second visit to the Ministry, the officer gave more details of what was expected from me. In addition to trying to get in contact with the leaders of the freedom fighters in Bali, especially with my former classmate Ngurah Rai, I was to talk to other revolutionaries, who for security reasons were being kept in prisons all over the island. I was also expected to hold public rallies in the capital towns to give information to the public at large about the political situation in Holland. Feeling the trickiness of such a mission and remembering Astri's advice, I put forward my condition, that I should be guaranteed complete freedom of speech and that if there would be something that might not be agreeable to the authorities, we would be transported back to Holland as free citizens. This was approved.

* * * * * *

Ten days later, after having gone through a series of interesting novelties such as inoculations, and having obtained our passports and other travel documents, we boarded an old twin-engine Dakota for the flight to Rome and Cairo, the first leg of our long and exciting journey to Bali. It was our very first travel by air, and since everything was new to us, we enjoyed every moment of the trip. We felt we were having a second honeymoon! Used to simple meals at home, we were impressed by the luxury lunch with wine at Rome's airport on a spotless white tablecloth, served by neat waiters clad in black and white. Our festive feeling found its height at the Grand Hotel in Cairo, where we spent the night in a huge, majestic bedroom suite, surrounded by heavy curtains adorned with tassled cords in red and gold. I was filled with awe, but the nurse in Astri discovered immediately that all that luxury could do with a lot of cleaning!

The next day we touched down for lunch at Basrah airport, where we amused ourselves by looking at a large kind of cupboard, in which a couple of fans were blowing air through a shower of water into the hall, driving the murderous hot air out of the restaurant with its cool wind. The next stop was Karachi where we spent the night in another luxury hotel. In those years the planes did not fly higher than 7,000 feet, so that we could see every detail of the landscape below us. We could not stop looking down, wondering at the immense vastness of the barren Arabian desert; we were surprised to see numerous camel tracks crossing the sand in all directions, and now and then a caravan of Bedouins with their camels and their mules.

Approaching Calcutta, where we were scheduled to land for lunch, we were suddenly flying in the midst of big birds by the hundreds, zigzagging above, under and on all sides of the aircraft, some of them so close by as we could have touched them with our hands. They were huge, measuring about two metres between the tips of their wings, and we could clearly see that they were vultures. We shuddered with disgust when the steward informed us that they were feasting on the thousands of bodies of those killed in violent clashes between Moslems and Hindus in the town for the past few days. Fortunately the airport was situated far from the town, but even from there we could still see the creatures hovering above the town in the far distance.

After two more short stops—in Bangkok and Singapore—we arrived in Jakarta to be met by an elderly gentleman, Mr Van der Plas, who presented himself as an old friend of my father. He had been Governor of East Java for many years before the war and had visited Bali several times. Now a high official at the Ministry of the Interior of the newly-established Provisional Netherlands East Indies Government, he was considered the right man to meet his friend's son. At the briefing session the next morning the Deputy Governor General, Mr Koets, confirmed the approval of the conditions I had put forward at the Ministry of Overseas Territories in The Hague two weeks before.

Over the next few days we made excursions by jeep in the surroundings of Jakarta, escorted by another car with heavily armed soldiers. Mr Van der Plas wanted us to see the confused state of affairs in the areas around the capital, where, despite the armistice, clashes between the Dutch and the Republican forces continued to occur, while on both sides the authorities were trying to draw the demarcation line between their jurisdictions. Special attention was given to the deplorable conditions of the poor population in the area as result of the continuing war.

We were not only curious but also eager to see the situation and we did not think about the risks and dangers involved. Because of the fluidity of the so-called borders we must have penetrated several times the Republican Territory. Once we were nearly thrown out of the jeep, when all of a sudden the driver, discovering a deep trench over the whole width of the road, made a sharp U-turn, and before we realized what had happened the car raced back at high speed to escape an ambush. We saw the other jeep lingering for some time near the trench before it turned around to join us. Our driver told us, that as he had been driving on that road safely the day before, the trench must have been dug that night. We heard no shots or anything and felt relief.

* * * * * *

The flight from Jakarta to Bali was made in a Boeing fighterbomber. On arrival, all high civilian and military officials were lined up to meet us with all the honours due to a high visitor. Was I not a prince, the son of the most venerated of the Rajas of Bali? Had I not come with the important mission to bring peace to the island? And then, there was my Dutch bride. Was it not something to be proud of?

We were housed in a luxury suite at the Bali Hotel, and on the first night we had dinner with the Resident, Mr Boon, and his wife. After the luxury meals during the trip thus far, I was struck by the plainness of the dinner. We had spinach, rice and fried pigeons. The Boons talked with nostalgia about the past, of the time when Mr Boon had been Controleur in Karangasem, where he had built a tennis court and how much fun we had playing tennis together.

A busy programme was prepared for us, consisting of public rallies in all the towns where I would give speeches, informing the public at large about the political changes all over the world and about the situation in Holland. Also I would make visits to political detainees in prisons and in detention camps. I was also requested to talk to key persons of the community and to traditional leaders on the island.

The first public meeting, held in Denpasar, was for me quite embarrassing. Not having spoken the official Indonesian language for a long time, I was unable to make a speech in public in my own language. I spoke in Dutch, translated, phase by phase, by the Assistant-Resident, Mr Major Polak. It was not a bad choice because he was one of the few Dutch civil servants who was trusted by many young Indonesians.

By the second rally, held in Gianyar, I had picked up my Indonesian again and spoke quite fluently. About twice a week, rallies were held in the other cities, sometimes in community halls, other times in fully packed large movie theatre buildings. I had no complaint of too little interest from the public. For me, the visits to the prisons and detention camps were more interesting. There I had the opportunity to discuss the political problems more in depth with my former schoolmates. The discussions with the traditional leaders of the community in the villages did not reveal much to me. They respected me as the son of my father and they were generally of the opinion that a return to the old system, which they were familiar with, was the best for Bali. Strikingly their interest was Bali-oriented while political detainees were eager to discuss the future Indonesia.

I cautiously avoided the controversial issue of a centralized Indonesia, as demanded by the Republicans, or a federation of autonomous Indonesian States, as advocated by the Dutch Government. The Republicans regarded this as a ploy for a divide-and-conquer policy. I thought it better to state that this should be decided later by the various groups after we had gained our independence.

Before the audiences I remained consistent in my recommendation to fight for independence by peaceful means, by campaigning for the political rights of the Indonesian people, thereby seeking the help of powerful nations like the USA, Britain, France and the Soviet Union, because decolonization was in the air all over the world.

On our first trip outside Denpasar we were provided with an armed escort of a couple of soldiers in a separate jeep, because there were reports of clashes everywhere with freedom fighters. I felt protected and honoured by this, but Astri, with her Dutch common-sense, reasoned that the soldiers were inviting danger because the guerrillas would be tempted to seize their weapons, which they badly needed. So we made all following trips without escort up to the most remote villages on the island. Astri was right, nobody ever did us any harm.

Once, in Klungkung, as we were walking to our guest-house at dusk in the afternoon among the crowd on the street, after an hour-long speech and answering questions from the audience in a fully packed movie theatre building, I felt a slight slap on my shoulder. A man jumped from his bicycle, stopped at my side and pressed a roll of paper into my hand. Everything went so fast, and I was so astonished, that I did not see the man's face in the half-dark. Before I could ask anything, he sprang on his bicycle and raced away, zigzag-ging between the crowd out of sight. I thought: "It might be a message", but since it was too dark to see, I put it in my pocket. Arriving at the guest-house I curiously opened the roll. It contained a neatly handwritten letter in Indonesian, saying:

"My dear friend, I fully approve of what you are doing. Please carry on with your mission. I will not follow your steps, because I have <u>vowed</u> that I will con-tinue our armed struggle until my last drop of blood! Let us fight together, each in his own way. We remain brothers. Destroy this piece of paper, Ng. Rai".

I read the letter three times, translated it for Astri, and lit the paper above the kerosene lamp, stunned and filled with sadness. I knew that my friend would perish. His captured fellow fighters had told me how hard their lives were in the field. Out-gunned and out-manned, they were always on the run, they had never enough food, and were suffering from malaria and other diseases. They had often no medicines at all. Later I found out that he died with ninety-five of his guerrillas in an ambush in November, one month after we left Bali.

Nevertheless, his message reassured me that the he and his group believed in my sincerity and did not regard me as a traitor. It meant that we could go everywhere safely. But still, I had to be careful with my words. The content of my talks did not meet the expectations of the hardliners among the Government officials. For example, I never condemned the armed struggle for political independence, politically I sounded strictly neutral and I literally con-formed to my terms of reference: to try to win the hearts of the nationalists for a peaceful settlement. My only hope was that, at the highest political level, set-tlement would soon be reached, before my friend perished in battle.

It was obvious to everyone that our sympathies were on the side of the free-dom fighters. Army Intelligence Officers mistrusted us and their agents moni-tored our contacts and movements carefully. From our public performances they could not find reason to restrict our freedom. The enthusiasm and cor-diality of the local Dutch authorities waned quickly and turned into mere for-mal courtesy. Typically and entirely unforeseen by us at that time, an incident of a purely personal and private character turned their attitude into a silent and secret hostility, the far-reaching consequences of which we would experience only many years later.

CHAPTER 29

A Matter of Colours

Before starting our programme of rallies, talks and visits to villages, we took a few days off to be with our family in Karangasem.

My father came to fetch us from Denpasar, curious to see what kind of bride his son was bringing home. The encounter was emotional, sweet and happy. It must have been quite surprising for Astri not to see my father and me rushing into a wild embrace. As was my father's way of showing affection for a son, he only ruffled with his fingers through my hair. I saw tears welling up into his eyes. My lips trembled and not being able to speak, I bent my head to hide my moist eyes. For a few minutes we said nothing to each other until my father spoke. It struck me later that I had automatically adopted the traditional custom of not starting a conversation until asked by one who is older or higher in rank. I performed the traditional *sembah* gesture, clasping my palms together and holding them at the level of my chin during the conversation. From my father's face I could read satisfaction that tradition had not been lost.

I felt immediately that my father liked Astri and that he accepted her. On her side Astri seemed attracted by the old man's charming manners.

Father had come with two cars from Karangasem. The welcoming party consisted of my eldest brother Gedé, his mother Mekelé Trena, Manik, my only sister by the same mother, her husband, who to my surprise had become a priest, and many others from the Puri. Transport was still a difficult matter and of course when the opportunity was there, everyone wanted to be part of the event. Father had not succeeded in keeping two seats free for us and so there were about 20 of us cramped in two sedans making the long, hot and dusty journey to Karangasem. News and experiences were exchanged, and several times my father tried to speak a little Dutch to Astri. All my brothers still spoke Dutch fluently, which was a great help for Astri.

Along the road people stopped and bowed their heads deep down every time they saw our cars nearing and continued on their way only some time after we had passed. This had not been the case before the war. Gedé explained that it was a practice left over from the Japanese occupation.

A large crowd was gathered at the border of the Regency of Karangasem, where beautiful offerings were placed on temporary bamboo platforms and shrines, erected for the occasion in the middle of the road. We stopped and left our cars, and took part in a colourful welcoming ceremony in the blazing sun, conducted by a priest with prayers of gratitude to the gods for our safe homecoming. The trip further to the east was very hot and dusty. It was toward the end of the dry season and the roads had not been maintained well for the past five years during the occupation.

At our arrival in Karangasem we had to take part in another thanksgiving ceremony with colourful offerings on a bamboo platform on the street in front of the palace gates, with our Court Priest officiating. Astri got plenty of attention during these ceremonies. All my sisters scrambled to be as near as possible to her and to help her make the standard manual gestures for prayer, for receiving blessing, and how to drink the *tirta* (holy water) from the hollowed palm of the hand and to sprinkle it with flowers from the beaker over the forehead. Standing next to Astri before the priest I could not help laughing when I saw the disorder and merriment caused by my sisters. It must have been confusing for her that first time, to notice the absence of solemnity in what was supposed to be a serious and holy business.

At last the ceremony came to an end and we walked up the stairs and through the gates to our quarters, with everybody rushing behind us close to our heels. My homecoming with a blond Dutch girl was too sensational! Manik and all my elder sisters looked elated and flocked all the time around her, cheerfully commenting in Balinese. Ayu Djelantik was the only girl who could speak Dutch fluently. She explained everything to Astri. My brothers were happy to see me alive and well. For some time there had been rumours that I had been dropped from an allied aeroplane by parachute near Padangbaai, had been captured by the Japanese and executed as a spy!

We were housed in the old Chinese building near the pond opposite the Maskerdam and we celebrated our homecoming by showing the film of the *maligya* festivals which I had made ten years earlier.

Father insisted that our wedding ceremony should be a grandiose occasion. We preferred it to be small and only within the family, but for him this was out of question. It would be shameful for him not to invite the whole community and all the rajas and the notables of the island. The High Priest consulted the ancient horoscopes. By chance the appropriate days according to the horoscopes fell within the last week of our stay in Bali. We could therefore first return to Denpasar to start our work.

* * * * * *

Four weeks later, when my mission was completed, we came home to the Puri. Preparations for the wedding were in full swing. Hundreds of people came every day from various villages to pay tribute to my father, bringing with them, according to tradition, all kinds of produce from their lands, firewood, coconuts, and the like. Appropriate reception of these crowds had to be arranged, they had to have drinks and food. It was clearly Father's festival, in which we felt ourselves more or less as passive subjects. We did not mind at all, because we would not be able to organize anything ourselves. Besides we found everything most interesting and wanted to share Father's happiness.

One evening we had, as the introduction for the religious event, a *kekawin* session at the Maskerdam. A large number of priests and literary men were gathered. They sang strophes from the Mahabarata, relating to Arjuna's wedding night with Princess Draupadi. Strophe after strophe the recitals were translated into high Balinese language in a musical and dramatic fashion. On behalf of Astri somebody translated the most important passages in Indonesian and I tried to pass the meaning to Astri. She enjoyed the performance intensely.

Most touching was the session we had to attend the following day in the Gili, a pavilion in the centre of our large pond, held by a group of mullahs, clad in white gowns and turbans. The Moslem community of Karangasem did not want to be behind in asking God's blessings for our wedding. They held prayers and read strophes from the Koran considered appropriate for the occasion. At the end they all stood up and gave us the *salaam* of congratulations. We were very moved.

On another evening the Chinese community treated us to a surprise. They organized a large procession of lampions (Chinese lanterns) through the town, displaying a wide variety of beautiful, colourful creations in the shapes of fantastic dragons, fishes, horses, boats and aeroplanes, followed by singing schoolchildren and bursts of fire-crackers. It was all exciting and cheerful. The spontaneity of those gestures impressed us particularly and filled us with respect for the bond which still existed between Father and his people.

One day, however, I lost my temper when Father's secretary proudly informed me that he had sent off a messenger to Denpasar with a great number of invitations for the reception to be held the day after our wedding ceremony. They were addressed to the highest authorities in Bali, which included besides all the rajas, also the Resident, the Assistant Resident, all the *Controleurs*, police officers, the Military Commander and to our shock even the Head of the Military Intelligence Service. Not one Dutch official was forgotten. I was furious. I thought of all the political detainees in the camps and of what political consequences these may have in future. On the other hand, I realized that it would hurt my father very much if I argued with him about the matter. He would probably not understand my feelings. In any case it was already too late.

Luckily, Astri calmed me down, saying: "Well, it is your father's festival, not yours! Don't spoil it now. Let us take care that our sisters will have their share of the fun, and not as I have seen on the first party here, that they could only see the affair going on by stretching their necks from behind the walls".

* * * * * *

The elaborate wedding ceremony took place in our family temple, the *merajan*, which was profusely decorated for the occasion. As family tradition demanded, the function was conducted by two High Priests, one of the Siva and one of the Buddhist sect. Three of my sisters, who had had great fun that morning dressing Astri in the traditional Balinese wedding attire, now had the joyful privilege to assist her in performing the long series of rituals of the *manusayadnya*, a preliminary to the real wedding ceremony. The whole family attended the prayers in the temple. From several courtyards in the Puri sweet *gamelan* music filled the air, mixing with the ringing of the bells and the Sanskrit prayers recited by the priests, and the hectic sounds of a *wayang* puppet performance from one corner of the temple yard.

By noon the ceremonies came to an end. We shed our uncomfortable costumes and joined our brothers and sisters in a large communal kind of banquet. The pavilion in the centre of the large pond was reserved for the priests and the Brahmans. Seated on the floor in groups of four to five we ate from *dulangs*, on which the most delicious dishes were served on banana leaves.

At the same time all my father's other guests were served communal meals in the same way, in several courtyards in the Puri. For the common people, banquets were arranged in the outer courtyards and due to lack of space in the Puri, also in two neighbouring *banjars* (community buildings). All together there were according to Father's secretary about 5,000 guests. Father was radiant with happiness and pride. This was the first occasion for him to treat the community grandiosely and it was his way to show his affection and love for his people.

I was marvelling at Father's organization. The whole affair went smoothly, with everybody seeming to know exactly what to do, when and where.

In the evening my brothers surprised us with a *topeng* performance (masked dance drama) in which all of them took part, even those who had never had any classical Balinese dance lessons. Three professional dancers took up the key roles, by which they succeeded in keeping the story and choreography flowing smoothly. It was an evening of great fun and a lot of hilarity.

* * * * * *

The next day we were awakened very early in the morning by noises from outside, sounding like people chopping bamboo and digging in the ground.

"What is it?" Astri asked.

"I think they are putting up bamboo poles around the pond," I replied.
"What for?"

"I don't know. I think for decorations. Father is fond of them. We will have this gala lunch today with many high officials as guests".

Astri eagerly jumped out of bed, still in her pajamas. I followed her to the front porch. There were indeed a great number of people working along the edges of the large pond. Some of the poles were already set up and flying the red, white and blue Netherlands flags. We looked amazed at each other. Although I would have preferred to see beautiful Balinese decorations of bamboo and arcades of palm leaves, I found it quite understandable that Father wanted to pay honour to the Dutch officials. But Astri exclaimed:

"No, we can't do this. It is a mistake. Madé, can we stop them? We must remain neutral. What will your friends, the freedom fighters, think of us? No, we must stop them".

For a moment I hesitated, considering that it was certainly on Father's orders. Could I contradict him? I called the headman and asked:

"Who gave you the order to put up all those flags?"

"Your father, Sir!"

"Stop it, bring them down!"

"Why? What is wrong with them?" he asked.

"It is wrong. You must understand me. Times are different now. We don't want to do something which looks as if we want to return to colonial rule."

"What shall I do then?" he asked.

I could not think of a good answer, but Astri had an idea and said: "Let us put up banners of all the colours of the rainbow, red, yellow, green, orange, violet, and so on. It will be very decorative, like at any festival. You have to explain to your father. He will certainly not object".

I translated it to the headman. He nodded his head and grinned jovially, and said, "Yes, it is a good idea. But you have to consult your father first!"

I went to the Maskerdam where I found Father supervising the preparations for the gala lunch, figuring out the placing of his guests according to protocol at the long table which ran from one end of the huge verandah to the other. The table had become much longer than usual because Astri insisted that all our adult brothers and sisters should be at the party. When I explained the matter to him, he looked very concerned. He realized that he should honour his Dutch guests. On the other hand, he did not want to disappoint me. After a long silence he asked: "But what about Astri? Will she not be offended?"

"Not at all!" I said, "it is actually her own idea to replace the flags, because we should be strictly neutral politically. It is a private party".

Father smiled with a sigh of relief. He told the headman to go to the town, to buy cloth in all colours available, in order to make as many flags as were needed. I told my younger brothers about the change. Madé Karang saw its merit, went to the front gate of the palace, cut the ropes from the big main flag-poles and hid them away, to prevent the large official red, white and blue flags being hoisted.

Thus, when the high official guests arrived, the Netherlands colours were nowhere to be seen. Instead the most colourful banners were flying in the wind around the large pond and everywhere else. It was a great festive sight.

At the official gala lunch everything went smoothly and wholly in Father's style, pleasant, agreeable, with polite speeches to which Father now and then added some witty remarks. One of the main speakers was Gedé Agung, the young Raja of Gianyar, an old school friend of mine. He toasted us with a glass of champagne, congratulating Astri and me, and mentioning our bond as symbolic of the eternal bond between the Dutch and the Balinese people. He was at that time a staunch supporter of Van Mook's concept of a Federation of Indonesian States, and later became the Prime Minister of the State of East Indonesia, of which Cokorda Sukawati, his father-in-law was the first President. He was a strong opponent of the freedom fighters in Bali. This made him unpopular among the Balinese young revolutionary generation.

As expected, Astri drew special attention from the Dutch officials. From their conversation and looks I could easily pick out the progressive staff from the diehards who still adhered to the pre-war concepts of Dutch Indonesian relations. This distinction escaped Astri. She was not accustomed to diplomacy and, straightforward by nature, she expressed her opinions freely. Her ideas did not always meet with the approval of the conservatives among them. The Head of the Army Intelligence Service, especially, took sharp notice of her innocent remarks.

My brothers and sisters enjoyed the party very much. For most of the girls it was the first time that they had had the opportunity to sit at an official dining table with European guests. My brothers had great fun instructing them how to handle a knife and fork and to eat with their mouths closed. After lunch we all enjoyed a *legong* dance performance in the palace grounds.

Late in the afternoon, when all the guests had left, my father came to me and took me to his bedroom. He looked distressed and I was afraid that he was ill. When we were alone, he talked softly to me: "Madé, I was summoned by the Resident and the Military Commander before they left. They asked me why I had not raised the flags of the Netherlands at the gate in their honour."

"And what was your answer?" I asked.

"Well, actually I had not been aware of this neglect myself. What a shame! I had failed to check. I made my excuses of course and had the responsible watchman called before us for an explanation".

"And what did the man say?" I was curious.

"He was very nervous," Father said, "and told us that a few minutes before the expected arrival of the guests he wanted to hoist the flags, but saw to his shock that the ropes were missing. While he was searching for them the guests arrived. So we assumed that there had been an act of sabotage, perhaps by one or other agent of the freedom fighters, who might be among our servants."

I hardly could suppress a smile coming up on my face and kept silent. Madé Karang's "act of sabotage" would never be disclosed to my father. We knew that our watchman had been informed and that he had been acting his role in the play perfectly well. Father asked me if something had to be done to prevent further acts of sabotage in our Puri by agents of the *Pemudas*. I assured him that it was unnecessary, that the freedom fighters still respected him and that they would not do him any harm.

* * * * * *

Our departure from Bali the next week was totally uneventful, completely different from the spectacular reception at our arrival six weeks before. There was not one single Dutch official to see us off at the airport. A large number of our family came with us, and Father could not hide his emotion when he ruffled through my hair and gave Astri a kiss on her forehead.

On the four-day trip to Holland we had to go through moments of anxiety only once, when our plane was caught in a terrible thunderstorm over Greece. Arriving back in Holland at that time was more of a homecoming for me than when we had arrived in Bali.

We left the whole affair behind us as if it had been a lovely but hectic dream.

The Plates

Plate I: The author's great uncle, I Gusti Gedé Djelantik, *Stedehouder* of Karangasem from 1896, with the author's father, I Gusti Bagus Djelantik, who succeeded him in 1908.

Plate II: The author's father, I Gusti Bagus Djelantik, in ceremonial dress.

Plate III: Anak Agung Madé Djelantik Brayawangsa, second son of the Raja of Lombok. In exile, in Bogor, probably c. 1920.

Plate IV: Photograph to commemorate the author's 210th day (1st *odalan*) after birth. He is sitting on the lap of the Pedanda Gedé Madé Punia, while his half-brother Ketut (on left) sits on the lap of his grandmother.

Plate V: The author (right) at the age of three, with his elder brother, Gedé (centre) and half-brother Ketut (on left). The children are all wearing elaborate gold headdresses, and ceremonial clothes.

Plate VI: A. A. Madé Djelantik Brayawangsa.

Plate VII: The house in the Puri of Karangasem allotted to the author's mother, Mekelé Selaga. The author was born here in 1919.

Plate VIII: The author's father with three of his wives from the nobility. This formal portrait was taken in Karangasem, some time in the 1920s.

Plate IX: A 1922 photograph taken in front of the Chinese Pavilion at Karangasem. The author's father is surrounded by all his children at that time. The author is held by his Nanny (back row, far right), while his elder brother, Gedé, is fourth from left in the front row.

Plate X: From left to right: Gedé, their father, and the author in the official Dutch gala dress. Kayumas, Denpasar, 1925.

Plate XI: The author and his brother (in the gala dress their father insisted they wear) on the top step. They were photographed in 1926 with other family members at the first *odalan* of A. A. Gedé Karang (first row).

Plate XII: Family gathering, photographed in 1928. The author is on right (in tie, shirt and sarong), while Gedé and their father stand on the left, at back.

Plate XIII: Formal portrait of the family, 1928.

Plate XIV: School years in Malang, 1931. Future freedom fighter, Ngurah Rai, is on the left; the author and Gedé are on the back step in the centre.

Plate XV: Members of the "Bali Dharma Laksana" (Balinese Cultural Society) formed at the M. U. L. O. school in Malang, with their flag. Sitting far left: the author; second from right: Gedé.

Plate XVI: Formal portrait of the author, taken in July 1938, just before he left for University in Holland.

Plate XVII: The author's extended family, 1952, photographed at Gedé's house in Karangasem. Astri, his Dutch wife, is sitting on the wall on left.

Plate XVIII: The author and Astri, wedding day, 31 May 1946.

Plate XIX: Karangasem, 1952. The author with his first two children, Trisna (left) and Surya. Surya was not happy to don ceremonial dress for this photograph!

Plate XX: The author and hospital staff at the new hospital he built in Kotamobagu, North Celebes, 1953.

Plate XXI: With Dr Schlesinger, consulting physician from Vienna for President Sukarno, at the Bonnet Museum "Ratna Warta" in Ubud. Standing far left: Astri; standing in front: the Cokorda of Ubud, between Widur (author's son) and Madelief (author's third daughter); and second from right: Surya (author's second daughter).

Plate XXII: The eruption of Gunung Agung, 1963. The author took this photograph and captured the hot gas escaping from the fresh lava running down the north-east slopes towards Kubu and Tianyar.

Plate XXIII: The author, in Kut, Northern Iraq, March 1970. By this time, Dr Djelantik had taken up a position as Malariologist with the World Health Organization.

Plate XXIV: Dr Djelantik (right) with a member of his WHO staff, conducting fieldwork in Somalia, 1972.

Plate XXV: Disseminating fish in Somalia, 1972.

Plate XXVI: Fred Cristal (left) and the author taking a well-deserved rest in Somalia, 1972.

Plate XXVII: Astri with Gedé in Puri Gedé, Karangasem, 1992.

Plate XXVIII: Sita's six-month age ceremony at temple in Karangasem Puri, 1992. Foreground, left to right: Astri, Marika (Widur's wife), Sita, Widur and the High Priest.

Plate XXIX: The author receiving an award for his activities in the field of arts and culture, from Professor Wardiman (the Minister of Education and Culture) June 1993.

Plate XXX: With Suteja Neka, owner of Neka's Museum of Art, Ubud, who received the same award at the Ministry of Education and Culture, Jakarta, June 1993.

Plate XXXI: Dr Djelantik and his wife, 1995.

Plate XXXII: Dr Djelantik's daughter, Trisna, at her graduation ceremony, 1992.

Plate XXXIII: Dr Djelantik's son Widur, 1994.

Plate XXXIV: Trisna dancing in the temple courtyard, 1995.

Plate XXXV: Golden Wedding family reunion in the garden behind the mountain house in Kintamani, August 1995.

BOOK IV

A Doctor in Indonesia

Exile

After World War II, Astri and I settled into an idyllic life in Deventer. We found a small apartment close to the hospital and I was stimulated beyond belief with my medical training there. On 8 September 1947 our first baby was born. We named her Bulan Trisna after my half sister (Bulan means Moon, and Trisna means "faithful"), because it sounded very sweet in our ears. Like any young parents we revelled in our happiness with our first child. She grew very slowly, but seemed from a very early stage to have an abnormally quick under-standing of the world around her. However, she seemed to have no desire to stand up, and when there was no improvement by the time she was 18 months old, we were really worried. Eventually, a pediatrician told us not to worry—Trisna was simply too interested in intellectual matters to concentrate on phys-ical ones. Astri found this a reasonable explanation, but I remained sceptical.

After my return from Bali, I lost all interest in politics, even though great political developments were taking place in Indonesia. I was too much absorbed by my professional training and followed the news from Indonesia only haphazardly. I knew that there had been many negotiations between the Netherlands Government and the Republicans, often with the help of other nations like England and the U. S. A. Many times arrangements had been made for a ceasefire, but the guerrilla war continued. The Dutch Government pushed ahead with creating separate States in the Archipelago, to counter the Indonesian Republic, which showed expansionist tendencies. Successively the states of Borneo, West Java, East Indonesia, North Sumatra, and eleven others came into being. Bali belonged to East Indonesia, with Makassar (since 1960 renamed Ujung Pandang) in South Celebes as its capital.

In the fall of 1948, my tutors found that after two and a half years' training I had acquired enough knowledge and skills to be able to stand on my own feet in the faraway tropics. There were advertisements in the papers from the Ministry of Overseas Territories, asking for doctors to be sent to Indonesia on "short contract" assignments of two years. I went to The Hague to register myself and was immediately accepted.

Under the terms of the "short contract" I had to go alone first. Astri and Trisna were to follow three months later. This provision was made in general to ensure that the incumbent had already found a house for his family at his duty station and had adapted himself to local circumstances. I was given the standard outfit for civil servants to be sent out to the tropics: four long-sleeved khaki safari suits, khaki underwear, two pairs of soldier's boots, socks, a green raincoat and a khaki helmet. In addition there was a khaki mosquito net, a box with emergency medicines, anti-malarials and insect repellents. I found it marvellous, and somehow I got a proud feeling of being part of a great and efficient organization. Having assured myself that Astri would be able to manage on her own for the coming three months, I left for Indonesia early in September 1948.

My position was that of a Netherlands civil servant, seconded by the Dutch Government to the Ministry of Health of the "United States of Indonesia" in Jakarta. I applied for a position in Bali, but the Ministry of Health felt I would be better placed in Namlea on the island of Buru. I had never heard of the place before and consulted the map of Indonesia which hung on the wall at the Minister's office. It was indeed far away, near New Guinea, twice as far from Bali as Bali from Jakarta. I accepted.

I flew by military plane to Ambon, and stopped over in Makassar for one night in order to report to the Minister of Health of East Indonesia. To my great surprise, that evening I received a visit from Gedé Agung, previously Raja of Gianyar, now Prime Minister of East Indonesia. We had known each other since the early 1930s during our school years in Malang, East Java, and the last time I had seen him was when he had made an emotional speech at our wedding reception in Karangasem two years ago. Our meeting was very cordial, but it struck me how much his political career had changed him from a cheerful jolly person into a very cautious diplomat. It made me feel uncomfortable.

After the usual formalities, he told me that I had not received a medical position in Bali for "political" reasons. "We considered it not safe for you to be placed in Bali," he said.

"Why?" I was astonished.

"Please, don't ask too many questions. The political situation in Bali is very tense. The *Pemudas* are very active supporting the Republic, they are planning something".

It was clear to me that because of the flag incident I was an unwanted person in Bali. I did not enter into arguments, as it would be of no help. Moreover, lured by the unknown, I was already determined to go to Namlea in Buru, Beb Vuyck's "Last House of The World".

CHAPTER 31

Suffering, Life and Death in Namela

After my first successes with the treatment of patients, the attendance at my policlinic in Namlea grew fast. The District Officer, a very young Dutchman, fresh from the Indology Faculty of Leiden, was very pleased to see progress. He succeeded in getting funds for me from the Health Ministry to build three hospital wards, one for males, one for females and one for children, and a small operating room for surgery. He was wise enough to leave the planning of the construction of the buildings to me and not to interfere in technical matters. I was happy to have the freedom of pioneering and learned a lot by experience. The building of the small hospital took less than two months.

Because of a lack of electricity we had to use kerosene lanterns and pressure lamps. Since the hospital was built on high ground where no well could be dug, water had to be brought twice daily from a well down in the village by *strapans*, the convicts from the local prison. I also had a free hand in training new nursing personnel as needed. It was marvellous to see how these youngsters, having had very poor schooling before, acquired new knowledge and skills so quickly.

By the time Astri arrived in Namlea, I had already performed my first surgery, an old man, who had been immobile for more than a year because of an enormous hernia. While I examined the patient, the village medicine man, who came with him, explained to me that the noises which we could clearly hear coming from the swollen scrotum, were the utterings of an evil spirit. My first intention was to tell him a bit about anatomy and peristaltics, but then I thought it better to follow his thinking and I said:

"You are right, the spirit is angry. He wants to be free. If I can help him out of there, he will no longer bother your friend".

The man looked amazed at me, perhaps wondering how I could understand the oracle so quickly, while he was pondering on the rhythm and intonations of the sounds. "I think I can do it!" I said. "You can stay and watch the operation from the outside through the window".

The operation was easy and went well. The man recovered soon and after fourteen days he was able to do his work. The medicine man was so impressed that he became a good propagandist for modern medicine.

Work became more busy every day and was not without adventure. One night I was called out for a delivery some way from the village. With my midwifery kit on the back of my bicycle and holding a small hurricane lamp in one hand, I rode over a grassy dirt path, enjoying the cool night air. The sky was clear and beautiful and the sight of the bright stars above my head evoked in me Marsman's famous poem. While I was happily humming: "Ik, die het stuifmeel der planeten fangs de melkweg blies" ("I, who blew the planets' pollen along the milky way") my bicycle suddenly bumped in the air, nearly throwing my lamp out of my hand. By stopping on both my legs I prevented a nasty fall. Making a few steps back to see what the obstacle was, I saw to my horror a huge python lying across the path. I sped away as fast as I could.

The delivery took place in a primitive thatched hut on a shaky bamboo structure, from under which I first had to chase away three goats and a few chickens. Then followed the routine of preparing a pail of boiled water, sterilizing instruments, and giving the necessary instructions to the family. The greatest difficulty was to keep out the onlookers, who came from everywhere in great numbers. The baby came without trouble. On the way back in the morning I made a detour along the coast to avoid another encounter with the python.

* * * * * *

A doctor, working in those remote places, was not supposed to stick to his duty station all the time. He was expected to visit the hinterland also, where, as in the coastal areas, malaria, yaws and other tropical diseases were rampant. Roads did not exist. All travel was to be done on foot, or along the coast in small boats, and over the rivers on rafts when possible. It happened more than once that a village which was shown on the map, appeared to be abandoned and was overgrown by bush vegetation. The population had either left the place (usually because of lack of food), or had been wiped out by malaria. An overcrowded graveyard was often the only indication of this.

I got used to walking through the jungle, covering about ten miles a day, thriving only on rice and dried fish, while the porters who carried the medicines, tents and household equipment, preferred to eat only sago cakes, made from the marrow of the sago palm, a very inadequate diet.

On one of these trips we came through an abandoned hamlet consisting of about twenty thatched huts standing in two rows. From the fair condition of the huts it was obvious that the hamlet had been abandoned very recently. Reaching the end of the lane my eye was struck by a strange black heap covered with leaves, against the side of one of the huts. My curiosity was aroused because I saw movement under one of the big leaves, or so I imagined. I walked up to the hut, lifted one of the leaves and instantly reeled back in horror, when a thick swarm of black flies flew up from the heap. The sight of what came to light was horrifying: the naked emaciated body of a girl, wholly covered with open Framboesia (yaws) ulcers, upon which the flies had been feasting. Most terrifying of all, the girl was still alive! Stirred by the noise of my footsteps she gave a very faint sound like crying, and moved her frail ulcerous arm towards a tin plate placed near her head. On it was a filthy piece of sago cake. She could not reach the plate. Left with her was also a rusty tin with some water. It was full of ants! I shuddered and was so shocked that for a few moments I was unable to move my legs. When I turned round, I saw my assistant and the porters standing there, gazing with horrified eyes at the skinless ulcerated body. When I asked them to bring the cases with medicines and bandages, they stood as petrified and I had to repeat my request twice before they moved.

I put up my camping bed, spread a rubber sheet over it and with the help of the nurse lifted the girl on the bed. Our clothes got spoiled with blood and pus and the stench was indescribable. For more than one hour we worked, cleaning and dressing the wounds. Giving an intravenous injection with Salvarsan was easy since the veins were exposed by ulceration of the flesh. When all was over, I had spent almost all of my Rivanol solution, and half of my supply of bandages. I found myself faced with the problem, what to do next? We could not leave the girl alone in the abandoned village. There was no point continuing our safari, carrying the patient with us all the way through the thick jungle. I decided to return to Namlea, which fortunately was only two days away. The safari could be repeated as soon as circumstances allowed.

Using my campbed as a stretcher, with my mosquito net over it to keep the flies away, we marched wearily back through the same villages that we had just visited. At every stop we cleaned the wounds, and distributed more malaria pills to the population. Salvarsan injections were given again to Framboesia patients who came to see us.

With good food and patient care in our new hospital the girl's wounds healed marvellously. Unfortunately, since the areas affected were extensive, ugly scars developed later. Some of them caused contractures, impairing her movements considerably for the rest of her life.

* * * * * *

Christian missionaries had been active in the Malukus for more than three centuries. They founded schools on the main islands, especially on Ambon. Therefore the Ambonese were more advanced than the population of the surrounding islands, one of which was Buru. Here the indigenous population, who were Alifurus, had not been christened and did not have any schooling. In some coastal villages Mohammedan traders had settled and had converted a few into Moslems. In these regions the Ambonese functioned as administrators, teachers and managers and became the notables of the community.

One Sunday morning we were invited for lunch with the Ambonese manager of an estate on the outskirts of Namlea. His house was like ours, made of local material, small and primitive, but impeccably clean. Furniture and everything in the house breathed the quiet discipline and soberness of the Christian church. My male nurse Pelu, was also invited. He had come with our hosts from the church and they were discussing the sermon of the speaker of that morning who was also the principal teacher of the school.

We were enjoying the excellent meal, which our hostess had been working hard on the day before. She was explaining to Astri the peculiarities of the Ambonese cuisine and all of us were listening with great interest. Nobody had noticed that her dog had slipped inside the room and hidden himself under the dining table. At one moment my nurse, Pelu, felt the dog moving against his leg. Being a regular visitor of the house, he knew the dog very well. He reached under the table with his hand to caress its head, but a menacing growl made him pull back his hand in surprise. Shifting his chair he looked under the table and called in astonishment:

"Hey, what's that? Hush, hush, Tommy, give it here! Tommy, Tommy, leave it, give it here!"

Tommy growled much louder. We looked amazed at each other. There must be something strange happening! I kneeled down to have a look under the table. I could not believe my eyes! Tommy held between his teeth the decapitated head of a newborn baby! Pelu grabbed the dog by his neck and pulled him loudly growling and sputtering from under the table. Tommy let loose his horrible treasure and while Pelu held him fast, I took the grisly, bloody, little head out of the dark. The ladies cried in anguish and turned their heads. Pelu threw a small table cloth at me in which I swiftly wrapped the head and brought it out of reach of the dog. The scene was so gruesome and shocking, that we were not able to continue our meal. When Pelu released the dog, it sniffed the air and ran out of the house. Pelu and I followed him. He ran over the field to a spot where people used to throw away garbage and started to dig in the refuse. We found there the body of the baby with its umbilical cord and placenta still attached. The head had apparently been severed with a sharp knife by the mother who did not want the child.

When we returned home, Pelu and his friend took care that the body had a normal burial and reported the case to the police. People told us later that homicide of this kind quite often occurred in Namlea, but never before had a dog presented a lunch party with a severed baby's head.

* * * * * *

Another chilling experience befell me on one of our boat trips. Early in the morning we left Leksula on the South coast and sailed westwards to reach the last village on our schedule. Somehow I had an uneasy feeling. Perhaps it was because the boatmen looked tired and worn out after nine days of rowing. Perhaps I had sensed their reluctance to take up their oars for the seven-hour journey lying ahead. At the beginning we were lucky to have the right wind blowing and the men regained their spirits. Relaxed they started to chew on their sago cakes. When after three hours the wind stopped they were still in a good mood. They started to sing and rowed on the rhythm of their songs with powerful strokes. An hour later we turned around a rocky cape into a beautiful bay, lined by thick tropical forest with tall trees, casting a deep shadow over the narrow beach. A sailing boat, much bigger than our canoes, lay on the beach. The odd thing was that it lay halfway on its side, and there were no sails and no ropes. My men became curious and so was I.

They asked if they could have a look. I nodded. We went ashore and two of the men climbed up on to the ship, but jumped immediately back on the sand and ran away quickly shouting: "Mati, mati, mati!" ("Dead, dead, dead!") At first I was stunned, but driven by curiosity I climbed up, followed by the rest of my men. My heart stood still at what I saw: sprawled on the bottom of the boat lay a Chinese man, dead, with the shaft of an arrow sticking out of his chest. My men, stricken with fear, fled in panic. I was overcome with an awful feeling of helplessness. I stood as if nailed to the ship, trying to make up my mind what to do next, but Lamusa, my houseboy, shouted at me: "Doc, please come, quick, the men are leaving us here alone!" Indeed, I saw some of them already climbing into our canoes. Lamusa ran down shouting: "Stop! Stop!"

He was just in time to get hold of one of the boats before it took off to the sea. I was furious, but I felt helplessness and panic at the same time, and my knees were trembling. Imagine if they had left us there alone! It was clear that we could not do anything or save anything. The ship was completely empty. I thought that at least we could dig a grave and bury the poor man. I shouted at Lamusa: "Bring all of them here, let us bury the dead man first!" But Lamusa did not share my humane feelings.

"Please, Doc, come here, quick. I can't hold them any longer. Let us leave this place as fast as possible. Our men are very scared. They will not help us to dig and when we are busy digging they surely will leave us alone here".

Although I did not like the situation, I felt that there was no way out, the men were utterly restless. To save my face I climbed as quietly as possible into my boat. I was hardly seated when the men, who had been waiting impatiently, yelled out, and with swift powerful strokes they rowed us out of the bay.

The next village was still two hours away. For a long time I was furious for not having been able to bury the dead man. Perhaps more so because of my feeling of losing command over my men. When I had calmed down at last, I asked Lamusa why the men were so afraid of a dead body. It was apparently a stupid question. Lamusa smiled. He came nearer to sit next to me.

"Doc," he started, "last night people in Leksula told me stories of gangs armed with arrows and spears, roaming about in certain parts of the south coast, robbing lonely merchants and fishermen, and they are hiding in the thick jungle. The Chinese had obviously been robbed by such a gang. You have seen that they had taken away everything, even the sails and ropes. Our men were scared to death. They thought the gang might still be hiding nearby in the bush. So it was not the dead Chinese they were afraid of".

It dawned on me that probably these stories had caused the reluctance I sensed among the crew that morning.

CHAPTER 32

A Blessed Dog

The Government Doctor's house in Namlea, the capital of Buru Island, had the reputation of being one of the best buildings in the village. At least it had a sturdy foundation which could withstand the recurring inundations by sea water. This occurred often at high tide when strong winds from the south raged over the Bay of Namlea and swept the water in waves over the coastal road in front of the house and down into the garden. After the water had receded, the approximately half an acre of low ground around the house would remain submerged for a few days. When it dried an awful nauseating smell of a mixture of salt and organic decomposition would emerge from under the ground through hundreds of holes made by ugly and menacing-looking crabs creeping everywhere.

The concrete floor of the house stood three feet above the garden grounds and was on the same level as the sandy coastal road from where an elevated gravel path led to the three cemented steps of the open front porch. The walls of the house were made of split sago branches fixed to each other by the sharpened veins of its leaves and held in place by wooden frames which went along the eaves at the upper end and close along the floor below. Wooden laths fixed horizontally at various heights served as enforcements for the frail structure. Similar walls also formed the partitions between the porch and the two bedrooms. They did not last long because the material attracted woodworms and white ants. The roof was thatched with palm fronds which were laid too sparsely upon each other, so that it did not give sufficient protection against the tropical rains. During rains of any significance we had to spread our raincoats over our beds in order to remain dry.

On that memorable day in September 1948, when I arrived in Namlea for the first time, I was not in the least shocked by the miserable state of the house which was assigned to me as my residence. I did not pay much attention to its very poor condition. Having experienced so many kinds of deprivation and shortages during the German occupation in Holland and during the post-war period, I was used to discomfort, and I neither realized nor felt the urgency of doing something about it. My priorities were then more decided by my professional responsibilities than by personal considerations or the need to prepare a decent home for my wife and little daughter who would be coming from Holland in a few weeks time. There was on my part actually a gross ignorance concerning the requirements for setting up a home for a young Dutch housewife, in which she could find not only comfort and happiness but also security and privacy in an alien and sometimes hostile environment.

Three months after my arrival on Namlea, it was organized that Astri and Trisna would board the plane from Holland to Jakarta and from there they would travel by boat to Ambon where I was to meet them. A Higgins motorboat, a leftover from World War II, was the only means of transport between Ambon and Namlea. It maintained a more or less regular cruising schedule, running from Ambon first to the northern islands Buru, Saparua and Halmaheira, then back to Ambon and further to Banda and the Kei islands, returning to Ambon for a short period for checking and repairs. It came to Namlea about once in a month, while at occasional intervals a second Higgins boat was available for special visits by Government officials. The boat used to arrive in Namlea in the afternoon and return to Ambon early the next morning. One had only one night for answering letters received that afternoon, or for finalizing official reports, if one did not wish to wait for another month.

The boat, measuring only 12 by 3 metres, had a strong motor and a body entirely made of thick steel, giving an impression of indestructibility. There was no cabin, so passengers and goods were cramped together on the flat steel deck, protected by a low canvas roof against sun and rains. The passage between Namlea and Ambon was usually quite rough because of the strong currents running south to north between the islands. I had to undertake the crossing to Ambon in mid-November in order to be there to meet Astri and little Trisna who were to arrive there in December. That crossing was unforgettably rough. The boat jumped and fell down on the high seas so wildly that for many a moment I found myself praying, fearful that Astri and little Trisna coming fresh from Holland could well be entirely left on their own in Ambon. At one time the pilot of the Higgins was able to avoid being overturned by manoeuvring the vessel quickly in a circle before a 6 metre-high wave. The following moment the boat was taken high up in the air and smashed down in a deep valley of turbulent water. Despite it being turned around over 180 degrees the pilot succeeded in keeping it on the right angle ahead of the waves, which every time frighteningly lifted us up from behind. In the end we found ourselves suddenly on smooth waters and when we reached Ambon's harbour we were thoroughly soaked but we were most grateful for having arrived safely.

The two weeks that I spent in Ambon waiting for Astri and Trisna to arrive by plane proved to be very useful, for I found plenty of work in the main hospital. I learned a great deal from my colleagues who had had many years' experience of tropical diseases, and from the nursing staff, particularly concerning the ways to deal with the work in circumstances where, due to scarcity of medicines and material and the low educational level of the community, a doctor had to be inventive and commonsensical in order to achieve the best possible results. I also had plenty of opportunities to discuss with my superintendent the problems and experiences I had during the three months in Namlea. Dr Siregar was of Batak origin and was a great idealist, who had served for many years as a medical officer in remote places in Borneo. I was most impressed by his devotion to his profession.

When at last Astri and Trisna arrived safely in Ambon my joy was indescribable. That day a miracle was bestowed upon us: at the moment we entered our hotel Trisna stood on her feet and started to walk! She made her first steps without falling or stumbling, showing a remarkable equilibrium and coordination of movement. (She was to become a famous dancer later.)

The Chief Medical Officer of Ambon managed to arrange a special motor boat for our journey to Namlea. This time the crossing was extraordinarily smooth. When we arrived in Namlea the tide was exceptionally low, so that the boat could not be aligned to the pier. It had to land with its bow in the sand at some distance from the landing bridge. The passengers had to wade through the shallow waters or to be carried by porters on their backs. We saw our luggage and cases being carried by porters up the dry shore sands and were not in the least aware of what was going to happen later on.

When we arrived at our house I saw to my great relief that the garden had not been flooded during the month. It looked even quite nice because of the abundant mass of pink flowers on its higher borders. This plant, (botanically known as *Lochnera Rosea (L.) Rebb.*) was the only flowering plant which was able to survive on that salty piece of land.

We tried to arrange ourselves as comfortably as possible and it was only then that I discovered that I had not thought of ordering a nice cot for our little girl. However Astri's practical mind did not flounder for one moment. She found that a small table when put upside down with a mosquito net over its legs would suffice for the time being, until we would find a carpenter to make a proper child's cot. With an assured competence gained during her nursing career, she assessed the various other inconveniences of the house and figured out in a few minutes what improvements had to be carried out in the immediate future. Her happiness at the reunion of the family prevailed, and above all she was, even more than myself, imbued with that missionary ideal of bringing the blessings of modern medicine to the destitute population of the island.

Even the great disaster which befell us the next morning when our goods were delivered to our house did not disturb her too much, nor could it depress her sturdy mind. What had happened?

The previous day the porters were too lazy to carry the heavy cases from the shore over the 300-metres stretch of sand to our premises, and they had selected only the lighter trunks and suitcases which we needed immediately. During the night most of the remaining cases and wooden boxes were flooded by the incoming tide. In the early morning the porters chose to wait until the water had withdrawn low enough for them not to wet their feet when picking up those crates which contained our new kitchenware, plates, bowls, cups and other earthenware, our sewing machine, a bicycle, a children's carriage and other useful household items. When we opened the crates and laid the contents out, the thoroughly soaked assemblage was a dishearteningly sad sight. The wet cartons and papers, in which the earthenware had been neatly packed, looked an awful discoloured mess through which we saw many broken pieces of porcelain and glass sticking out. When we had everything unpacked and laid out in the open, it appeared that those items of metal or with metal parts, looked the most distressing. Worst of all was our old sewing machine, which Astri had inherited from her mother, and to which she was emotionally very much attached, since it had been used in the past by her grandmother. That most important part of our new household had been completely immersed in sea water for more than 12 hours. When uncovered from its wrappings it showed an awful body of red rust, with thick red-brownish fluid dripping down from all sides. The newly purchased Raleigh bicycle was luckily only affected in its wheels. Fortunately the children's carriage had not been in contact with sea water, having apparently been folded up in the upper parts of the crate.

The only person with some technical skill was the Ambonese chauffeur of the Dutch H. P .B. (Hoofd Plaatselijk Bestuur or Chief of Local Government) who had the only motorcar on the island, a wartime Willy's Jeep. He came to our rescue and proved to be an invaluable handyman and mechanic. After drying and cleaning the most visible rust from the sewing machine he took the largest of our oval pails (used as a bathtub for Trisna), put the machine in it and poured a jerrycan of kerosene over it until it was completely submerged. When he came back the next morning the rusted screws had become moveable and it was now possible for him to take the whole machine apart. He patiently cleaned all its parts, one by one, with kerosene and glass-paper. Towards the evening he had our sewing machine already reassembled, greased, and, with a gleaming smile, he handed an even brighter, gleaming machine to Astri who was more than delighted. And it functioned wonderfully well!

Trisna continued to use her legs efficiently and we used the carriage only for the longer walks over the dusty roads along the beach to the village. A primitive sort of a baby cot was produced by a local carpenter and our house assumed gradually a more homely appearance. Still the necessary major improvements could not be carried out before the start of the rainy season, due to some bureaucratic regulations, and we had to continue spreading our raincoats over the beds every time it rained for a long time.

On an elevated part of our garden, in front of the house a few yards from the sandy road, there was a *waru* tree which provided some shade. Here we built a sandbox for our little girl where she used to play in the early morning after breakfast before the sun became too hot. Astri could then attend to household matters while I was already off to the Hospital.

One morning while Trisna was playing in the sandbox, Astri, busy cleaning in the large bedroom, was suddenly startled by a penetrating and prolonged shriek. It came from outside in front of the house and sounded like a dog in anguish. Running out of the room and coming out on the front porch she was shocked by what she saw: our neighbour's black dog was screaming and desperately struggling in the mouth of a huge crocodile, a few yards from the sandbox where little Trisna was quietly watching, as if she was surprised at what was happening. In an instant Astri had her in her arms and had run back to the house. Standing on the porch she could observe the crocodile retreating quietly over the sandy road to the beach with the now still feebly screeching dog between his teeth. The next moment she clearly saw how the dog disappeared into the crocodile's mouth and how peacefully the crocodile disappeared into the sea, as if it were completely unconcerned by the shouts and noises made by the people who came running out of their houses aroused by the screams of the poor animal.

From the crocodile's imprints in the sand it was later found that from the point where it came out of the sea, it had crept in a straight line to the sandbox, and if there had not been a stray dog crossing its path, one can only with horror imagine what would have happened...

Among the crowd nobody seemed to dare discuss the miraculous event aloud. Only soft murmurings of *Takdir Allaah* (God's Providence) could be heard. As was still common in many primitive societies in those days, such miracles tended to enhance the respect and awe for the persons involved. I felt that after that event the population of Buru became more responsive to our modern ideas about health and disease. It was not so difficult any more to muster their co-operation and voluntary work when I later undertook to build a new hospital in Namlea, more suitable for the care and treatment of patients, than the temporary thatched structure which I had originally set up.

CHAPTER 33

Rats

On clear days the land on the opposite side of the Bay of Namlea could be seen from our house as a vibrating image of green and blue through the warm air above the tranquil and smooth sea. Since the beginning of my stay in Namlea the sight had always evoked a strange curiosity in my mind. I knew that somewhere on that shore the biggest river of the island of Buru, the Waingapu, was discharging its muddy water into the bay. The area of Waingapu was the notorious habitat of the disease Filariasis, which is caused by a nematode (worm-species) invading the lymph vessels of man. Its ultimate symptom is elephantiasis, the spectacular swelling of the lower parts of the body, which I knew only from pictures in textbooks on Tropical Medicine. I was excited by the thought of such an adventure, since I heard that no medical doctor had ever before entered the area any further than the coastal strip. Usually, the elephantiasis patients were brought by small sailing vessels to Namlea for treatment.

An opportunity to visit the area came when the local Raja of Waingapu came to Namlea for some urgent reason. He reported to the authorities that heavy rains had caused extensive floods in his area and that the Waingapu River had already changed its course for the third time that year. For our intended trip to that area there was no better guide than this Raja who also had some of his tribesmen with him. Few people from Namlea would venture to those shores, where hundreds of crocodiles lay in wait for their prey.

Travel by sea was full of risks because sudden rainstorms could play havoc with the frail sailing boats; overland travel was more hazardous, and could only be done on foot. Roads or regular footpaths did not exist and one had often to orientate oneself either by the sun, by river tributaries or by certain landmarks only known to the local population.

Buru was, in 1949, part of the autonomous State of East Indonesia. The Dutch Head of the Local Civilian Administration was delighted when he learned of my plans. No better propaganda for the benevolent Dutch-controlled government could be thought of than their medical doctor going from village to village to bring relief to the population from so much suffering.

After being assured that the Raja with two of his men would be our guides, we made preparations for our medical safari. The only male nurse I had could not go with me since I just had managed to build a small temporary hospital on the grass field behind the policlinic with thatch walls and roofing and some twenty discarded metal beds left by the Japanese soldiers after the war. In my absence he would have to take care of the in-patients, which had started to function with increasing numbers of patients attending. These could not be left to the minor auxiliaries whom we had given the most elementary of basic medical training. Fortunately my own houseboy, Lamusa, an immigrant from Buton in Southeast Sulawesi, who had been helping with the setting up of the Hospital, was eager to accompany me on the trip. He was of extraordinary intelligence, had great stamina and was of more use than any of the auxiliaries. Moreover, he could help me with the cooking and other household work.

We had to recruit about twenty porters, because we had to take everything with us: food, salt, medicine, instruments, camping material and so on. Food had to be limited to the most essential items, such as rice, dried fish and salt. For the porters we took sago cakes which they preferred as a staple food to rice. Sago is however most inadequate as food since it consists only of starch and does not contain any vitamins or protein. Thus we had to bring with us a large amount of multi-vitamins which had to be given to them, often by force. Since rice was not grown in Buru and had to be imported and was therefore often very scarce on the island, we welcomed their preference in one way. Vegetables and beverages also were not available. Of course, a large stock of medicines, medical equipment, bandages, and tablets to make water safe to drink were essential. Of the medicines more than half consisted of anti-malarials (at that time only quinine and atabrine) and Salversan for the treatment of yaws. One could safely assume that everyone was suffering from Framboesia (yaws) and that the percentage of the population harbouring malaria parasites in their blood was over 90 per cent. A bulky part of our luggage was our tents, camping beds and mosquito nets. The nets later appeared to be unnecessary, as I discovered that most of the porters were too lazy to put up their nets. They were used to mosquito bites and in any case were already infected with malaria parasites. It was a true expedition.

We were to cross the Waingapu valley on foot in a circle, starting from the northeastern side and would after a march of 14 days arrive at the shore on the southeastern side of the valley opposite Namlea and there we would embark in small sailing vessels to cross the bay on the way home. It was the first time that I had ever gone on a big safari through the wilderness. And a real jungle it was without doubt. For most of the time two of our porters had to go in front with big sharp *parangs*, long-bladed choppers, to hack a passage through the thick bush for our troupe. At the end of a day's exhausting march we would arrive at some "village" which was usually not more than a cluster of about 10 to 20, but sometimes as many as 40 huts made of sago palm leaves. While we prepared our bivouac and some food, putting up our tents and camping beds, the Raja would gather the people, urging them to come for medical treatment early the next morning. This was not always easy. There was still much superstition regarding disease and a doctor was a complete novelty. This time we were lucky to have their own Raja with us whose words were powerful enough to overcome their fears. On past safaris on this island, the population fled away into the jungle or onto the seas, so that we had to wait for one or more days and hope that some of them would have enough courage to come back. Even now the Raja had some difficulty in persuading his fold. He had to talk very patiently and elaborately about our intentions. Exercise in patience was of course also demanded from us. I could not speak Alifuru, the local dialect of the island, and I tried my best to put the people at ease by gesticulating in as friendly a way as possible.

On the whole we were quite successful that morning and achieved a nearly complete coverage of the diseased population, treating about 100 patients. The Raja was most happy. Actually, ignorance was still much on my side at the time. I silently congratulated myself with the achieved results, having treated more patients than the Raja had expected. However, I did not realize the very little impact which our great efforts actually had on the health of the population. Years later, I would understand that the one Salvarsan injection that we could give to the patients that day, would help their Framboesia indeed, but only temporarily and not completely. Complete cure could only be achieved in the very early cases. And in such an environment—saturated with germs and where hygienic habits were minimal—patients would soon be infected again. Those who already had the disease in an advanced stage would only be helped for a short while.

About the same can be said in regard to malaria. Without the possibility of combatting the mosquitoes effectively, the distribution of quinine to the population—perhaps only once in a period of one year if not more—would only give to the sufferers a temporary relief, before they would be reinfected with the parasite. Nevertheless, we were at that time most happy to see that sick people got better, without worrying about the future. Conditions did not allow us to undertake measures which would have lasting effects in those totally undeveloped jungle areas.

It was during that first safari that I had my first great adventure as a medical doctor working in the wilderness.

We had been walking for eight days when in the early morning we arrived at a very low depression of the Waingapu valley which was still completely under water. This had not been foreseen by our guides. We had to cross the vast flooded area and there was no way to find out where this could be done with the least possible risk except to try. After proceeding along the edge of the water very slowly, stumbling over uprooted trees and debris for more than three hours, the Raja discovered at some distance a number of dry pieces of ground emerging above the water level. He decided that it would be possible to make the crossing by hopping from island to island. This appeared to be easier stated than executed. All the time we had to probe the depths of the water between the elevations and in many places it was too deep to wade through. Many times we had to do balancing acrobatics over floating tree trunks, during which some of our porters fell into the water and had to be dragged out. It was a very long and tiresome struggle and in the meantime it was getting dark. Our porters got frightened, and soon they were most reluctant to go any further. Although our troupe was scattered over several islands we decided just to stay where we were and to wait until the next daybreak.

I found myself on my own on a small dry piece of flat ground just large enough to put up my camp bed, which my house boy Lamusa very ingeniously managed to pass over to me from another island quite a distance away. He threw to me a piece of wood which he had attached at the end of a long rope. At the other end of the rope he bound my camp bed, mosquito net and my backpack with clothes, neatly bundled on a piece of driftwood, making a small vessel. By carefully pulling at the rope I was able to get the driftwood with its load safely on my island. Putting up tents was out of question. We were too exhausted to even think of preparing food. Our first concern was to get to sleep and to make ourselves as comfortable as possible in those miserable circumstances. Each carrier had his ration of sago cakes, so some food was available. Lamusa called me from his island asking me if I was hungry. I was indeed, but called back: "No!" If I had said "Yes" he would undoubtedly have started to work on the kerosene burner to prepare food. That would be not an easy undertaking since the necessary items were scattered over several islands and had to be retrieved first. I was happy to be left alone and to be able to get out of my thoroughly wet trousers and underwear and to slip into my dry pajamas. My camp bed with its four poles at the corners was easily set up.

It is impossible to say how long I had been sleeping when I was awakened by a violent shaking of the mosquito net above my head. Flashing on my small electric torch I saw a quite odd shaking of the net, but being still half asleep I assumed that it was the effect of a stiff breeze coming up in the night. After assuring myself that the poles of the net were in place, I turned over, switched off my torch and immediately fell asleep again. After a while I was again half awake when I felt something sharp on the back of my head. Assuming that I had forgotten something at that end of the bed I reached out with my hand but instantly withdrew for I felt something bite my finger. "Oh God," I thought, "a snake!" I sprang up and in the light of my torch I saw a *rat* springing up from the bed against the ceiling of the mosquito net in an effort to escape, and to my great surprise I saw three other rats at the other end of the bed, looking at me and immediately springing up against the inside of the net, trying to get away. As an automatic reflex I pulled up the net and let them disappear in the dark. Perhaps I was too exhausted to realize that I had a definite problem. Not for one moment did I question the situation. I just put things in order, fixed the mosquito net firmly to the four posts of the bed, and fell asleep peacefully. But the sight of the three rats staring at me remained in my subconscious.

Some time later, I was awakened again, this time by something which I felt creeping up against my thigh inside my pajamas. When I felt a bite, I fully awoke with the shock, sprang up and threw off my pajamas. I snapped on my torch and was horrified to see the inside of the net full of rats, crawling and jumping! Strangely enough, I did not feel any fear or panic, but I had a clear idea that the situation was serious. When some of the rats started to attack I was filled with something which I had never experience before: a rage to survive. It was also quite abnormal that I did not scream for help, it just did not come into my mind. Without realizing what I did I had instinctively pulled one of the wooden sticks, which was fitted at each end of the bed to stretch the bed canvas, out of its sheet and used it to defend myself. While most of the rats were trying to escape, a few were furiously attacking as if out of despair. One sprang on my head and bit in my hair, fortunately not in my ear, and while this happened I managed to hit another rat straight on its head when he jumped up to my face. Blood spattered on all sides when it fell dead on the canvas. I just went on striking wildly to the left, the right, up and down. I did not know if I had struck other rats as well, probably I did. But a miracle happened. In a very short time all the rats were gone.

I was very puzzled when all was cleared up. Had it been a dream? It seemed as if I awoke fully after a sort of trance. For a short while I sat on the bed trying to find out what had really happened. Then I remembered everything clearly. *And there was a dead rat on the canvas bed!* Splashes of blood were everywhere, on the bed, on the mosquito net, and on the ceiling. I took up the cadaver and threw it away just outside the net under the bed, because then I was scared to take more steps outside. Still it did not occur to me to call for help. Inside the boundaries of the mosquito net I felt somehow quite safe again and fully at ease. I wiped the bed canvas as clean as possible, slipped again into my pajama, and fell soon in a sound sleep.

I felt as though I had a good rest when I awoke that morning. Remembering the events of the night before, I consoled myself that all had been a bad dream only. The next moment the splashes of blood on the netting and on the bed canvas convinced me of the reality of my experience. I started looking for the dead rat that I had thrown under the bed but found only some remainders of it about two steps further away. Apparently other rats had started to consume their mate. I started to pack up my equipment.

The water level had in the meantime fallen very much during the night and we were able to reach dry ground at the other side of the valley easily. There we had a rest to prepare our breakfast before continuing on to the next village. I asked my companions if they had been troubled by rats or other animals that night. None had been in trouble, but some of the porters reported having seen a number of dead rats in the water near my island and on another island we saw a strange phenomenon, which we could not explain. There was an open field which showed a strip of about two metres wide where the grass and other vegetation seemed to have been trampled down as if a heavy object had been dragged over it. Was there perhaps a fallen tree which had been pushed along by the stream or by strong winds? We were too busy picking up our luggage and getting ourselves ready for the march, and nobody pondered much further about the matter. When I told my story, everyone was just happy that I had not been harmed and that their fears for evil forces threatening them during the night were over.

After work in three more villages during the last four days of our trip we reached the southern shore of the Bay of Namela a few kilometres from the mound of the Waingapu river. A number of sailing canoes had been waiting there for us for some days, arranged beforehand by the Raja who had sent a messenger across the bay when we started our safari. There was very little wind and we had to row or to paddle with any possible bits of wood to get moving.

Later in the afternoon we arrived at low tide on the beach of Namlea. My adventure with the rats has often kept me awake at night since, but out of fear of being disbelieved, I hardly ever talked about it. Years later, however, when I told the story to a biologist friend in Holland, he hypothesized that I could have been camping exactly on the track of a migrating colony of rats in search of a new habitat because of the floods. This would explain the strip of land that had been severely trampled on. He also told me that in such circumstances—because of hunger—the animals could be very aggressive. I think this was the correct explanation for my horrendous experience.

CHAPTER 34

A Godsent Aeroplane

The hardships of life in Namlea put an almost unbearable strain on the civil servants working on the island. On average, they went down with malaria within one month after arrival and would never be completely cured, because soon after recovery they would get a new infection. Being conscious of the danger of malaria we meticulously took our prophylaxis. In those days chloroquine was not yet known. The drug of choice was quinine, since atabrine made one yellowish and there were reports of mental disturbances after long use of the drug. Our neighbour, Hetharia, the police chief, had never been able to do any work at all. He fell sick ten days after he set foot on the island and after six weeks of repeated attacks of fever he was so bad that he had to be evacuated.

I myself remained healthy, but both Astri and little Trisna fell ill despite the prophylaxis. After recovery from her third series of malaria attacks Astri became very weak. Soon thereafter, she became pregnant and suffered from hyperemesis. She could hardly eat anything and lost weight rapidly. I became very worried and wrote to the Ministry of Health, asking for a transfer. Since we had already spent more than a year in Namlea, my request received due consideration. Earlier than expected, I was informed by cable that we were being transferred to Sumbawa, one of the Lesser Sunda Islands, east of Bali. The autonomous Regency of Sumbawa was ruled by a sultan, who had much influence on the ministers of the East Indonesian cabinet. He needed a doctor immediately. The cable specified further that we had to leave at the first opportunity, so I should not wait for my successor who was already on his way.

We packed our belongings and boarded the Higgins motorboat to Ambon. Lamusa, our devoted houseboy, insisted he go with us. Being an orphan of parents who had come as migrant workers from Buton in Southern Celebes, he had no family in Namlea. We were happy to have him on hand.

I found it a great pity to leave behind the small hospital that I had built, and the work, which was progressing well. Pelu, my chief nurse, was very sad. I was confident that he would manage the routine work as well as any doctor. He was very intelligent and had learned a lot during the past year. But for other reasons I was glad to leave. The harsh life, the poor food, the climate, the ugly crabs, the mosquitoes, the white ants, the cockroaches and other unsightly insects, all together had become too much for Astri and had started to wear her down. Her pregnancy came on top of this general decline. It was perhaps her diminished physical resistance which was decisive for the course of the illness which struck her soon after our arrival in Sumbawa.

The first week on the island was not free of strain and struggle. Compared with Namlea the capital Sumbawa was a real town, having asphalt roads, lined by shadowy tamarind trees and Chinese shops, stocked with all sorts of commodities. There was a hospital of 60 beds with a reasonably complete staff and a policlinic with an attendance of up to 100 patients daily. So there was plenty of work to do for a single doctor.

Our housing, however, was worse than we expected. Situated in the crowded downtown area, it was even worse than our dwelling in Namlea. It was so dilapidated and filthy, that we were greatly shocked when we saw it. We decided to stay in a hotel until the local authorities had found a better place for us. After a few days I had a chance to meet the District Officer. Speculating that as a servant of a Sultanate he might be sensitive to descendancy, I told him about my ancestry. It seemed to help. The next day we were moved to the Sultan's private country house on the hills outside the town and I got a Chevrolet sedan as my office car with a driver. It was a luxury that we had never dreamed of.

A steep winding road over barren slopes led to the green forest on the top of the hill, where the Sultan's villa was cozily nestled between huge trees inhabited by hundreds of monkeys. They were very excited when we arrived in our limousine followed by an open truck with our luggage. When we came out of our vehicles they fled noisily screaming into the trees. We felt happy getting rid of them, but while we were unloading our cars they came back in great numbers. They pulled at our luggage and at everything loose and we had difficulty in keeping them away. Luckily and to our surprise little Trisna, then three years old, was not at all afraid of them. She laughed heartily every time they fled as Lamusa chased them with a stick. When at last all our cases and packages were in the house, we had to shut all the doors and windows.

Astri was still tired from the events of the last days and went to bed with a bad headache. Migraine was a family trait, and headaches after such strenuous days were not uncommon for her. Lamusa was quick in unpacking some of our kitchenware and started to prepare a meal for us in the kitchen. When the meal was ready, Astri preferred to stay in bed. Considering that nausea was a common feature of migraine, I found it wise to leave her alone and let her have a good rest. In the morning she felt better but developed a fever. Immediately suspecting malaria I took a blood slide and went to the hospital for routine work and to have the slide examined in the laboratory. It was negative. I was assured, the more so when in the afternoon the fever subsided.

The next morning, Astri seemed reasonably well. I found no reason to cancel my trip to a faraway village in the mountains, where cases of smallpox had been reported. It was urgent that I check the situation and, if necessary, take measures to prevent an outbreak of an epidemic. Fortunately, it turned out to be chickenpox. Back in the capital I reported my findings to the authorities and hurried home. Arriving there late in the afternoon, I found Astri in bed with a high fever that had developed during the day. I took another blood slide and sent it to the hospital. It was negative again. However, Astri's headache became much worse and she could not move her head. In the evening the fever went up very high and her neck became rigid, a symptom which was characteristic of meningitis. Having had only bad experiences with meningitis in Holland, I became very worried and scared. Modern antibiotics were not yet known. The only drug we had in Sumbawa which could be of help was sulfadiazine. Thus we set our hope on this medicine, although we knew that it could have bad side effects.

During the night the fever remained high, the neck remained stiff, and the headache unbearable. Astri got pain in her kidneys, an indication that she could not tolerate the drug. In the early morning she could not move her right arm; a little later also her right leg. At noon she had difficulty in swallowing when I tried to give her something to drink. She became sub-comatose and could not speak any more. I felt my heart bouncing wildly and cold sweat broke out over my body. I was desperate. Little Trisna had climbed on the bed and held her mother's hand. I did not dare to look at the lovely little girl. I could not think of anything, all thinking seemed blocked, and my energy was just ebbing away. Just when I was going to weep, I heard the sound of an engine in the air. Looking out of the window I saw a small aeroplane circling downwards around the hill as if it would make a landing on the grass airstrip near the town.

Suddenly, my head cleared. I jumped up from my chair, grasped the telephone and called the hospital, asking the staff to send the ambulance. Frantically I turned at the telephone (it was still that old-fashioned instrument like a box with a handle at one side at which one had to turn to get connected to the operator in town) and got the airport, from where the staff informed me that an unscheduled plane had landed there on its flight to Makassar, the capital of East Indonesia. I asked to talk with the pilot, got him straight away, and explained to him the urgency of my situation. My wife should be immediately transported to Makassar. He promised to wait.

Quickly I got some necessities ready for our flight and made arrangements with Lamusa and the hospital staff for the next few days. Lamusa should stay in the house and wait for me to cable him from Makassar.

The ambulance arrived. We carried Astri with Trisna at her side on the stretcher into the ambulance and raced to the airport.

There was enough room for the stretcher on the floor at the rear end of the cabin. I sat down next to Astri to feel her pulse and listen to her breathing. The pulse was hardly palpable and the breathing was very superficial. The pilot contacted Makassar airport to get an ambulance ready. The flight seemed to me endlessly long. When we landed, Astri was in coma. We rushed her to the Military Hospital, where the Chief Internist, Dr Gans, was waiting for us. After hearing my story and making a short examination of Astri, he addressed me in a very unfriendly manner, actually cursing me: "So, my dear colleague, you could have killed your wife!"

I was stunned. Not knowing what to say, I stammered something of symptoms indicative of meningitis and negative slides, but Dr Gans interrupted:

"That meningitis of yours is nonsense! Don't you know that in cerebral malaria one rarely finds the parasites in the peripheral blood?"

With a profound shock, I realized my failure. I knew very well that Falciparum Malaria parasites tend to clog together in the small capillaries of the brain. How could I have been so stupid? How could I have just dismissed that possibility straight away?

Without saying a word, Dr Gans opened an ampoule of Atabrine and gave Astri an intramuscular shot. Two Dutch nurses were standing by. He ordered them to bring Astri to the room which was reserved for her and not to leave her during the night. Then he spoke to me, this time in a more friendly manner: "Well, boy, let us wait and see how it works. The chances are 50-50". He did not have to explain to me how grave the situation was. I thanked him and picked up Trisna, who was waiting outside in the corridor with a nurse. Silently we followed the nurses with the stretcher. While they were putting Astri in her bed, she opened her eyes and seemed to recognize us. She smiled faintly and closed her eyes again, painfully, perhaps because of the unbearable headache. We were allowed to sleep in the adjacent room. Trisna was surprisingly quiet and calm when I laid her down in her cot. She was looking at me as if she understood everything that was happening, and she soon dozed off.

I could not sleep and went every five to ten minutes to see Astri and check her pulse and breathing. The nurses looked at me with apprehension. They had read from Dr Gans's notes about my error in Sumbawa.

A miracle took place. Three hours after the Atabrine injection Astri came out of her coma. She looked around her and asked: "Where am I?"

I whispered: "In Makassar, in the hospital".

She closed her eyes again, and I assured myself that she was sleeping. Her pulse became gradually fuller and her breathing deeper. Early in the morning Dr Gans gave her another Atabrine shot. Astri awoke because of the prick and could even move her head to have a look at the doctor, but fell asleep again.

When she woke up at noon, the fever was subsiding. There was that tingle of life in her eyes. I felt relief, but remained worried because she still could not yet move her right arm and leg. She could not swallow and spoke only with great difficulty. It was clear that she was paralyzed after the infection in her brain. I was still very worried since she was then seven months pregnant.

In the afternoon I phoned some friends, Gusti Bagus Oka and his wife Gedong, whom I knew from my school years in Java and had later met in Bali during our political mission. He had since been transferred to Makassar, as Secretary at the office of the President of East Indonesia. They came immediately to see Astri and offered to take Trisna home, where she could play with their three pre-school children. I found it a great idea and Trisna was happy.

I stayed as a guest at the hospital, where Astri recovered slowly but steadily, except for her paralysis. Because of this paralysis it was out of question to bring her back to Sumbawa. I went to the Ministry of Health and asked for a transfer to Makassar where further treatment could take place. By coincidence there was a doctor needed at the Labuan Baji Missionary Hospital in the southern suburb of Makassar. The two Dutch doctors working there, a surgeon and an internist, could not cope with the volume of work, which had much increased. When they heard that I had had intensive training in surgery and internal medicine in Deventer, they were most happy to have me there as their assistant. Soon after my assignment, we moved Astri to our place. There were two Dutch nurses at the missionary hospital. They had that devotion and love which I felt missing at the Military establishment.

During the following months Astri's condition improved greatly and in January our second daughter Surya was born. All the time the two sisters had devoted themselves with loving care to Astri, day and night.

CHAPTER 35

Escape from Makassar

Labuan Baji Hospital was a haven where I found the tranquillity I needed after almost a full month of turbulence and anxiety. Astri was in good hands with the two devoted Dutch sisters and recovered steadily from her malaria and the paralysis of her arms and legs. My fears that her pregnancy might come to an abrupt end proved unnecessary. Although the work at the hospital was very busy, I was not responsible for administration and management and could therefore concentrate on the medical problems only. It was like an extension of my training in Deventer, now confronting real situations in a tropical setting. I had great luck in having two senior supervisors, Dr Hoekstra, the internist, and the surgeon, Dr Veldstra, both of whom had had many years experience in Tropical Medicine. Since I wanted to be near Astri all the time, I had a room in the hospital. It was very convenient for the two doctors to have their assistant at hand at any time for any emergency.

After Surya's birth Astri gained in strength quickly and with exercises the movements of her arms and legs improved gradually. When the baby was three months old, she could move around slowly and it was no longer necessary to keep her in Labuan Baji. We found two rooms in town in the State-owned hotel, which was used as a transition camp for civil servants, waiting for assignments.

Meanwhile, great political developments were taking place in the young Nation. In December 1949, the Dutch handed over the sovereignty over the Indonesian archipelago to the "Federation of States of Indonesia", except for West New Guinea. The "Republic of Indonesia" which was proclaimed in 1945, became one of the states in the federation. From the beginning it was evident that the federal concept of Indonesia would not last. The fervour of nationalism, generated by the Republican slogan: "One Country, One Nation, One Language!" was firmly implanted into the hearts and minds of the Indonesian people, especially among the youth. The Republicans were quick to exploit this strong nationalism to undermine the other states in the federation, aiming at the proclamation of the unitary "Republic of Indonesia". All over Indonesia groups of young people formed paramilitary organizations, called the "Laskar Rakyats", to counter the local police and armed forces.

In Makassar, large bands of Laskar Rakyats soon roamed the streets and started to attack remote police posts to obtain weaponry. One day, while I was busy at the clinic, there was a great upheaval on the street in front of our hospital. Looking out of the window I saw two policemen being chased by a mob of about twenty youth armed with sticks and knives, wearing red bands around their heads. They were moving with great speed towards our gate. I sprang up from my chair and just before I reached the front door the two policemen, their rifles firmly gripped in their hands, fled into the crowded waiting hall. Fortunately, the gang, seeing me in my white doctor's uniform in the entrance, hesitated for a few seconds at the gate. It gave me time to overcome my panic. When they came near I could calmly stop them and asked their leader who, to my astonishment, had a hand grenade in his hand, not to enter the hospital. When they insisted, I stood firm and asked: "What do you want?"

The wild-eyed leader burst briskly: "Their weapons! Let us get them, otherwise... and threatening with his grenade he tried to push himself past me. I stopped him, saying: "Wait a minute. Stay here! We will get them for you!"

Alerted by the tumult Dr Hoekstra arrived in the hall. With the help of two male nurses, he succeeded in persuading the policemen to hand over their rifles. By some miracle the Laskars at the front door remained quiet, and when they saw Dr Hoekstra coming back with the two rifles, they cheered. We handed them the guns. They went off cheering triumphantly and we phoned the police station, asking them to collect the two poor men. They were apparently very new recruits, totally inexperienced and were obviously happy with our protection. Soon a police van appeared with six heavily armed men. We explained what had happened and they approved our course of action. Bloodshed in a crowded hospital was the last thing they would have liked to see.

For a few weeks the air was filled with rumours that there would be an invasion by troops of the Republican Army from Java. But nothing happened. There were negotiations between the Republic and the other States of the Federation, which came under great psychological as well as political pressure, not in the least from within their own ranks. One by one they yielded to merge with the Republic, first West Java, then East Java, Madura and Borneo. Only North Sumatra and Celebes remained. The Malukus proclaimed themselves a sovereign State, independent from Indonesia. Negotiations at the highest level were continuing. There was chaos. Nobody knew what was going to happen.

During this period of uncertainty all the Regional Heads of Government and the Rajas of Celebes were summoned to Makassar to discuss the situation. The conference lingered on and on, without any decision being taken, because the Prime Minister was in Java, negotiating with the Republic.

The Raja of Bolaang Mongondow, a remote enclave in North Celebes, took the opportunity of being in the capital to ask the Minister of Health for a doctor for his kingdom. This autonomous Regency had been without a medical doctor for many years after the death of the last one. The President's secretary, Bagus Oka, brought us the news. I talked the case over with Astri and we decided to volunteer. I went to the Ministry of Health and the transfer was arranged. The Raja was most happy.

But things turned difficult. A contingent of the army under the leadership of Colonel Andi Azis, declared themselves opposed to the Republic. The threat of war between army factions provided a reason for the Republican army, the T.N.I. (Tentara Nasional Indonesia), to land in Makassar. Fierce fighting broke out in several parts of the town. Our hotel was one of the first targets to be taken. The armies were fighting each other on the street in front of the hotel. We huddled in our rooms, lying flat on the floor between our suitcases and as many mattresses as we could gather, while the bullets smashed against walls and flew through windows. Fortunately, the ordeal did not last long. The troops of Andi Azis were out-gunned and retreated towards the town centre. While the battle in the town raged on, a messenger from the Ministry of Health arrived at the hotel, telling us that a K.P.M. vessel, the *Swartehont*, would leave the next day from Makassar to Menado, the capital of North Celebes. We should get on the boat because it would be the only and last ship to sail to Menado, but the Ministry could not provide any transport to the ship. All vehicles had been requisitioned by the military. We faced a great problem. Even if we could get transport, to travel to the harbour we had to cross the town's centre, where fighting was still going on.

Coincidentally, my cousin, Mantik, who was a Major with the Republican Army, had also landed in Makassar and he visited us. He promised to arrange something. The next morning a T.N.I. Captain came with an open army pickup to our hotel. He had orders from Mantik to take us to the boat. We did not know the man, but were confident that it was all right. We loaded our luggage in the back. Astri, little Trisna and the baby sat in the cabin next to the Captain who drove the car himself. I climbed on the pile of trunks and suitcases and held above my head a stick with my white handkerchief attached to it as a flag, hoping that it might guarantee us free passage through the streets. Pockets of resistance by troops loyal to Andi Azis were still everywhere and several times our car, carrying emblems of the T.N.I., was shot at from a far distance, forcing our Captain to turn swiftly into unknown side streets. After a hectic ride of nearly one hour we arrived at the harbour, which was crowded with Republican soldiers. It was not difficult for our T.N.I. officer to get soldiers to help us with our luggage and to secure a cabin on the ship for us. Hardly had we made ourselves comfortable in our cabin when the ship's siren blew three times and we were off at sea.

The two-day journey to Menado was quiet and relaxing. It was the last journey of the Dutch vessel before returning to Holland. We enjoyed the Dutch meals which we had been missing for a long time. It was the last time for many years that we enjoyed the cleanness, comfort and luxury of a Dutch passenger ship.

The first horror befell us when in the harbour of Menado we were transferred from the *Swartehont* to a small coaster to bring us 100 miles further west to Inobonto, the harbour of the kingdom of Bolaang Mongondow on the north coast of Celebes. The filth we found on the coaster was indescribable. People were very friendly to us, the captain himself put his berth, the only one on the whole ship, at Astri's disposal for the night. However, it swarmed with cockroaches, rats and hundreds of mosquitoes. For the whole night Astri had to keep them away from the children. The restless crowd on the boat, the noise of the engine, the heat in the cabin and the stench of rotten fish kept us awake most of the time. Fortunately, the travel took only one night. It was still early in the morning when the boat slackened speed and approached Inobonto. We saw only three buildings with thatch roofs on the beach, which was totally empty. There was not even a pier for our ship to land. There seemed to be no life at all. The coaster stopped about 50 metres from the shore near the largest building and blew its siren three times. After a while we saw people moving around the buildings, and outrigger canoes were dragged to the sea. A big bus appeared on the road along the coast. We were struck by the sight of the crowd in the bus. There were about twenty men in the vehicle, all clad in black uniforms and wearing red bands around their heads.

We got in one of the canoes, while the captain took care of our luggage. When we set foot on the beach we found ourselves suddenly surrounded by the twenty men in black. Each of them had a rifle in his hand. We had no idea what was going on, but the menacing gestures of the men and their wild looks made me suspicious. They were Laskars for sure, but we did not understand what they were doing, until their leader spoke and told us that we were taken prisoner. Some of them, trigger-happy, started to shoot in the air. When I showed them my papers, the leader snatched them out of my hands, chuckling viciously and bragging: "I see, these are recommendations from the Raja of Bolaang Mongondow. You should know that there is no Raja here any longer, we have taken the Government in our hands. We are the boss now. Since you have cooperated with the Raja, you are our enemy. You are our prisoners now".

It was too much for us to comprehend all at once. The Laskars ordered us to mount the bus, all the time closing in on us as if we would try to escape. These young so-called revolutionaries were especially suspicious because of Astri. Anything Dutch was for them the symbol of colonialism and the cause of all evil. We were not allowed to get our luggage. After a ride of two hours we arrived at the capital Kotamobagu. During the whole trip the trigger-happy youngsters were shooting in the air, especially when we passed through a village. Realizing that we were completely in the hands of irresponsible half-educated rascals, drunk with power, we kept quiet. They searched our luggage several times thoroughly. We got the impression that it was more out of curiosity than for security reasons. After that, they behaved miserably. Astri was not even allowed to get water for the baby.

In Kotamobagu we were put in one room of the *pasanggrahan*—a Government guest-house at the corner of a square—around which the Government Offices were built. We were not allowed to leave the room. Heavily armed guards were placed at the door and outside under the windows. When we went to the toilets one of them went with us. It was ridiculous. Sometimes I found it difficult to keep silent. The hostess of the house was a very nice lady, but obviously she was very afraid of the Laskars. She helped Astri with getting boiled water for the children and prepared food for us. Surprisingly our children withstood the turmoil remarkably well. They never cried, just looked around with wide open eyes and showed no signs of panic. They went to bed on time and slept quietly. Although Astri found the men's behaviour most offensive and annoying, she managed to keep her head cool all the time. Her admirable courage and calmness kept my spirits high.

CHAPTER 36

The Doctor's House

Bit by bit we gained a clearer picture of what had taken place in the Kingdom of Bolaang Mongondow during the past month. The first revealing information was given by the Chief Male Nurse of the Hospital, a nice elderly man, who visited us the morning after our arrival. He looked ill-at-ease when the two Laskars who stood guard at the gate brought him to our room, but was visibly relieved when they let him in while they remained outside. Our clever hostess had told the boys that coffee was ready for them in the kitchen. She came in, introducing the man to us as "Ziekenvader" (The Father of the Sick) as he was locally known. Apparently a most respected citizen, he looked impeccably clean in his white uniform. He welcomed us heartily. But before he spoke further, he looked suspiciously towards the door. It was evident that the new men in power did not earn his sympathy. In a very subdued tone, almost whispering, he started: "Doctor, be careful. These boys are very dangerous. They are drunk with power. Don't do anything which might displease them!"

"What has happened?" I asked, "Why have they taken us prisoner? What wrong have we done?"

"Actually, nothing. Like everywhere else in Celebes, bands of Laskars have been created in the name of the Revolution by the supporters of the Republic, also in our Regency of Bolaang Mongondow. When our Raja was called to Makassar to attend a conference, they took the opportunity to proclaim Bolaang Mongondow as part of the Republic and the Raja was denounced as a puppet of the colonialist power. They took the police garrison, seized their weapons and put all the men who refused to vow loyalty to them in jail."

While he spoke, Ziekenvader tried to keep calm, but we felt that inside he was raging with anger. We heard later that he was a staunch supporter of the deposed Raja.

"Look!" he said, leading me to the window and pointing to the opposite corner of the large green square, "that is the Doctor's house, we had just finished all repairs and we were cleaning it for you and your family. They took it and are using it as their headquarters. What a shame!"

We saw a nice small villa under big trees and some Laskar boys in black moving around in the garden, guns over their shoulders. An open army jeep stood in the driveway.

Ziekenvader then went on to explain that both the District Officer and the Chairman of the House of Representatives had been put in jail and released only after they pledged loyalty to the Republic. The hospital was continuing to operate as best as it could under the circumstances, but Ziekenvader did not rate our chances of release highly.

"They regard you as a Royalist," he explained. "Unless there are instructions from the Republican Government nothing will happen. Nobody knows. The officials are afraid to do anything. Everything is chaotic. Meanwhile these rascals are robbing the population."

There was a knock on the door and the Laskars told Ziekenvader to leave. He went, reluctantly, with his greying head bent in sorrow.

As the days passed the vigilance of our guards waned gradually. Our hostess came more often and became more talkative. She told us that the Laskars extorted money and goods from the shopkeepers. Especially the Chinese were rudely subjected to their whimsical terror.

A new local Government, the Revolutionary Council, consisting of people who had no experience in public administration, was set up. They were also afraid of the Laskars and made no effort to call them to order. Without anybody having authority over them the boys indulged in their power and made forays to the gold mines up in the mountains, where people stood for days on end in the water, trying to sieve some precious metal from the sand and gravel they dug out from the river beds.

After ten days, the Laskars seemed more interested in the gold mines than in the doctor they still held in captivity. When in the early morning all of them, fully armed, drove up to the mines in two jeeps, our guardians, anxious not to miss their share, ran up the street and joined them. I peered at the nice doctor's house in the far corner of the square. It seemed abandoned and peaceful. I determined to carry out a bold plan that had been ripening in my mind for some time.

"Now or never!" I thought, and told Astri of my intentions. She agreed fully and when I asked her if she was afraid, she smiled: "Of course not! I will follow you everywhere, let happen what will happen. We must make an end to this silly ordeal!"

I asked our hostess to call Ziekenvader and two men from the workshop of the Public Works Department with a big axe and hammer. She was excited, sent her two gardeners out with the message and to my great surprise the men came in less than half an hour. I told Ziekenvader that I wanted to occupy the

Doctor's house and asked him to bring as soon as possible some furniture from the hospital for temporary use: two beds, a baby cot, a table and some chairs. The old man was perplexed, he shook his head and tried to convince me that it was madness.

"Not madness, but justice!" I replied. "I will do what is right. We cannot stand this humiliation any longer. Please get those things. I am now Director of your hospital, and your boss. Take it as an order!"

Ziekenvader gasped at me, but his eyes started to brighten, expressing confidence. He obeyed happily and as he went, I told Astri to stay until I returned to fetch her later. In an exalted mood I crossed with the two men from the workshop the large open square to the Doctor's house and asked them to force open the lock of the front door. Sensing my determination they obeyed after some hesitation. They were very handy and performed the job easily, without causing much damage to the house. I thanked them and entered the building, feeling like a king at the head of a victorious army.

The house had a small living room at the front, from which a wide corridor led to the back door. Four French doors, two at either side, gave entrance to four bedrooms, each having a folding door, opening into the garden. I was surprised to find no furniture at all in the house. There were mats on the floor on which the Laskars had been sleeping. All their belongings were stacked against the walls in a most disorderly manner: clothes, shoes, caps, boxes, and quite a large amount of ammunition. There were no plates or pans. They had apparently taken their meals outside. No restaurant or coffee-shop would dare to refuse them any food or drink.

Ziekenvader and some hospital personnel arrived with two bull-drawn carts, loaded with much more furniture than I had ordered. With their help I moved quickly all mats, clothes and everything else out of the house. They heaped them somewhere under a tree and brought the furniture in. All was done in a matter of one hour. By noon we had cleaned the rooms and went to the guest-house to fetch Astri, the children and our luggage. The hostess brought our food. She and Ziekenvader stayed with us for lunch.

Some time later an orderly from the hospital came to get Ziekenvader for an urgent patient. The old man went reluctantly—he wanted to be with us when the Laskars returned. Eager to see a patient, I wanted very much to go with him, but found it better not to leave Astri and the children alone.

Late that afternoon two jeeps pulled up on the driveway at great speed. With brakes screeching and wheels grinding over gravel they stopped in front of our door. There was loud shouting and stamping of heavy boots on the ground. The door burst open and a Laskar in green fatigues and a red band around his head thrust himself inside the room, brandishing a revolver in his hand. I felt a shock through my body, but managed to keep calm. Pointing his weapon at me he shouted: "Get out of here, or I'll kill you!"

Suddenly everything became unreal to me and it was like in a dream, when I heard my own voice saying: "No, we are staying here. This house is destined for us. I have come here to help your people. If you want to kill us, kill my wife and the children first and then me!" It seemed to me as if somebody else was speaking with my voice.

The Laskar hesitated. I saw clearly that his hand was shaking when it put the gun back in its holster. Looking up he started shouting again: "We will burn you to death. I'm going to put kerosene around the house. I'm giving you five minutes to leave, otherwise you will go up in flames!"

Once again, with that same sense of unreality, I heard my voice saying: "Okay, go ahead. We will not move!"

He turned on his heels, went out of the house, leaving the door wide open. In the half dark I saw with chilling clarity the men in their black uniforms and red headbands moving around the two jeeps, shouting and wildly gesticulating. One of the vehicles drove away while the men positioned themselves around the house, as if to prevent us from fleeing. I seated myself next to Astri on the rattan bench and took Trisna on my lap. Astri was giving Surya her bottle of milk. I put my arm around her shoulder and we looked into each other's eyes. Hers shone with that intense love so characteristic of her, that gave me courage, strength and confidence. I thought: "We will never be separated, not in this world, nor beyond".

The jeep came back, we heard men jumping to the ground and the clatter of jerrycans. I guessed that they were indeed throwing kerosene around the building. The Laskar in fatigues stepped inside the room and shouted to us: "Get out, otherwise I give the order to my men to light the kerosene".

I looked straight at him and suddenly I had again that strange feeling of unreality, while I heard my voice saying calmly: "Go ahead!"

The wild-eyed man stood there in front of us as if nailed to the floor. He hesitated for a while, turned round and left. He called something and there was a burst of shouting of which I could not make out the words. The men seemed to be arguing with each other. We waited for things to happen. Those were some of the most tense moments of our lives. From the noises outside I realized that some of the men were gathering their belongings from the backyard and loading their jeeps. For more than five endlessly long minutes we listened intently, trying to figure out what the Laskars were doing. Nothing happened. Suddenly we heard them start the engines, all of them jumped into their vehicles and, still loudly arguing, they drove away in the dark.

We looked at each other in disbelief.

We had a quiet night. Early in the morning I went outside to have a look. There were indeed traces of kerosene spilled haphazardly here and there under the walls, but not very much. Apparently they had carried out the job halfheartedly.

It was perhaps innocence that gave me the courage to walk down the one-mile stretch to the hospital that morning. Ziekenvader was delighted to see me healthy and well. I felt happy to work again with patients. It was not long before Ziekenvader rushed in, urging me to hide because the Head of the Laskars was at the gate. I looked out of the window and recognized the man in fatigues. He had no red headband, but instead had donned a military cap. I asked Ziekenvader to meet him and ask him what he wanted. While he was impatiently waiting for me to run for a hiding place, one of the Nurses came in, trembling with fear, saying: "Ziekenvader, the Laskars want to arrest the Doctor. They say they will punish him by tying him at a pole in the sun for the whole day!" Ziekenvader went to the door.

"No," I said, "don't go. I will go and meet him!" and with my white doctor's coat still on, I walked straight ahead towards the man. He was still sitting at the steering wheel of his jeep, apparently waiting for Ziekenvader to deliver me to him. When he saw me approaching on my own, he looked rather surprised. I came nearer. Aghast and without giving me the chance to rail at him, he started the engine and drove away in high speed. I did not see him again.

There was no car, so I walked every day to and from the hospital and found great happiness in my work. A week later the same military jeep stopped at the gate and a Laskar carried on a stretcher by four comrades was brought in. He was in great distress and crying loudly from unbearable pain. That morning in Inobonto he had fallen from the jeep and was smashed against a tree. The rough ride from Inobonto to Kotamobagu had done him no good. I found a complete luxation of his shoulder. Swiftly I gave him some ether, took off my shoes and with the boy still on the stretcher I put my left foot in his arm-pit, pulled with all my might at his arm and swung his shoulder back in place. It was done in three minutes, and he awoke with a broad grin. His terrible pain was gone. He thankfully shook my hand and walked happily out of the room.

It was the beginning of better terms with Bolaang Mongondow's unruly revolutionary youth.

CHAPTER 37

Consolidation and Pacification

Since the happenings that first week in the hospital I became the idol of my personnel, who were happy to have at last somebody whom they could fully trust as their leader and adviser. I had no difficulty in getting things done, no matter how much work had to be accomplished, or how poor the facilities. Everyone was eager to volunteer for overtime work. Their enthusiasm rose even more later when I started to set up training courses in basic medicine, in nursing and midwifery.

With the continuing unstable situation in Indonesia during the first years after independence we received very few medical supplies and equipment from the Government. I applied for help from a voluntary organization in Holland, S.I.M.A.V. I. (Steun In Medische Aangelegenheden Voor Indonesia) and soon started to receive great quantities of medicine, instruments, baby food, baby milk and medical supplies. By training volunteers we soon had enough personnel to cope with the increasing volume of work.

I designed a new hospital—with three polyclinics, two operating rooms, a maternity and children's ward, and plenty of storage space—to replace the ramshackle 30-bed existing hospital. Since no Government funds were forthcoming, we raised money by several means. Voluntary contributions flowed in from all sides, and the Chinese community resorted to their favourite gambling games, which yielded an unexpected amount of money. We knew that it was not a conventional way of fund-raising, but we also knew that the Chinese would be gambling anyway, so we may as well extract good use out of their entertainment.

Later, Astri initiated the building of a Maternity and Child Health Clinic together with the Kotamobagu Ladies Club. The clinic was named ASTRI and we found it still functioning when we visited the place 30 years later.

After the completion of the main hospital we had to give attention to the rural areas. By that time many rural village chiefs had heard of the progress in the medical care of their people in the town. They showed much interest and all wanted to have a clinic. I told them that they could easily build one for themselves and send candidates to be trained by me. By the time the building was finished nurses and midwives would be ready for them. I had no difficulty in recruiting youngsters from the twenty-eight districts for basic medical training and nursing in Kotamobagu for two years after which they would return to their villages. But to implement this scheme I first had to visit all these places.

Communication with those remote areas was very poor or non-existent. Travel had to be done over land by foot or on horseback through jungles and marshes, or along the coast by boat or canoes. One of the areas where I initiated a polyclinic scheme was in the beautiful Dumoga Valley which stretched over some 25 to 30 km between two mountain ranges west of the plateau of Kotamobagu. My first visit there was unforgettable. The Ziekenvader and two senior male nurses accompanied me on the trip to assess the feasibility of establishing a polyclinic there. Dumoga Village, in the centre of the valley, was our destination. The Dumoga Village chief arranged horseback transportation and we arrived safely before dark in Dumoga Village, where a large crowd had gathered in front of the Chief's house to welcome us.

The next day was spent working in an ad-hoc polyclinic and selecting the site for a permanent one. I chose the ground near the market which would make it easy to reach for the population.

Over the course of time, atrocities in Kotamobagu occurred less and less and we were able to continue our work unhindered. It was several months after the "revolution" by the Laskars that a police detachment from Menado arrived in Kotamobagu, reoccupied their office and freed the policemen being held there in custody. They did not, however, disarm the Laskars for fear of appearing anti-republican. This was done a few months later by the T.N.I., the regular Indonesian Army. In February 1951, Brigadier General Gatot Subroto was dispatched to North Celebes with a battalion of troops to pacify the region. After two months of travel, he arrived with his troops in Kotamobagu. He was a jolly and energetic fellow, who joked about everything, but when it came to military action, he was a man of no nonsense. He visited the hospital that I was building and I joined him on his trips to rural areas.

It was an impressive show of force. The population had never before seen so many soldiers and military vehicles pushing over the nearly impassable roads through the jungle. The Laskars surrendered meekly. There was a sigh of relief among the people. He left a garrison of 150 soldiers in Kotamobagu to restore law and order, and as a gesture of appreciation of what we had done thus far, General Gatot Subroto stayed in our house instead of the palace of the deposed Raja, which had been reserved for him. Perhaps it was also meant as a public relations move. He had heard about our popularity with the people.

Before he left to continue his mission, he appointed me a Major of the

Armed Forces. I was perplexed because I had never been in the army and had never held a gun in my hand. Seeing my frown, the General smiled, saying: "Dr Djelantik, the commander of the garrison that will stay here on duty for about six months is a Captain. Being a Major you must be respected by him. If necessary he could even be placed under your command. It is a precautionary measure. You are not required for any combat, but I trust my men under your medical care!"

He handed to me the golden badge of a Major and a military uniform, which luckily I never needed to put on. That cordial appointment took place in April 1951.

CHAPTER 38

Happy Pioneering

Our house became a safe haven for the European planters and their families, who came regularly to relax after weeks of hard work. There was a German family at the Modayag coffee plantation high up in the mountains east of Kotamobagu, and three Dutch families at the coconut plantation of Lolak, west of Inobonto. The Dutch missionary Langeveld and his wife, and two Catholic priests, were among our frequent visitors. One Dutchman, a lonely coconut planter in Poigar near the Minahassa border never came up to Kotamobagu. After years of solitude in faraway places he had become very shy and self-contained. The educated elite of Bolaang Mongondow loved to visit us and have a chat in Dutch, a language which many of them spoke very well. Without restraint they sometimes aired personal and general grievances against the recent changes in the country.

Astri was happy, gained in strength and in the cool climate of Kotamobagu she became as energetic as she had been in Holland. She initiated all kinds of social work with the ladies, organized with them bazaars for fund-raising. Special milk for babies, medicines and other supplies which came regularly via S. I. M. A. V. I. enabled her to devote herself entirely to the health of mothers and babies, which had always been her hobby. In these activities she was enthusiastically assisted by the Kotamobagu Ladies' Club. When I was away on medical safaris, which lasted from two days to two weeks, the nurses would often seek her advice in difficult cases and she had to act as a medical doctor.

In 1952 our third daughter Madelief was born and one year later our son Widura. There was of course no other doctor present. Having seen three daughters being born one after the other I was so surprised when I saw a boy, that while holding the baby by his feet upside down, I burst into convulsions of laughter and completely forgot to cut the umbilical cord. Astri had to remind me!

On these and other happy occasions like birthdays the whole community shared our happiness, expressing it in a way that was very enjoyable but extremely exhausting. The abundance of flowers transformed our house into an overladen flowershop and we had to shake hands with an endless stream of well-wishers. We received a huge amount of cakes, sweets and delicacies, most of which we passed on to hospital patients, orphanage children and prison inmates. Once we had a professional photographer take a family picture for us to send to friends and family in Holland. All the people who saw the picture in his shop wanted to have one! Proudly the photographer told us later that he had sold a few hundred copies. Twenty-five years later people returning from Kotamobagu told us that they saw our picture still hanging in many houses.

* * * * * *

The Dutch who had built the main roads in Mongondow in the late 1920s had also built beautiful bridges over the main rivers. They were sturdy wood constructions with a roof of plate wood or corrugated zinc over the whole length and double banisters at each side for pedestrians, while the gangway consisted of planks fixed on cross beams lying one yard apart. Since the Japanese occupation, these roads and bridges had not been maintained. In the 1950s most of the smaller bridges had disappeared and on the bigger bridges most of the wood was rotting away.

Once two crossbeams in the middle section of a bridge halfway between Kotamobagu and Poopo were found broken. Labourers of the Public Works Department had taken them away together with the planks, so that a gaping hole of three yards remained on the gangway. None of the workers had thought of closing the bridge or placing a warning signboard somewhere on the road.

It was already dark when a teenage boy from Poopo drove his cart with two oxen at great speed down the road. Swinging to the left upon the bridgehead he did not see the gaping hole and plunged with oxen and cart 6 metres down onto the stony riverbed. People of the nearest village were alarmed by the thundering noise of the crash followed by the terrible bellowing of the bulls. By the light of torches they went cautiously down to the river and rescued the boy from under the wreckage and the dying bulls. Two men cycled to Kotamobagu for help. They came to our house with Ziekenvader just as we had finished dinner. I got my first aid kit and jumped with Ziekenvader into my jeep. Arriving at the bridge we found the boy lying on a makeshift stretcher, crying from pain. It was a terrible sight.

His arms and legs looked oddly out of place, indicating that he had fractures in several places. Blood gushed from his forehead. I gave him a painkilling shot and stopped the bleeding with a pressure bandage. Fortunately the wound did not involve the bone and none of the fractures was of the open type. Since we could not do much more on the roadside in the dark we put the boy with the make shift stretcher on the back of my jeep and I drove cautiously down the bumpy road. Unfortunately, the bulls could not be saved; carrying them up the steep riverbank was impossible. To make an end to their suffering the people called the butcher to slaughter the animals on the spot. It was done to conform with the Moslem religion and the meat was divided among the people.

The boy was still moaning from pain when we arrived at the hospital, so I gave him another shot. He had 11 fractures in several places over arms, legs, hips and shoulders. As we had no X-ray apparatus, I had to rely entirely on my tactile and visual senses in treating the fractures. They had to be done one by one, using splints, bandages and traction from four angles. By midnight I was able to leave the boy in the care of the night nurses. The boy was strong; he was able to drink and soon recovered from the shock. Every day during the following week I had to make adjustments in the bandages and tractions. It was an exciting experience of experimenting and learning. Two months later the boy climbed without help onto a new ox cart by which his parents, broadly smiling, took him home.

* * * * * *

Much more patience was required when a Chinese family desperately asked me to cure their emaciated father who was heavily addicted to opium. During the first week I had to visit him two or three times daily, later nearly every day for one month. Miraculously he recovered. After three months he could do his work normally. Funnily enough, thirty years later I met by chance his son in Jakarta. He had become a successful businessman, with offices in Jakarta, Singapore and Sydney. He recognized me immediately and treated me lavishly every time I happened to be in Jakarta!

Great success befell me also with operations on patients with goiters. Although I had never before learned the technique, circumstances compelled me to perform the surgery with the help of surgical manuals. It was as if my fingers knew what to do, and the work went smoothly. The belief grew among the people that I had *tangan dingin* (literally "cold hands") meaning that anything would grow well and heal under my hands. Eleven young girls were operated on and married soon afterwards.

Superstition still prevailed among the people at large. One day four men in one village near Kotamobagu committed suicide at about the same time. They were in no way related to each other and lived in separate locations. It was a very strange phenomenon. Nobody was able to give any reason for their action. Eyewitnesses told me later that suddenly a man became mad, took a knife and with a terrible shriek cut his throat, falling to the ground, and bleeding to death. A few minutes later the same happened some 100 metres away and some time later another man did the same at the other end of the village. Of course people rushed from all sides and tried to stop the men. On the last occasion one young man among these helpers, who happened to have a knife with him, suddenly went mad and hysterically screaming slashed his own throat. Fortunately many people were close by. They grabbed him and prevented him from running his knife through his belly. The three other madmen died within minutes, but this last one was still alive. They carried him to our hospital, tightly tied with ropes onto a divan, still bleeding from his throat when he arrived. While the nurses carried him to the operating room, the village chief took me aside and solemnly told me the story:

"Doc, our village is under the spell of a witch. This happens about every five years. This is the third time that I have seen it, there were four of them the first time, later five and today there are four. All of them died except this one, because there were many people around him".

"How did it start?" I asked.

"Who knows," he replied. "It was all of a sudden, for no reason at all. Doc, I am a Moslem, and I should not believe in this kind of things. But this must surely be the work of witchcraft!"

He sounded so convinced that it was pointless to argue with him. Moreover, first of all the patient needed my attention. The nurses had put him on the operating table and were trying to clean the wound. It was not easy, as new debris kept emerging out of the wound. Apparently both the windpipe and the gullet had been cut through. I removed a mass of clotted blood from inside the windpipe. The patient started to cough and sprayed us with a hail of blood and mucus, after which he could breath freely again. But regurgitated food particles soiled the wound again. I nearly lost hope, but succeeded in inserting a rubber tube through which I rinsed his stomach clean with a lot of water. At last I got the wound as clean as the circumstances allowed. There was remarkably little bleeding. The large carotid veins and arteries were intact, thank God!

The problem was what to do next. From the textbooks I knew that sewing a gullet was one of the most hazardous things to do. It was stated that stitches would just not hold. But I had no choice, I should just try what commonsense dictated. I replaced the rinsing tube with a much thicker and longer one, inserting it this time through the mouth. Into the opening of the severed windpipe a metal canule was inserted, which was attached to my automatic narcosis cap, filled with ether. With two strong hooks the windpipe was bent forward and held fast by a nurse, giving me free access to the gullet. Meticulously I sewed both ends of the gullet together around the stomach tube, layer by layer. Work on the windpipe was much easier. The operation went satisfactorily.

After the operation I met the village chief who was waiting in the corridor. I told him to forget about witchcraft. "What then was it that made my people crazy?" he asked. I could not find a good explanation.

"Maybe something happened which made your people very excited", I said. "In such circumstances people can be induced to do things unwittingly, like imitating others doing suddenly extraordinary things".

But actually I did not know. I thought of *latah*, an hysterical imitating phenomenon I had often seen in Bali and Java many years earlier. But those involved harmless actions like undressing, uttering obscene words, and so on.

The next morning the patient was in good condition. He smiled at me. Then he grimaced painfully, pointing with his finger to the trachea-canule I had fixed on his throat. I understood that he felt uncomfortable with the device, so after assuring myself that he could breathe normally without it, I removed the canule and closed the wound. After one week I removed the stomach tube through which he had been fed with baby food all the time. He was very happy and was able to eat porridge with a spoon. Strict instructions were given that for the time being he could only have fluid baby food. But Nature was stronger than any doctor's instruction. In the evening of the next day he managed to slip away in the dark. We found him in a *warung* (eating house) enjoying a full meal of rice and hard fried whole peanuts! I was furious and scolded him most severely. He cried pitifully and with tears in his eyes he sobbed: "Please Doctor, don't be angry, I was dying from hunger!"

My anger melted away. I put my arm around the boy's shoulders and led him back to the hospital, promising him the best food we could obtain. Surgically there were no complications.

He survived!

CHAPTER 39

Clouds over Mongondow

The happy and fruitful years in Bolaang Mongondow did not last. Continuing upheavals in the new Indonesian nation soon had their repercussions as far as the remote areas in North Sumatra, North Celebes and the Malukus. Plagued by political instability the central government could not maintain effective management and control over these faraway territories.

In these outer provinces the initial euphoria in the wake of the merger of the Federal States into the Indonesian Republic, was soon dampened by a general feeling of neglect. The welfare state promised by the politicians after the expulsion of the colonial rulers did not materialize. Even among the staunch nationalists who had high places in local government, there was widespread dissatisfaction in regard to the allocation of development funds to the peripheral provinces. There was no apparent mass movement by which dissatisfaction was expressed, but small groups of dissent had formed underground. We citizens could only guess at their existence from rumours circulating among the population. Sometimes there were acts of sabotage among the workers on the plantations, especially where Dutch people were still in charge. Gradually the confusion among the population increased, the authorities were losing credibility and political opportunists made use of the prevailing dissatisfaction for their own purposes. Most disturbing was the emergence of armed gangs in remote areas who seemed not to be under the control of any authority or any recognized organization and operated freely according to their whims. Nervousness and anxiety ran high among the families of the few expatriates living on the remote plantations, whom we met regularly.

Once, at midnight, we were awakened by a frantic banging on our front door and a loud excited voice calling: "Doctor, doctor, please come, quick, please. Your help is needed, quick, it is very urgent!" I jumped out of bed and rushed to open the front door. I saw a policeman, wide-eyed with panic, trying to talk to me. But he was out of breath and could not speak. Behind him, I recognized my medical assistant who was on night duty at the hospital. He told me that here was indeed an emergency and a very serious one: About 10 km east of Inobonto, where the road was winding sharply around high hills that reached the coastline, a police patrol consisting of two open jeeps manned by ten policemen had been ambushed that night by an armed gang, apparently with the purpose of getting at their firearms. After a short exchange of fire the gang was driven off but one driver and two policemen were badly wounded. The commander had decided to send one jeep with two men to Kotamobagu to ask for help while he and the other men stayed behind with the wounded.

Meanwhile, Astri had joined me at the front door and had heard the story. I was caught up by a compelling sense of urgency and without thinking of anything else or saying goodbye to Astri, I was in my clothes in a few seconds. I motioned the hospital assistant to follow me and jumped in my jeep. We rushed to the hospital to collect some emergency surgical equipment and drove at high speed down the 40 km road to Inobonto. There I stopped for a minute at the polyclinic to give instructions to the medical assistant in charge.

The ride took more than two hours and it was already dawn when we reached the place. The three wounded men were lying on the grass under the jeep with the five others positioned around them combat-ready. The driver had broken his leg while jumping from his jeep into the gutter. The other two men had several bullet wounds, one of them with a badly severed shoulder. It was clear that I could not do much on the roadside. With the help of one of the policemen we cautiously lifted the wounded one by one into the vehicles. While doing this, I saw the other policemen crawling swiftly over the ground changing their positions. Their faces looked grim. Suddenly I felt eerily uncomfortable, as if we were being observed by the invisible armed gang from behind the trees waiting for the right moment to open fire. I looked at the commander who seemed to guess my thoughts He comforted me, saying: "Doc, don't worry, we are watching and as long as they see our readiness they will not attack". I made an effort to produce a smile.

Working on the open jeep, I took care of the wounded as well as circumstances allowed. It was not possible to perform any surgery on the spot. We decided to transport them to the polyclinic in Inobonto. Fortunately nothing happened while we were busy rearranging the wounded policemen on our jeeps in order to make it more comfortable for them during transport. Meanwhile, the other police jeep arrived with another five men.

We drove cautiously, expecting a hail of bullets at every corner. I drove my jeep with the three wounded men in the middle, feeling protected by the armed policemen in the vehicles in front and behind me. Nevertheless a deep sigh of relief escaped me when I saw the first houses of the village before me.

The medical assistant of Inobonto had prepared very well for our arrival. He had transformed the only table available into an emergency operating table.

Scalpels, hooks and other necessary instruments had been sterilized so that I could start work immediately. I started first with redressing the fractured leg and treatment of the open wounds. Later on I removed a bullet from a shoulder. With the help of my two assistants the work went smoothly. By noon we were ready to move back to Kotamobagu. When we arrived there the wounded men looked fine and were in good spirits. I put the three men in our hospital for further treatment.

During the following year more and more rumours reached us about armed gangs which were active against the police force and we heard that even some military personnel were behind the separatist movement. Nobody knew for sure what was actually happening. The central government in Jakarta was plagued by a series of cabinet crises in succession. Political parties intrigued against each other fighting for political dominance and favours of the President.

From the Minahassa district the irregularities soon spilled over to Bolaang Mongondow Regency. Armed groups established their hide-outs in the thick forest on the mountains surrounding the Dumoga Valley. From there they took control of the valley, where for many years a number of migrants from the Minahassa with more or less success had settled themselves as farmers. Many of these migrants had perished from malaria and other diseases. Others returned home after having lost part of their families. More than once we met them in Kotamobagu on their way home to the Minahassa with mothers cuddling their dying babies in their arms. The few remaining continued to struggle for their existence. Those who were successful attracted new migrants from their villages. So in the course of years their numbers grew steadily but slowly. Accustomed to a perilous life, the arrival of armed gangs did not bother them much. Moreover, since they were of the same ethnic group they cooperated. The official administration was still in the hands of the Mongondow authorities, but the armed gangs or *Pemuda* (youth) as they were called, behaved as the rulers of the District. Their attitude towards the local authorities was both suspicious and hostile. However, they welcomed me heartily every time I visited the area to perform my routine medical duties. They were always friendly and hospitable to me so that at one time the Regency Chief confided to me that he felt safe in the area only when he was in my company!

Once I was asked as a guest of honour to address a mass rally which they organized in the District capital. Hearing their emotionally laden rhetorical speeches I was rather shocked and when I saw their huge red banners flying over the paddy fields I silently drew my own conclusions, associating them with the Communist Party. I found it wise, however, not to refuse, but found it also better not to involve myself in politics. When my turn came I climbed the shaky bamboo platform and spoke at length about health prevention and health care, trying to convince everybody that health is the first priority for any community in order to make good progress.

As was to be expected from revolutionary youngsters they were very anx-ious to take good care of their guest of honour. In their imagination they were always surrounded by "enemies of the revolution". Armed guards followed me everywhere I went, even to the bathroom, to protect me. I remained calm and behaved jovially, but inside I felt a little bit uneasy. I imagined that if it really would come to a clash between them and the government, they certainly would need to have medical help available at any time. What would be easier than just taking the doctor with them to their hide-outs?

These secret concerns grew stronger and stronger with time, since more rumours filled the air about pending revolutions in other parts of the vast Indonesian archipelago. When I mentioned my worries to Astri, she confessed that she had had the same feelings for a long time. Without my knowledge she had always a sum of money ready at hand during my long trips away from home, expecting that at any time during my absence an armed gang could knock at the door.

Other concerns came up. The cat of the Catholic priest who lived near us around the corner died of rabies. A week later a man was bitten by a dog which the next day died with obvious symptoms of rabies. I asked the police to kill the dog and sent the skull to the virus laboratory in Bandung, West Java. Following my textbook carefully I treated the man with fourteen daily injec-tions of serum in the muscles of his back and his belly, which to my astonish-ment were incredibly painful. It was the first and also the last time that I ever treated a rabies patient. He survived. One month later we were informed by cable that the test was positive. Meanwhile, our anti-rabies campaign was suc-cessful, thanks to the cooperation of the dog owners, the police and the mili-tary. There were no new rabies cases reported in the area, but we could not get rid of our rabies scare. We could not help but look with suspicion at every dog we met, since it was not possible to keep our children at home all the time. They went out happily to play with our neighbours and with other children at the kindergarten. We started also to think about better schools for our children and that they needed to grow up in a normal and peaceful atmosphere.

After long deliberations, we decided to request the Ministry of Health in Jakarta for a transfer to Bali when our contract with the Regency of Bolaang Mongondow was due to expire in August 1954.

BOOK V

Pioneering Work in Bali

CHAPTER 40

Return to Bali

It was not easy to disengage ourselves from the people of Mongondow. They begged us to stay. The Regency's House of Representatives even sent a delegation to the Ministry of Health in Jakarta requesting to annul our transfer. Since we were on contract with the Regency on a voluntary basis, there was no legal justification for the Government to prevent us from returning to our home island. Moreover the Ministry had already promised the Governor of Bali to provide a doctor to fill the long standing vacancy of Regency Doctor for the large district of North Bali.

Nevertheless, it was with a heavy heart that we took leave from all the personnel with whom we had been working most harmoniously all those years, from all our friends and the people who had put their trust in us. We felt especially uncomfortable since we knew for certain that for them political tumult and social disturbances were lying ahead. (We heard later that not long after his arrival in Mongondow the doctor who replaced us was abducted by unnamed guerrilla groups and was held hostage for some time in the jungle.)

On our last day many visitors came to say farewell. It was an emotional event, and very exhausting, especially because that day Madelief and Widur came down with fever from malaria. However, we did not postpone the trip, because our first port of call was going to be the Catholic Missionary Hospital in Tomohon, where we would be under the care of our friend Dr. Annie Barten.

She immediately made us welcome, and cheered us up with her good humour. She was the prototype of the missionary doctor, fully dedicated to her work. We had a couple of days rest in Tomohon, waiting for the boat that would carry us from Manado to Makassar and further to Buleleng, the harbour of North Bali. Widur and Madelief recovered from their malaria and Astri felt much better in the cooler climate.

The boat which carried us from Manado to Bali was one of the few ships remaining from the K.P.M., the old Royal Dutch Shipping Company, that after independence was taken over by the Indonesian government. For the time being they were still under the command of a Dutch captain. The change from deprived life in Mongondow to the luxury of a Dutch passenger ship was for us a great event, which we fully enjoyed. Unfortunately, on the third and last night on the ship, Widur became suddenly ill with a very high temperature. What worried us was that there were no signs or symptoms which could give us any clue about his illness. We assumed that it was just a severe cold.

When we arrived in Buleleng the next morning, Father, my eldest brother Gedé, his mother and his wife, my sister Manik and other family members were at the harbour to meet us. Father was delighted to have us back in Bali, although he could not hide his disappointment at the fact that I was not assigned as a doctor in Karangasem. He had hoped that my activities as a doctor in his previous kingdom would serve to regain prestige for the family which he felt had been eroded by the recent political developments. Since 1950 the government had abolished the self-governing Kingdoms—and the still functioning Rajas or their successors had become government officials. That was the case also with my eldest brother who succeeded Father when he retired in 1950. For Father it was really a bitter pill to swallow.

Our reception in Buleleng by the authorities was lavish, partly due to the fact that many of my friends from before the war now held important positions in government. Dr Nuridja, the head of the hospital in Singaraja, brought us straight to the doctor's house that had been made ready for us with furniture temporarily on loan from the hospital. He had also arranged for people to unload and transport our luggage. After we had settled ourselves in our new home, Father and the rest of the family returned to Karangasem.

Towards the evening, Widur became hot again, and what was worrying, he became lethargic. By chance, a Dutch doctor was visiting Bali and as a matter of course we consulted him about Widur. On account of his low pulse rate and lethargy, he suspected typhoid and gave us a bottle of chloramphenicol, a new drug which was not yet available in Bali. I gave Widur the recommended dose of the medicine. Two hours later—at midnight—the boy was icy cold and sophorous, reacting hardly to stimulation. I was terrified that I may have given him an overdose. Not having the courage to tell Astri my fears, I kept silent, while trying to hide my panic. In an attempt to restore his body temperature we took the boy between us in bed. I didn't really know what else to do, other than keep my finger on his pulse and put my stethoscope on his chest now and then. The night seemed endless. Towards dawn, however, his pulse became stronger and his body temperature returned to normal. In the morning he seemed better, and in a few days he recovered completely, despite the fact that I had stopped all medication. Who knows, it may just have been the flu!

* * * * * *

As the District Medical Officer for North Bali it was my duty to go to the field and visit all the polyclinics and the leprosarium at least once a week. There were eight polyclinics in the district at distances ranging from 10 to 80 km from town. Other field trips had to be made in connection with several public health campaigns, such as the yaws campaign, smallpox and BCG vaccinations, and the treatment of leprosy patients. In the past few years Dr Nuridja had been in charge of the field work in addition to his main duty in the 100-bed hospital in the town. Obviously that was too much for his frail body and most of the visits had to be done by medical assistants. No wonder then that when word came through that the polyclinics would be visited by a real doctor, the people flocked in great numbers to seek medical help.

Although I had a good car to make the visits, the work was quite strenuous. The roads were very bad. Potholes in asphalt made a much rougher ride than the dirt and gravel roads I was used to in Celebes. Asphalt lured our drivers to drive fast and thus bump harder over the potholes. After having covered not more than 20 km in one hour I arrived with a completely rattled body at a polyclinic where 200–300 patients were waiting. Then the real battle would begin—battle against time, against poverty, against ignorance, and most frustrating of all, against shortage of medicines and other medical provisions. The sheer numbers of patients caused the quality of medical work to deteriorate well below the acceptable level. One had to judge and make a diagnosis in seconds, since there was just not enough time to be spent on each patient. One had very often to be content with giving substitute medicines, knowing that they would be of little or no help at all. Nevertheless, in the light of the tremendous short-comings one may in hindsight marvel at the progress that was made.

In those years, yaws, malaria and tuberculosis were still rampant. There was a great deal of malnutrition, and more than half the school children had chronic tropical ulcers on their legs. However, with the advent of penicillin in the mid-1950s, the UNICEF "yaws campaign", the BCG immunization programme and the introduction of DDS against leprosy, great improvements in public health were made. Although there were far too few doctors on the island to take care of the population of one and a half million, the medical and health services were much more advanced than in Bolaang Mongondow. In Bali there was a district hospital of between 50 and 100 beds in each of the eight Districts, one main central hospital in Denpasar with a number of specialists, one mental hospital in Bangli and four leprosariums at coastal sites. A number of nursing schools and a midwifery school were already established. About forty polyclinics were spread over the whole island, each manned by one or two medical assistants. To remedy the shortage of doctors, the government recruited foreigners on short-term-contracts. When I arrived in Bali in 1954, there were only seven Indonesian doctors on the island, six of them senior to me. By 1957, we had nine foreign doctors as well.

Being involved as District Officer in the various mass campaigns and seeing their spectacular results, I became more interested in Public Health, although I found clinical medicine still most intriguing. With time my inclination towards Public Health grew, and when in 1956 the Bali government needed a doctor to be trained as a nutritionist at the London School of Hygiene and Tropical Medicine and none of my colleagues was willing to go, I volunteered. I did not question why nobody was interested to go for such a training course which seemed so attractive to me.

It was only some years later, after I had become Bali's Chief Medical Officer and had as one of my tasks the supervision over the work of my colleagues that I realized why their general attitude towards the medical profession was so different than mine. Already during the first weeks in Bali I was shocked by the lack of scientific discourse among my colleagues. At social gatherings I felt embarrassed every time they or their ladies asked me how I was faring with my private practice. That was apparently a very normal question among them. But it embarrassed and confused me at the same time, leaving me wondering whether it was only a formality or sincere interest or malicious curiosity. I usually managed to give vague answers and quickly changed the subject. Later as Chief Medical Officer it dawned on me how wrong I was to expect that everybody who had chosen to become a doctor was an idealist. In the circumstances prevailing in our country in the 1950s and 1960s, where everything was uncertain, and no security for the future existed, everybody—including our doctors—was trying to obtain as much wealth as possible in as short a time as possible. Nevertheless, despite the difficult circumstances and political upheavals there was enough sense of responsibility among our colleagues and our paramedical personnel. In general, they performed their duties well, thereby fully respecting the ethics of their profession.

Unfortunately this was no longer the case in the following two decades.

CHAPTER 41

Life in Bali

Medical Work in Buleleng Regency

Balinese society always had and still has great respect for tradition. A great part of my success in my work in Bali as a medical and public health doctor must be attributed to the trust and respect the people accorded to the Karangasem royal family. For the people of Buleleng, the large District of North Bali, the family links between the traditional rulers of Karangasem and Buleleng were of great significance. In addition, there was that mystic belief that a doctor who had studied in Holland must be of a higher order than his colleagues from an Indonesian medical school. These favourable attitudes made it easy for me not only to win people over to modern medicine and to combat superstition, but also—with regard to medical and paramedical personnel—to get things done.

Once UNICEF introduced the anti-leprosy drug DDS, the great number of lepers on the island were encouraged to seek medical help. They had to be convinced that leprosy was curable and more easily so if the patient could be treated as early as possible. Detection of patients at an early stage was therefore very important. For this purpose it was crucial to overcome their shyness about appearing in public and to convince people that the disease was not a punishment by the gods for committed sins in a previous incarnation. To show that leprosy was not contagious I had my hair cut in public by a known leper.

General fear of contact with leprosy patients started to wane and was later further diminished when in 1958 people saw that we chose to build our house next to the leprosy hospital in Denpasar and allowed the patients to enter our premises and play with our children. The British doctor in charge of the leprosy campaign was most happy with the remarkable change in attitude of the public at large. At times he became too enthusiastic in his work and having only in mind his patients, he overlooked his personnel's certain deep sentiments. This lack of sensibility turned out later to have grave consequences.

My colleagues cooperated fully. Although my main duties were in the field, Dr Nuridja was especially happy with my experience in surgery and on my suggestion made the necessary improvements at the surgical department of the hospital. I was most happy to be able to perform surgical operations regularly.

One time on a visit to Denpasar I saw a brand-new Rontgen apparatus standing unused at the office of the Medical Superintendent of Bali and the Sunda Islands. It was a typical instance whereby UNICEF provided a health service with an apparatus for which there was still no trained personnel. Since I had been trained in Rontgenology in Holland, I asked the Superintendent if it could be used in the hospital in Singaraja. He approved immediately. Thus within a week a small X-Ray department was installed at the hospital. Of course this meant extra work for me, but I took it up as a hobby and people benefited from it.

I had always loved clinical work much more than public health. Therefore I took voluntarily every opportunity that presented itself to work in the hospital. Soon, with the exception of my fieldwork, I was fully engaged at the hospital. Gradually however, more and more I realized that in circumstances where a shortage of funds made it impossible to provide adequate medical help for everybody, public health activities would indirectly be of more benefit for the population as a whole. This motivated me to accept the offer for a fellowship from the Food and Agricultural Organization of the U.N. to be trained as a Medical Nutritionist in London for a period of eight months. We also thought it would be good for Astri to be in Europe for a while after seven years of tropical climate. It was decided that I would travel to London according to the F. A. O. schedule in August 1956 and that Astri and the children would go to Holland in November. They would stay there with the Tjebbes family in Bussem until I finished my training in May. I would then join them in Holland and we would travel together by ship to Bali.

Dancing

It was in 1952 during our short vacation in Bali that at a family celebration in Karangasem Trisna saw the Balinese classical *legong* dance for the first time. The dance fascinated her so much that after the performance she stepped resolutely up to Astri, saying: "Mammie, I want to learn that dance!" We were of course very surprised and at the same time very happy. The week that remained of our vacation was too short to arrange for a teacher and for her to follow any training. We therefore promised her that she would have it later when for sure we would return and live in Bali permanently. At the time we did not yet have any idea when that would be.

After that evening, Trisna started dancing by herself. It was as if all the time she heard the music in her head which directed her steps and movements of head and limbs. On the ship as well as in the hotel in Makassar on our journey back to Mongondow, whenever there was time and space was available, she was dancing. She astonished us by the way she could perform the dance movements and poses of the *legong* almost perfectly. During the remaining two years in Mongondow the dancing gradually waned, but now we were back in Bali she reminded us of our promise.

Soon after we had established our home in Singaraja we asked the dance teacher Ida Bagus Raka whom we saw two years before in Karangasem to come and stay with us in Singaraja and instruct Trisna. A young musician—a teacher in town—brought his *gender*, a Balinese metal xylophone for the accompaniment during the lessons. Trisna was extremely happy, enjoyed her training and progressed marvellously. It drew the attention of friends, Balinese and non-Balinese alike. Among the latter, many who regarded Trisna as half-Balinese were impressed that she mastered Balinese dancing so easily. Soon their daughters of Trisna's age joined and a class was formed. Spurred on by Trisna's talent, Raka developed his teaching methods. He became the first dance teacher to give Balinese dance lessons not only by the traditional individual method, but also by taking a group as a whole. This required systematic analysis of dance movements, which at that time was a completely new venture in Bali. The success he achieved became known to the teachers in the other schools in Singaraja and drew the attention of the authorities. He was invited to teach other classes. At the National Independence Day celebration, a mass demonstration of collective teaching of Balinese dance with 100 school girls was performed on the soccer field with Trisna dancing as prima donna in the middle.

Trisna was soon advanced enough to perform in public with a full Balinese orchestra and made her debut by dancing the *kebyar* at a religious festival in Karangasem. Soon afterwards she mastered the classical warrior's dance, the *baris*, and still under the tutorship of Ida Bagus Raka she learned the female part of the *temulilingan* duet. Professionals and laymen alike hailed her as an extraordinary dance talent. For Astri it was a most exciting experience. With our trip to Europe in mind we purchased the various appropriate *gelungans* (headgear) and costumes for the dances and made tape-recordings of the accompanying music. We anticipated that our friends in Holland would like to see our little girl performing.

Privacy

Every time we entered the Puri in Karangasem we heard exclamations like "Ooh, how cute!" or "Look, how fair, how beautiful!" from our sisters and the female community in general, as they saw our children. In the beginning we felt proud, but when people just could not keep their hands off our little ones it became more of a nuisance. I found nothing strange in their behaviour, but it was hard for Astri to get used to. Family and servants alike could not stop carrying our children around and giving them sweets all day.

My brothers had already been given houses with their respective families in the Puri complex, usually in the same compound as that assigned to their mothers. Since I had no mother there was no compound left for me. This did not matter, as Astri did not want to stay within the Puri complex when we visited, since for her it would mean a loss of privacy.

During one visit to the Water Gardens ("Tirtagangga") that Father had built in 1948 as a recreational park for the people and where he had erected a small bungalow for himself, Astri pointed out to me an idyllic empty plot at its north-eastern corner, consisting of a stony hill and some low marshland. One day when Father was standing on the verandah of his bungalow overlooking the wild marsh vegetation I asked him: "Father, may I ask you, what are your plans with this piece of ground?"

"Do you mean this marshland?"

"Indeed," I answered, "and that rock in the back".

"Nothing. It has no soil at all. Nothing will grow there!"

"Can we have it? I mean, Astri and my family, to build a home there!"

"Of course, but how will you do it? By the way, that rock belongs to Mé Gunakse, your stepmother. You can buy it from her. She won't object."

"Thank you so much. You will see results soon!"

Thus we paid a token sum for the piece of rock and hired labourers to dig a large round pond in the middle of the marsh, drawing the water there in order to make the surroundings dry. The rock was levelled out and Astri designed a Balinese-style house with a large verandah and four small rooms. One of Father's best helpers, I Jendela, was assigned as foreman. Because we lived in Singaraja, my brother-in-law (the husband of my only real sister and a priest), volunteered to be the supervisor. Digging the foundation in the rock was the toughest job, but after six months the house was completed. It was inaugurated with the required religious ceremonies, and we were sure that in addition to the house being "spiritually safe", it stood on solid rock.

On a round elevation in the middle of the large circular pond we put up a wooden octagonal pigeon-house, which a Chinese carpenter in Singaraja had made for us. Water lilies completed the beautiful setting of our own water garden, later enlivened by twenty white pigeons, while the terraces around the pond were decorated with flowering bushes and trees.

On holidays, weekends and events for which we had to be in Karangasem, our compound in Tirtagangga became an inexhaustible source of enjoyment for us and our children. The children roved endlessly over the five acres of garden grounds, the surrounding hills and paddy fields, and plunged themselves ten times a day in the pure spring water of the swimming pool. We found there the privacy we much needed.

Tirtagangga

In 1948, Father—who was still Raja of Karangasem—built the complex of ponds and gardens around the natural spring of Rejasa, which he later named Tirtagangga after the Ganges, the holy river in India. Its water has always been and is still regarded as holy and is used for all kinds of religious ceremonies both in temples and by families. The religious significance of the spring, the pleasant cool climate and the scenic beauty of the surroundings inspired my father to build a small country house there and a recreational garden for himself and his people. Making water gardens of all sorts had always been his hobby. He not only did the designing himself, but he also used to work together with his labourers, digging in the ground, standing knee-deep in the water, dirty with mud. It was a great surprise for visitors, after watching the work in progress for some time, to discover the tiny figure of the Raja among the workers. People liked it, as it was one of his charming traits. During the first years the work gave him only enjoyment.

In 1950 with National Independence and the ensuing Indonesian Constitution, the government started to abolish the institution of the Rajas, made them civil servants and stripped them of the privileges previously bestowed by the colonial power. Father lost the means by which he could indulge in hobbies such as the building of water gardens. Work had now to be done on a very modest scale and with the cheapest of materials. He suffered, not so much from the material loss, as from the sense of powerlessness and humiliation. It was as if a whole world—his world—had crumbled. More and more he spent his time in Tirtagangga. On weekends when we came over from Singaraja, we often saw him standing on his verandah, staring into faraway distances, dreaming of past times of glory. He was always happy to see us there. Astri was for him the embodiment of whatever he felt as the favourable attributes of anything Dutch: trustworthiness, practicality, genius. While in the past he was entirely charmed by my eldest brother, he came to realize in later life that his second son could better satisfy his interest in world affairs. He asked about everything. Despite his lack of schooling, Father knew a lot thanks to his bright intellect. He was of that type of people who understood situations with a minimum of factual knowledge. Often he surprised us with the questions he asked; they were always relevant and exact.

Once I discussed with him the subject of land ownership because I knew from reliable sources that the government would soon introduce Land Reform over the whole country. I was not able to convince him about the necessity of taking steps to save at least some of the huge property for his family. It was just beyond his imagination that a government would take somebody's property and distribute it to other people. For him "the other people" meant the people living on his property, therefore "his" people.

"Why should the land be distributed to them?" he asked, "They already enjoy all the produce, and, moreover, they do not pay taxes".

I frowned and asked: "How is that? No taxes?"

"No, because I am paying it for them".

I suddenly realized what I had thus far only vaguely imagined. Now I understood why Father, with all his 500 hectares of land had trouble paying expenses for his lifelong hobby of building water gardens. He never demanded anything from his tenants, leaving all these matters to his *sedahans* (bailiffs). Apart from rice and coconut, necessary for the upkeep of the household of some two hundred inhabitants of the Puri in Karangasem, and for our family's well-being, contributions were asked from the tenants only for religious ceremonies to be held at certain temples that related to our family. This complete lack of supervision from Father's side had spoiled his bailiffs. Father became poorer by the year, because for the payment of taxes he had to sell a piece of land every year. This of course went through the managers who knew how to make profit out of everything. Knowing how Father loathed to check anybody, I came to the conclusion that the forthcoming Land Reform Bill would after all be good for Father and for us.

My younger brother Ketut happened to have good relations with the Agrarian Affairs Department. He also knew of the forthcoming Land Reform Bill, and received information that, before its enactment, land could still be given legally as inheritance to direct male descendants. This could take place at a rate of seven hectares per person living in the same District or three hectares for those living outside the District. He got access to a complete list of Father's properties, and worked out a way of distributing Father's land among his ten sons. Even after this distribution, about 400 hectares still remained.

With great effort we succeeded in persuading Father to make use of the short time still available. He instructed Ketut to make arrangements for distributing as much of his land as would legally be allowed. One day, Father called me and led me into his bedroom. After making sure that we were alone, he said: "Madé, I think you are right when you told me that Land Reform is after all not a bad thing. Honestly speaking we must admit that we have not earned our property by our own sweat or hard work. As Rajas our fathers had the right to confiscate land from anyone who died without legal male inheritors. They then took care of their wives and children."

Little did I suspect that Ketut would take advantage of his position to assign for himself the better pieces of land. I knew that his task was not an easy one. Apart from the prospect that some of the bailiffs would certainly try to hide papers of land ownership, Father had often impulsively given away land to people out of compassion or as a contribution for the maintenance of temples. Many times the necessary paperwork had been neglected. My other brothers were happy to allow somebody else to do the tedious work, but years later they blamed Ketut for having been too generous to himself.

CHAPTER 42

Balinese Dance
in London

In 1956 I spent a year training as a Nutritionist at the London School of Hygiene and Tropical Medicine. While I was there I met by chance a former classmate from the A.M.S. -B in Yogyakarta who had finished his medical studies in Jakarta. Asked what he was doing in London Dr Moerdowo surprised me by saying that he was assigned to the Indonesian Embassy as the Cultural Attaché. I remembered from school that he could paint well and that we together performed Indonesian dances at a school festival, he a Javanese *wayang orang* and myself the Balinese *baris*. However, knowing that he was always very straightforward in his utterances, I had never thought of him as a diplomat. Actually he had not become a member of the diplomatic staff, but through influential friends at the Ministry of Foreign Affairs had got this job, giving him the opportunity to specialize in Internal Medicine in London while working at the Embassy. Talking about dances I told him about Trisna's success with Balinese dance. When he found out that my family was in Holland, he insisted that Trisna should come to London and perform on behalf of the Indonesian Embassy for the diplomatic corps. As Cultural Attaché he could easily arrange a venue for the performances and take care of the invitations to the embassies and all other official necessities. Although it quite overwhelmed me, I liked the idea.

Thus, it was arranged that the performance would take place in May when I finished my studies. Astri's father would accompany Astri, Trisna and Surya to London, while the two younger children would stay with the Tjebbes family in Bussum. In England there was no age limit for performing in public. In order to make the show long enough to fill a whole evening, Dr Moerdowo made arrangements to have an Indonesian dance event in the Albert Hall that would be attended by the whole diplomatic corps of London. Both Dr Moerdowo and his wife would perform Javanese dances in addition to some Sumatran dances by staff members of the Indonesian Embassy.

Unexpectedly, we met with a bureaucratic problem. The immigration officials would not allow Astri to travel abroad with only Trisna and Surya because the names of all our four children were written on her passport! Thanks to Hans Rhodius having good connections with high officers at the Ministry in The Hague the problem was solved after an exchange of telephone calls.

At the Albert Hall the applause after Trisna's performance was tremendous and prolonged. The leader of the Sadler's Wells Ballet came to see us in the dressing rooms. They asked our approval for Trisna to perform for their ballet group in their studio. We felt very honoured and a little shy. But Trisna who had spent one week with the ballet group of Sonja Gaskel in Holland was enthusiastic. She wanted to see more of ballet rehearsals.

The meeting with the Sadler's Wells dancers in their studio was most interesting. The dancers found the Balinese music and dance movements simply fascinating. Many of them tried to perform some passes together with Trisna while others took paper and pencil and made quick sketches of Trisna's dancing positions and gestures of head and limbs in minute detail. Being a lover of drawing myself I was particularly impressed. That night we were invited to watch their group performing Petrouchka. We enjoyed the ballet profoundly. Trisna was much impressed by the perfection and discipline of the seemingly involuntary movements of the puppet. Not having seen anything like that in Balinese dance, she found them both funny and admirable. When some time later her mother asked her: "Tris, would you like to learn ballet?" she thought for a while and answered; "No, Mams, I don't know precisely, but I do miss something in it. It is too much physical exercise".

At the time I had not yet been long enough involved in the arts in Bali and I did not pay special attention to her words. With hindsight, however, it must be said that naturally enough a girl of nine years age would not be able to express her feelings exactly in such matters. At a later stage after some years working with dance groups in Bali, I realized with astonishing clarity that our daughter had indeed already at that age grasped—be it unconsciously—the essential difference between the mechanical perfection of Western ballet and the transcendental quality of even the simplest Balinese dance.

CHAPTER 43

A Move to South Bali

A Surprise Promotion

After I finished my studies in London, Astri and I enjoyed a short vacation in Paris, then we all returned home to Indonesia on a freighter aptly named *Bali!* After a very enjoyable trip we disembarked in Surabaya, and then boarded the connecting boat, the *Valentijn* to Buleleng in Bali. Dr Nuridja met us at the harbour and brought the news: "Madé, we have all agreed that you will be our boss, the Chief Medical officer of Bali."

"What?" I asked, "Has Dr Subadi been transferred?"

"No! He was murdered! About a month ago!"

"What??" I was perplexed. "What happened?"

I was completely taken by surprise. Knowing Dr Subadi as a very sympathetic person, it was the last thing that I expected to hear. I asked Dr Nuridja to tell what had happened.

"Well, it is a very sad story indeed," he said. "You know Dr Reed, our expatriate leprologist. He succeeded in getting three motorbikes from the Ministry for his personnel to visit the leprosy treatment points all over the island. He recommended that the motorbikes be assigned to the three most active and reliable fieldworkers in the Leprosy Campaign. Dr Subadi had to distribute the vehicles. One of the seniors of the field workers who was known as very lazy was of course not on the list. He came to Dr Subadi's office and complained. Somehow a heated exchange of words followed. Then the man ran away, came back with a knife and attacked Dr Subadi. There was nobody else in the room. When office personnel dashed into the room because of the noise, Dr Subadi was bleeding to death on the floor. The murderer came to his senses and surrendered willingly. Dr Subadi was rushed to the hospital but did not survive."

I fell silent for a long time. It was too abrupt a story to digest. I had the feeling of a totally unnecessary loss of life which could have been avoided.

"But why me?" I asked, "there are other colleagues who are more senior and who have been working in Bali for much longer'.

"Because we know that you are an organizer. You are honest and everyone will listen to you!'

"Stop!" I interrupted, "that is too much praise!"

"Not really," Dr Nuridja continued, "we mean it!" Looking straight into my eyes, he said softly, "To be honest, Madé, everybody is scared to take up the job."

This remark made me laugh inside, but I was careful not to show my contempt. Many thoughts were flashing through my mind. I had enough self-confidence and knew well that I was able to do the job. For the moment, however, I had to concentrate on taking care of my wife and children, putting our household in order and arranging for the children to get to school properly after an absence of so many months. Fortunately, these matters were easily organized, and our children were bright enough to catch up with the lessons they had missed very quickly.

At Headquarters in Denpasar everything appeared to have been prepared for my taking up the Chief Medical Officer's job. A replacement for me as Regency Medical Officer of North Bali had been secured by the Ministry of Health. Even the difficulty of housing had been overcome, although there was no house yet in Denpasar for the Provincial Chief Medical Officer. A large piece of ground was made available by the Government to build a Leprosy Hospital and Rehabilitation Centre in the northern outskirts of the town. It was meant for the treatment of adverse reactions on the new drug DDS and surgical treatment of disabling effects of leprosy. Having seen the site of the project we found that one fourth of that piece of ground could be reserved to build a house next to the Leprosy Hospital. When everybody, including even our doctors, frowned upon this, we argued that it would be a very effective way making people understand that leprosy is not contagious and thus not to be feared.

We were allowed to design our official residence ourselves, very much to Astri's delight. The construction of the house took about eight months. During that time I had to go every other day to Denpasar to fulfil my duties. Much of the work consisted also of inspection trips to the other Districts of Bali and to the island of Nusa Penida in the south. But by mid 1958 the building work was completed and we moved happily to the capital.

Peliatan

Our transfer to Denpasar turned out to be of great significance for Trisna. Her former dance teacher Raka advised us that she should continue dancing and be trained by the old lady dance teacher, Biang Sengog, at Peliatan, a village about 25 km from town. The Peliatan Legong Dance group was already famous because of performance in 1929 at the International Fair in Paris, and later per-fomances with a European tour in 1952, described by John Coast in his book

Dancing out of Bali. When we made our visit to Peliatan, the leader of the group, Anak Agung (Prince) Gedé Mandera, a prominent nobleman of the village, felt very honoured having Trisna as a student and club-member, for he regarded her as a real Balinese princess. His delight knew no bounds when he saw Trisna having her first lessons with Biang Sengog. Being a musician and dance teacher himself he immediately sensed her extraordinary qualities.

Soon Trisna became the idol of the company. In three weeks she mastered the intricate and most difficult dance of the *condong*, which Biang Sengog had been training other girls for with great patience for three months without satisfactory results. Biang Sengog was not a "soft" teacher. She trained her pupils rigorously in the traditional way and demanded the utmost from them. Luckily, Trisna had the right attitude for learning Balinese dance. She could give herself completely to the teacher, letting herself be moulded into the movements and shapes of the classical art forms handed down from generation to generation. In less than one year she mastered several classical Balinese dances and became the prima donna of the group. A surprising discovery was that she had that natural stage presence which made the audience watch her only and hardly glance at the other dancers as soon as she entered the arena.

Soon it became known over all Bali that the *sekeha* (the music and dance club of Peliatan) was in the fortunate position of having a wonderful dancer among them. Later we heard that even President Sukarno could not resist the temptation to test the news and came incognito to see her dancing on our twelve-and-a-half year wedding anniversary held at the Segara Beach Hotel in Sanur.

Being Bali's foremost group, Peliatan was always asked to perform at the Presidential Palace in Tampaksiring before President Sukarno and his State guests. Being her parents, Astri and I always had to accompany Trisna to Tampaksiring where we were introduced to personalities such as Kruschev, Norodom Sihanouk, Ho Chi Minh, and the Presidents of India, West Germany, and many other celebrities. Trisna always drew special attention from the guests, and once after a performance the crew of a Yugoslav naval vessel enthusiastically lifted her and carried her around on their shoulders. Norodom Sihanouk from Cambodia, who was a frequent guest often brought his palace band with him in which he himself played the trumpet. As a special treat Sukarno then picked out some of his guests to dance with the beautiful Cambodian ladies who formed an indispensable part of Sihanouk's retinue. On such occasions I tried hard to be somewhere else, but I never succeeded.

Later, when cultural missions were sent abroad, Trisna was asked almost every time to join as a guest dancer. In a few years she travelled to many countries including Pakistan, India, Cambodia, Thailand, China, Vietnam, North Korea and Japan. It was a miracle that with all the rehearsals in the village, the frequent night performances at religious events and before guests and the long absences from school during her trips abroad, Trisna always managed to be in the first of her class at school.

An episode that we will never forget occurred when once in the middle of the night two buses with about fifty people stopped in front of our house in Denpasar. Three men in traditional dress knocked at our door and asked if we would allow Trisna to come with them to the village of Sukawati to perform the *legong* dance in their temple. We were perplexed. The headman explained: "Please excuse us. This is very serious. We are having the *odalan*, the yearly celebration of our village temple tonight. Just an hour ago during the most sacred ritual in the inner temple our temple priest fell suddenly in a trance, uttering the following: 'Our gods want to see Trisna Djelantik dancing the *legong!*' and so we have come here with our sincere request." When I replied: "Trisna is used to dancing to the music of the Peliatan Group," they answered: "Yes, we know, and we have already asked the group to come too."

We found it a difficult decision. Astri suggested that we should ask Trisna herself for she was to have her school examinations the next morning. We woke her up and when we told her what was on hand, she immediately said: "Mams, don't worry, of course I will go, it will be good for everybody". The delegation assured us that they would bring her back the next morning. Still a bit sleepy Trisna climbed happily in the bus. We had much confidence in the people so that we did not bother to accompany her. She came back home at five in the morning and at seven she was already in her classroom.

Through Trisna's membership of the *sekeha* (music and dance club) of Peliatan we got involved in the routine activities of Balinese artists, dancers, musicians and teachers. From the dance teachers and musicians at Peliatan I learned a great deal of technical detail concerning Balinese performing arts. Astri shared my delight and she busied herself with the improvement of the girls' dance costumes and succeeded even in reviving the use of the most classical and appropriate outfit for the *gabor* (old temple dance.) Our involvement with the Sekeha kept us busy all the time, travelling up and down the road between Denpasar and Peliatan, often until late after midnight. We became the principal advisers of the Club.

Involvement in the Arts

President Sukarno was a great lover and promoter of the arts. Once he brought a group of Javanese dancers with him to perform dances to Bali before the Balinese public. For the exchange programme our group was asked to perform the classical *legong* that evening. A temporary open stage was erected in front of the Bali Museum in Denpasar. Equipped with wire-framed large silken wings on their backs a group of beautiful Javanese girls performed the Butterfly Dance. The dancers could move their wings to the rhythm of the music through a mechanical device by manipulating a handle at the front of their girdles. It was indeed a most beautiful show. The members of our group were completely fascinated. In the dressing rooms at the end of the evening they urged me to order such wing devices for our Peliatan group. I was perplexed!

All of a sudden I realized that with all their natural artistic talent the members of our group had not grasped the difference between Art and Kitsch. I was faced with the problem how to explain it to our friends. Even their leader A. A. Mandera voiced the opinion that to match the beauty of Javanese art we ought to acquire such equipment. I was determined to wash away that misconception once and for all immediately. Asking one of our girls to dance with our traditional leather wings fixed on their arms and next to her at the same time one of the Javanese girls to dance with their silken wings, I asked our friends to try to feel the difference and spoke about the Balinese concept of *taksu*, the magic of the spiritual force, behind the dance movements. They instantly understood and decided to drop their request.

The episode struck me and remained worrying me for a long time. I had the strong feeling that something important had to be done. Our Balinese artists had to be made aware of potential dangers of deteriorating influences on their art by what they might see as "progress". There must be a way of establishing intensive contact with all of them, not only with our Peliatan group. But how? Fortunately at that time the Konservatori Karawitan or Music Conservatory (abbreviated to KOKAR) had just been opened in Denpasar as a branch of the Conservatory of Solo, in Central Java. The Government felt the need for this institution of Javanese music and dance to have a branch in Bali for the preservation of classical Balinese dance and music. The teachers were drawn from alumni of the Solo Conservatory as well as from traditional dance and music teachers in Bali. With the help of the then Deputy Governor of Bali and the Director of KOKAR I succeeded in establishing a consultative council for the arts and culture, (abbreviated LISTIBYA) to advise the Government and groups of artists in all matters relevant to the preservation of the values of the arts in Bali. The Council consisted of volunteers and worked very hard, visiting art groups performing in the field, monitoring their developments and constantly giving the needed information and advice. It organized exhibitions and competitions and put forward proposals to the authorities for extending awards to artists of extraordinary merit.

Our Council was tested heavily when in 1962 President Sukarno wanted to have a spectacular dance performance at the opening of the Asian Games which would be held in the huge Olympic stadium in Jakarta, newly built with Russian assistance. His idea was to match the Russian mass gymnastics show that he had seen in Moscow, which was to come to Jakarta for the same occasion. I was appointed as Director of the Project. With our Balinese dance and music teachers we choreographed a colourful mass dance programme to be performed for twenty minutes by 960 girls and 80 boys. We trained them for three

months in six different places in Bali. It was an enormous organization and a
novelty, requiring a completely new approach to Balinese dance. New costumes had to be invented. A passenger ship was requisitioned to transport our
dancers, musicians and officials and provide accommodation during their stay
in Jakarta. At the grand opening in the stadium all went remarkably well, with
perfect precision of time and space, even though the Russians had marked the
whole field with confusing lines and signs for their own show. Nevertheless
thanks to the skill and discipline of our dancers we made a most spectacular
performance.

In the course of time it became apparent that the Conservatory was organized only for the practical training of performing artists, aiming at the delivery of practising dancers and musicians who would be able to teach dancing
and music at schools and in private. It did not give the students the academic
background needed for them to be able to reflect on the developments of the
arts in general and to see Balinese art in a wider perspective. Thus, at the initiative of LISTIBYA, the Art Academy for Dance and Music (ASTI) of
Denpasar came into being in 1967. My friend and colleague Dr Moerdowo
played an important part in this endeavour. In my capacity of Dean of the
Medical Faculty of the University, I had him transferred to Denpasar in 1966
to become Head of the Department of Internal Medicine. Seeing my involvement in the arts he immediately became an enthusiastic member of our
Cultural Council. I became a lecturer at the Academy on the subject of
"Aesthetics" and, being a physician, also on "Kinesiology". Starting with voluntary teachers only and using classrooms at the Conservatory, ASTI was soon
recognized and financed by the Provincial Government. In 1969 it became a
National Institute under an Directorate of Culture and thus financed by the
central Government. In 1976 it was taken over by the Department of Higher
Education. With the purpose to develop it further towards the establishment of
an "Institute of Indonesian Arts" (Institut Seni Indonesia, or ISI), in 1988
ASTI's status was raised to university level and named STSI, "Sekolah Tinggi
Seni Indonesia" (College of Indonesian Arts), as the precursor of ISI, which
will eventually include not only Dance, Music and Theatre, but also the Visual
Arts (Painting and Sculpture, Photography and Film-making), Ceramics and
Handicrafts.

CHAPTER 44

Family Planning

My position as a high official in government service meant I had to attend a host of formal occasions, while my ancestry entailed the traditional obligation of being present at many family and religious celebrations. These were all time-consuming events. Astri in the beginning had some difficulty in coping with the traditional separation of the female and male guests. In the course of time she learned to adapt and with better command of the language she found such occasions increasingly interesting.

She had to comply with the limited range of subjects that was possible between her and the Balinese ladies, who usually started with asking about her land of origin, how long she had been in Bali, and always how many children she had, how old they were, and so on. These exchanges of the same information were boring but unavoidable. After some years, however, Astri discovered that the ladies were most impressed whenever she mentioned that our youngest was ten years old. It struck her that it often triggered off a lively whispering among them in Balinese which she could not follow. But it took some more time before one of them ventured to ask: "How do you do that?"

"What do you mean?"

"No baby any more? Have you not been pregnant again? But of course, your husband is a doctor, he must have given you the right medicine for that!"

"Medicine? No, we don't take any medicine. But it is quite difficult to explain, I am afraid my Indonesian is not good enough, you had better ask my husband."

Such a conversation happened again and again.

Once, after attending a tooth-filing ceremony, Astri told me her discovery: "Madé, I think that your ladies are in need of some method of birth control. Do you know a good one that would be suitable for them?"

I had no ready answer for her. It was a subject that for some reason I had never studied seriously. For ourselves, we had applied the calendar method, although not always consistently. We decided to give the problem some serious thought and started to study from available literature. Circumstances were not very favourable. Politically our President was against it, in the belief propagated by the Communists, that the West was promoting birth control in the developing world to keep these peoples small and thus weak in order to hold them forever under its supremacy. Also Islam, the religion of the greater part of Indonesia, was at that time still strongly against any form of birth control.

Among the wives of the military, use of the diaphragm was known secretly. Nevertheless most of them still became pregnant after their husbands' short visits during leave from duty on the outer islands. Apparently these devices went from hand to hand and moreover they didn't fit well.

The Hindu religion in Bali would as far as we knew not pose a big problem, but although there was no official ban on Family Planning we had to start very cautiously.

Through visitors to Bali and friends abroad we somehow got in touch with the Pathfinder Fund. A great opportunity opened for us when Mrs Edna McKinnon, Field Representative of the Pathfinder Fund and Family Planning for the Far East, came to visit us in Bali. We received the right literature and contacts were made with the Planned Parenthood Federation in London, from where we received our first material assistance in the form of foam tablets. Meanwhile, Astri with the help of a few interested ladies, had started with the creation of the Balinese Family Planning Association. The Balinese community appeared to be very responsive to the idea. Despite a host of difficulties we made good progress. The number of participants grew steadily. A very energetic lady in Jakarta, Mrs Juwari, founded the National Family Planning Association. The realization that there were more people in Indonesia pursuing the same objectives strengthened us in our undertaking.

Our association received a boost after my return from Singapore where under the auspices of the Planned Parenthood Federation I was trained by Dr Shusila Gore in the technique of inserting intra-uterine devices (IUDs). Dr Kessler of the Pathfinder Fund came from Boston with a suitcase full of Lippes loops. It appeared that in Bali the IUD was readily accepted by the women as well as by community and religious leaders. I immediately started to train my midwives, knowing that our too few doctors were too busy and had no time for it. Moreover the women, especially the Moslems, would feel more comfortable to be helped by midwives. There was less reluctance among Balinese women, since traditionally our midwives had always been male. I trained two doctors in the technique to enable them to supervise the Programme. The Planned Parenthood Federation continued to provide us with material, which had to be brought into the country by messengers.

Astri was very successful in promoting the acceptability of the programme. In collaboration with the Dutch pharmaceutical firm ORGANON she introduced among the women the use of the contraceptive pill. She discovered that the pills that were manufactured at that time were of too large a dose, causing side-effects in our women who weighed on average only 40 to 45 kg. In her report to the firm she proposed to make them smaller. ORGANON complied, reduced the strength of their pill by half and it turned out that Astri was right. Later the use of even much smaller doses was recommended worldwide.

While, in the beginning, the Health establishment and the majority of the doctors were opposed to my training of midwives in IUD insertions, it was proved later that midwives were quite able to master the technique. Being the most practical way to follow in mass programmes it was gradually adopted by all Health authorities. Doctors were needed for supervision and where problems of a medical nature occurred.

Although not officially recognized our programme drew the attention of the outside world. After the upheavals in the wake of the abortive Communist coup in 1965, the new Indonesian Government saw the need for Family Planning in the country and recognized the National Family Planning Association. In 1967, I was invited to read a paper at the Family Planning Conference in Taiwan organized by the Population Council.

Under the auspices of the Planned Parenthood Federation, delegates from the Indonesian Family Planning Association were sent for a seminar and training course in Chicago in 1968, followed by a study tour to the Middle East and India for three months. Astri took part in the delegation. After the presentation of her paper in Chicago, the experts were amazed at the results of our association in Bali. Computerization of her statistical figures and graphs showed by extrapolation a remarkable trend of a declining birth rate for the future in Bali.

On her return from the trip, Astri was struck by a severe form of hepatitis which she appeared to have contracted in India. She was ill for many months and was thereafter no longer able to participate in the activities of the Association. However, she had laid a solid foundation for the Programme and there were already enough trained personnel to continue with the activities.

In the 1970s, in recognition of its complexities, the Government took charge of the family planning programme and integrated all relevant Departments and private organizations together into the National Family Planning Board (BKBN). All local authorities from the provincial Districts and down to the village level were made responsible for the implementation of the programme. With the assistance of US AID it has become the most successful family planning programme in Asia.

CHAPTER 45

The Good Ship HOPE

From the verandah of a bungalow at the Sindu Beach Hotel in Sanur we looked over our after-dinner coffee at the wide sandy beach glistening in the bright moonlight. We enjoyed the tranquillity of the bamboo bungalow, the cool sea breeze and the soft rippling sound of the water. My guest, Dr Walsh of the People-To-People Foundation, Washington, had invited me, head of the Bali Health Services, for dinner at his hotel. He wanted to hear my opinion on his plans for sending a fully-equipped hospital ship around the world, manned by various specialists who would volunteer for a period of time on the ship to fulfil a great humanitarian mission: that of providing medical help to sick people and giving specialist training to local medical staff. When he elaborated in detail about his programme I was impressed by his enthusiasm and enthralled by his idealistic humanitarian intentions. The beautiful beach under the full moon was too inviting and we went for a walk along the shore. Both of us were silently reflecting on our discussions. The wet sand giving in under our feet gave us the feeling that every step brought us physically nearer to our common goal.

"I already have the agreement in principle from your Ministry in Jakarta," Dr Walsh continued, "the problem is will it be operable. I have to find out what medical and other facilities there are locally, your manpower, equipment, road conditions, and whether the people themselves could be motivated to seek help on our ship".

"I am sure there will be a rush. But our harbour in Benoa, ten km from Denpasar, is not deep enough for your ship; you will have to moor at Padangbai, a natural harbour fifty km away and stay about two-hundred metres from the coast."

"Then transport of the sick people will be a problem."

"Sure, and therefore I think that your work in Bali will have to be different from that in Jakarta and in Surabaya, where you can moor the ship in the harbour, easily accessible to the people. In those towns there are medical schools with advanced medical staff and many more paramedical personnel. Specialist training of these staff will be very useful. The professors can pass their new knowledge and skills to their assistants and students. In Bali, providing medical help will be the greater part of your work and it should not be done only on the ship but also in our rural hospitals, which are more easily accessible for the people. I think that your doctors may also like to have experience in working in rural hospitals in the tropics in primitive circumstances. It should be challenging for them too!"

Now it was his turn to find my idea exciting. Walking leisurely on the white sand we discussed further details and later in the hotel we specified our plans on a map. We arrived at a solution by which about half of the ship's medical staff would go ashore on rotation and be dispersed over five hospitals—the Central Hospital in the capital and four rural hospitals—while the remaining personnel would stay on board for the treatment of cases that needed sophisticated equipment and good aftercare.

Six months later Dr Walsh's dream became reality.

Early in October I received the message that the hospital ship had arrived in Jakarta. At that time I had no idea at all of the many difficulties Dr Walsh had had to overcome to get his project off the ground. An old, indeed very old, World War II navy hospital ship called the *Consolation* that later had also served during the Korean war, was donated by the Government of the United States. It was of course already out of date and in very bad shape. How Dr Walsh succeeded in getting it renovated, getting volunteers as medical and nursing personnel, the medicines and equipment, was a series of exciting stories which I learned later and enhanced my admiration for my American colleague. An old friend of his invented the motto "Health Opportunity for People Every-where" making the acronym HOPE to name the ship. It was just marvellous!

Pressing medical problems in Bali did not allow me to go to Jakarta, so I decided to wait for the ship in Surabaya where it was expected to arrive two weeks later. For me it was crucial to know about the facilities, the doctors and other personnel on the ship in order to finalize our work in Bali later. Being used to our poor conditions, needless to say I was very impressed by what I saw on the *HOPE* ship. Their Surabaya programme was about the same as in Jakarta, selecting patients from the local hospitals for treatment on the ship and teaching in the ship's classrooms while demonstrating methods of treatment. It formed a most valuable addition to the medical training of students and staff in our medical schools.

Returning to Denpasar after a few days I was convinced that I should go ahead with the original plan which we outlined at the hotel in Sanur. The necessary arrangements were made with the five selected hospitals, our personnel and the best possible provisions were made for transportation of patients from anywhere at any time.

As it turned out the plan worked very well. There was excellent co-operation from the authorities. Despite some language difficulties our personnel enjoyed fully the work with their American partners. Many friendships were made between colleagues who extended their correspondence for many years afterwards. The HOPE people did not restrict their activities to the medical field only: they helped us to solve technical problems such as water supply and sanitation and repairs of equipment.

Bali provided, of course, plenty of opportunities for the HOPE people to enjoy the beauty of the island and to witness the great many colourful socio-religious events. During the Galungan (Balinese Thanksgiving) festivals on the 17th of December almost all of the HOPE personnel went ashore to see the beautifully decorated villages and various temple ceremonies. Thereafter, they were invited to attend a celebration at the palace of the Cokorda in Ubud. It was a grand festival with classical dance and music performances. As if by premonition Harriet Jordan, the HOPE midwife, felt that she was needed and returned early in the evening to Padangbai.

A few days before a very sick woman from Singaraja, with a huge tumour in her abdomen had been admitted on the HOPE ship in Padangbai. The surgeon removed a completely abscessed kidney as big as a coconut. To his surprise he discovered that the woman was pregnant. Because of her illness she had not menstruated for many months, so it was impossible to know the exact stage of her pregnancy. Moreover the womb was badly compressed at one side by the kidney abscess. He decided to close the abdomen and wait and see what would happen.

That evening when we were enjoying the party in Ubud, the woman went into labour. Harriet Jordan arrived on board just in time to attend to her. She delivered a premature baby who weighed only 5 lbs and named her Madé Jordan Hope Merta after the mother's, her own and the ship's name. As result of the compression by the tumour, the baby's face was severely dented at one side. Her skull had the shape of a half-moon. The delivery went normally without any complications. She was put in the incubator. A messenger was sent to Ubud and when we heard the news we cheered and celebrated the birth of the first HOPE baby born on the ship.

Under the loving care of Harriet Jordan the baby girl thrived in the incubator. A problem came up the following week when the ship had to sail further to its next destination. She could not stay on the ship. After the *HOPE*'s departure we had to nurse her in our main hospital in Denpasar.

The following day I told Astri about the baby. She knew the conditions in our hospital and worried that we might not be able to keep the baby alive. The next morning she went with me to the hospital and seeing that after two days the baby's weight had fallen, she decided to nurse her herself at home. I reluctantly agreed.

Thus, from that moment, her inborn nursing instinct found a new impetus after a few years of inactivity. She had the same drive and energy as I felt before when we were working together in Buru and in Northern Celebes. The baby was placed with a series of hot water bottles and cushions in the old cradle, in which she herself and all our children successively had spent their babyhood. The baby was placed in our bedroom, next to Astri, so that she was able to feed her once every hour, day and night, with the right mixture of milk from a dropper pipette. This went on for one month. When the baby gained weight the feeding frequency was gradually reduced to once every two hours from a normal bottle, and much later still to once every three hours, and so cautiously further to normal schedule. The HOPE ship luckily had left behind enough baby formula for her. A most rewarding moment was that after two months the first smile appeared on the baby's still severely deformed face. Astri knew that she had won the battle.

Our daughters Trisna and Surya first received the baby with curiosity which, perhaps induced by what they felt emanating from Astri, soon turned into love. They loved to help with bathing, changing of diapers, and later with feeding. When Madelief got older she too joined her sisters in their love for the little baby. They competed with each other in the care of the child which they soon regarded as their own little sister.

I must confess that my approach to the baby was of a very different kind. Struck by the bad deformation of the skull, I was most interested in the baby's physical and mental development. To my surprise her sight, hearing, and the reflexes of the eyes were normal. The motor functions showed clearly an increased excitability compared with normal babies. My mind was too much preoccupied by medical phenomena and I often wondered when pathological symptoms might emerge. Fortunately none of these occurred.

The mother was very ill after the operation. Although the wound healed reasonably well, her condition deteriorated when her other kidney malfunctioned. She died in the hospital in her home town two weeks after the ship left Bali.

When the baby was five months old, she was so healthy that we thought it was time to return her to her father's home. There were two grown-up girls to whom we could trust the care of their youngest sister. So we brought Merti with a sufficient stock of milk and other necessities to Singaraja and gave the necessary instructions to the two elder sisters as how to feed and to take care of the baby. All looked fine and well and the family was happy.

We had misjudged the situation. Two weeks later when we returned from a trip in the evening we found the baby back in the cradle in our bedroom! The family had brought her because of diarrhoea and Trisna had lovingly taken care of her as the baby did before. When we saw Merti we were severely shocked.

She was entirely dehydrated and stared at Astri with hollow eyes deeply sunken in their sockets. She hardly breathed. The father had told Trisna that the baby had had diarrhoea for the past three days. Astri took the baby in her arms and wept. We were back to square one.

Astri's battle started anew. For more than a week she was busy feeding every hour, day and night. The critical phase subsided and soon Merti could be given the normal feeding for her age and weight. She grew normally except that her face was still deformed. We told the family that she could stay with us and that we would send her to school when she reached school age. Her father and the whole family agreed.

Our children were very happy to have Merti back at home. Soon they took over most of the care from Astri. Since they had to go to school in the mornings, we also took a babysitter into the house. I continued with my medical observations on the girl. Physically she appeared completely normal. A striking trait was that she was very easily distracted from anything she was doing both physically or mentally. If she was eating or playing with her doll she would jump up and run to the door if a vehicle passed by. At school it was impossible for her to concentrate and stick to her work. She always became too excited, more than others, in anticipation of something happening, such as going to town or to the beach. This hyper-excitability diminished gradually in the course of the years.

Although the custom of taking children into one's house was and is still common in Indonesian and Balinese families, especially in case of relatives, our care for Merti drew much attention among colleagues and our own family. Our Balinese family could not understand how we could treat like our own offspring a child who was not from the nobility. In their eyes Merti was just a *Sudra* belonging to the fourth caste; she should be with the servants in the servants' quarters, and not have the privilege to have her meals with us together at our dining table. Often a member of our family when entering our house and seeing Merti playing in the room would innocently remark: "Hey, is this the child you picked up from the boat?" Of course, it was not meant maliciously, but we were always shocked and wondered if such remarks would harm the child. Among the doctors' wives there was some gossiping that we were crazy to have taken in such an ugly girl, and moreover one with such a dark skin!

One day, when Trisna's dance teacher came to our house to give Trisna some extra training, she happened to see Merti, still a baby at that time, in her cradle. Great sympathy for the baby with the ugly deformed skull welled up in her and she asked: "Doctor, will you please allow me to straighten that face?"

"How do you want to do that?" I asked in reply.

"Well, that baby is still like a twig, it can be moulded."

Knowing that we doctors could not do much, I said: "You can try if you like, I don't object at all".

So, after Trisna's rehearsals, Biang Sengog took the baby on her lap and playfully massaged the face with her fine delicate hands, while humming Balinese childrens' rhymes. She came to our house more often not only for Trisna but especially because she was sure that she could help Merti. And indeed, to our astonishment Merti's face started to straighten out after three months. Biang Sengog found that no more massage would be needed. Merti developed later into a very pretty girl.

In the course of time, my medical interest in Merti's development diminished while my affection towards her grew. We enrolled her in the best private school in Denpasar, the CIP school, the head of which was a Dutch-educated lady. Dutch education was still believed to be a guarantee for quality and discipline. But here also the teachers had to be reminded specifically and repeatedly that they should not make any distinction between Merti and our other children who had been at the same school in previous years.

A problem regarding Merti came up in 1968 when after many requests from the World Health Organization I received the government's approval to join their services as a Malariologist. I had to leave the country to take up my assignment elsewhere. Astri and the children were entitled to go with me. But Merti was not, since she was not our child. We decided to adopt her as our own, a plan her father and family readily agreed to. Hastily, adoption papers were made and by a Court Decision on November 28th, 1968, Merti became officially our legally adopted child. She was named Merti Jordan Hope Djelantik.

CHAPTER 46

Tampaksiring

Duties

Bali's Chief Medical Officer had the privilege (and duty) occasionally to have breakfast with President Sukarno at his palace in Tampaksiring. Officially it had an obvious purpose, since it was natural that a Head of State wished to receive information about health matters concerning an area where he happened to be for a time. Since President Sukarno's mother was Balinese he had a special affinity for the island. He had a Presidential palace built with a large auditorium and a stage for art performances at one of the most beautiful spots in Bali. It was built on the same location as the old colonial government's guest-house, perched on a steep hill above the charming Tampaksiring temple complex. From this idyllic point one has a bird's eye view of the public bathing place outside the temple, consisting of two separate open shallow ponds for male and female visitors, who let the fresh water of the holy spring that is spouting into the ponds splash profusely over their naked bodies. Such daily shows of human beauty did not fail to attract the attention of even the President.

From my predecessor I learned that I did not have to bother about health statistics or anything of that kind: "You just present yourself and offer your services as a doctor. But please don't forget to take your stethoscope and other useful things like blood pressure manometer, and so on", he advised.

"But doesn't our President have his own doctor with him?"

"Usually he does, but sometimes he comes without one".

When I went up the palace for the first time I had of course prepared myself for all sorts of questions. But my colleague was right. It was a very pleasant informal breakfast. Sukarno was indeed a charming personality, friendly and he liked jokes. Most of the time he talked about art, music, dance and history, about which he was very well informed. He seemed also to have been briefed about myself. He told me that according to his hypothesis my forefathers were refugees from Cambodia, who in the 9th century had fled the country after an abortive coup and landed by boat in Bali. They established a dynasty on the island. In the 11th century, one of the Balinese kings married the daughter of the King of Kediri in East Java and became the famous King Eirlangga, reigning over East Java and Bali. I confessed to him that it was the first time that I had heard the story. My father had indeed told me many years ago that we are descendants from Eirlangga and not from the Majapahit dynasty as most of the Balinese nobility claimed, regarding it as superior. He never had, however, mentioned to me any connection with Cambodia.

"Well, Doctor, you have been educated in Holland, but now you should read more about your own family's history and that of Indonesia," he said.

He did not touch on politics and I found it wise not to do so either. His personal health was of course a topic which was dealt with extensively. I noticed that a whole pharmacy was on a tray next to him on our breakfast table. His account of his kidney troubles did make me think of kidney stones in the first place and I marvelled at the presence of a large bottle of lactas calcicus tablets (a calcium supplement) on the tray. The remainder consisted of all kinds of vitamins and other health stimulants. I saw also tranquilizers and sleeping pills. There were three small boxes apparently containing ampoules for injections, but I could not read the print.

After breakfast he stood up and picking up one of the small boxes he asked me to come with him to the bedroom. He took an ampoule out of the box and handed it to me. "Doctor, please give me this injection!" he requested.

I read the label—"Testosterone"—and stared at his face.

"What is the matter, Doc?"

"Well, I think this is bad for you, so according to my medical conscience I have to refuse your request!"

It was perhaps an honest, but the most stupid answer that I could have given him. His face grew instantly red and, raising his voice, he said: "How come? You are the first doctor who ever refuses me what I ask, how do you dare?"

We landed in an argument. I braced myself to remain calm and explained my reasons. I repeated his complaints about his kidneys and associated it with the many hormone injections that he surely had had already. I mentioned the lactas calcicus that might have promoted the forming of kidney stones and the heavy overload of vitamins A and D by which he was poisoning himself.

He calmed down, saying: "Well, you are the doctor and I have to follow your advice. But why have none of your colleagues told me this before?"

Timidly I answered: "I don't know. Perhaps they are afraid to tell the truth".

The result was that he asked me to remove from the tray all medicines that I considered harmful for him. The big bottle with lactas calcicus was sent to Peliatan as a present for one of our dancers Siti, who was at the age of accelerated growth and had a frail body. He inquired more about the functions of the kidney and asked me about acupuncture that was being applied on him by a team of Chinese doctors, sent by Mao Tse Tung. Very much to his disappoint-ment I had to tell him that I was totally ignorant of such matters. Somehow, he was no longer upset and I felt more and more at ease with him. In the course of the following years we became quite close to each other.

It became routine on his following visits to Bali that President Sukarno called on me to accompany him on his many tours to studios and art galleries. He had heard of my activities with the Consultative Council for the Arts and Culture and wanted to hear my opinion about products of art that caught his attention. After a few occasions when he met Astri he seemed to be impressed by her personality. He often asked Astri's opinion on matters of interior design, about the colours of curtains in the VIP waiting room at the airport, and so on. It was remarkable that he always addressed her in the Dutch language while Astri tried her best to speak Indonesian.

His appreciation became stronger after my success with the mass dance per-formance at the opening of the Asian Games. Some time later it was due to his insistence and persuasive power that I overcame my reluctance to undertake the difficult task of starting a Medical Faculty at the Udayana University, for which the existing conditions were most unfavourable in all respects at that time.

A Discarded Canvas

From our porch in Tirtagangga we were enjoying the sight of our garden. In the large round pool the water lilies were opening their flowers fully in the late morning sun. Some of our white pigeons were fluttering around high up in the air, others were flying to and fro between the trees around and the black thatch roof of the yellow pigeon-loft in the centre of the pool, bringing life into the lovely landscape.

Towards noon the sky darkened and it looked as if rain was in the air. I wor-ried about the brand-new Opel Sedan I just received from the Ministry of Health that would have to stay outside in the rain for a whole night. I went to look for a canvas cover. My father was sitting with some attendants on the large open verandah, discussing plans for urgent repairs at the water gardens. A strange bundle of what looked like canvas perched on wooden rafters under the roof at one corner of the verandah caught my eye. I asked father: "Excuse me, could that be a piece of canvas that you have there up in that corner?"

He looked up and said: "I think so".

"Would you mind if I borrow it for one night? I have a brand-new car from the Ministry outside. I just received it last week and I would not like it be spoiled by the rain to-night".

"All right," replied Father. "Here boys, help my son get that canvas down and carry it to the car".

It was a heavy load, even for four boys to carry it all the way over the vast water gardens through the gate to the driveway. When we opened the bundle to spread the canvas over the car, we stared at each other with open mouths. Before our eyes a beautiful painting unfolded, depicting the old Indian epic Ramayana, so popular in Bali and over most of Southeast Asia.

We quickly folded the canvas and carried it back to Father. I asked him if he still remembered what kind of canvas it was. He looked somewhat puzzled, and said: "You had better tell me!"

"Well it is the Ramayana painting that I saw being painted by a group of painters at the *bencingah* (outer compound) of the Puri in Karangasem during our vacation from Bolaang Mongondow in 1952. Was it not for the *maligya* ceremonies on behalf of our late uncle Putu?"

My father thought for a while. "Of course, now I remember also how it came here. After use at the *maligya* ceremony we brought it here to serve as decoration at another ceremony, the *tirtayatra*, the obligatory follow-up one month after the *maligya*. Our people must have folded it up after use and found that corner convenient as temporary storage".

"And as usual," I interrupted, "it has been forgotten and has been rotting there in the wind, dust and rainwater these past ten years!"

"Well, calm down!" my father put me straight, smiling charmingly, "in any case we have the beautiful painting back".

"But it is beautiful no longer," I replied, and unfolding it piece by piece, continued: "Look here, what a disaster! There is hardly anything left of the painting, you can throw it away or use it as a cover for something".

"Well, it has fulfiled the function for which it was made. For my part it is no longer of any worth".

"In that case, may I have it?" I asked

"Of course, you may have it. What will you do with it?"

"Perhaps I can find the painter who did it. Do you remember who it was?"

"Yes, Gusti. Ketut Kobot, I don't know exactly where he is living now. Perhaps near Ubud".

"Thank you, I will try to find him".

The next morning we brought the canvas bundle home to Denpasar. When we spread it on the lawn of our garden it measured 4 by 6 metres. Assisted by two men I rolled the painting over a long piece of bamboo trying to straighten out the folds by cautiously pulling all the time as hard as possible at its edges.

From friends in Ubud I learned the location of Kobot's house in the rice fields far away from the village. To reach the spot one had to walk over small dykes between the paddies. Gusti Ketut Kobot, a friendly middle-aged man, remembered very well the three months he spent with seven apprentices painting in our Puri in Karangasem. When I told him about the purpose of my visit, he was deeply moved and was eager to start with the work. The problem was how to get paint that was not available in the country. It needed to be tempera, specifically Rembrandt or Greco. In any case I could bring the painting so that he could assess the damage and see if something could be done. He would then wait until I got the paint.

One week later I went to Kobot with three men carrying the long bamboo pole with the painting on their shoulders. When we spread the canvas on his courtyard, tears welled up in his eyes. Four of the seven apprentices were still with him. They also were full of admiration for their own work of ten years ago. With caring hands they rolled and stretched the painting over a long wooden pole made from the pinang palm, which was more evenly rounded than my bamboo and hung it high above the ground in Kobot's studio. For the time being the canvas was to wait there for me to bring the paint.

During this period Bali was struck by a major disaster. The largest volcano on the island, Mount Agung, erupted in February 1963, followed three months later by another volcano, Mount Batur. As Chief Medical Officer of the island I was in charge of the medical and health aspects of the relief operations. Astri volunteered to take care of the logistics of the relief aid for the 300,000 refugees who fled their homes. It took more than two years before life in Bali started to become normal again, although roads, bridges and waterworks took much longer for their rehabilitation. Because of our hectic involvement in disaster relief work we completely forgot about our painting in Kobot's studio for two and a half years, until one memorable morning in mid-1965 when I was having another breakfast in Tampaksiring with President Sukarno who needed relaxation after a strenuous week in Jakarta.

"Doc," he asked me, "who is now according to your evaluation the best painter in Bali?"

"Do you mean among all the painters or among the Balinese only?"

"Of course I mean among the Balinese".

It was not easy to give an answer, because among the better ones they were about equal, only their styles were different. Having in mind the paintings I had seen in various art galleries and museums lately I mentioned Kobot.

"Can we go to his studio?" he asked.

"Well, it is not easy, we have to walk a long distance over the paddy dykes, it will take time to get there".

"Is he working on a painting now?"

"Yes," I said, "a painting of the Ramayana".

Hearing of the Ramayana, he became more interested and asked: "How large is that painting?"

"Very large, Mr President," I replied. Suddenly something inside me clicked a warning, and I hesitated, before I continued, "it measures four by six metres".

"WHATTT?" he exclaimed, "It must be something very special. He can't have started it by himself, somebody must have commissioned it".

"Well, actually it is an old painting which I got from my father some time ago. In 1952, Kobot and seven of his apprentices worked on it in our Puri in

Karangasem for three months. It was used as a decoration at a *maligya* ceremony which my father held on behalf of his late nephew. It is heavily damaged because of neglect. Kobot is repairing it, I think he is now doing the outlines only and we have to wait until I manage to get a lot of paint that is required. It will not be easy".

Sukarno was obviously deeply intrigued. He would have liked to go and see the painting immediately, but he was too tired and considering the difficult terrain he asked: "Is it possible for you to get the painting here?"

"Of course it is, but I need four people to carry it and a truck".

He instantly gave instructions to his adjutant. Five minutes later I drove down to Ubud followed by a truck with too many people on it. After two hours we were back at the palace and spread out the canvas in full on the beautiful green lawn. Sukarno was overwhelmed by what he saw. Kobot had just finished redrawing with Chinese ink the outlines of the figures. As a genuine Balinese artist he kept himself quietly seated on the grass at a distance while palace personnel were unfolding the canvas. For a long time Sukarno stepped cautiously around the canvas, his thoughtful eyes admiringly wandering over the parts depicting the sequence of the Ramayana story. After having an amicable chat with Kobot he asked me to come with him to the porch outside his suite.

"Doc," he said, "I think I must help you, perhaps I can".

He asked his adjutant to bring the Health Minister who was at that time with him at the palace and temporarily acting as Minister of Foreign Affairs. To my great astonishment I heard the President giving the Acting Foreign Minister the following order: "Dr. Azis, here is Dr Djelantik whom you know already. He needs paint and I want to help him get it. Send a cable to our ambassador in Rome and tell him to dispatch as soon as possible a complete set of the best quality of tempera paint, Rembrandt or Greco, for a painting sized four by six metres. No, to be on the safe side, better mention two complete sets!"

If President Sukarno could not believe his eyes when he saw the huge painting, now I could not believe my ears! It was too wonderful to be true. While I was stuttering a few words of thanks he interrupted: "Nonsense! We must rescue this piece of art!"

Three weeks later in Denpasar I got a telephone call from the Head of the Public Works Department: "Doc, we have received for you from the President's palace a package with the paint President Sukarno promised you".

It has never been clear to me what connection the Public Works Department had with the whole affair, but I did not wait a moment to pick up the materials. The following morning I brought them to the painter. Needless to say, Kobot was very happy. He called his apprentices and they started work immediately.

President Sukarno never saw the finished product. He did not have the chance to visit Bali again. In Jakarta political tensions were building up, keeping him busy finding a solution to the growing hostility between the army and the Communists, who tried to draw Sukarno into their fold. The crisis found its climax in the killing of six generals by the Communists and their abortive coup on 30 September 1965. Sukarno found himself in a most controversial position because of his sympathetic attitude towards the Communists. In the wake of this tragic event, upheavals were set in motion over the whole country, whereby thousands of Communists, sympathisers and innocent relatives were killed. Bali, due to its numerically strong Communist party, experienced a great portion of this havoc. It lasted until March 1966 before life returned to normal. In Jakarta radical changes took place in the political situation that led to the ousting of President Sukarno. We brought the painting home. It was indeed a magnificent piece of art.

CHAPTER 47

Eruption of Mount Agung

Unawareness

In November 1962, when I saw the crater with the small yellow pond deep down in its centre, I was struck by surprise. I had not expected to see a crater at all! At school we had been taught that Mt Agung was an extinct volcano. After a strenuous seven-hour climb, from our improvised base camp in the "Sanggar Agung" temple at 1,000 metres on the southern slope, up to the mountain top at 5,000 metres above sea level, we needed above all to rest for a while, stretch our legs and relieve ourselves from our heavy backpacks. My companions were a ballet dancer Hazel Chung from New York, Dr Meylius, an Australian, and one of my seven expatriate assistants. We sat down on the rocks and enjoyed our breakfast and drinks from our backpacks.

I scanned the rugged crater rim, and estimated its diameter at less than 60 metres. At one side where the rim was highest, a rock formation looked very much like an altar and I fantasized that it could have been built there by people by way of an open offering shrine.

My Australian colleague was the first to regain his energy and was descending into the crater. Remembering that on our school excursions our teachers were always on guard for possible poisonous gases, I called him back. He did not hear me, and I sprang my feet to try to reach him. He did not get far down, however, before being stopped by the stench of sulfuric gases rising out of the yellow pond. Bubbles came constantly out of its depth, breaking at the surface, letting free that awful smell. No smoke was visible. Back on the crater rim I told him of my surprise, but we did not elaborate further. Had I known (what volcanologists told me later) that the bubbling of the yellow liquid was a sign of an impending eruption, I would have warned the authorities. We quietly ate our lunch and enjoyed the view around us from the top of the island of Bali. It was already past midday. The mounting sun had meanwhile evaporated the waters on the rice fields and the vegetation on the plains, making the sight beyond the clouds drifting below our feet quite hazy.

Looking at my watch, I found that it was time to start climbing down if we wanted to be at the base camp before dark. Our backpacks were now much lighter, and the trip down less strenuous, but at many points much more difficult. Especially on the smooth steep stretches of barren rock between deep abysses it was frightening and we often let ourselves slide carefully on our bottoms. Completely exhausted we reached the base camp at dusk, where we fell fast asleep without bothering about food.

Early the next morning we walked another four hours down to the village of Sebudi where we had left our cars. One hour later we arrived at Tirtagangga where Astri was anxiously waiting for us. She was quite shocked by our appearances. With some exaggeration she described us later as walking ghosts: emaciated, pale, dirty and dishevelled creatures, sluggishly mounting our porch and slumping limply into our rattan easy chairs. She was quick with lots of grapefruit juice, which we gulped down greedily. After a refreshing bath and a real breakfast we slept for most of the day.

The Eruption

Two and a half months later, on 19th February, 1963, the volcano erupted totally unexpectedly. Accompanied by loud and heavy rumblings, thick columns of smoke rose up to 1,000 metres in the air, followed by rains of boulders, stones, gravel and ash. The people in the surrounding villages fled their homes in panic. In the beginning it was on a relatively small scale. After one day the eruptions seemed to die down and people began to return to their homes. But the rumblings inside the mountain continued, getting louder and louder.

On the third day an army officer burst into my office and alarmed me. He had just arrived from the disaster area, had gone to the Governor's office but could get no response from the authorities. Now he made an appeal to me as head of the Health Service and of the Balinese Red Cross Society. He described the situation as very critical. He explained to me that at any moment a great eruption could take place. He urged me to organize the evacuation of the population before it was too late. He was over-excited, and his alarm did not sound very convincing. Reluctantly I went with him to see the situation myself. It was frightening indeed! Thick smoke was blowing high up from the crater and terrible rumblings were heard from below the earth mixed with a cacophony of metallic sounds like that from hundreds of blacksmiths working in a huge forge. The population was in panic: Some of them were already far away from home, others wanted to stay in their villages. Many people wanted to rush back to rescue their belongings. Clearly, something had to be done.

Back in Denpasar, I reported to the Governor himself and convinced him of the urgency of the situation. I urged him to requisition school buildings outside the dangerous zone to serve as temporary shelters for refugees. He telephoned the Military Governor, the Head of the Police and several other Depart-ment Heads. Rushing back to my office I started work immediately. I plotted twenty-four points on the slopes of Mt Agung where I put up Red Cross stations and manned them with my Health personnel and Red Cross Volunteers. They were to provide emergency medical aid and to help evacuate people and cattle.

It took another week before a Disaster Relief Committee was set up by the Governor in coordination with the Military Authorities. Called Komando Operasi Gunung Agung (KOGA), its job in the first place was to organise the evacuation of the population out of the dangerous area. In addition, KOGA would be responsible for food and clothing. The evacuation of people to the hastily erected refugee camps in schools and community buildings was much more difficult than anticipated. Many people refused to leave their homes and properties, preferring to die together on the spot. The intermittent occurrence of the eruptions, with quiet periods lasting from one to seven days or even longer, made things more difficult. If the quiet period lasted for more than two days, people started to rush to their homes and villages on the mountain slopes, and to flee back again to the refugee camps when the intense rumblings and earthquakes heralded a new eruption.

Emergency Aid

Up to the second week, publicity about the disaster was very poor. Our government at that time, because of its confrontation with the west and the United Nations over Malaysia's independence, had assumed a policy of isolation and "self reliance". Nothing bad that happened in the country was to be known to the outside world.

Paradoxically, the first news about the calamity came from BBC television in London, which showed a film of the eruption, made by Denis Mathews, an Englishman who happened to live in a bungalow built in the 1930s by the late German painter-musician Walter Spies in Iseh at the foot of Mt Agung. This footage incited countries, international agencies and charity organizations to send emergency aid to Bali. The first to arrive was a medical team from the Philippines consisting of a medical doctor, five male assistants and three nurses. The Australian Government sent eleven pick-ups and a large quantity of blankets, medicines, and medical supplies. There came food and milk in great quantities, donated spontaneously and generously from all corners of the world, clothes, blankets and a great many other items, before we had any chance to make specific requests. The magnitude and variety of material aid overwhelmed our authorities who had no experience in such kind of emergency logistics.

Astri volunteered to take care of the logistics of food and clothing. She organized about fifty volunteers to sew hundreds and thousands of pieces of clothing for the refugees who were in the eleven refugee camps set up by KOGA and in the many village community buildings spread over Bali. She also assisted with the supervision of the stores and, to ensure orderly distribution, she often delivered the goods by truck to these camps and the village distribution centres herself.

Everybody worked very, very hard day and night. Our Red Cross Teams performed wonderfully. The Universities of Jakarta, Bandung and Surabaya sent doctors and medical students to assist us in this gigantic and often dangerous work on the mountain slopes. It must be mentioned that the Philippine team had set a magnificent example for our people.

With the arrival of help from the outside world a host of correspondents visited Bali, competing with each other in getting information for their papers. *Medical News* from Britain asked me to write an article for them, which is quoted here in full:

MEDICAL NEWS, July 5, 1963.
HUNGER IN THE WAKE OF THE BALI DISASTER
It had never occurred to anyone that the Gunung Agung might erupt. Even at school we had been taught that it was a dead volcano. When, on February 19, this year, a request from the authorities came to me, as Head of the Bali Red Cross Society, to send a rescue team to the mountain which was reported to be erupting, I complied only with reluctance and disbelief.

But the eruption was a fact although its implications were not realised. Something inherent in the character of the Balinese made them ignore the serious danger to which the island and its population was suddenly exposed. The whole community believed that by observing a series of religious ceremonies prescribed by people who spontaneously went into trance, calamity would be averted.

Recalling it now serves to emphasise how fortunate it was that no more than 1,600 victims were killed by lava, clouds of burning gas and hot floods; and only 215 patients burned and scalded seriously enough to have to be hospitalised. This is all the more remarkable as about 40,000 people lived within a radius of 10 km (just over 6 miles) of the crater and about 150,000 within a radius of 15 km.

From the beginning, the Bali Red Cross and the Government Health Services took responsibility for the care of the thousands of people who fled in confusion from their houses and their fields and later returned. This they did several times in the course of the disaster.

Twenty-four Red Cross stations forming a chain around the mountain were set up to meet the many kinds of emergencies. Doctors were not available for each station, so a male nurse and one or two auxiliaries did the job, assisted by a few voluntary workers. Three doctors were in charge of the supervision of these stations.

The emergencies were: (a) direct victims: of lava, clouds of burning gas, hot floods resulting from heavy rains which mixed with fresh lava or other volcanic material; and, further away in the plains, of cold floods; (b) all kinds of diseases which naturally occur when great numbers of people are on the move without proper food, sleep or shelter—such as bronchopneumonia, gastro-enteritis, eye and skin diseases.

With thousands and thousands of refugees moving to and fro mainly on foot, it was remarkable that the only injuries found were those from burns. There was only one single case of other injury: a dislocation of the knee of a young woman who ran too fast before the lava. Heavy rains of stone and gravel did not cause injuries of any importance. Burns were located mainly at the extremities, caused by running through hot lava, hot ash or hot streams, and many times by falling on the hands. They were mostly second-grade burns, which with proper care and antibiotics healed remarkably quickly within fourteen days.

Burns over larger areas of the body or where contractures could develop will need grafting and a certain amount of physiotherapy. Only nine cases of this kind were considered serious.

The standard treatment given to burns was a prophylactic shot of anti-tetanus serum, penicillin for at least five days and local application of ointment, usually containing boric acid or cod liver oil.

Close attention was given to the general condition of the patients, especially to nutrition and intestinal diseases. Much use has been made of intravenous fluid administration on patients who were dehydrated or in shock.

Nearly half of the hospitalised patients came from the area of Sogra and Badeg on the southern slopes of the mountain, where on March 17 a huge cloud of burning gas at one and the same time engulfed the people who were holding religious gatherings at several different places. Some 1,100 people who could not escape the cloud must have died at once. The process must have been very short, judging from the remains found on the spot about four weeks later when at last it was considered safe to enter the area. Many bodies were found in the position in which they must have been overcome by death, holding something in the hand, or sitting facing each other as if still having a chat, or with both hands stretched forward while falling.

Interesting though all this is, attention has to be concentrated on the living. There are 75,000 people who cannot return to their homes, either because their homes are no longer there or because if they return to where their homes are, they would starve because they cannot begin cultivating lava-covered soil.

There are another 150,000 people more or less seriously affected by the eruption. While crops have been destroyed, irrigations demolished and fertile land covered with fresh volcanic material. More than 20,000 acres of wet rice fields are destroyed and about 100,000 acres of dry fields; 40,000 acres of forest outside the immediate area of the Gunung Agung have died and reafforestation of 600,000 acres of mountain slopes for this year have been set at naught by the destruction of the whole area of seedlings.

This disaster is all the greater because of the role forests play in the watering of the land. It is also important to remember that not only people are suffering from hunger, but pigs, cattle and other animals also.

Thus the most serious result of the eruption is not the death toll, but hunger, hunger for thousands and thousands of people for whom there is no prospect of any kind of livelihood unless they are willing to migrate to other parts of Indonesia, such as Sumatra, Celebes or Sumbawa. A great deal of careful planning and preparatory work will be needed for this vast enterprise, and it will take time.

Meanwhile these hungry masses have to be fed and comprehensive measures have to be taken to prevent outbreaks of epidemics and hunger oedema. Steps are now being taken to re-establish administration in the devastated areas, transmigration is being successfully encouraged, and the Health services are continuing the vaccinations which they began in the first days of the eruption and which have played such an important part in preventing epidemics.

The health care of these helpless people is putting a heavy burden on our doctors and nurses of whom there are far too few. Hungry masses dispersed over large areas of agriculturally useless soil have to be fed and protected from the dangers of epidemics by vaccinations and intensive surveillance.

The hard work has only just begun!

Epilogue

That article was written in June. Meanwhile, Mt Batur, an active volcano in Central Bali, had been erupting violently since May, but it did not cause much of a calamity. Situated in a deep caldera 12 km in diameter, its lava ran down along existing courses towards the crater lake to the east and over solidified lava from the 1917 eruption to the west. The inhabitants of the few villages along the lake were out of reach of the hot lava streams but they were evacuated because of the rains of hot ash. There were no casualties. From the rim of the caldera we could safely look at the spectacular scenery of the erupting volcano at night like huge fireworks spitting glowing material upwards in the air and red hot lava flowing slowly down the slopes. Inside the caldera four new smaller craters came into being on the norther slope of the mountain.

The eruptions of Mt Agung continued for another four months. In September 1963 both mountains stopped erupting, but still produced smoke and intermittent rains of ash. By the end of the year volcanic activity had died down and most people had returned to their villages. However, since their fields could not yet be cultivated for a long time, they continued to need food aid, medicines and other forms of assistance. There were a great many patients with hunger oedema who took a long time to recover. In the course of the following year the refugee camps were abolished. Some 2,000 families had chosen to transmigrate to Sumatra, Borneo and Celebes. Repairs of roads, bridges and irrigation works took another five years to complete. Soon the land became productive again.

. However, large previously fertile areas, like the famous rice fields on both sides of the Yeh Unda river south of Klungkung remained covered by an up to ten-metre-thick layer of volcanic material: ash, sand, gravel and boulders, brought there by the floods. It was estimated that it would still be at least 50 years before the material would wear and become fertile soil for agriculture. Fortunately, ten years later, when as result of the economic recovery of Indonesia as a whole, reconstruction work in Bali gained momentum, it was found that after having cooled off and solidified for some time, the deposited lava provided good building material for the roads, dams and other building projects. People, who at the beginning of the disaster wept at the loss of their land and property, started to excavate sand and stones either themselves or had it done by contractors, and made good money from it. Moreover they had the prospect of regaining their good earth in the end.

Today (in 1996), over 30 years after the eruption, excavation work is still going on in many places. This gives an idea how much of material came down from Mt Agung. The holy mountain has nearly stopped producing smoke, its crater is now about 400 metres wide, but its height has been reduced to 2,800 metres from the 3,142 metres it measured before the eruption.

CHAPTER 48

Sacred Ceremonies

Confusion

The highest mountain of Bali, Mt Agung, is for the Balinese also the holiest dwelling of spirits of their forefathers. It is the most supreme of all sites in Bali where at certain times the gods come down from Heaven to attend the rituals and ceremonies performed by devotees. The over 800-year-old temple of Besakih, at an altitude of about 1,000 metres on its southwestern slope, is regarded as the "mother temple" of the island. According to the holy scripts, once in a century the most sacred of ceremonies—the *Eka Dasa Rudra* ("ceremonies for the divine representations of the eleven directions: east, south, west, north, southeast, southwest, northwest, northeast, zenith, centre and nadir")—should be performed there. This consists of a series of ceremonies lasting for two months.

Plans for holding the great temple festival from March to April 1963 were initiated in January, and when Mt Agung erupted in February much of the preparations for the rituals were in full swing. Great confusion and anxiety swept the responsible authorities and religious leaders, which might be the reason why the authorities did not take any action during the first days after the eruption.

The volcano made people accept the events as the will of superhuman forces. In the context of the Balinese religion such acceptance was entirely normal. But many religious leaders went a step further and after consulting the scripts and horoscopes and reviewing recent actions taken by the government they concluded that a great mistake had been made by starting to organize the *Eka Dasa Rudra* rituals in the temple of Besakih for 1963, evoking the wrath of the gods. Rightly it should be held in 1979. Despite all the warnings by prominent religious leaders the Governor refused to postpone the grand ritualistic festival. There was never any explanation given for this stubborn attitude, but privately word circulated that our ambitious Governor, Suteja, wanted it to happen during his term of office. By organizing this festival he wanted to show the people how strongly he adhered to the Balinese Hindu religion and so rid himself from allegations of being a sympathizer of the Communist Party. Preparations were at the same time in progress in Jakarta for a big conference of PATA, the Pacific-Asia Tourist Association and the distinguished delegations would be given the golden opportunity to visit Bali. What would be more spectacular for them than this grandiose once-in-a-hundred-year temple festival? According to many, the main motives behind the government's arrangement were not purely religious.

The Balinese community was confused but nobody protested against the Governor's decision. Moreover, when at last responsible religious leaders pronounced the inappropriateness of the date, it was too late and the preparations were in full swing.

The grand ceremonies, attended by a 100,000 people, took place in Besakih on March 8th with the volcano raging with all its might close above the Great Temple. The sounds of the *gamelan* orchestras, the ringing of dozens of bells accompanying the prayers of the priests and the *wargasari* hymns sung by hundreds of devotees in the temple yards were at times completely drowned by the terrible rumblings underneath, while massive columns of black clouds bulged out of the crater and rose hundreds of metres high in the air, spreading over the sky and transforming the sunlight into something eerie and unreal.

The real climax on the last day on April 20th, the worship of all the gods who descended from Heaven, was more grandiose, more colourful and magnificent than any Balinese temple festival I had ever seen. The sight of the prayers executed by some fifty priests all at the same time was most impressive. The ceremonial dances, the music and other art performances together contributed to a wonderful and spectacular event. Despite the slightly dirty rain, and the muddy grounds of the temple yards, all proceeded well.

My father and family members from Karangasem took part in the ceremonies, ostensibly outwardly undisturbed. During the prayers and the rituals with the holy water dispensed by the priests, I could not concentrate on its religious content. My thoughts went to the raging volcano and the dangers to which my Red Cross teams on the nearly inaccessible mountain slopes were exposed.

We felt great relief when the ceremonies came to an end. Slowly we drove back to Denpasar in a long column of vehicles over the roads covered with volcanic sand and ash. On arrival at home our clothes were full of black spots and we discovered to our great surprise that our blue car in which we had been driving had turned green!

During the following weeks our relief work started to become better organized. The refugee camps were set up, storage and distribution of goods were better supervised and gradually most of the work became routine. Aid from abroad continued pouring in. I could devote myself more to the medical and the public health aspects of the disaster.

At a later stage, steps were taken by the Governor and the military authorities which made us wonder. Under the pretext that my capacities were overstretched, they relieved me from my duties as Head of the Red Cross. The stores of the Red Cross Society were moved from the premises of the Health Department to the Military Headquarters. From that day on all supplies and equipment received from abroad were to go to there. The Government had proclaimed the State of Emergency, so the military took the dominant role and everybody complied.

Apparently to circumvent any objections from my side they appointed my nephew Gedé Agung, who was then Director of the Department of Information, as the new Head of the Red Cross, under the command of the military. Astri, who all this time had assisted me with the logistics of the emergency aid could no longer have free access to the stores. Her sharp intuition made her suspicious. Gedé Agung's wife was a sister of the wife of Puger, the Chairman of the Bali Communist Party. The Military Commander in Bali was known to be a sympathizer of the Communists. Our Red Cross volunteers saw themselves gradually replaced by military personnel. One day, when we needed bandages for treatment of patients with burns in one of the rural hospitals we were told that the supplies were depleted. We knew that there was still plenty! Suddenly, there was also shortage of certain kinds of medicines and disinfectant. We continued working with great idealism and devotion, but had to struggle as a result of these dwindling supplies.

There was much secrecy about the incoming disaster aid. Rumours abounded, especially when a large consignment arrived in Benoa from China, via the harbour of Ceribon in West Java, apparently consisting of chinaware for the victims. The peculiarly long rectangular cases appeared to contain rifles and ammunition. Since they came into the hands of the military, nobody could get any information. None of these rumours could of course be substantiated.

Some time later, after having addressed our medical students at a rally at the Udayana University, I was called to the office of the Jaksa (Chief Prosecutor) who reprimanded me that I was too liberal and independent in my speech, bringing wrong ideas about freedom into the heads of my students. Astri told me to be careful, warning me that there must be something being planned by the Communists. I dismissed her suspicions as emotional.

But how wrong I was! In the face of events taking place two years later there were strong indications that the Communists in Bali were stockpiling medical and other emergency supplies and preparing for the follow-up of the Communist coup in Jakarta in September 1965. As is known, the coup in Jakarta failed. Puger, Suteja and Agung fell victim to the anti-Communist purges in the wake of the failed coup.

Miracle around a Bridge

After some time we understood that the eruptions of the mountain had followed a certain pattern. The smaller eruptions emitted smoke containing volcanic ash and sand that came down on the slopes and—depending on the winds—reached areas 80 km away. The bigger eruptions were usually preceded by heavy earthquakes and loud rumblings below the earth. Then, with a tremendous explosion, huge columns of black smoke emerged out of the crater, rising high up in the air. In the ever widening clouds of smoke high above the crater an erratic flurry of lightning developed, caused by the discharge of electricity generated by friction of volcanic material, and heavy rains followed caused by condensation of its huge content of water vapour. These heavy rains would sweep down all the ash and debris that had been falling on the slopes in heavy torrents, causing floods known as "cold *lahar*". Fresh hot lava that might be expelled with the eruption would turn the floods into "hot *lahar*". By the time the torrents reached the plains they usually had lost momentum, so that often people were able to flee ahead of them. But in other cases—as in the north because of the steep slope and narrow coastal plain—hot lava could reach the sea producing steam at contact with the water. The heavy viscous lava did not always follow like water the lowest path, but being pushed by more heavy mass from behind, would often surge upwards beyond river banks, forming long stretches of hills after solidification.

One morning in Karangasem, while my father was having his breakfast on a verandah in the Puri, our guards at the gate were pushed aside by a group of men, wildly gesticulating with drawn krises in the air. People rushed to the scene and tried to stop them. According to witnesses the intruders were obviously in a state of trance. They shouted and demanded that my father should come with them to perform a sacrifice at a river in their village. Our guards and the others were able to master them and wanted to push them away. My father who had seen the tumult from a distance sensed that this might be something serious, worth his attention. He gestured to his guards to bring the intruders nearer. Still in a trance, the men, by then recognized as coming from Subagan, a village 2 km from Karangasem, said that they had been dispatched by the priests of their village temple to fetch my father to perform a ritual as the only means to save their village from disaster.

The priests had received a heavenly message that only my father was entitled to perform the ritual. The voice from heaven predicted that in a few hours time the holy mountain would erupt again and send *lahar* down the slopes which would destroy their village. Their task was to carry my father on their shoulders to the small old-fashioned bridge in the village where the community was already waiting with the sacrificial animals: a black goat and a black hen. Father was to pray to the god of Mt Agung, and to throw the animals in the river. My father did not hesitate. If that was the message of the gods, why should he not go and perform his duty? He mounted the shoulders of the strongest of the gang and, followed by a large crowd, he was carried away in a noisy procession to the place of the sacrifice.

Subagan was a prosperous village of about 600 families of which half were Moslems. Two rivers flowed from north to south at 200 metres distance from each other. The road to Denpasar crossed the eastern river over a small old bridge and the broader western stream over a bigger one recently built of concrete. This river flowed near the big mosque where the Moslem population were gathering and praying day and night asking Allah to spare them from disaster. The mainly Hindu part of the population was assembled at the old bridge where the men put my father down. He prayed with great care and concentration of mind and dutifully flung the goat and then the hen in the fast-flowing water under the bridge. The men came out of their trance as if nothing particular had happened and paid their respects to my father. The community was satisfied and reassured.

As predicted, the volcano erupted two hours later most violently. A tremendous avalanche of thick muddy *lahar* consisting of a mixture of ash, sand and lava came down the rivers, bringing down everything on its way such as fallen trees and huge rocks. It spilled over the river banks and swept away the large concrete bridge, but the small old one on the eastern river was not at all affected. The speed of the flood at the village was not very high and people could flee ahead of it to safer grounds where they spent the night.

The next morning they returned to their houses to collect what could be saved and the Moslem community gathered again in the mosque for prayers. Suddenly another avalanche struck the village, this time much larger and more violent than the day before. The mosque was swept away together with some 200 people who were inside. Further south, nearly all the houses were engulfed by the tremendous flood. Fortunately, most of the population had already fled to nearby villages. It was a disaster of major proportions. The extent of the calamity became evident the next day: most of the houses were destroyed, and the whole area was covered by a layer of debris and mud up to 3 metres high. More than 1,000 people had to take refuge in refugee camps nearby.

People were impressed by the fact that the old, rickety, partly wooden bridge, where my father had performed the sacrifice two days before, was completely intact in the midst of the colossal devastation! After the sacrifice at the bridge, however, many eye-witnesses had seen the black goat retrieved from the river and slaughtered by some Moslems downstream. The people attributed the calamity that befell the village, and that which befell 200 Moslems during prayers in the mosque, to this act of sacrilege. The small bridge miraculously survived until the end of the disaster and long after the volcanic activity had died down

CHAPTER 49

Divine Influences

The Trembling Valley

During the first weeks of the disaster we met with great difficulties in evacuating people out of the danger zones. The mainly illiterate population of the mountain areas were still under the influence of local temple priests whose belief in the holiness of the Mount Agung was absolute. It was unthinkable for them to accept that the volcano could do them any harm as the evacuation officials had warned them. Facing the emission of columns of smoke out of the crater and feeling the earth tremble under their feet, they would gather in their temples and ask their priests to communicate with the gods and the spirits of their forefathers requesting their advice. Usually one or more temple priests would go into trance and their utterances would be interpreted as the will of the gods. Often the pronouncements of the entranced men were indeed positive and there would be no problem in persuading people to move. But sometimes the advice was to the contrary and the people surrendered themselves to the inevitable as happened on March 17th in Badeg and Sarga, where 1,100 devotees perished in their temple yards in a huge gush of hot gas.

Once during my inspection tour to the Karangasem area the District Head of Abang came to me asking me to help evacuate some fifty families from Laga, a village on the eastern slope of Mt Agung, saying: "We have been trying for three days to bring these people down. They are refusing to move because they have not yet received instruction from the *Batara* (local deity)."

"Can't you force them," I asked, "you are in command and in the right position as a government official."

"After trying for three days, I really don't know what to do. They, strongly believe in divinity. That is why I have come to you. As you know, according to their belief your father has inherited that divinity that made him ruler of this area. I am sure that their belief in this inherited divinity is passed on to you. I mean that if you tell them to come down to a safer place, they will obey. Please come with me."

"Is it faraway?" I asked, looking at my watch.

"Not so far, but it is heavy climbing, about one hour."

"Well, okay!" and we started the climb. We passed through a steep winding valley, walking over the riverbed which was covered with volcanic sand. The persistent rumbling inside the mountain, sounding so close to our ears, was frightening. We saw the smoking crater just above our heads and now and then small flames were visible over the crater rim. It was very hot under the blazing sun and I was philosophizing about what thoughts and feelings my six companions might have at those moments and why it was that I did not feel any fear at all. Then I heard one of them calling in excitement: "Doc, stop! Please feel the sand!" I turned round and saw him kneeling with his hands on the ground, calling again: "It is hot, it is boiling!"

I checked, and indeed, the ground under our feet was hotter than could be expected from the warming by the sun and...it was moving! I felt that a quick decision should be made, either go back or move on. I asked the District Head how far we were from the village.

"Not far, just over this hill in front of us. We can be there in five minutes".

To return now without having seen the people would be ridiculous. We decided to move on. We quickly left the riverbed and continued climbing over the rocks. I was frightened to death. The most terrible thoughts raced through my head. I imagined the earth splitting along the riverbed and fire and gas engulfing us at any moment. But it would be unwise to show any sign of fear, my companions would run away. So I kept on joking and chatting.

Beyond the hill, about 200 men, women and children were gathered at the outer yard of the village temple, waiting for the priest to come out of the sanctuary to bring the divine message. Although the village was more than 1,000 metres below the mountain top, it looked as if the heavily smoking crater was looming just above our heads. The noise of the volcano was terrible and the ground was trembling under our feet. I was very relieved when the head of the village recognized me; he originated from Pidpid, my mother's village of origin and was closely related to her father. He ran to me, kneeled down and affectionately hugged me around my thighs. (It would be against traditional etiquette to throw his arms around my shoulders). I asked him to get the temple priest. He ran into the temple and came back with a man clad in white. The poor priest looked very depressed. He had not been able yet to communicate with the gods. The believers were left in limbo.

I asked all the people to come nearer and explained why I had come. It was of course nothing new, the District Head had told them the same. But he was right, not what had been said did matter, but who said it. The whole village replied in a chorus: "*Inggih, Dewagung, Tityang ngiring*! My lord, we follow you!"

I saw that most of the families had already some of their belongings in bundles with them. I saw also some cows held on ropes and even chickens in palm leaf baskets. Apparently they were prepared to come down and were only waiting for the outcome of the priest's prayers. Not wanting to waste any time I ordered: "Come, let us go!"

They obeyed silently. There was a great sense of relief. We walked down over the rocks as fast as we could, avoiding the valley. When we reached the refugee camp in Abang an hour later, we saw the people there in great distress, many houses were destroyed and walls were smashed to the ground. There had just been a heavy earthquake that we had not been aware of during our hasty retreat.

An Ignorant Photographer

Tirtagangga appeared to be a very special spot on earth!

A few weeks after I first climbed Mt Agung, our houseboy Bandolan, for whom we had built a small house behind the kitchen, reported that one evening a fireball fell at one corner of our ground. He could not tell from where the fire came but many people from the village nearby claimed to have seen it coming straight from the top of the mountain. According to their accounts it was a strange greenish transparent fire which lingered for some time on the spot and died down slowly. As usual the people attached a supernatural meaning to such a phenomenon. I myself was a little sceptical and regarded it as something quite natural: gas that escaped from marshes and ignited by oxygen in the air. Was our ground not a swamp before? However, in order to reassure the population of the area we complied with their request to have a ceremony and erect an offering shrine on the spot.

The same volcanologists who told us some time after the eruption that the boiling sulphur we saw in the crater was a sign of an imminent eruption, found that we should not dismiss straight away the accounts of the fireball coming from the top of Mt Agung. It could possibly have been a sign of activity starting in the volcano. The people in Karangasem had a different explanation for the phenomenon: A fireball coming from the top of the holy mountain is—for them—a well-known motif. It is found in the legend of the immaculate conception of the princess of the Puri Kelodan of Karangasem leading to the creation of the Karangasem dynasty.

During one of my tours to East Bali inspecting the Red Cross posts and refugee camps, Astri and the children went along with me and we spent the weekend in Tirtagangga. That whole week the mountain had been relatively quiet and we enjoyed our weekend house and water-gardens and had a swim in our swimming pool. Tirtagangga was considered safe from lava streams or *lahar* floods, because of the chain of high hills stretching from east to west behind the garden complex, forming a natural barrier between our grounds and the mountain. Any lava or flood would follow the existing valleys and water courses at both ends of the barrier, leaving Tirtagangga unaffected.

That Sunday after lunch I climbed into my Landrover and started my inspection tour of the northeast coastal areas. My ten-year-old son Widur insisted on coming with me. The day was beautiful with bright sunshine and the monsoon winds bringing the cold from the Australian winter. It was a gorgeous ride over a magnificent landscape, especially where the road went in a hundred sharp curves up and down through a narrow gorge crossing the high pass between the Mt Agung and the twin-mountains of Seraya in the East. Just as we left the gorge, descending into the coastal plain a most spectacular event occurred before our eyes.

Below in front of us the half-barren savannah landscape displayed its typical charm, enhanced by the shadows cast by the declining sun hidden just behind the mountain. The mighty volcano rose high and dark at our left side, its crater partly covered by a cloud of smoke. Its steep pyramidal slope that continued with gradually lesser inclination to the far right, was beautifully silhouetted against the bright sky. Suddenly from behind that silhouette, starting from the left, a series of frightening outbursts of huge dark clouds rose high in the air as if from a battery of atomic bombs. Automatically I stopped and reached for my camera and was able to take a number of photos of the event. I noticed that the series of cumulus explosions took less than five minutes to cover the whole ridge from the mountain to the far right end where the coastline was, a distance of about 7 km. The whole western sky became dark, covered with clouds from the series of what looked to me as eruptions, but eruptions of what? There were no craters there! Due to the strong eastern winds the sky straight above us remained clear. For several minutes both Widur and myself were speechless, awestruck. I tried hard to figure out what we were witnessing. Suddenly I realized that it must be a huge stream of lava running with high speed down from the crater just west of the ridge so beautifully silhouetted against the sky. There must have been an enormous eruption of the volcano just when we turned around the corner coming out of the narrow gorge. The sound of the engine in low gear might have masked the noise of the eruption, which was perhaps also dampened by the high wall of the gorge and the strong eastern winds blowing in our ears.

But now I found myself facing a dilemma: to go further and run the risk of landing in the lava or the flood of *lahar* which was to be expected coming very soon, or to return and leave my Red Cross people to take care of themselves? And if I went further would I be able to drive back to Tirtagangga later?

In such circumstances one just cannot think clearly and unconsciously one follows human instinct. I looked at my son, who was still silent and was looking with awe at the mighty clouds within which some lightning had started. I knew from experience that within fifteen minutes heavy rains would fall, causing floods down the riverbeds, hot this time because of the fresh lava. Deciding to go further, I drove carefully over the sandy road until the coastal village of Kubu, where our Red Cross volunteers had already been alarmed by people fleeing from the west. Among them were people with burns over great parts of their bodies, carried on improvised stretchers to our polyclinic. I went to the clinic to attend the wounded. There were six of them, two were children. They told us how they got their burns. They were peacefully sitting in their houses, when suddenly the air became incredibly hot and their bamboo huts—as if by themselves—burst into flames and fell down on them. While they fled they saw the red lava stream passing at about 500 metres distance from them. Other people who were in the fields got burns from their clothing which suddenly ignited. During the time that I attended to the six patients, the crowd around the clinic had swollen to a hundred distressed people. There were more reports about people still trapped in their burning houses, scattered at great distances from each other. I assembled my Red Cross volunteers and asked each of them to form squads of four men to go and search for those victims. They went with the best of spirits. The head of the village of Kubu had already started with the arrangements for temporary housing of the refugees.

The lava stream stopped about 100 metres before the shoreline. At first, it had followed the riverbed in the existing gully but due to its speed, volume and viscosity it overflowed the valley further downwards. Fortunately, it took its own course westwards along the distant bank of the river. The Kubu water-course which usually had a dry riverbed passed about 500 metres west of the vil-lage and was more than 1,500 metres wide. Therefore, in Kubu itself we did not feel the heat of the lava.

(Later when the lava had cooled down and solidified, it became a stony hill range more than 100 metres wide and 25 metres high.)

Curious to have a look at the lava, I drove westwards through the village but could not reach further than the eastern river bank where the hot flood was flowing fast and was more than one metre deep. The villagers told me not to go further. From the highest spot of the river bank I could see from a safe dis-tance the long wall of steam rising at the far side of the river where the flood water touched the still hot lava. It was most impressive!

Meanwhile, it was getting dark. Seeing Widur next to me looking with the greatest interest around him, I thought of Astri and the other children in Tirtagangga and I turned my car. In Kubu, I assured myself that there were enough medicines, food and other supplies, then headed back to Tirtagangga. Astri had been very worried about us, and was extremely relieved to see us back safe and sound.

Volcanologists from Java, sent by the government to monitor the situation in Bali, frequently came to visit us in Denpasar during the following months. Sometimes there were also experts from abroad coming with them as consul-tants. During one of those visits I showed them the remarkable photographs I took on that Sunday with Widur, on the other side of the Mt Agung. Actually all the time I had been cursing myself about a white streak running from left to right across the picture, which I attributed to a fault in my photography. Had I perhaps not noticed a disturbing lightbeam reflected from somewhere inside the Landrover and hitting the lens or was it something else? Nevertheless the whole of the picture was so breathtaking, that I took pride in having made that extraordinary photograph. The visiting volcanologists exclaimed in great excitement: "Who took that picture?"

"Me!" I answered in surprise, "What is the matter?"

"You ask what is the matter? Well, you must have a good guardian angel watching over you! Do you know what that white streak is?"

"Sorry, perhaps I had made a mistake or maybe there was something wrong with the camera!"

"No, Doc, that was *hot gas*! If you had been a little nearer you would not be here now!"

Both Astri and I were speechless while we were listening to their explanations. I was remembering the hot gas of the 17th of March killing 1,100 people on the temple grounds of Badeg and Sogra. I was also remembering the wind blowing hard from behind us from the east when I took the photograph. It left me wondering. It was just luck!

Or was it the wind? Was it my birthmark protecting us? Who knows?

CHAPTER 50

Transmigration

A Bold Plan

There was the disconsolate picture of the land: whole areas covered with vol-canic ash, valleys and rivers plugged with debris from lava and *lahar*, bridges swept away by torrents, and vast stretches of road covered by boulders and other material deposited by successive floods. There was the terrible picture of destitute people in the refugee camps, hungry faces, emaciated, anaemic, many with hunger oedema, in idleness waiting for the daily food distribution, griev-ing of lost homes and property, dreaming of better times, and wondering in despair what the future might hold for them.

Confrontation with these realities time and again, on my routine inspec-tion trips to the disaster-struck areas, forced me to think about possibilities of moving these people out of Bali. The government was carrying out a regular transmigration programme for the densely populated islands of Java and Bali, which went on according to the budget allocated for the purpose. I knew that there was always too little money for transmigrating adequate numbers of peo-ple, to lessen overpopulation of these islands. I started to wonder if the present calamity could not be a good opportunity to give a boost to the programme. Consultation with the governor did not lead to any action. Since the country's administration was very much centralized, our local authorities lacked initia-tive and were very quick in answering: "That is a matter of concern for the *Pusat* (Central Government)."

In my case perhaps Providence was again at work. Friends working at the Ministry of Health in Jakarta, leaked the information to me that Representatives of Bolaang Mongondow Regency, North Celebes (where I had worked from 1950 to 1954) were in Jakarta with a request to the Minister of Health to reassign me to their Regency. The Minister knew of course about the volcanic eruption and my work with disaster relief and could not comply with their request. That news brought back in my memory the Dumoga Valley, where migrants from the Minahassa Region had tried in vain to settle. I remembered again the destitute migrants from Dumoga coming to our house in Kotamobagu on their way back to the Minahassa asking for medicine for their babies who appeared to have died already while underway in their arms. I knew that malaria was the main cause of failure of their efforts.

Having succeeded in eradicating malaria in Bali just one year before in 1962, I imagined that if I could prevent migrants from getting malaria by applying the techniques I had acquired in our Malaria Eradication Programme, it might make transmigration successful. A bold plan developed in my mind: if the Mongondow people could not get me in person as a doctor, perhaps they would be served by getting migrants from Bali to develop their still backward agriculture. I thought of transforming their fertile but marshy Dumoga Valley into productive rice terraces. The Governor found my plan excellent and made contact with the Bolaang Mongondow delegation while they were still in Jakarta. Suddenly things moved very fast, the military authorities promised to make a transport ship from the Navy available. I held talks with the refugees about fertile grounds in Dumoga. In a remarkably short time 216 families volunteered for migration to Bolaang Mongondow, more than half of them people from Karangasem Regency. It was all the more remarkable because the area was unknown to them and people had not yet heard of experiences of migrants from that place, only from me about my experiences working there as a doctor.

For the protection of the migrants against malaria, I selected one team of five men for insecticide spraying, five men for surveillance operations, and two microscopists from our Malaria Eradication Programme to go with them and stay there for at least six months, after which time they would be replaced. I provided them with the necessary equipment and enough insecticides and anti-malaria tablets for a period of two years. Their task was simple in theory, but most difficult to implement. First of all everybody had to be given malaria drug prophylaxis. To be sure of the intake of the drug this could not be left to the migrants themselves, but had to be given by our surveillance agents personally. Every case of fever needed to be checked by laboratory and—in cases where the blood was positive for malaria—patients had to have a full course of radical treatment. Every hut or house that would be built should be completely sprayed as soon as it was occupied by people, even if the construction was not yet complete. Spraying should be repeated thereafter every two months, not every half year as normally done in Eradication Programmes. As in any Surveillance Programme, all houses should be numbered and provided with the standard housecards used in Malaria Eradication. An intensive refresher course was given to our migrant malaria staff and regular information about malaria and other diseases was given to the migrating families. In addition to our malaria workers and with the full co-operation of the authorities, we had been able to recruit volunteer temple priests, paramedics, teachers, craftsmen and artists, to be transferred to the transmigration area. For the landless farmers the prospect of getting two hectares of land was better than the uncertainties for the future they had to face by staying in Bali. When the ship left the harbour of Buleleng with 216 families and about fifty volunteer workers on board I was somehow fully confident that our malaria staff would do their job well and their mission would be successful.

There was still little communication between Bali and North Celebes. Despite their Hinduism they were received very well by the Bolaang-Mongondowers, who were Moslem. From the scarce news we got, we understood that due to the discipline of our malaria personnel our migrants had not been affected by severe malaria. Of course life was very hard in the beginning. The area had not been prepared beforehand and they had to fell the trees, to dig drainage canals, build the roads all by themselves. As is customary in Bali they prayed and performed all the religious rituals and ceremonies before starting to work the soil, to fell a tree, or to build a house. A temporary village temple was erected which would function as a binding element for the community. The local government was taking care of the distribution of land, food supplies, agricultural tools, and other logistical matters in a satisfactory matter.

After a few years we received news from officials who had visited the new area that large stretches of marshland had been transformed into rice fields, and that the crops were excellent. Each year more good news arriving in Bali attracted more migrants from Bali to the Dumoga. Many went voluntarily, at their own expense, without waiting for the assistance from the Government. Our malaria personnel who went with the first migrants also were given a piece of land like the other migrants. They fared well and did not want to return home.

Dumoga Revisited

In March 1986, old UNICA friends from Holland, Ferdinand and Nitska Oldewelt, came to visit us for the third time in Bali, and they proposed we make a round trip to North Celebes by boat. Our knowledge of the area would be useful during the trip. Actually, for a long time we had dreamed of such a vacation trip to Bolaang Mongondow and Dumoga. Fortunately the PELNI (Indonesian Shipping Company) had recently purchased four new airconditioned passenger ships from Germany and had started to operate a convenient schedule of round trips from Jakarta and Surabaya to Sumatra, Borneo, Celebes and the Malukus. The only snag was that the boat did not stop in Bali and we had to travel first to Surabaya by air. Therefore, we agreed that the Oldewelts would come directly from Holland by plane to Surabaya where we would meet them at the airport. That was not much of a problem. We had friends in Surabaya who arranged our boat tickets at Surabaya harbour.

The boat far exceeded our expectations, being very clean and neat. After the hot battle on the quay we found great relief in the cool air-conditioned hall. The journey was pleasant except that finding a place where we could sit quietly was difficult. Not only were there apparently too many passengers in the lower classes, but they were free to use all the decks. Being the only Caucasian passengers on the ship, Ferdinand, Nitska and Astri drew the attention especially of the youngsters who were eager to try their English!

My former medical assistant from Kotamobagu, Pratasik, now in his sixties and a prominent politician in the Minahassa, met us at the harbour of Bitung near Manado with three jeeps to bring us to Kotamobagu. And what a difference we noted from 1954!

Whereas, in the past it took us two days to travel from Manado to Kotamobagu over a dirt road full of potholes, crossing streams over stony riverbeds, now we covered in less than five hours the 200-km asphalt highway which ran beautifully with wide curves, between the mountains over the highland and the coffee plantations of Modayag, from where it went winding steeply down to the capital Kotamobagu. To my astonishment I could not recognize streets and houses when entering the town. There was nothing that reminded me of the 1950s. The town had suffered terribly during the *Permesta* years, when North Celebes was trying to gain its independence from the Central Government. The secessionist troops had applied the scorched earth tactic during their retreat before the advancing Government Armed Forces, burning and destroying everything on their way. After having quelled the *Permesta*, the Government swiftly embarked on rehabilitation. Roads and bridges were soon rebuilt and modernized. The roads were paved with asphalt. The beautiful old wooden bridges with thatched roofs made way for modern constructions of steel, stone and concrete. The returning population received help in reconstructing their houses with brick instead of wood as was the previous custom. The buildings now to be seen were not much different from those in other towns in Indonesia. Although we were impressed by the remarkable achievement, we felt great nostalgia for the elegant wooden mansions standing on poles that gave a typically rural atmosphere and made the residential areas of old Kotamobagu particularly pretty.

To our great relief we found that the retreating *Permesta* troops had spared the hospital that I had built. The front part had been renovated and provided with a concrete driveway and a roofed porch at the entrance. The wooden barracks in the back had been taken down. The hospital had been extended with two more wards and a modern operating room. My old operating room where I used to work under a Petromax pressure lamp was now functioning as an emergency clinic. There were now three doctors at the hospital and three doctors working in the rural areas. I saw with great satisfaction that the hospital was clean and in a very good shape.

We were particularly happy to discover that the old Consultation Clinic for

Mothers and Children that Astri had built with the Kotamobagu Ladies Club was still standing opposite the Hospital and still had the name ASTRI on its signboard. According to the midwives and nurses it was still very popular and very well attended. Family Planning had been introduced and widely adhered to. It was still being run by the Kotamobagu Ladies Club, and got much support from the government doctors and the Health Services.

Almost all of the hospital personnel were new to me. Of the old guard most were on pension and since they came from the Minahassa many of them had gone. That evening a get-together with our old personnel was held at our hotel. It was a happy and emotional event. The faithful old head male nurse, Ziekenvader, had died, but his wife was still very healthy and active as a nurse-midwife. Old memories were nurtured and the evening was a great success.

The next day we proceeded to the Dumoga Valley. Driving in a comfortable jeep over the broad highway from Kotamobagu along the Dumoga river was a far cry from the hazardous ride on horseback 35 years earlier. The landscape had completely changed. There were no more marshes. Forest and wild bush which had covered the valley were gone and instead we saw beautiful rice terraces with the paddy in various stages of growth like we were used to seeing in Bali. The forest had been pushed back higher up the hilly sides of the valley and there preserved for the maintenance of the water supply of the area. Where tributaries of the Dumoga River entered the valley we saw the most enchanting vistas of winding ravines with narrow rice terraces climbing up the steep slopes on either side. The poor settlements of three decades earlier had been transformed into prosperous villages with good houses and lively markets. It was evident that all these changes had been brought about by our transmigrants from Bali who arrived here 23 years ago.

In honour of our visit the village elders, who were the first migrants from the Mt Agung disaster, assembled themselves in the temple where we again had a most emotional gathering. The older women who immediately recognized Astri embraced her and wept. The men told proudly about their first adventures in their new land and how hard they had had to work to reshape the environment. They have succeeded. The Dumoga Valley has become the main rice producer for the whole of North Celebes. The members of my old Malaria Eradication teams were now on pension and each had his own business. Their children had received higher education, and some had become lecturers at the University in Manado. They were especially proud of their achievement in having kept the community free from malaria by strictly observing the instructions from the beginning until the end. By the time they went on pension the Malaria Control Programme had entered the maintenance phase and a good surveillance system had been established. I believe that their work had been indeed the basis of the successful transmigration programme.

CHAPTER 51

Bali's First University

A Reluctant Dean

Sutedja, the young Governor of Bali, was a highly ambitious and devoted government servant and worked with a vigorous idealism. His patriotism was so strong that at times it blurred his vision, making his perception of the world verge on the ridiculous. When rumours were circulated by certain influential people that the CIA was sending submarines to Indonesia for subversive activities, he had the whole coast around Bali guarded by "people's vigilantes" causing among the population a state of alarm and anxiety. His experiences as a guerrilla freedom fighter had imbued him with a certain amount of xenophobia, especially against the West.

From the beginning he often voiced to me his dislike of the fact that we still had expatriate doctors working in the Health Services. Of course he knew that the Government was compelled to seek help from outside since we still had too few qualified Indonesian doctors. For more than three years he pressed on me his idea of setting up a Medical School in Bali in order to get rid of those foreign doctors as soon as possible.

Knowing the realities and the requirements for a modern Medical School I found his idea grossly premature. All my reasoning could not convince him. He held me in high esteem because of my hard work and he was convinced that the brilliant student he remembered from his school years must be able to accomplish his ideals, if only I was willing to make the effort.

He took the opportunity to voice his dream at an informal get-together with President Sukarno held at his house in Denpasar in early 1961. The President knew that I had great reservations about the scheme, and asked me to explain them.

"Considering the realities," I said, "I don't see it as a possibility in the near future. Perhaps after ten years if the Universities in Java have already produced sufficient numbers of doctors and other scientists such as physicists, chemists, biochemists, biologists and medical specialists, we can think of creating a medical school here in Bali. Moreover from where could we raise the money?"

President Sukarno turned on his seat so that he could look at me straight in my face. We looked into each other's eyes for some time and suddenly the intensity of his scrutinizing eyes turned into a most charming smile and he said: "Well, Djelantik, I know that you have had your medical education in Holland. I guess that you would like to accomplish the best that you could according to the high standards you have learned in Holland. However, don't forget that we are a new and still developing Nation. You have still to learn to live to my motto 'vivere in pericoloso' and be aware that we cannot make progress if we always wait until all the conditions for an ideal set-up are met. We have to take risks."

Although I understood what he meant with his favourite motto which he had used in so many speeches, the motto of a guerrilla fighter, my question escaped from my lips: "What do you mean?"

He laughed, saying: "Doctor, take this as an order from me, the President of Indonesia. I think that you are the right person and the only one who can fulfill my wish. It is my wish that you establish this medical school in Bali as soon as possible. I will instruct the authorities to give you all support you need. I repeat, this is an order!"

That was all too clear! I had to follow or to submit my resignation. That would be ridiculous, meaning that I was afraid to take up the challenge. I was just at the beginning of my career. I looked at Sutedja. He grinned with delight. I sensed the same expression on the other faces around us. There was no return possible. I swallowed a few times before I could answer: "Yes, Mr President, I have understood!"

In preliminary discussions with the authorities involved, it appeared that their ambitions reached further than only a medical faculty. They wanted a university! By adding a Faculty of Medicine and a Faculty of Veterinary Science and Husbandry to the existing Faculties of Literature and Science at our institute of Higher Education, they proposed to create Bali's first university.

I set to work immediately. From memory of my student years in Amsterdam I made the designed and constructed the work benches for Physics, Chemistry, Biology and Physiology and arranged them neatly into two laboratories. As Director of the Denpasar Main Hospital I made the aula of the hospital available to serve as a lecture room. We could perform our essential functions as a hospital without an aula. Then problems of personnel and equipment arose. Still without administrative staff, I had to write personal letters to the Deans of the Medical Faculties in Jakarta and Surabaya, inquiring about physicists, chemists, biologists and physiologists available for our first-year students. Fortunatly four enthusiastic, young assistants were willing to be assigned to Denpasar. They were marvellous young men who did not ask what they could get from us, but how they could contribute to the creation of our new Faculty. They were satisfied with modest salaries and modest housing. When the need came later for laboratory animals, the physiologist himself went with the students before dawn to the rice fields to catch frogs for their physiology practicum. The physicist had to support himself by working as a taxi-driver in his free time. With the little means available all of them were very inventive in preparing and taking care of their laboratories. In addition, I transferred some of my most experienced administrative staff from the hospital and from the Health Services to the new Faculty.

By President's Decree of 17 August 1962, the Udayana University in Denpasar, with its four Faculties, was established. As a natural course of events when the Faculty of Medicine was ready to start, I became its first Dean. I lectured in the subjects of Public Health and Nutrition.

In deviation from the normal curriculum at the other Schools of Medicine, we started giving Public Health studies to our students from the beginning of their first year, continuing to the end of their studies. I was convinced that in developing countries Public Health should be given priority over clinical medicine. It has become the trade mark of our Medical Faculty, especially after affiliation with the University of Hawaii. Prof Volgaropaulos from Hawaii assisted our Faculty in setting up as part of the Public Health curriculum the UCHP or "Udayana Community Health Programme", which began functioning in 1972. With this UCHP, our Medical School distinguished itself as the spearhead of Community Medicine in our country.

Udayana Revisited

Due to my assignment to the World Health Organization from the beginning of 1969, I could not take part in this Community Health Programme. At the end of 1979 I returned to Bali after completing my tour of duty with WHO. Although I was already on a pension from the Indonesian government, the Udayana University asked me to rejoin the Medical Faculty as a lecturer in Public Health with Malaria as my main subject. I took great pleasure in this job, and discovered that no textbook could match the effectiveness of teaching by telling people from one's own experiences.

In 1975, the Government embarked on an ambitious plan to build 5000 Health Centres over a period of five years, spread over all the islands of the Archipelago, which should form the frontline of the Basic Health Services. With the increasing numbers of doctors graduating from medical schools it appeared that it would not be difficult to man these Health Centres with qualified doctors. Since 1980, inspectors from the Ministry of Health were travelling all over the country to evaluate the work of these Health Centres. Their reports were not satisfactory. Most of the Health Centres were not functioning well or not functioning at all, for many reasons. Bad communications, shortage of medicines, inadequate equipment, low salaries, frustration among the personnel and many other explanations were at hand. However, when they made comparisons among the various Health Centres, they found that most of those Health Centres which were doing well, even in the most remote places, were managed by an alumnus from Udayana University in Denpasar! This led the Ministry to the question: "What was there at the medical school in Denpasar that was different from the other schools?" They came to the conclusion that it must be our Udayana Community Health Programme, and in 1982 the Ministry asked UNICEF to have an evaluation study made of ten years activities of the UCHP by an independent consultant.

UNICEF started to look for a consultant who knew Udayana University and at the same time had the required distance from the present situation to be objective. Somehow they knew that I had returned to Bali after many years work with WHO abroad. They asked me to perform the difficult task of evaluation. I accepted.

The job which included historical background, analysis of the curriculum, and critical evaluation of its implementation and of the various elements involved in the Programme, appeared to be a quite demanding enterprise. At that time we did not yet have the convenience of a computer, so that all the data had to be worked out manually. It took me one year to complete the study.

It resulted in the recognition that the Community Health Programme was essential for the medical curriculum in our country. At the national seminar shortly thereafter organized by the Health Ministry and the Ministry of Higher Education all the other universities in Indonesia resolved to revise their Community Health Programmes using our model.

CHAPTER 52

Our House in the Mountains

A Deal and a Windfall

Ever since we went on weekends to Kintamani to escape the heat of Singaraja and enjoy the cold, the mist and the quietness of the pine forests, we longed to have our own small hut in the mountains. On every trip we used to look around the village for spots with beautiful views and had our dreams glued to one hilltop after another. The problem was that we did not yet have the money to buy land. For the time being we indulged in our dreams and spent the weekends in Kintamani in the guest-house of the Forestry Department. On one of our reconnaissance walks, Astri found a beautiful spot on the top of a hill just outside the village. However, since the land belonged to the Forestry Department it could not be bought.

By sheer luck the Forestry Department of the Ministry of Agriculture needed in 1957 a piece of land in the Karangasem Regency to plant a nursery of pine trees for reforestation of the slopes of the Mt Agung. After investigations of the local soil and water supply they found 1.5 hectares of land in a valley near Tirtagangga that was specifically suitable for the purpose. They were faced with the problem that the owner was not willing to sell the land. The Head of the Forestry Department, Komang Tjau, a good friend of ours, asked if we could help him to make the deal with the land owner who happened to be our niece Anik. Astri was smart. Aiming at the hilltop she had marked for our mountain house she proposed to Komang Tjau a deal, that if we could get the land from Anik, we would exchange that piece for Forestry land near Kintamani. Since the outcome of such a deal was obviously in the interest of the Forestry Department, Komang Tjau agreed.

I went to Karangasem and had a talk with Anik. At first she refused to think of any deal. Since she had never been to school, she did not know anything about forestry and agriculture. I told her about the purpose of the nursery, about how good it would be for the population if the arid land north of the mountain could be transformed into rice fields in future. I told her of the duties of our family towards the population of Karangasem and to the welfare of the country at large. She appeared to be responsive and listened attentively. When I finished she said: "Tutek, (that was my nickname) I have always liked you, because you are a good boy. Now that you are a doctor, we are proud of you. Regarding the piece of land, please take it as my gift to you personally and you may do with it whatever you like!"

My heart bounced with joy and the success of my mission.

At the same time I anticipated that our dream house would come true. The deal worked perfectly well on two sides. The ground in Karangasem was much larger than the half hectare piece of forest that we wanted in Kintamani. It was agreed that the Forestry Department would pay the sum of Rp 15,000 for the balance. Komang Tjau took care of the necessary bureaucratic procedures. Even though the deal was soon officially approved in writing by the Ministry of Agriculture, it took more than 20 years (until 1988) before the legal transfer was finalized by the Department of Agrarian Reform and we received the Land Certificate.

We did not wait for the red tape and started to plan the building and gather little by little the building materials since we could not afford to employ a contractor. From the old house in Singaraja we took the tiles of the demolished terrace we had built in front of the bedrooms; from a village near Denpasar we bought limestone blocks for the foundation and lower parts of the walls; from a village near Klungkung we bought the best quality roof-tiles that we could get in Bali. The eruption of Mount Agung in 1963 brought an abrupt end to our building preparations and we had to put the project on hold.

It turned out that later an unexpected windfall befell us from the disaster. Thousands of pine trees on the mountain slopes around Kintamani were destroyed by the volcanic ash. We could buy the wood from those dead trees for virtually nothing and had to spend money only on labour to cut them into planks and to transport them to our hilltop. When at the end of 1964, we could start with the construction, we had first to recover the stones we had stored on the hill out of one-metre-deep volcanic sand and ash!

Build a Chimney First!

Once while buying building materials after our success with the Forestry Department Astri remarked suddenly: "I don't want the house if the fireplace that we are planning to have there does not draw well!"

I looked up, somewhat baffled, but soon understood her concern. There were in Kintamani three buildings that were equipped with fireplaces: the PELNI (formerly KPM) Hotel, the Government Guesthouse and the "Strasser" House, an annex to the PELNI Hotel some 200 metres outside the village on the rim of the caldera. We had spent some weekends in each of them and in all three we sat in smoke for part of the evenings. None of the chimneys was drawing satisfactorily. Astri's wish put a great question mark over our undertaking. There was nobody in Bali who could give us advice in the matter. Friends at the Public Works Department had no idea what was wrong with the existing fireplaces.

In August 1959, on one of our walks in the forest of Kintamani, we met with a group of students of the Bandung Technical Institute in West Java who were on a study tour under the tutorship of a Swiss architect, Walter Hunzicker. After the usual initial chit-chat I asked him: "Well, if you are an architect and you are originally Swiss, then you should be able to tell me how to build a chimney which you can guarantee will draw well," and I explained our problem to him further. He seemed much interested, smiled at me sympathetically and promised to have a look in his books in Bandung and send us a sketch from which we could make the construction drawing.

His letter came two weeks later and carried a hand-drawn sketch as promised. It was indeed complicated, involving the construction of a smoke chamber inside the chimney and several slanting walls and corners at certain points. Nevertheless, with a little mathematics I succeeded in making the construction drawings, including views from the front and from the sides, and vertical cross sections. I was proud of my achievement and we decided to build the chimney first. Only if it drew well, would we start building our house around it!

When I showed our workers in Kintamani my blueprints of the chimney and fireplace their reaction was blank. They were simple bricklayers and carpenters, and they could not read or understand what was on the paper. That was a problem that I had not anticipated. For one night I mused, pondering on a solution. There must be one! All of a sudden I had an idea. I bought large sheets of ordinary wrapping paper. They were cheap and large enough for my purpose. Calculating from the blueprints, I drew horizontal cross-sections of the fireplace and the chimney on the paper to scale. I made twenty of them, starting from the bottom, proceeding every time 20 cm upwards to the next cross-section. When all was finished I brought them to Kintamani and put them before my workers. They looked with great interest and listened intensely. I explained that they just had to start at the bottom, proceed upwards and adjust the masonry as they went. With happy smiles they nodded approvingly. I left and let them discuss among themselves how to proceed with the work. The next morning I returned and checked to see if they had met with some problems. There were none and they started with great fun and enthusiasm. It was the novelty that spurred them on to show their craftsmanship.

Within two weeks a beautiful chimney with a fireplace stood erect in the middle of the flattened hilltop.

Then came the trial. How anxious we were to see the result! The more so because it was to take place outside with free winds all around. We put plenty of wood in the fireplace and lit the fire. The chimney drew very hard immediately. All of us cheered with delight. Our workers looked very proud!

With the building of the house there were more novelties which excited our village carpenters and bricklayers. Built almost entirely of wood, our partly two-storey house demanded resourcefulness from them: there was a staircase which at a certain height had to make a right-angle turn at the corner between the living room and one of the bedrooms; there were built-in cupboards in the bedrooms; and under the stairs, a built-in storage room between the kitchen and the porch at the entrance, and an open space and two bedrooms on the upper floor. They had never before had any experience with that kind of construction.

The more refined parts, like the Dutch-style doors and windows, we had made by a Chinese carpenter in Denpasar. An antique Balinese front door was obtained from an art collector in Sanur by bartering for it with a painting by Bonnet which we were not very fond of. We went up to Kintamani every Saturday to supervise the work and pay the workers. It took exactly one year for them to complete the building.

It turned out to be a unique house, giving the impression of a Swiss chalet, especially later when it lay hidden between green pine trees and cypresses that we planted around it.

A dream had come true!

CHAPTER 53

The Killing Squads

During a weekend in our Kintamani retreat not long after the house was finished, we were awakened early in the morning before dawn by frantic knocking at the front door and excited whispering voices through our open window.
In the half dark we recognized our old house caretaker, Rai, from the village.
With him were three men who had come on foot all the way from Kalanganyar,
a village some 5 km down the road. They came to ask help for the delivery of
a baby at their neighbour's house. The poor mother had been in pains since the
previous night and there was nobody else in the house. I found it a strange
story, because in Bali a house with a woman in labour was usually full of family members and curious neighbours.

"Where is the family?" I asked. They told me—in whispers—that the
woman's husband had left the house the day before because he had been ear-
marked as a collaborator with the Communist Party. Anticipating that he
would be found by one of the "killing squads" which, according to rumours, had
been active for several days in the region, he fled and went into hiding. Since
everybody in the community knew this, nobody had dared to come near the
house. One never knew if by chance an over-enthusiastic member of the squad
would suddenly become hysterical and feel the urge to kill. Even the mere fact
that out of kindness one might have once provided lamps for a festival, or a
rally of the local branch of the Communist Party, was enough to be suspected
as a member—or at least a follower—of the Party and so run the risk of being
killed. It was a most sinister situation, one that prevailed in many villages in
Bali after the news of the abortive Communist coup in Jakarta had filtered
down to the Provinces. We had vaguely heard about these killing squads, organized by political opponents of the Communists, but only now after hearing
the story told by the frightened men, did I realize the seriousness and sadness
of the situation.

I discovered at the same time that I myself had changed. Unlike ten years before in North Celebes, when without hesitation I jumped in my jeep to rush to the wounded policemen after an ambush by guerrillas, this time I felt inhibited by second thoughts: "Would it be safe? Should I take the risk?" But eventually professional and humanitarian considerations prevailed. I gathered the necessary instruments in my emergency bag and joined the three men in my Landrover. The road was eerily empty and when we arrived at the house nobody came out on the street. I imagined, however, seeing people peeping from behind their windows. Somehow all my apprehensions evaporated and I went to work. The delivery was easy. In the meantime, the neighbours found a distant relative who was willing to take care of the woman and the baby. He happened to be a friend of a member of one of the killing squads and it was considered a safe solution. I agreed and returned home in great relief. One month later the husband came back from his hiding place after having been assured by the community that nothing would happen to him.

Such happenings, under circumstances of a mysterious vague terror, occurred almost every day and everywhere in Bali, some of them ending terribly. No one who had been, or was supposed to have been, associated with the Communist Party or with its social or cultural organizations, was sure of his life. Out of the 1,500 men and women working in our Malaria Eradication Campaign, about 500 went into hiding, but more than half of them were caught and killed by killing squads.

One morning a troupe of five men clad in black overalls and wearing red bands around their heads burst into my office at the Main Hospital demanding that I hand over six patients who were, according to them, Communists. They presented me with a list of the names and the wards where they were being treated. While I was greatly shocked, I was impressed by their accuracy, but seeing their big swords and two of them brandishing revolvers, I realized that they meant business. I felt my knees trembling.

"I am sorry," I replied as calmly as I could, "I am afraid that you don't understand the situation and especially my position as a doctor. When would taking up my profession, I took an oath that I would never do anything harmful to my patients who have entrusted their fate into my hands. Therefore, I just cannot consider your request. I know that according to your conviction you are doing good for our Nation. But as long as these people are under my medical treatment they are my responsibility. If they are cured and are away from the hospital, I will be no longer responsible for them. So I must ask you to leave the hospital now and do your duties elsewhere." The tense looks in their eyes gradually disappeared, the two of them with revolvers relaxed visibly. They became very polite and with a friendly smiles, they thanked me for my "advice" and walked quietly out of my office.

I took no chances and told my colleagues that those marked patients be kept under treatment as long as possible. However, the incident had of course not escaped the attention of people at the hospital and by word of mouth the news quickly spread over the wards. The next morning some of the intended victims appeared to have been taken away by their own families into hiding. We had, however, no further visits by death squads.

One afternoon, while driving home from the hospital in my Landrover, I found the main street mysteriously empty. Shops were closed and I saw people running hastily on the sidewalks and disappearing into the houses. In the far distance I saw three small groups of men clad in black and wearing red headbands roaming the street, knocking at one or two of the shops and one group forcing open a gate. When my car came nearer, it seemed to me that they recognized me in the vehicle. They shouted at me excitedly, but they did not sound menacing. Although I noticed that they had all sorts of weapons in their hands I found it wise to pretend not to have seen them. What should I do? Be heroic and stop them and run the risk of being branded as pro-Communist? I thought of my wife and family at home. Would the children be back from school already? When at last I arrived at the house the kids and Astri welcomed me with cheers. I was later than usual and Astri had been worrying. I did not tell her what I had seen. But she already had been informed that black squads had been roaming several streets in town. She asked: "Have you seen them?" and I replied: "Yes, they have recognized me. Maybe that was a good thing!"

Some days later it was 12-year-old Widur who came home racing at high speed on his bicycle. He was trembling all over and he was very pale. On the street one block away he had come upon a black death squad attacking a man who, screaming terribly, tried to get loose. He did not stop to see the end.

Widur was a very sensitive boy and had a talent for painting. For a few days after this event he was very silent. Without telling us anything, he had been painting in his room. We later found a remarkably expressive painting presenting demonic masks in various positions on a black background with false grins, protruding tongues and menacing eyes, decorated at several corners with fires, amputated limbs, skulls and severed heads.

On another occasion it was already nearing dusk when a large group of black-clad men came to our house and asked my permission to burn down the abandoned house of our neighbour, a wealthy Chinese merchant who had left for China a few weeks earlier. Knowing that the Indonesion Communist Party was closely associated with China, he had anticipated upheavals and felt it would be safer out of the country. I was baffled, and asked why they should have permission from me especially. Their explanation was as simple as it was ridiculous. "They would do it anyway, but they wanted only to make sure that we would not be too much shocked when seeing a house next to ours ablaze; that we should know that it was part of their duty as a patriotic revenge against the Communists." Of course I could not stop them, but I told them to first make sure that there was nobody in the house who could be burnt to death. It was a gigantic bonfire.

Meanwhile, the killings went on and on. Alleged Communists were hunted down out of their hiding places. For some hours every night we were kept awake by the frightening noise of trucks driving north. They travelled along the road at the other side of the river next to our house on the way to the killing fields at Peguyangan some 5 km distance. There the squads would deliver their harvest of the day to a professional butcher who performed the execution by beheading their victims with a Japanese samurai sword.

We would not have been that much emotionally affected by these events, were it not that our nephew Gedé Agung was one of the innocent victims. He was the Head of the Provincial Department of Information, and as such he had to follow the instructions of the Information Minister in Jakarta, who was closely associated with the Communist Party. A few weeks before the failed Communist Coup in Jakarta, the Information Ministry despatched to the Information Departments in the provinces all over the country pamphlets which should have been distributed immediately after the Coup. It contained instructions about the transfer of authority by the Provincial Government to the Communists. As a disciplined government civil servant, he did just what was ordered by the Minister. That was enough to implicate him and he was one of the first who was taken away from his house. We heard afterwards from eyewitnesses how the execution had taken place. Agung was very quiet, having apparently accepted his fate as the "Law of Karma", and before he was beheaded he took off his wedding ring and his wrist watch, asking the executioners to deliver them to his wife. He died peacefully. The delivery of the goods was done properly.

Governor Suteja and his family had been called (or fled?) to Jakarta quite soon after the abortive coup and had escaped the local killing squads. But nothing has been heard of him since. Rumours circulated later that he had been taken away in an Army Police jeep. But actually nobody knows. No harm was ever done to his wife and children.

This uncertainty continued for some time in Bali. When I had to go out in the evenings I used to put on all the lights in my car so that people could recognize me. Somehow I was sure that nobody would do me any harm. But this did not mean that we did not have to take precautions. My younger brother Gedé Karang who was Police Chief of West Bali provided me with a big Colt revolver. Although I took it with me on my duty tours, I never had to use it.

One night we were awakened by one of the killing squads asking for the doctor to come with them to see their team leader who was sick in bed with high fever. We had already taken the precaution that Astri was always the one who went to the front door in such cases and only if she considered the matter safe, would she call me. Otherwise she would signal me to escape. The black uniforms and the red headbands made her apprehensive and she asked them to wait outside. When she told me I telephoned the Bupati (Regency Chief) who had close links with the leaders of the killing squads. I wanted to be certain that indeed there was a sick squad-leader in bed with high fever. The sick man turned out to be his own younger brother who had been brought into his house that afternoon. We felt relieved. I went with the black troupe in their car and treated the patient for a relapsing malaria.

Eventually, General Suharto and the military establishment in Jakarta, who had initially unleashed the Communist hunt, realized that it was crucial to restore law and order as soon as possible. Special elite army units were dispatched all over the country to put an end to the manhunt and its terrible consequences such as looting and the endless series of reciprocal acts of murder among the population to revenge old scores.

For more than two months after the abortive coup, the political situation in Bali remained confusing. We knew from the radio broadcasts from Jakarta that General Suharto with his New Order was firmly in command and had introduced many changes in the government. We did not understand why, after such a long time, they had not yet replaced the left-leaning military commander in Bali, nor the pro-Communist Attorney General. There must be some reason for this. Perhaps the government, knowing that the Communist Party had been very strong in Bali, was not sure how many of the local military officers were to be trusted. Perhaps they cautiously wanted to prevent an outbreak of civil war. While people knew that the Military Commander in Bali had been secretly pro-Communist, they were amazed that he did not take action to stop the killings. Perhaps he found it wiser not to oppose the anti-Communists among his ranks. Encouraged by these anti-Communist elements among the Military, the killings increased week by week, later day by day.

At last a regiment of paratroopers was assigned to pacify Bali. This elite army unit succeeded in putting an end to the killings and other irregularities by their determination and their spectacular display of skill, which impressed the public deeply. One eyewitness told me what he saw at the main shopping street in Denpasar. During a looting spree on the Chinese shops, their sharpshooters shot the goods out of the hands of the looters without hurting any of them. The looters gave themselves up with their goods voluntarily. Soon the Attorney General and the Military Commander of Bali were replaced by pro-Suharto officers. The killing squads were disarmed and life in Bali became normal again.

That such horrible mass killings could be committed by the Balinese, who were renowned for their peacefulness and cordiality, remained for a long time incomprehensible to the outside world. Only after having grasped their deeper philosophy on life and death, and their dependency on and adherence to the village community, which is based on their religion, may one understand the mass hysteria which exploded after the series of events that for many years had caused despair, suppressed anger and frustrations.

Within the Balinese community there was a strong belief that the Communists had made the earth "unclean" with their propaganda against religion throughout the previous years. There were other grievances that had been suppressed for a long time and led to a deep sentiment against the Communists. One of these was the illegal occupation of farmland by landless people instigated by the Communists. Most of the landowners concerned were members of the Nationalist Party. Clashes occurred and in some instances the owners and their families were killed. The Governor, the army and the police did nothing. This had caused great frustration and hate. In remote areas, other acts of violence committed by the Communists occurred with impunity.

All of these had contributed to the build-up of animosity among the population. No wonder that once the Communists lost their protection and their grip on the authorities the storm broke loose. The Balinese accepted these horrible killings as acts of purification. In some instances—in Sukawati and other villages—the Communists clad themselves in white and marched to the police to give themselves over to be killed on the spot. Killers and the families of the killed alike believed that these happenings were manifestations of transcendental forces.

Later on, when all the killings had stopped, all over the island the people organized purification ceremonies and cremations to render the land clean of all evil. In general the families of those some 40,000 people who had been killed, kept quiet. They would never talk about their lost fathers, brothers or sisters except to each other. Therefore, it has never been possible to establish exactly how many people died. They would never make any claim over lost property or other wrongdoing inflicted on them during the horrible period of mass hysteria. That was all according to the will of the gods.

BOOK VI

Work Abroad and
Back to Bali

CHAPTER 54

Unauthorized Action

In 1968, I was approached by the World Health Organization to take up a position as a Malariologist. After a three-month refresher course at the beginning of 1969, I received a cable from WHO Headquarters, stating: "In view of his broad experience, Dr Djelantik should immediately to sent to Basrah, Iraq, because of a great malaria epidemic in the wake of floods occurring over the greater part of the area". Two days later, I boarded a plane to Alexandria to report to the headquarters of the Eastern-Mediterranean Region, to which Iraq belonged. From there I travelled directly to Basrah.

The office of the National Malaria Eradication Service in Basrah was housed in an old two-storey building along the Shatt-El-Arab River not far from the harbour. Our small WHO staff consisted of only two persons: myself as Malariologist and my Palestinian assistant Hathat, a Sanitarian from the Gaza Strip. We occupied a large room on the upper floor with a high ceiling which was very convenient in the hot climate. From our windows we had a nice view of the boats on the river which at that point was about 200 metres wide. We usually kept the large windows open to allow as much fresh air as possible into our working space. This had the disadvantage that our room in a very short time became dirty with dust from the town and sand from the desert and needed a complete clean-up every other day. This happened seldom!

During the first week, I did not bother much about cleanliness, because for most of the time we were in the field with our spraymen, trying to stop the epidemic by an intensive spraying of all the houses scattered over the whole flooded area where more than thirty villages were affected. That was easier in theory than in practice, because to get to the houses we had to row in small boats with all our personnel and equipment, and to row back and forth many times to refill our spray cans at the supply stations. It was extremely cumbersome and time-consuming and—with a little arithmetic—I realized that we would never succeed in quelling the epidemic.

One morning, we had to stay in the office and wait for our Iraqi counterparts to get our transport problems solved. The thick layer of dust in our room upset me too much and I asked for a few workers to clean up the mess. During the work an old man who climbed on a chair to clean heaps of old papers on top of a cupboard slipped and fell with a loud crash on the floor. Together with him a bunch of papers fell apart under the chair. I looked up and saw the poor old man kneeling on the floor, gathering the scattered papers in a whirling cloud of dust. I could not help feeling pity and went to assist him. The first paper that I took up from the floor struck my eyes! It was a WHO-publication of some years ago, bearing the title: "Aerial spray with insecticides during a malaria epidemic on the Salomon Islands". I ran back to my table to read the paper. It was an extensive study with a lot of information about the reasoning, the techniques and the evaluation of the operations, all very new to me, but to my mind very convincing and apt to our situation in Southern Iraq at that time.

I was deeply impressed by the article and that same evening I discussed the matter with my counterpart, the Chief of the Southern Iraq Malaria Eradication Campaign. He fully agreed with me and the next morning we went to the Military Commander to ask for his assistance. (At that time Southern Iraq was in a state of military alertness and everything had to be approved by the Military.) The Military Commander was most enthusiastic. He saw in my proposal an excellent opportunity to do something spectacular and good for the people. He also saw real possibilities for the execution of the plan. He had three small aeroplanes at hand. They were equipped with spraying apparatus and were being used regularly for pest control on the date palm plantations. And there was plenty of the insecticide Dichlorvos (DDVP) in stock, which he could make available for our programme. That afternoon we went to the airport with the pilots and inspected the aeroplanes. To my great delight those were the same aeroplanes with the same spraying equipment that were described in Salomon Islands' study. And also DDVP had been used in the Salomon Islands. We discussed the whole plan with the pilots and the Iraqi malaria staff and made up the final plan of action, which took into account the exact times of spraying. That should be during the hours when most mosquitoes were out of their resting places in the houses and would be swarming in the air or busy laying eggs on the waters. Our entomological team knew from experience those times to be between 5 and 6 am and between 6 and 7 pm. The pilots learned at what altitude they should fly, how to take into account the direction and velocity of the winds. They calculated from the maps, and the width of their spraying swathes, how many rounds they should make in one hour's time during the morning and the early evening. We decided from the life-cycle of the mosquito that one and the same area should be sprayed once every three days, and thus the whole affected area was divided into three parts and each part again into three sub-areas for each of the planes. The pilots seemed to like the new task, which required great precision in timing, techniques and logistics. They needed only one day to make their preparations and the next morning we were all in the field before dawn to start the operations.

Perhaps because of its novelty, I found our undertaking both exciting and challenging. In order to meet epidemiological criteria I made provisions for monitoring parasitological and entomological data by establishing a scheme of blood surveys and mosquito-catching stations. Since we were using an insecticide that had never been applied before, I felt that tests of the mosquito's sensibility for this insecticide should be carried out. Our entomological team in Basrah was not qualified for such work, so I asked my supervisor, the WHO Senior Malariologist in Baghdad, to send to us the WHO Entomologist.

The entomologist came, but I was shocked by the rebuff I got from my supervisor. I didn't know that I should have obtained his permission to start aerial spraying operations. It was perhaps because I had been used to being my own boss in Bali and used to make decisions myself, that I had not for one moment thought of asking the Senior Malariologist's approval. This method was beyond WHO's policy in malaria eradication, regarded as dangerous because of possible toxic effects on the population, and therefore should have first been studied and approved by WHO headquarters in Geneva.

What to do? The WHO decided to let the local government make a decision as to whether to stop or to continue. My Iraqi counterparts used their commonsense and were all for continuing our efforts. Our local entomological team established that after two days of spraying, the mosquito densities in the inundated villages had dropped from over 300 per room to less than 20. After six days it had dropped to zero in many places, but after two days without spraying it increased again, but not alarmingly. The WHO Entomologist was satisfied with the results and made sensibility observations on the mosquitoes placed in cages at intervals of 200 metres along the aeroplane routes. To our great joy the number of malaria cases stopped increasing and later dropped remarkably with medication. We decided to continue with the aerial spray for one month. Meanwhile the water receded and the epidemic was regarded as over. The Malaria Eradication Programme resumed its routine activities and my Iraqi counterparts were delighted.

In the course of the epidemic the WHO Senior Malariologist came over from Baghdad together with the WHO Chief Sanitarian and the Chief Entomologist from headquarters in Geneva. Remarkably both the Chief Sanitarian and the Chief-Entomologist congratulated us; the Senior Malariologist did not!

CHAPTER 55

Fieldwork in Southern Iraq

The rebuff of our aerial spraying made me understand better the functions of the field worker in such a tight system as the Malaria Eradication Programme of the World Health Organization. We were only the executioners of a work scheme of which the policy was entirely determined by headquarters in Geneva. Apparently there was too much at stake in terms of time and money to let people in the field follow their own schemes. Deviation from prescribed methods could also jeopardize long-term results of the Programme. All policy was therefore directed from headquarters; the in-house spraying operations should not fall short of the fixed time schedule and should be done with great precision in order to achieve total coverage and maximum effect. Besides, to supervise the national staff on the proper application of the field techniques we had to monitor the results, to evaluate the effectiveness of the methods, to follow closely the sensibility of the mosquitoes towards the insecticides in use, and other epidemiological indicators.

From time to time we had to try out new insecticides in small pilot projects because resistance against the most extensively used insecticide, DDT, started to emerge in other countries. We were among the first to conduct trials with Carbamate and later also with Malathion in parts of Iraq. I had one very interesting experience when working in the area of the Marsh Arabs. These people lived isolated from the rest of the country in a marsh area of 6,000 square miles, located around the town Qurna, where the rivers Euphrates and Tigris join to form the Shatt-El-Arab. The Iraqis didn't like going there, not only because of the difficult terrain but also because of the attitude of the ethnically different population who, like all isolated people, were suspicious of intruders. They formed an almost independent part of Iraq and had their own traditions to which they adhered fanatically. Travel in the area could only be done by boat or canoe, of which they had several types, from the most beautiful and sturdy wooden *tarada* measuring up to 40 feet, to the most primitive ones consisting of merely a bundle of reeds and rushes. Reeds and rushes were the only vegetation over the enormous area of water and were the only building materials available.

We were travelling on three boats, each carrying one squad of four spraymen and their equipment, followed by a fourth carrying the insecticide. The boats were especially made with flat bottoms because of the abundant growth of underwater reeds in the numerous narrow canals between the hundreds of small islands, most having only one or two houses on each. There was plenty of wild fowl—ducks, pheasants and partridges—which flew up noisily at our approach. When we passed houses there were always lots of dogs barking ferociously and following us along the banks until they could not go any further. While I found the whole environment most interesting, I was very worried about getting lost. In many places the reeds were so high that we could not see anything beyond, even when we stood erect in our boats. How our rowers could find the right direction and which tributary to follow was for me a great mystery. We could not use outboard motors since these would immediately get stuck in the vegetation under the water. Our men used long poles to punt the vessels forward. At last we came on a large open lake where the bottom of the marsh was apparently too deep to use the poles and our men rowed farther with paddles. They steered to a large island where a brick house was standing between a number of reed huts. That brick building was to be used as our base camp, where we arranged safe storage for our insecticides and equipment and made all preparations for our daily spraying operations.

Lunch was served at our camp. After a short nap Hathat looked at his watch, talked with the foreman and decided that we could only finish twenty houses on three islands not far away that day. We boarded our canoes. Our guide and rowers were Marsh Arabs themselves and knew the area very well. I could not understand their dialect which was quite different from the Arabic which I had been learning in Basrah. The boat trip was delightful. Despite the summer, there was always a cool breeze except when we were between high reeds. Half an hour later some of our spraymen started to pump up their spray cans. Before us we saw a small island with two reed huts. While the other two boats disappeared into one side canal each, ours steered straight onto the island and landed with its stern on the bank. I expected a crash, but nothing happened. The bank gave softly way to the stern and seemed to hold it fast. We stepped onto the island. Great was my surprise when I felt as if I stepped on a soft mattress! The ground under my feet gave way a little at each step. Hathat laughed when he saw my puzzled face.

"Doc, I did not tell you beforehand because I wanted it to be a surprise. This is not a real island! We are now standing on something artificial. Because there is not much land here, the people have bound the tops of the reeds together to make their islands on which they build their houses".

"Very interesting!" I nodded, "but when the reeds grow more, will the islands not capsize?"

"Well, because of the weight of the people and the cattle and all the debris they heap on this ground everyday, the growth adapts itself and the substance under the island becomes more dense with time. This island is relatively new, so you feel as if you are walking on a cushion."

I examined the ground, and saw indeed no earth, only crushed reeds and rushes and leaves and twigs and debris and not one piece of stone.

The houses were very primitive structures, entirely made of reeds. Each house's skeleton consisted of four arches, each arch made by binding to each other the tops of two opposite pillars formed by the stems of tall reeds, bundled together to two feet thick at the bottom and tapering off upwards. The roof and the walls on either side consisted of strong and thickly woven reed-mats fixed to the arches. At each end of the tunnel-like space mats made up the back wall and the front where an opening served as the door. Spraying of these houses was very easy compared with the many rooms in the houses in the town, and there was barely any furniture or other household items to be taken care of. The population was very co-operative and I was struck by the absence of special precautions to hide the womenfolk. They moved around freely, chatting and giggling. I was also struck by the sight of so many of the men carrying rifles.

Before we were finished with our work we saw two men with a herd of cows wading over a shallow part of the canal towards our island. Our rowers gesticulated to them and told them to stay with their cattle at some distance from the freshly sprayed houses. They stood patiently waiting at the bank while the cows grazed at invisible vegetation under the water, from time to time raising their heads above the surface, chewing on some green. After a while some of the cows seemed to have had enough of the water and stepped ashore just next to our boats where they shook off the water from their bodies. Concerned that our insecticides might be wetted I walked down to our boats. I found myself in the midst of the cows all curiously gazing at me. They came slowly closer. To my great surprise I saw that they had webs between their abnormally long hoofs. I attributed this phenomenon to the cows having to spend their whole lives in the marshes where they often had to swim and their feet never came in touch with a hard surface.

We caught up with the second spraying squad on the next island and finished our work there at the same time as the third squad finished spraying the houses on their island. The trip back to our camp was most relaxing. One of the rowers proudly showed us a huge fish which he had managed to catch with his fishing line. Roasted on a fire, it was a delicious addition to our evening meal.

CHAPTER 56

A Bloody Spectacle

Translation from Dutch of a letter from Madé to Astri

"Basrah, 8 March 1971.

Dearest!
To-day is Ashura, the 11th day of Maharram (the first month of the Islamic calendar). It is a holiday in Iraq. Last night until this morning spectacular events
took place in town.

Out of curiosity, for the past two days I had been trying to get information
about what was going to happen, but nobody was able to tell me. My Iraqi mosquito collector only said: "It will perhaps last until the morning with its climax
at about 3 am" and about its location he indicated vaguely: "Everywhere, you
just look around!"

Anxious not to miss anything I was there at 7 pm. There was, however, still
nothing particular to be seen. Like all other evenings all the streets in the
market area were closed to traffic and occupied by vendors behind all kinds of
little stalls. The shops, restaurants and tea-bars on both sides of the streets were
open and it was very crowded everywhere. As usual the public consisted almost
only of men and boys. I saw a few veiled women in black gowns doing some
shopping. The stalls were illuminated by kerosene pressure lamps which gave a
rural taste to the scene. Numerous small children played and romped about on
the sidewalks and between the stalls, which displayed a great assortment of
cakes, fruit, and also *tikka* or *kebab* (pieces of meat on a stick) being roasted on
charcoal. I kept on stumbling over small boys with their shoe-polish boxes. So
I strolled in between the stalls looking at shoelaces, plastic purses, razor blades,
cigarettes, and secondhand clothes. The place became more and more crowded. People were strolling, chatting or shouting at each other and there was a
kind of expectation in the air. By 10 pm the smaller children who had been
romping and mock-fighting became tired and started to whine and nag at their
elder brothers who were visibly fighting sleep.

Suddenly, a loud and heavy drone of drums filled the air. Running into the side street where the noise came from I landed at a brightly illuminated open space where four men were beating with sticks on huge drums which hung in front of them on ropes around their necks. Around them two groups of men were dancing to their rhythmic beats. They were clad in black *dishdashis*, the traditional long loose Arabic shirts, which apparently for this occasion were cut open from behind, leaving their backs and shoulder blades exposed. The dancers moved around the drummers in opposite directions, making two concentric circles and followed with their steps the rhythm of the drums . . db dbbb . dbdbdubb . . db dbb dbdbdubb . . db dbb . dbdbdubbb . . db dbbb . dbdbdubbb . . db dbbb . . . dbdbdubb . . db dbb . . swaying to the left at the first and to the right at the second "dbb" and coming forcibly with the left foot on the ground at the third "dubbb" whereby with a deep yell they hurled with great force a big iron chain which they held fast with both hands over their right shoulder, hitting their back with a frightening crash. They hit themselves alternately from the left and from the right side to the rhythm of the drum beats. It was not long before their backs were red and started bleeding. Nevertheless the beating went on and on, and while singing "Allah Akbar" the men seemed to be in a trance and not feel any pain. It was most fascinating! The monotonous sound of the drumming and singing and the rhythmic crash of the chains on human flesh made a gripping experience. After a while the public joined the singing and many came under some sort of auto-hypnosis.

Some time earlier I had indeed seen a similar spectacle also in Basrah, however without blood. People were singing and dancing on the beat of drums, hitting their chests with their fists. Their movements were better coordinated and there was great joy but nothing of a trance. It was a jolly good show at a wedding party. About this evening my informant had told me that after the performance with the chains there would be another spectacular event when the dancers would exchange their chains for big swords and hit themselves on their heads. Great was my disappointment when after less than one hour dancers and drummers suddenly disappeared into one of the buildings. A loudspeaker crackled and announced something in Arabic. Amidst the noises of the dissolving crowd I only could catch the words: "At four o'clock in the morning!"

I could do nothing better than walk a little more around, hoping to see something worthwhile. After one hour or so, I felt tired and strolled back to my flat. Before going to bed I put on my alarm clock at 3 am.

I was fast asleep when it rang. I listened intently to see if there were sounds of drums. Nothing! One moment of hesitation, then I dressed hastily. After gulping down a glass of chocolate milk, I was within ten minutes at the market place again. It was already crowded there, but most of the people looked tired and worn out. They gazed at each other with sleepy eyes or stared expressionlessly in the dark. Others shuffled aimlessly around, waiting for something to occur. On the pavement groups of men were lying down, yawning and half asleep. There was much less movement than last night but I saw more women in black gowns between the few remaining and now half empty stalls. Other women sat together in small groups on the edge of the sidewalks. To be sure that I would not miss anything I strolled systematically over all the streets which came out on the market. All the time I heard people asking each other: "Where? When?" Nobody seemed to know.

By 4.30am I had covered all the streets twice and flopped down on a low bench in front of a teahouse at the corner of the main street. Fortunately it was still early in spring and the temperature was nice. I ordered a cup of tea, the famous Iraqi tea: a very sweet concoction in a small glass with golden rim. Looking around I could not find any one whom I could expect to know enough English to give me some information. The Iraqi elite and educated citizens were never to be seen in this part of down-town at these kinds of occasions. These were the common folks, peasants from outside the city, workers at the harbour, and townspeople of the lower middle class. After some time a man who had been curiously looking at me for a few minutes sat himself down next to me on the bench and ventured to address me in Arabic. He asked me where I came from, and in which hotel I was staying. I tried to speak Arabic as best as I could and asked him if the procession of the men with the swords would really take place and when. "Ba'ad Sa'a," he answered (meaning "in one hour") and that the procession would be passing exactly where we were sitting.

I looked at my watch: still half an hour to sit and wait. That did not appeal to me but if I would go for another walk my nice place would immediately be occupied, so I thought better to stay and pay for the tea as well. Great was my astonishment when the waiter told me that it had been paid for. He laughingly pointed to a tall Iraqi standing against the wall in the back of the teahouse, who grinned jovially at me. My my! To my greater astonishment I recognized him as the errand-boy at the office of the man who managed the flat building where I lived. I was really touched by such hospitality. That was one of the charming traits of the common people of Southern Iraq. My Arabic was not good enough to express my gratitude in formal terms to him, when he later came and sat himself down next to me on the bench. He explained to me in English that the procession would soon pass by and that it consisted of four groups of about fifty men, each representing their own village. The owner of the teahouse, an old, jolly fellow, joined us and told me that I should rather stand on the bench to have a better look at what would be going on.

It was already 5.30 am when suddenly a group of men emerged from one of the streets, gracefully swinging huge green banners above the heads of the crowd. They were followed by a troupe of drummers who filled the air with their powerful drumbeats, and immediately behind these were about fifty men and boys wholly clad in white and all of them shorn completely bald. Each of

them had a frighteningly flickering big sword in his hands. They danced forward to the mighty beats of the drums dbb . dbb dbb dubbb . . dbbb . dbbb dbb
dubbb . . whereby with every forceful "dubbb" they hit their bald heads with
their swords. Since a head wound always bleeds profusely, their faces and
clothes were instantly drenched in blood. It was a terribly fascinating sight.
The crowd became hysterical and started to sing, to lament, to cry, to howl, to
yell loudly, while the sound of trumpets and loud-speakers mixed with the
drone of the drums. After the first troupe of swordsmen another bunch of green
flags followed by another fifty self-castigating men and then a third, a fourth
and a fifth column of fifty bloody human forms, all passing slowly and rhythmically along in front of us. More and more people joined in and walked along
with the bloody procession. The third column carried with them huge pictures
and paintings, depicting scenes from the story of Hussein and the battle where
he had been betrayed by his followers. Crying hysterically, women ran into the
procession and tore pieces of bloody white cloth from the men's garments,
wrapping these soiled pieces around their heads. Other women put bloody
cloth that they could snatch on the heads of their babies which they held in
their arms, expecting their children to be cured from some disease. Others ran
away with a piece of bloodstained white cloth, apparently also for some magical
purpose. More and more people were possessed by the breathtaking spectacle.

The procession went on and on, the mighty thuds of more than 100 drums
and the atmosphere of religious ecstasy among the crowd, the crying of the
women, the singing of the men, all could not fail to stir emotion. The sun
meanwhile had reached higher in the sky and although I started to feel the
heat, my legs kept moving . . . Moving?? . . .

Suddenly I realized that I had been marching with the hysterical crowd all
the time for more than one hour. It was as if I had not felt that I was walking,
I was just there, witness—and without being aware of it—also participant.

I came to my senses. The procession came to a halt at the same marketplace
as where it started. We had been marching in a circle around down-town. The
end of the occasion was more prosaic than I expected. There were no ceremonies, no priests, no orchestras, there was no singing, no music. The drums
just stopped all of a sudden, leaving a void in the air. The participants in their
blood drenched clothes separated without greeting each other and stepped into
their buses with an astonishing matter-of-factness. People were silently rolling
and wrapping the huge banners in brown canvas bags. The large pictures were
folded together and loaded upon trucks and off they went.

The marketplace was empty in a few minutes. I found myself alone and lost
on the wide open square. Completely exhausted from the march, the heat, the
dust, the hysterical crowd, and the imperishable gripping memory of the bloody
spectacle, I dragged myself home.

CHAPTER 57

On the Home Front

After I left Denpasar, Astri immediately started designing a new home—a real hobby of hers—this time without the restriction of an official budget. But our means had its limits of course. We had nothing to put aside from our savings. She had to wait until my WHO transfers came through.

At the same time arrangements had to be made for Surya's travel to Holland for her studies at the Hotel Academy. There had to be money for the plane ticket, for the school, for clothing and other necessities. With great effort Astri managed first of all to secure Surya's entry in the Hotel School. But a host of difficulties emerged during the process of obtaining her visa for the Netherlands, and when at last that problem was solved, the Dutch immigration authorities required her to have a return instead of a one-way ticket. With the help of friends in Holland who worked with the Royal Dutch Airlines we got the ticket changed and everything else arranged well on time, even for Surya to have a stopover in Kuwait for a few days so that she could visit me in Basrah on her way. Astri had to arrange everything, also for friends to pick her up at Schiphol airport and for temporary accommodation. Luckily we had good friends in Holland who all the time assisted Surya with every problem.

I met Surya at Kuwait airport and brought her to my flat in Basrah. It was just delightful to have her around. I showed her some interesting places in Basrah and later we spent two days in Kuwait where her miniskirt caused excitement among the young men who could not refrain from trying to pinch her buttocks. She arrived safely in Holland on the 6th of August 1969.

In Bali meanwhile, Astri finalized her building plans. To have the house built by a contractor was out of the question. It would cost a lot more and the quality of the material would be very questionable. Astri preferred to buy all the materials herself: stones, cement, bricks, tiles, nails, hinges, door-locks, pipes, faucets, toilets, and so on. How lucky we were to get help from my younger sister Ayu Mas, whose husband owned a timber-trade and factory in East Java. He provided us with first-class teak for the whole house at cost price: doors, windows and the whole roofing construction. In addition, with the wood he sent two experienced carpenters from his factory, to set up the roof skeleton that had already been prepared neatly by his workers according to Astri's blueprint.

With her practical instincts, Astri knew very well how many and what kind of rooms and spaces were needed, their position in relation to the sun, how to achieve the right cross ventilation, and so forth, so I did not need to bother about anything. Only with one exception: there was that huge Kobot painting to be considered. I had been thinking of the problem, and came to the conclusion that we should have a hall with a six-metre-high wall at one end. At the opposite end the house would have two levels. Astri found my suggestion ridiculous and most unpractical. Without hesitation, she cut the painting in two halves to fit precisely on the walls of the living and of the dining room respectively. Miraculously, the cut did not disturb any scenes in the painting. The result was fanstastic!

I applied for a short Christmas holiday at home, since during wintertime there was not much anti-malaria work to do in Basrah. I received Headquarter's approval and had a fantastic homecoming. I fell straight into the midst of Astri's construction activities. Truckloads of earth were being brought to raise the level of the middle part of the terrain where the foundations of the main house would be built. Stones and wood were neatly stacked in a temporary shed on our piece of land, faithfully guarded by an old man, Djendela, who in his younger years had assisted my father with loyal devotion in all his building activities. Later when we were building our mountain house in Kintamani he was of great help to us.

It was remarkable how Astri had managed to take care of so many technical, logistical and financial problems in the very poor circumstances prevailing in Bali at that time. It was very difficult to get good material, to arrange for transport, even to get petrol for the car. At the same time, because of her commitment to the Family Planning Programme (for which she had been on a study travel to the USA, the Caribbean, the Middle East and Asia), she had to teach a family planning training programme for doctors and midwives.

We celebrated Christmas as usual in our mountain house in Kintamani. We used to chop off the top of one of our cypresses, and compose a beautiful Christmas tree, which our children loved to decorate. Since there was no electricity we always lit candles. The morning after Christmas, while we were sunning ourselves in the backyard, Astri noticed that Merti was missing. We could not find her anywhere in the garden, nor in the house. She must have gone on her own to the village. When after one hour she still did not turn up, we sent our boy to find her. She was just nine years old and Astri was worried that something might have happened to her. After half an hour she returned... but how! She was in her panties only and did not have on the brand-new jeans she had been given for Christmas. Just when Astri was going to reprimand her for being late and going out without telling us, she saw to her great surprise that Merti was affectionately cradling in her arms a very small monkey! When Merti, with tears in her eyes, sobbing and gasping for breath, told her story, Astri's anger melted away. On the street in the village Merti's attention had been drawn to a troupe of boys chasing after a monkey. Somehow they killed the monkey which appeared to be a mother with her baby. The boys grabbed the baby monkey and with great hilarity tossed the poor animal as a toy from one to the other. With great compassion for the small creature Merti stopped the boys and demanded that they gave it to her. One of them, sensing from her good clothing that she must be from a rich family, demanded money. Merti had no money on her and the boy demanded that she barter her jeans for the monkey. Merti did not hesitate for a moment, took off her jeans and the monkey was hers. When she finished the story Merti wept. She felt guilty about the jeans. We were impressed.

Astri took the baby monkey in her arms. It was still very young, perhaps about two weeks old. It was a miracle that it was still alive after such abuse by the boys, and that no bones were broken. The monkey had to be fed with milk from a bottle and soon it recovered and developed into a cute naughty pet that got especially attached to Astri. Tungtung, as we named him, moved freely in our house, still the government doctor's house next to the Leprosy Hospital in Balun. When visitors came or there was lightning in the air and a storm broke loose, he fled into Astri's arms and had to be rocked to sleep. Later, when he got much bigger, he was sometimes bound to a chain with a wide ring at the end that could move along a three-metre stretch of bamboo in the garden. Merti and Astri loved Tungtung so much that they found it very hard to leave him in Bali when later they had to move to Somalia.

My Christmas holiday was of course too short. But I came again to Bali on home leave in December 1970. Astri had already moved out of the government doctor's house and proudly showed me our beautiful new premises which she had completed a month earlier. She had it fully furnished with all our cherished belongings. It was incredible how she had managed to arrange those buildings on a piece of ground with such difficult proportions, being 110 metres long and only 15 metres wide. In addition to the main house with the garage and the servants' quarters she had also built a pavilion with two bedrooms, a sitting room, kitchen and bathroom. Intended at first as my private surgery, it could serve also as a guesthouse. Between the main house and the pavilion she had erected a beautiful Balinese open *pendopo*, consisting mainly of antique carved woodwork, charmingly set in a small pond with water lilies.

It was a wonderful homecoming. Astri had recovered well from a bout of hepatitis, and the children were doing well at school. Even Merti who formerly was very easily distracted by the slightest event, had made good progress. Her monkey Tungtung had grown fast and was happily roving around in the house. His naughtiness was human, so we had to take care that he did not spoil anything. With incredible speed he used to snatch away the best food from our dining table and then look triumphantly at us before he started to nibble at the meat. He gave us and the children a great deal of fun. However, from the first moment he saw me he was incredibly jealous. Every time I came near Astri he made threatening noises and if I did not pay attention he really attacked me. I had to refrain from being too near Astri in his presence! It was not easy for me but it was impossible to change his behaviour.

His affection to Astri grew so strong that a few months later, when Astri was packing and preparing for her travel to join me at my new duty station Mogadishu in Somalia, he seemed to feel instinctively that she was going to leave him alone, and two weeks before she left he sat all the time in a corner of the house, sadly hiding his head between his hands and refusing to eat unless Astri fed him herself. Then he would look at her with an intensely sad look in his eyes. When she at last, with Widur and Merti, actually got in the taxi to go to the airport he refused to come near and hid his face behind his hands. Ketut, our boy, who was to stay behind and guard our house, brought him to his house in Balun. To his great distress, Tungtung went on a hungerstrike, refused all food, and died soon after.

During my vacation there was still more work to do. According to the Hindu religion and Balinese custom the house had to be blessed by a priest in an inauguration ceremony. Otherwise our family and the servants would not feel happy and safe to enter or live there. Astri had already built a shrine at the northeast corner to meet religious requirements. Our brother-in-law who was a priest consulted the old books, found the appropriate date for the *pelaspas* or inauguration ceremony, and was more than delighted to officiate at it himself. Trisna, our daughter who was studying medicine in Bandung and whom we had not seen for the past two years, came back to attend the festival and to see us before we left Bali. Our niece Raka took care of the whole set of offerings needed for the occasion and a group of musicians from her *banjar* came with their instruments to perform the *beleganjur*, the music traditionally for the exorcism of evil spirits. The priest performed his prayers and the whole family, friends and relatives who attended the ceremony joined in prayers for the well-being of the community and the environment.

The remainder of my leave was spent helping Astri complete and beautify our home and garden. Christmas was spent as usual in our mountain house in Kintamani with a Christmas tree by candlelight. It was even harder than the previous year to leave Bali for Basrah. But when I arrived back in Basrah, I found a letter from Regional Headquarters in Alexandria telling me that I was to be transferred to Mogadishu, Somalia, and not to Afghanistan, as was promised before!

The next morning I informed Astri by cable about the transfer, so that she could adjust her preparations for the change. What a hard time for her to change again. Moreover, she was busy preparing Widur's travel to Holland to attend the School for Engineering and Architecture in Delft. A hectic time for her followed, sending letters and cables to Holland and Basrah. At the same time she had to look for opportunities to rent or to lease our house on contract to a foreigner. A good friend of ours who was director of a government bank offered his good services to take care of any deal. And there were again the bureaucratic obstacles for obtaining visas, but this time Astri had learned from experience. Eventually all fell well in place and on the 15th of May Astri, Widur and Merti boarded the KLM flight in Denpasar to Bombay. From there Widur would fly further on his own to Amsterdam, while Astri and Merti had to find seats on the plane to Mogadishu via Aden, which as yet had not been confirmed.

After Widur's farewell kiss in Bombay, Astri felt a great void around her. However, she could not dwell for long on her sense of loneliness. Airport ground personnel ushered her and Merti into the waiting bus for transport to the lounge, where they were informed that there was no connecting flight and that they had to stay overnight in a hotel. Their seats on the plane to Aden the next morning had not been confirmed. Great confusion ensued, not in the least about their luggage. The flight to Mogadishu was quite complicated, involving three different airlines carrying them first to Aden, from there to Hargeisha and further to Mogadishu. The stopover in Hargeisha, a small town in the middle of nowhere in North Somalia, where the airport consisted only of a barely visible grass airstrip, was in itself an experience of sorts.

After a trip with so many delays and confusions, Astri and Merti were completely exhausted when their plane landed at Mogadishu airport on 19th May 1971. It was a miracle that none of their luggage was missing.

CHAPTER 58

A Taste of Terror

Before I moved to Somalia, I had a very unpleasant experience in Iraq. After a bout of strenuous fieldwork undertaken in the murderous heat south of Basrah, Dr Rishikesh, our Indian entymologist, Hathat and I sat in his comfortable cool hotel suite in Basrah discussing material for our reports. We had just finished when Mrs Rishikesh entered the room and told us that dinner was served. We had not enjoyed a decent meal for three days and devoured the variety of Iraqi dishes put before us.

"Well," Mrs Rishikesh remarked, "from the way you are eating, I guess that you must have been starving down there in Fao!"

"Indeed," Dr Rishikesh answered, "and it is now time for a little relaxation. Let us make a pleasure trip by boat over the marshes. It is pleasant and cool there, with the winds blowing over the waters and there is plenty of wildlife to see: wild ducks, all kinds of birds, even swans if we are lucky. People have told me that it is the season now".

I was more than eager to join them, but Hathat had an appointment with his wife's family. As a longtime citizen of Basrah, he knew addresses and promised to arrange a charter motorboat for us. After dinner, we dispersed, and I walked back to my flat a few blocks away.

Early the next morning the three of us, equipped with tropical helmets, sunglasses, cameras, sandwiches and a lot of drinking water, followed a man by the name of Yousuf to the shore of the Shatt'el Arab River and boarded his small motorboat which was waiting at a wooden pier. Yousuf steered his vessel diligently to the north between the numerous boats and ships lying criss-cross in the Basrah harbour. When we left the port, a beautiful wide panorama of blue and green unfolded before our eyes. There was indeed a pleasant cool breeze blowing from the vast marshes extending on both sides of the river. We passed a great number of large and small tributaries through which we now and then caught glimpses deep into the mysterious reeds. While I was wondering if and how there could be people living in these marsh areas the boat turned into one of the larger watercourses and before long the stream widened into an open lake. Scattered over the vast plain of water were patches of reed forming small islands of various sizes. A flock of ducks flew up with noisily flapping wings and Yousuf slowed down the engine. As silently as possible the boat glided along the edges of the lake and we discovered that the place was full of many kinds of birds. My powerful Russian binoculars, recently bought in Kuwait, made birdwatching particularly delightful. We made profuse use of our cameras.

We were so absorbed by the beauty of the scene that none of us had noticed that another motorboat had been following us for some time. All of a sudden we were startled by a sharp whistle and a loud command to stop. A Navy craft drew up alongside our boat, a soldier hurled himself over the railing and landed with his boots heavily on our deck.

By chance, Dr Rishikesh had already used up all his film and had put his camera safely in a plastic bag under his seat. I was busy zooming in on a group of white swans. The man came straight up to me and roughly grabbed my camera from around my neck, shouting furiously that we were in a military zone where photography was forbidden. Yousuf made excuses, arguing that there was nowhere any sign with "Forbidden Area" to be seen, which was true. But it was to no avail. Three other soldiers jumped down from the craft on our deck and one of them took over the wheel. Yousuf was visibly frightened. Dr Rishikesh went pale and attended to his wife who had nearly fainted.

I could do nothing else than surrender my camera and calmly wait and see what would happen. I expected that no greater harm could befall us than losing our cameras and my precious binoculars.

The soldiers did not search our boat. They were apparently satisfied with Yousuf's explanation about our identity and considered us innocent visitors. We landed at a camouflaged pier where an army officer emerged from a nearby tent. he approached us in a friendly manner and explained to us in English that we had entered a forbidden zone. Handing over my camera to me, he said politely: "Since we have to do our duty, we must see what you have photographed. Will you please take out the film and give it to me? We will develop it and if there are no sensitive pictures on it, we will return it to you. If there are, we will cut those out and you may keep the rest".

I found him very reasonable and did what was asked. He invited us for a cup of tea in his tent, but we excused ourselves because it was already late. With a sigh of relief we boarded our boat for the journey home.

I had that night, the sound sleep of the innocent. As a routine I walked the next morning to my office at the National Institute of Malaria and Communicable Diseases where I shared a room with Hathat. It was nearly lunchtime when Dr Hendow, the Chief Executive of the Malaria Eradication Programme, entered my office with a grave look on his face. He talked softly in

Arabic with Hathat. I could not follow the conversation. They eventually turned to me and told me that it seemed that I was under arrest!

I could not believe my ears. "Yes, it is true," they said. "There are two officers from Army Intelligence downstairs with a warrant for your arrest. We don't know what to do!"

"Why?" I asked.

"They said that they found harmful material on the film you gave them yesterday. Please advise us, what shall we do?"

"Nothing," said I. "Let me go with them. There is nothing serious; they told me that if there are pictures of forbidden areas, they will cut them out. I agreed because it is their duty. Come, let us go downstairs".

I put my files in order, went down to greet the two officers, and was somewhat horrified when they said we needed to go by my apartment to collect things for an overnight stay. I was very suspicious, but complied with their wishes and went with them in their jeep.

At the Army Intelligence Office, I was handed over to two armed men in civilian clothes. It gave me a strange feeling. I was led into a hall in the centre of which, three officers were seated on one side of a large table with a red cover. They ordered me to sit down on the empty chair at the opposite side. The officer in the middle started to address me in a rough and most vulgar manner: "Don't try to lie to us! We have discovered that you are a spy! You have been spying for the Iranians and for the Zionists!"

The words sounded so unreal in my ears, making no sense at all. I had the feeling that they were not addressed to me, but to someone standing behind me. I started to look around and this infuriated the man.

"Don't be so silly," he shouted. "I have here the evidence, and I will show you. Look here!" and he produced out of a file six enlarged photographs which he put before me on the table. It took me a few seconds before I realized what I saw, and when I recognized the photos, a deep shock went through my heart.

The man was obviously pleased when he saw my startled face. Noticing his victorious smile, I immediately recovered from my shock. I was convinced that this was a very serious matter and told myself that I should not panic for one second and keep my head clear to be able to find a way out somehow.

He cried: "Do you see the evidence? Now, answer me, did you take these photographs?"

Putting on a blank face, I answered as calmly as I could: "Yes, but may I explain..". He cut me short and shouted: "No, we don't want explanations. We know enough!" and to the guards: "Take the spy away!"

I found it wiser not to make more trouble with that dangerous madman and followed by guards. They led me to a wooden structure with a roof of corrugated iron, standing in the centre of an empty square between the office buildings. I saw at the wide entrance gate a number of heavily armed guards. Some of them wore civilian clothes. I speculated that these were Party members serving as Intelligence agents.

In my wooden cell which measured three by two metres and had no ceiling under the iron roof, it was terribly hot. Fortunately, there were two small windows on opposing sides through which movement of air brought some relief. The door was noisily shut and locked behind me and each of the guards placed himself under one of the windows. All the time they kept playing ostensively with their guns. Now and then, they looked inside, grimacing to me, calling out with nasty delight: "Hey, you! Tomorrow, hanging!"

I couldn't make out if it was meant seriously or merely as a joke to frighten me—and decided to believe the latter.

I sat down on the wooden cot which was the only furniture of the cell and thought of the six photographs shown to me on the table. I had completely forgotten that my camera which I had not used for three months still contained a film from a trip I had taken early in 1970 to Pakistan as a WHO consultant. On the return flight when we were above the border between Kuwait and Iraq, I was enthralled by the beauty of a cloud formation on the left side of the plane and got the urge to take some photographs. About half of the small plane was occupied by military officers returning home from Karachi to Baghdad. Since I knew that photography in the Middle East at that time was hazardous, especially from planes, I went to the officers and asked if I was allowed to take pictures of the clouds. After some discussion, they gave their permission.

On the photos, the clouds showed very beautifully indeed: they could be prize-winning photographs. But there was more to be seen: the tip of the plane's wing on top must have aroused immediate suspicion. Since the plane was already descending towards the airport of Basrah, down below the Iraqi fortifications on the border with Kuwait were clearly visible! I had of course not thought of asking for a written permit from the officers on the plane. How could I now convince these fanatics? Even if they accepted that I had the permission from the officers, they could always assume that I had cunningly tricked them by pretending to take pictures of the clouds only. If I did not succeed in talking sense into these men, what would happen next? The gallows were ready. Execution by hanging in public was routine business at the time in Baghdad. I thought of my wife and children and of Bali, and suddenly I felt very tired.

I lay down on the bare wooden planks, hoping to get some sleep and rest. However, I could not prevent my mind from yielding to frightening fantasies about what could happen in the following hours. Only a month earlier, while conducting spraying operations in Fao, one of our labourers showed me his mutilated fingers. He had been caught after visiting his family in Iran without the appropriate papers and was put in jail for a few days. They had tried to draw confessions from him by extracting the nails one by one from all his fingers.

The poor boy had nothing to confess, even after torture with burning cigarettes and electric wire. He was set free at last and recovered in a hospital. I was fully aware that my photographs were compromising. Although there was no war between Iraq and Kuwait, there was a dispute going on between Iraq and Iran about the Shatt'el Arab waterway and Kuwait was considered to be on Iran's side. I could not think of anything which could be brought up in my favour. At the time political sentiments in Iraq were highly charged, especially among the younger generation. Once while doing fieldwork near Basrah I was approached by a group of students who were curious about what this foreigner was up to, making house-to-house visits in the village. They asked where I came from and when they heard that I came from Indonesia, they became hysterical and shouted: "American agent! Your President Suharto killed many Communists on the orders of America!"

Sensing the futility of argument, I had kept silent and continued with my work. I did not bother to listen to their further enquiries with my Iraqi assistants, which anyhow went on in Arabic, and were for me incomprehensible.

Before long, I was led again to the interrogation hall with the large table in the centre. There were three reflector lamps on the table which lit up immediately as I sat down on the chair. Blinded by the intense glare, I could not see the faces opposite me, but recognized the nasty voice of the speaker. I did my best to answer their questions as clearly and as concisely as possible, explaining how and why I took the photographs from the plane. When they showed me two other pictures which I recognized also as mine, I hesitated. I did know when, but did not remember where the photos had been taken. It was somewhere in the *souk* (market) in Basrah on a Moslem Holy Day, the Id'l Adha, and it depicted a ceremony with Shia mullahs and a huge picture of Ali, Mohammed's son-in-law, in the background. Knowing the Iraqi government resented the Shia's veneration of Ali because of his association with Iran, I became nervous. My interrogators cried triumphantly: "Ha, there you are. Spying for Iran!" During the further questioning, I consistently stuck to my position that all the pictures were taken out of curiosity.

Toward evening, I was led for the third time to the interrogation hall. Again, those intense reflector lights were in my eyes. I had already prepared myself to be consistent in my replies and made no mistakes. For some reason, they did not resort to torture, they did not even touch me. In the end, I was told that I had to be interrogated by higher echelons of Intelligence at headquarters in Baghdad and that I was to travel the same night. Three endless hours of anxiety followed, during which I imagined all the terrible things that could happen to me. I was lucky that they had not robbed me of my watch, so that I knew the time and a little certainty was in some way helpful.

It was 10 pm when the same two civilian armed guards escorted me to the railway station. During the eight-hour train ride to Baghdad, I was seated in a separate compartment betwen the two men who were constantly playing with their revolvers, now and then poking their muzzles against my ribs. They must be typically ambitious party members to assert themselves and to show off their power. Their English was poor and conversation was not possible. Although they tried, I found it wiser not to be responsive, so that I would not say anything wrong.

Thousands of thoughts went through my head. I asked myself if I was afraid and was surprised to find out that I was not. Nor was there any feeling of panic remaining after those interrogations. Perhaps one gets used to that kind of thing. I observed my guards. They must have been in their late twenties. Apart from their showing off, they behaved correctly. But I had been warned earlier by people in Basrah that these activists used to extort money from their victims. I found their faces like those of criminals, able to do anything that occurred to them.

We arrived in Baghdad at six in the morning. They brought me to a restaurant, which was of course not open yet. But the hotelier let us in and led us to the empty dining hall. One of my guards indicated that he was sleepy, excused himself and disappeared. His mate ordered breakfast for the two of us, which to my surprise was served promptly. I assumed that they were regular clients. I was hungry and the food tasted good. The coffee chased my tiredness away and I felt energetic. After an hour, the first guard returned, clean and refreshed. He put down his revolver before me on the table. His mate excused himself for an hour of sleep. Breakfast was served again. I could hardly suppress my anger seeing the gun on the table, and hearing his sarcastic remark: "My friend... rest little, OK? You no need sleep? I know... spies go without sleep many days!" I did not reply, but helped myself to another cup of coffee.

An hour later the second guard turned up and they brought me by taxi to Intelligence Headquarters where we arrived at 8 am sharp. I was led straight away to a military officer who was apparently waiting for my arrival. We shook hands and the guards were ordered to wait in the waiting-room downstairs. I felt relieved. This was a very different reception. The officer was smart and I had to be very careful with answering his questions. He seemed not to believe anything I told him and kept shaking his head. I started wondering if it was genuine or whether he was play-acting.

I was led to another room where another military officer interrogated me again. The same questions again, now put differently, and the same answers adjusted accordingly. It seemed without end. At last, I was led downstairs to the waiting room where my guards received me with threatening remarks. They seemed to indulge in fantasies of seeing me hanging already. They continuously kept joking about me. I had never felt such an intense feeling of hate welling up in my chest than at those moments, but I kept silent.

I felt relieved when I was taken away for another interrogation in another room by another officer. Again, the same questions and answers. From his badges, I guessed that he was a Colonel in the army. I was struck by his friendly eyes. He scribbled a few lines on the margin of a typed paper before him, looked at me and said: "Dr Djelantik, I am sorry that we have caused you so much trouble. I am one of the officers who was on the plane. I have been able to convince the Intelligence Unit that you are innocent. On behalf of the army I apologize for all the inconvenience of the past 24 hours. You are free, but we have to keep your nice photographs".

He stood up, shook my hand and led me to the door. My happiness was indescribable. Instantly that awkward feeling of lameness in my legs and knees vanished. I thanked the Colonel, and ran down the stairs to the front door past the waiting room. Here my two Basrah guards stopped me: "Where are you going?" they asked.

"To the WHO office," I answered. "I am free now".

The two men looked disappointed. They shouted to the military guards at the door and ordered me to sit down. Protesting would have been useless, and seeing the door to the Colonel's office still ajar, I went back up the stairs. Hurriedly, the guards followed me. Apparently the Colonel had heard the shouting. He emerged from his room and talked to the guards. I left, but as I crossed the courtyard, the guards ran after me and caught up with me at the outer gate. They behaved differently, too polite to my taste, saying in broken English: "Congratulations, Doctor, we and you good friends, okay? We come to your house, okay? Have drink together, okay?"

I agreed, more to get rid of them than anything else, and said they could only come to visit me if they intended to be friends. I then hailed a taxi. At the WHO Office Mr Hathat was waiting for me. He had tried to visit me in my cell and, on hearing that I was being transported to Baghdad, had followed quickly. He had reported my arrest to the UN Representative, but before they could make contact with the military authorities, I had been set free.

In the office, I found a mirror and looked... Yes, the birthmark was still there!

At the UN, it was considered wise to play down the incident. No letter of protest was written. A week later a circular letter was sent to all UN personnel with a warning to be careful when taking photographs in the country.

One evening the following week, my guards came indeed to visit me in my flat. I was on the alert, and pretended not to notice their pistols protruding from their pockets. Offering each of them a large bottle of beer, I told them that they should keep their word and behave like good friends. They drank their beer silently, and left shortly afterwards. I never saw them again.

CHAPTER 59

Somalia

Settling In

Fred Christal, the WHO Technical Officer, met me on my arrival at Mogadishu airport. He brought me straight to the Malaria office to meet our Somali counterparts. Since there had not been a WHO Malariologist for the past two years, there was nobody from whom I should take over. It was clear that I would have to find my own way. This I did not mind at all since Fred assured me that I could easily find all the data I needed in the files.

Mogadishu struck me from the first moment as a charming, small historical coastal town. There were old Portuguese and Italian buildings along shadowy streets that gave the impression that time had stopped there. The cool sea breeze felt pleasant and the temperature was like ours in Bali. I thought of Astri and felt an intense longing for her because I knew that she would like the climate. Fred Christal was of the greatest help. He took me to a decent hotel, where he briefed me about Mogadishu, the capital of Somalia, the situation of our staff and about the other United Nations agencies in the country. I would see many United Nations people of different nationalities. That would be good for Astri too. There was a UN Club with various facilities.

But first of all I had to look for a house for my family. It was not easy to find a good one in this old city. But Fred had already secured for me—if I agreed— a good house near the beach close to the United Nations compound. The British expert who lived there was going home within the next two weeks. I was of course eager to have a look first.

His suggestion was in all respects a good one. There were four other houses in the same compound, all occupied by UN experts with their families. In Mogadishu more of such compounds existed, consisting of a number of houses together surrounded by a high wall with one common entrance gate, usually with a guard during daytime and a watchman during the night. However, one would find him sleeping in the sentry box most of the time. The houses were generally roomy and of good quality and had been built by rich merchants or landlords especially for expatriates. Their rent was of course far beyond the reach of the average Somali, but reasonable compared with United Nations salaries. After having seen Fred's choice I found it unnecessary to look further. Although it had only two bedrooms, one bathroom and a kitchen, the size of the house was enormous so that there was plenty of space everywhere. There was an open verandah with high pillars in the front over the whole width of the building. The high ceiling and the oversized windows allowed for plenty of sea breeze. Astri would need the services of a house boy. There were plenty of boys and girls available, but according to Fred, very few good workers. One had to train them several times again and again, and they needed constant supervision.

Water was the only problem. There was a deep well with an electrical pump to fill a large tank for all the five houses. The pump frequently broke down and the landlord was reluctant to install a new and stronger one, claiming that all the pumps in Mogadishu suffer frequent breakdowns because of the salty water. We, the five occupants of the compound, had to take care of the pump in turns and in case of breakdown, call the repairman.

Our compound was only 500 metres from the beach, where the United Nations Staff Association had a beach-house, efficiently managed of course by Fred and his Armenian wife, Nevaert, who did all the work voluntarily. The broad white beach was fantastic! It stretched about two miles from north to south along the Indian Ocean with its bottom sloping gradually from the shore to a broad coral reef about 500 metres away, which effectively softened the breakers.

Halfway up the road, actually a broad stretch of sand, from our compound to the beach was a large compound, with the office of the United Nations, and several houses occupied by UN Staff and their families. There were other buildings, one of which was the United Nations commissary where we UN staff could get duty-free goods such as drinks, cereals, cigarettes, canned meat and fish, and other household items. Fred's wife was the manager. That was a great improvement compared with Basrah. Last but not least, there was also a concrete tennis court.

Meanwhile, Fred told me that one could not do without a car in Mogadishu because, except for a few taxis, there was no public transport. He advised me not to buy a new one (because it would rust immediately and lose its resale value), but to try my luck with a second-hand vehicle from a departing expat. Fred happened to know a Danish expat who was leaving shortly. I did not hesitate, and bought his old Fiat-1600 sedan for US$300, a good bargain! I did not lose much time and looked for temporary furniture and some tableware and kitchenware, so that when Astri and Merti arrived a month later they would have at least a bed and a dining table. Fred and Nevaert offered to lend us other necessities for the time being. Astri could later quietly look around for items more to her taste.

When Astri and Merti arrived earlier than I expected on the 19th of May, she found our home more or less established. Nevaert was as great a help for Astri in household matters, as Fred was for me in the malaria office. Soon we felt completely at home in our new environment. For Merti the beach was the greatest asset of the place and there were plenty of UN children to play with.

There was, however, a problem with her education. The United Nations had no educational institution. The children of UN staff went all to the American School, the only option available. Merti first of all had to learn the English language. We were very fortunate that Fred knew a British lady-teacher at the American School who was willing to teach Merti privately. She did a wonderful job! Merti made such good progress that Mrs Gutale (her husband was a Somali) told us after two months that Merti would be able to follow the lessons at the Grade 3 level of the American School at the start of the school year in August. We were really surprised and of course very proud. Thus Merti entered the American School. The rather high school fee was no problem since it was partly covered by WHO.

Astri did not play tennis, but me, the tennis court in the UN compound was wonderful. Later the place provided another attraction. I borrowed a 16 mm film projector from the UN. We set up a UN film club at a very reasonable monthly contribution from our members and from a film agency in Nairobi, I got a regular supply of movies. I became the film expert and operator of the Club and twice a week we had an open air film show on the tennis court with the members bringing their own chairs. The shows were always very well attended. It was the only place where the expatriate community could see films in the English language. Since it was in the open air, I was much concerned about the rainy season. Although the season was very short, there could be sometimes heavy showers, especially in the evenings. The members found a solution by turning the tennis court into a "drive-in" theatre and watched the show from inside their cars. Sometimes we had to be content with films that we had not ordered or which we had already seen twice before. But on the whole it was very successful and met the needs of our rather isolated community.

The UN community busied themselves also with other kinds of entertainment. There were the parties at the Beach Club, and a music club. Because of lack of musicians we met together to enjoy taped music, mainly serious classical, with somebody as speaker and some discussion afterwards. Outings were very restricted. The bad roads did not encourage trips and the facilities such as restaurants and lodging were poor. The dunes along the coast to the south of Mogadishu were charming but otherwise the bush scenery in the rural areas was monotonous.

Malaria Work

Malaria work in Somalia was quite different from that in Iraq. The under-developed infrastructure in Somalia did not allow for the setting up of a fully fledged malaria eradication campaign. With the idealistic intention of wiping out the disease over the whole world in a not too distant future, WHO coined the term "Pre-eradication" for the varied combinations of measures which were feasible in primitive circumstances prevailing in countries like Somalia in the 1960s. More than half of the people in the towns and 90% in the rural areas were illiterate. For a greater part the rural population were (as they are still) nomads, moving all the time with their cattle and camels over deserts and bush country in search of water and grazing fields. Finding water was of such great concern that by nature people were suspicious. When they found a pond or other water source they would keep it secret, out of fear of losing it. When asked about which direction to go if one was lost, they would indicate the wrong way.

Road communications between towns and villages over the vast country were very poor. In some areas no roads could be seen over hundreds of miles. When travelling by car—only jeeps or Landrovers equipped with four-wheel-drive gears were usable—one often had to follow tracks left in the sand by earlier vehicles. Now and then such tracks disappeared for a long stretch or would suddenly fork into two or more branches and one had to rely on instinct, when deciding which to follow. Our Somali drivers seemed to have a fabulous orientation instinct. They always found the right track. The Somalis possessed other instincts as well. People told me that they could recognize from the hoof prints of a camel to which tribal clan the animal belonged. In our malaria work, I often wondered if that was perhaps why our Somali microscopists excelled in recognizing malaria parasites under the microscope.

The land, larger than Great Britain, consisting largely of savannah with thorny bush and vast areas of desert, was dry for most of the year. Where some agriculture was possible, like along the few rivers, the yield was poor due to the infertile soil and primitive agricultural practices. In the villages, houses were primitive structures of a round wall of dried mud, reinforced with a wattle-work of branches and twigs, with a thatched roof fixed on a pole in the middle. One opening functioned as the door and there were no windows for ventilation. There was usually a bare minimum of furniture: a bed, consisting of four rough wooden legs held together by four timbers and a network of ropes with a mat on top, and one or two low stools made of raw camel hide tightly stretched over four pieces of round wood. Cupboards did not exist.

Many villages had no fixed boundaries and often it was not possible to define the village where a house was located, a real problem for "geographical reconnaissance", an essential part of a malaria programme, and necessary for the orderly execution of spraying operations and surveillance. As a consequence, regular malaria-spraying operations aiming at the interruption of malaria trans-mission could not be done in the rural areas. That was reserved for the towns, but free movements of people from the rural to urban areas made re-infection with malaria parasites easy, and therefore the spraying operations did not have a lasting effect.

Spraying the movable houses or *akhals* of the nomads was not practical since it would have no effect at all. An *akhal* consisted of a number of strong wooden laths, of about four to six metres, which with their ends driven into the ground would form arches. Three, four or more of these arches, when crossing each other and bound together in the middle, would form a dome over which mats of grass were fixed to make out the roof and walls. When moving it was very easy to dismantle such an *akhal* and load it on a camel. Any insecticide sprayed on the walls of these *akhals* was lost by this action.

Because of these conditions, the malariologist had to investigate the local situation thoroughly before he could decide what steps to take to alleviate the malaria problem. Since no hard and fast rules for action could be prescribed, much depended on his inventiveness and common-sense to make the best of it and achieve the best possible results. Working in a pre-eradication programme was actually much more complicated and more challenging than in an eradication program where management, military discipline and precision were most essential. Considering the transient effect of our costly spraying operations and recognizing the country's infrastructure, I started thinking about other means of combating malaria.

I began to regard spraying operations in Somalia as a costly waste of time and energy. Memories from my childhood years in Bali came into my mind. I remembered that in the early 1920s the Dutch authorities seeded all our fish ponds in Karangasem with hundreds of small *Gambusia* fish, named *kepala timah* (tin heads) after the tiny silvery glistening disk on their heads. Bearing this in mind, I started to collect from every river or marsh as many species of fish as I could and selected fish that would prefer mosquito larvae for food, so-called larvivorous fish. For this purpose I had to raise mosquito larvae in our compound, using of course common mosquitoes which would not transfer malaria. The task was tedious but not difficult; we had only to count the number of larvae eaten per fish per unit of time. In a short time we could identify not fewer than six local fish species that met the required standard, at least in the aquarium. How they would behave in a natural environment was another matter; only field experience would be able to tell.

With the help of mosquito catchers from our office I found out that *Tilapia* was the most vigorous larvae consumer. In the course of my investigations, the malaria workers informed me that during the colonial period the Italians had indeed obliged the population of Mogadishu to raise *Tilapia* in their ponds for mosquito control. I was baffled. Why had they not told me earlier? It would have saved me much time and effort. In any case, I wrote to the WHO Head-quarters about my hopes of malaria control through larvivorous fish and got an enthusiastic response. Efforts would be made to send an ichtyologist to Mogadishu, but that would take time.

Meanwhile another problem came along. The nomadic population were especially vulnerable to malaria infection because they were always moving in the bush from one water collection to another, all mosquito-breeding places. When the pond dried up they moved further. They always got infected where they camped around the water source. The problem was that these temporary water sources could not be seeded with *Tilapia* because when they dried out the fish would perish.

Then it was as if Providence was at work again!

While I was cleaning up my office and re-arranging all old WHO publica-tions on their racks I came across a paper written by Prof Haas at the University of California, dealing with so-called "instant fish", popular among aquarists in the United States. I was fascinated by the fact that from special shops eggs were available which would hatch as soon as they were put into the water. Even more exciting was that in his paper Prof Haas mentioned the exis-tence of such a fish species, *Notobranchius*, in some regions of East Africa! I wrote to Prof Haas and got an enthusiastic reply with more particulars about "instant fish" and—most important of all—a slide photograph of the *Notobranchius*. He spurred me to look for the fish and advised me to look in the dry season for any sunken ground where water would stay for some time in the rainy season and dry up later. The *Notobranchius* was a beautiful small fish species, five to seven centimetres long and of a blue-tourqoise colour, with red fins and tail. It can eat 30 to 40 mosquito larvae in one day. The female lays its eggs in the mud on the bottom of the pond or lake and if the water dries up the eggs remain dormant in the mud and will hatch as soon as the rains start.

On duty trips in the country I marked as many hollow grounds as possible to be visited again after the rains came. Places frequently visited by nomads were particularly selected. During the following rainy season I went down to any temporary pond I found, equipped with long rubber boots and a fish net in search of the *Notobranchius*. There were some exciting encounters with hippopotami who did not like to be disturbed, and in some places I got entan-gled in weeds or other vegetation, but we never met crocodiles. These reptiles preferred the big rivers. At last, I caught the first three *Notobranchius* fish in my net. As Prof Haas advised me, I took notice of the vegetation in the pond, and indeed in a nearby pond with the same vegetation I got ten more of the fish. In no time we had collected plenty of *Notobranchius* and raised them in twelve large glass containers. It was a magnificent spectacle to see how these fish devoured the larvae which Merti was raising in earthenware pots in our back-yard, using a pipette to catch them. To simulate the mud in the pond as a receptacle for the eggs we had a piece of peat on the bottom of the glass container. Every week the peat was taken out and put to dry in the open air. Two weeks later we put it in a container with water and indeed, very tiny fish came out of the eggs, but... alas, we had no luck: they died the following day. The longest lifespan we got was three days.

We expanded our trials, using a pond in which we brought the mud and vegetation from the original lake 100 km far south of Mogadishu, to create the same ecological conditions for the fish. Even that failed. I realized that much more research had to be done, involving botanists, chemists and ecologists. The ichtyologist sent to Mogadishu by WHO, Dr Kovchasev from Varna, Bulgaria, agreed but was pessimistic if WHO would be willing to provide the necessary funds. I found it better to abandon my dream of having thousands of *Notobranchius* eggs distributed in small plastic bags to the nomads who should throw them in all the temporary waters they found in the bush. Instead I recommended to the authorities and the population to catch wherever possible fresh *Notobranchius* and to seed them in other temporary waters, just hoping that some would survive and multiply.

Meanwhile, we had more success with *Tilapia* distribution in permanent waters, such as lakes and marshes. On all our field trips we brought with us a number of jerrycans with fish collected from our raising fish ponds which we gradually had established in Mogadishu and some other towns. We tried to find the ponds and lakes frequented by the nomads. Sometimes they had to move not because of water shortage but depletion of the surrounding grazing fields. Over-grazing became a problem for the country, not only around the natural lakes and swamps, but also around the many artificial lakes.

Being more a Public Health doctor than a Malariologist I was convinced that a very important part of the fight against malaria should be waged by the General Health Services. It was the so-called PCD (passive case detection) of malaria cases in all the dispensaries and hospitals, and subsequent radical treatment which should play a crucial role in countries like Somalia. Co-operation between the Malaria Service and the hospitals was started. The Somali doctors readily understood and were of great help, as were the expatriate doctors.

Gradually, we succeeded in establishing malaria PCD posts in all the Government hospitals and polyclinics, by which we unwittingly spearheaded the integration of malaria control into the General Health Services. Years later this integration became the policy of WHO worldwide.

CHAPTER 60

Hunger

The prolonged drought of the early 1970s caused great disaster over most of the countries in East Africa. Famine struck Ethiopia several years before Somalia. Ethiopia's Emperor Haile Selassie ignored the suffering of his people and out of national pride did not want to seek the help from the outside world to allevi-ate the ever worsening situation. The people became restless and in 1974 he was overthrown. Somalia's President Siad Barre, realizing that the same might happen to him, swiftly asked for help from the United Nations for the more than 500,000 Somalis who were threatened by famine. It was actually already too late. On my field trips in 1973 we saw whole villages of hungry people and heard from the village chiefs about many deaths from starvation. In hospitals cases of malnutrition were left without treatment.

The United Nations, in this case UNICEF especially, acted with great speed and determination. UNICEF's representative in Mogadishu was a good friend and we heard first-hand about the relief operations. I was particularly interested in nutrition since I had trained as a Medical Nutritionist in London in 1957. While trying out the application of the concept of the integration of malaria work into the General Health Services I came in contact with many Somali doctors, among whom was Dr Abbas who had trained as a Nutritionist but had yet not had any experience in nutrition work in the field. On his request I advised and assisted him in the planning and execution of the first Nutrition Survey in Somalia from September 1971 to January 1972. It was a hard and time-consuming job. Again I did not first ask permission from WHO out of fear that it would be refused. But the survey was carried out successfully and the comprehensive report came out in beautiful print, published by the Somali Ministry of Health. I sent the book to WHO Regional Headquarters in Alexandria and received a lofty letter of praise from the Regional Director.

Due to my friendship with the UNICEF's representative I got first-hand information about the extent of the famine and about the refugee camps which

UNICEF had erected at selected places in the country. He said he would be very happy if I could have a look at one of the camps and give him my opinion. Due to the enormous distances I could not arrange special visits, but had to combine them with my malaria work. On my trip to the northern provinces of Hargeisa and Burao, I went to have a look at the relief work, awakening memories of our work in Bali during the volcanic eruptions in 1963.

There was a great difference however. The magnitude of human suffering from hunger in Somalia was overwhelming. In 1963 our people in Bali had little to eat, but help arrived at rather short notice, from family, the community, the government and from outside. Here in Somali there was real famine, involving hundreds of thousands of people who had lost their cattle and everything, and whose only hope of survival rested on the food they received from the United Nations.

We went to visit one of the refugee camps after we had seeded the last batch of *Tilapia* fish in a slow-moving stream which originated from a natural spring in the mountains and ended in a small lake in a beautiful valley near Burao, a small town in the highlands of northern Somalia. According to the population, there was always water in the lake, even after this prolonged drought. So it was a good place to raise fish for seeding other ponds. Feeling relieved from our malaria work we drove some 40 km down to the town over a winding road strewn with boulders, crossing numerous valleys by cautiously manoeuvering our cars over its dry river beds. The area was completely dry; there was not one piece of green to be seen. Here and there skeletons of camels and cattle lay scattered on the sand, witnesses of the tragedy of forlorn nomadic people walking, with hardly any food, for days and weeks from one empty watering point to another one—only to find it already dried up.

At one moment, when our driver had succeeded in driving our vehicle up the slope after crossing a dry river bed, I saw suddenly a lion just a few yards in front of us. The sight of the lion gave me a shock, but of a very different kind. It was an extremely thin and emaciated lioness that walked very slowly as if it could fall down at any moment. It had not the strength to run away or to turn round and attack us. She moved her head slowly to look at us, with such sad eyes that it struck me deeply. Automatically I reached for my bag, took out my bread, opened the door and stepped out of the car to feed the poor animal. But at the same moment I felt myself being forcibly pulled back into the car. Our two assistants held me tight fast at my arms and cursed me. "Oh, Doc, are you mad? You can't do such thing! Don't you see how hungry that lioness is? She would not grab only your bread but you too!" I came to my senses. Had I been dreaming perhaps? Because of the shouting in the car and the driver's frantic honking on the horn the lion had disappeared. I had not seen which way. Along the road we saw more carcasses of animals. After two long hours of bumping we reached Burao where we enjoyed a good sleep after a hot and strenuous day. The village chief informed me that 50 km farther to the west the United Nations had erected a large refugee camp where already 20,000 hungry people were housed and being fed. They came mainly from the areas near the Ethiopian border and every day still more refugees were coming. I knew about the existence of this camp, where according to my friend 10,000 refugees were being treated. The number had apparently grown since. Due to poor communications Mogadishu's statistics had lagged behind.

We started early in the morning to take advantage of the cool weather. After a three-hour drive we could see from the top of a hill the huge camp which was situated in a broad valley below us. It consisted of more than two thousand *akhals*, neatly arranged radially around a natural well in the centre of the valley. The *akhals*, glistening white-yellow in the bright sun, made really a breathtaking picture. In the centre there were some other structures, rectangular in shape and much bigger than the *akhals*. They served as a hospital, a dormitory for doctors and nursing staff, and as storage. While I was impressed by the beautiful layout of the camp, my Public Health instinct soon gave me concern. It was good that the people got food and water, but what about sanitation? I imagined that in the valley with the only water source located at its lowest point in the centre, it must be difficult to protect the water from contamination.

When we arrived at the centre of the camp hundreds of people were queuing with their pails and other containers to get a little water. The well was about 6 metres in diameter with muddy water 4 metres below. Four heavy wooden logs, two each at two opposite sides lying over the opening, served as bridges on which people stood while scooping water out of the well with a pail fastened on a long rope. According to one of the guards the water was only one metre below the rim and very clear one month earlier when they opened the camp.

Everywhere between the *akhals* we saw small children, helped by their mothers relieving themselves on the ground since there were no toilet facilities. Many of them appeared to suffer from diarrhoea and the doctors working in the camps told us that as many as twenty children died from diarrhoea each day. The "hospital" was a large barn with walls consisting of mere branches of bush under a crude roof of thatch and grass, supported by poles of tree trunks in a row at three metres distance from each other. From each of the poles two or three flasks of rehydration infusion sets were dangling with their tubes leading to the tiny arms of dehydrated emaciated children who were lying on mats or blankets on the ground. There was no water to wash them, and an awful stench hung in the air inside the hospital. Doctors and sisters were busy attending the sick. There were too few of them and all of them looked overworked and exhausted. I was impressed by their good spirits.

But I was appalled by what I saw. It was quite different from the reports that reached Mogadishu about ever-increasing numbers of people getting food aid and the proper distribution of supplies. Those good reports had brought the authorities and the UN Agencies into a kind of complacency. Nobody had ever reported about the appalling sanitary conditions and the many children dying every day from diarrhoea. My colleagues reported to their superiors in the province: there was an urgent need for medicines and nursing material; something had still to be invented to combat the thick clouds of flies generated from excreta, filth and garbage everywhere. I should return to Mogadishu as quickly as possible and inform my friend the UNICEF representative.

There was of course a lot of work to do in the camp, but I could not stay longer than two days. I assisted my colleagues in every way I could. First of all I advised them to take care of sanitation. There were many things which could be done easily. The meat after slaughtering the animals should be kept behind mosquito nets. The people did not like the biscuits which looked to me like old war rations. I advised them to pound them back to flour and make from it their traditional Somali pancakes. That was such a great success that the military camp commander insisted on being photographed between us with a pancake in his hands. A big problem was excreta disposal. Use of toilets was unknown among the nomadic population. To solve the problem would mean much education and organization. With the authority of the military camp commander we built primitive cesspits outside the camp, which served as toilets, in groups of one dozen for each of the twelve sections of the camp. Each toilet was separated from the other by a wall of bush branches. Each pit opening was provided with a slab made out of thick, flat stones. The first group of twelve was finished in one day. How proud we were with our achievement! The following day another dozen pits were dug and so the work continued.

However, I must admit that this activity, on which we had spent so much time and energy, led to nothing. The Somalis, used to squatting freely in the bush, felt uncomfortable in a closed environment. Moreover, knowing that somebody was doing the same close by, separated by a wall of branches which was anyway not completely impervious, was most disturbing. And the pit smelled after the previous user; in the bush one could look freely for a spot without any smell and no flies emerging from beneath. I was informed later that soon after the first attempts nobody made use of the toilets.

A good lesson for me with my theories about sanitation!

CHAPTER 61

Afghanistan

Encounters

After four years in Somalia, the WHO had me transferred to Afghanistan. In many ways life there was for us quite the opposite of what it had been in Somalia. While in Somalia the expatriate had to look for opportunities to enhance the quality of life in order not to fall victim to boredom or frustration. In Afghanistan the amount of interesting places and social events was overwhelming. The tropical heat in Somalia made work exhausting. Afghanistan had not only the seasonal changes like Europe, but the various parts of the country offered a wide variety of climates due to great differences in altitude. In winter one could travel in one day from the snowy Salang Pass in the north with temperatures of –25° C to the Helmand Valley in the south, where it was a mild +10° C during winter, but in summer temperatures could rise above 40° C.

In the capital Kabul at 1,800 metres altitude, where most UN expats lived, the climate was ideal. The high altitude made summers cool and although it could be very cold in winter, the air was dry and crisp, so that it was still comfortable even below –20° C. Astri's health benefited greatly from the cold.

Private life for UN staff in town was pleasant because of the abundance of goods in the shops and markets. There was a great choice of imported goods from Europe and America such as textiles, machinery, kitchenware, and canned food, and the markets were always full of land produce. All kinds of fruits and nuts were brought from the fertile valleys and also imported from Pakistan. Because of the diversity of climate one could find fruits of all seasons at the same time. For people with enough money there were the famous Afghan carpets to buy. One had first to consult somebody with expert knowledge of carpets because of the great differences in quality and—of course—the shopkeepers knew immediately whom they could cheat!

A unique feature was the so-called "second-hand market" downtown, where one could buy all kinds of clothing imported from Europe, mostly from

Germany very cheaply. Although some clothes were really second-hand, nearly all items were brand-new. They had been declared unfit for the European market, either because they were out of fashion or for some fault in the finishing of the product. These goods were dumped as unsaleable in Europe and transported in huge quantities by road to landlocked Kabul, where the big container-trucks in which they came found their way to second-hand truck dealers. The second-hand market was for us and many other UN expatriates a great place for shopping and bargaining, and also a place where one could find enjoyment in observing the Afghan people. We found there trousers, jackets and overcoats of the best quality, some of which we still wear on our travels over Europe today. How this tradition of second-hand sales came about, especially in Kabul, nobody could tell.

Afghanistan has been on the crossroads for trade and wars between West and East since ancient times. After gaining independence from Britain by the Treaty of Rawalpindi in 1919, the Afghan kings oriented their country's development towards the West. Culturally, France had the greatest influence, inspiring the kings to build palaces and gardens after French models. Even after the last king, Mohammed Zaher Shah, was overthrown by his Soviet-oriented cousin Daud in 1973 and the kingdom became a republic, the French Cultural Centre in Kabul was still very active in organizing language courses, exhibitions and cultural events like concerts and operas. All these provided excellent entertainment for UN staff and other expatriate experts working in the country. We never felt in Afghanistan the anti-Western sentiment that had been steadily building up during our four years' stay in Somalia.

In many other respects the Afghans were different from the Somalis: they had an inherent dignity as a result of their great cultural past. They were of a hard and sometimes violent race, but at the same time very humane, soft and friendly. On our walks on Sundays in the King's Gardens we always met families with children picnicking under the trees in the orchards, seated on a beautiful Afghan carpet spread on the grass. Without exception they would invite us to join them. The Afghans loved children.

On the other hand, we found them born crooks, unable to resist the opportunity to cheat a client. In summer we used to buy firewood in preparation for the winter from sellers who came along the houses with their wood and a pair of scales on a pushcart. For weighing the wood they usually had only one weight of 5 kg with them. To make 10 kg they weighed two or three pieces of wood to make 5 kg and put them together with the copper 5 kg weight on one of the scales. If the accuracy of this manoeuvre was already rather questionable, the weighing of the following batches of 10 kg each was always a sport. Usually there was nothing wrong with the first few batches, but the batches would become gradually smaller and smaller, until one discovered that the man had put his foot on a cleverly hidden extension of the scale! When the man saw that you had discovered his trick he would charmingly apologize with such a disarming smile on his face that one could not help but laugh. However, one had to insist that the whole process of weighing be done over again.

Once I was surprised and later very thankful for the way an Afghan colleague helped me out of a nasty situation. I was driving slowly and carefully on a very crowded street packed with men, women and children, fighting their way in all directions without paying attention to any traffic. Pushed by the unruly crowd an old woman fell head-first onto the street just in front of me. I stopped, jumped out of my car and helped the crying woman on her feet, but she fell limply in my arms. I could not do anything else other than lift her up and with the help of some people put her as comfortably as possible on the rear seat. I examined her and saw a few bruises on her leg. Fearing that something might be seriously wrong, perhaps a collum fracture, I told the people around that I had to take her to the hospital. Meanwhile, her family, two men and a woman, had before I could prevent them, climbed into my car. All the bystanders looked at me approvingly and although the car was severely overloaded, I felt happy and drove away carefully. At the reception room in the hospital my colleagues were most helpful when they learned that I was a medical doctor working with the United Nations. They immediately took X-ray photographs. There was luckily no fracture and nothing serious with the old woman. I could not follow the excited conversation between the doctors and her family who were waiting outside the X-ray room. One of the doctors took me aside to another room and asked what I intended to do. When I replied that I would gladly pay for the cost of the examination and the X-photograph and that I felt obliged to bring the patient to her home, he laughed heartily, saying: "Yes, I expected this answer of yours! But please, excuse me if I perhaps offend you! Don't do anything of what you had in mind. You would be blackmailed and robbed by my people. They are that kind of character. Believe me. So are the Afghans, especially if they know that they are dealing with unwary foreigners".

I was baffled and looked at him unbelievingly. "Yes," he continued, "I know what you are thinking. Don't bother about costs. All services are here free, this is a Government hospital".

"And what shall I do?" I asked, "Could you advise me?"

"Of course. We have already arranged things for you. My colleagues will keep talking with the family, while you go with me now through another part of the building to the parking lot. I will take you to your car and show you how to leave the hospital through the back gate, so that nobody will see you leaving. If, with all your kind intentions, you bring the women and her family to their house you would land into great trouble. We will call later a taxi for them which they can pay themselves".

It dawned to me that perhaps he was right. When, stopping at the back gate I thanked him for his help, he remarked: "I hope that nobody was smart enough to note down the number of your car, ha ha ha!" On the way home I kept wondering if I was doing the right thing. In the end a sense of relief prevailed over my guilty feeling of having been in some way unethical.

Malaria Control

In contrast to my counterpart in Somalia, the chief of the Afghan Malaria Control Program, Dr Nushin, was a very able and professionally trained malariologist and a good organizer who worked very hard and had his personnel under a strong discipline. I had the feeling that there was not much that he had to learn from us WHO experts. There were three of us. In addition to Fred Christal, the sanitarian who had worked with me in Somalia, there was in my team an entomologist, Jim Cullen, also a very able technician. I found it amusing to deal with the two completely different personalities in my team, one typically Scottish and one typically English in speech and attitudes. Technically speaking, I was in a fortunate position to have two able men as my assistants and a counterpart who had good understanding of the many problems which at that time had started to challenge malaria campaigns all over the world. As WHO advisers we had to find out new methods of operation to overcome the difficulties caused by increasing resistance of the mosquitoes to insecticides, and the increasing resistance of the parasites to anti-malaria drugs. We had to do much applied research in the field, monitor the effectiveness of new insecticides and drugs and follow the social impact of the epidemiological measures in the various communities: in towns, in villages and among the large numbers of nomads. Because of the great differences in the geographical and climatological conditions in the various parts of the country, to which the methods and timing of the work had to be adapted, the malaria control programme was of great variation and at the same time as flexible as possible. Therefore it was a most complicated programme, interesting and always challenging.

Under an agreement with the government of the Soviet Union, the malaria control program in the northern provinces of Afghanistan, bordering Russia, was taken care of by a large Russian team of malariologists, an epidemiologist, laboratory assistants and entomologists. They had their living quarters, offices and laboratories in Kunduz. Since I had not been informed beforehand about their malaria program, I went to see my Russian colleagues. They appeared to be very co-operative and agreed that the WHO malariologist should be responsible for the programme over the whole country. I was informed about all their activities and where necessary had to co-ordinate the two programmes. They worked very hard and were very disciplined. Some of their methods had to be adjusted to ours. On the whole they had good results with their operations over the years. They were most successful with the use of larvivorous fish, the Gambusia, which they had introduced for malaria control in the country many years earlier. For an area like northern Afghanistan, with its severe winters, the application of this method was not easy: during winter, the fish ponds were frozen and large openings had to be broken in the ice and maintained to allow air to oxygenate the water.

The doctors of the Russian team were fluent in English. Some of them had their wives with them, but the families did not live separated from the other team members. They occupied two houses in each of which one or two families lived with some singles. What struck me most was their rather primitive living conditions. The houses were neat and clean, but too crowded. There were no curtains at the windows. In several places paper was glued over the window glass to ensure some privacy. There were no lampshades, so that in the evenings they all lived under the glare of naked electric bulbs. Their meals were modest. Moved by their living conditions, Astri always gave me some items from our UN commissary for them, such as sausages, meat and ham. They were very happy every time we went to visit them. Our relationship remained excellent throughout, even later on when due to political developments in the country, the Afghans became hostile to the Russians. Unfortunately later the political disturbances affected the work of the Russian malaria team very much. When I once discovered that many places had not been visited by them as scheduled, one of them made the unmistakable gesture of moving his flat hand with stretched fingers like a knife squarely across his throat!

Touchdown in Kathmandu

Although we felt that the life of a UN expert in Kabul was very comfortable, UN bureaucracy considered the place as a "hardship post". We were therefore—in addition to the biennial home leave—entitled to a periodical "rest-and-recuperation leave" of two weeks to a nearby country. We chose Nepal for our R-and-R, firstly because of its cool climate, secondly because we heard about its cultural resemblance with Bali, and lastly because Nepalese friends of ours, a WHO malariologist, Dr Baidya, and his wife, lived in the capital Kathmandu.

Dr and Mrs Baidya were at the airport to meet us. We saw them at the entrance of the building, cheerfully and frantically waving at us with an unfolded newspaper, a gesture which bewildered us. Their enthusiasm appeared later to be twofold: besides the joy of meeting old friends again, by pure coincidence the morning edition of the local newspaper *The Rising Nepal*, (November 3, 1977) carried an article about malaria control in Afghanistan in which my name was mentioned. Proudly they handed me the paper and insisted that I should read it while waiting for our luggage.

Dr Baidya said proudly: "I was still living in Bali when WHO recruited you. Did I not tell you that they made the right choice?"

"Perhaps, yes," I replied, "but I am afraid that we malariologists are going to lose the war. There are too many difficulties for which there are no solutions yet in sight for the foreseeable future".

"Dr Djelantik is not here to discuss malaria problems," his wife remarked, "he is on R-and-R, so let us rather make plans for his stay here and advise him what is worth visiting".

Dr Baidya agreed. We enjoyed a real Nepalese lunch at their home and made up our vacation itinerary. After lunch they brought us to a nice hotel in town.

The following morning we boarded a tour bus that would take us on a sight-seeing trip up to the Chinese border. Since the abortive Communist coup in Indonesia in 1963, our country had no relations with China and no Indonesian was allowed to visit that country. China therefore had something of a mysterious attraction for us, especially because it was mentioned in the brochure that the participants would have the opportunity to cross the border and would have their passports stamped by the Chinese immigration authorities. We had hardly settled ourselves comfortably when to our great surprise we heard somebody calling from the rear of the bus in the Dutch language: "Dr Djelantik, Dr Djelantik, kent U ons nog? U bent het toch? Ja, natuurlijk!" ("Do you still remember us? Are you Dr Djelantik indeed? Yes, of course!")

Looking around, we saw a short stout gentleman and a lady struggling their way through the aisle and greeting us excitedly: "Well, what a surprise to see you in this place!" We had no idea whatsoever who they were. Only after the man told me his story, did I recognize him, or rather: I recognized, in the gentleman the face of his mother! It was way back twenty-five years ago, in the 1950s, in Kotamobagu, North Celebes, when I treated him, a boy of fifteen at that time, for pneumonia. Immediately his mother came to my mind: a round overweight lady with a most lovely and friendly face who used to walk up and down from our hospital to her house nearby. The sick boy of that time was now a famous pediatrician and professor at the University in Jakarta. He had been attending a medical conference in Bangkok the week before and was taking a few days leave for a visit to Nepal.

Still in great excitement Prof Tumbelaka took a newspaper out of his overcoat, and showed me the same article Dr Baidya had the day before. He continued: "Dr Djelantik, you can imagine how, being Indonesian, my heart was filled with pride after I read this article".

I was not much in the mood for talking about medicine, malaria or public health, and enquired about their plans for other trips. Unfortunately he could not stay longer in Nepal, there were too many commitments at the University at home. He had to leave the next morning, but for today he had been attracted, like us, by the promise of a Chinese visa stamp at the border. The trip was interesting. The nearer we came to the border the more we saw red flags with sickle and hammer adorning the houses in the villages. The people looked very poor and undernourished, their clothes were drab, many had merely rags around their bodies. It was not difficult to understand that Communism must have a great appeal to these destitute people. What we heard from the Baidyas about corruption in the higher echelons of government made us worry about the country. Nevertheless, we enjoyed the beauty of the mountains and valleys. We spent two nights in the small village of Pokara, surrounded by magnificent mountains, and made a round trip by air which delighted us with breathtaking views of snowy peaks one after another up to Mount Everest.

On another day the Baidyas took us to a cremation near a river, a very simple affair compared to those in Bali. No beautiful offerings, no music, and no colourful processions of girls and boys in their festive attire. The bodies were burned over a heap of firewood on a platform at the edge of the river, attended by a few family members who now and then moved the body with a long bamboo to facilitate the burning. At the end the ashes were thrown into the river.

They brought us also to an offering ceremony at a Shiva Temple where goats were being slaughtered after the traditional test by pouring cold water over their heads. Those which showed a particular way of shivering were chosen for sacrificial animals. The killing occurred before the eyes of the public. We could not stand the sight and shuddered. Blood was everywhere, and large quantities of rice mixed with blood were distributed to the pilgrims, who offered them to the deities by propping the bloody mixture against the mouths of the stone statues standing in a row along the wall of the temple. We found the ceremony rather awful, nevertheless most interesting. We could not help but compare everything we saw to our Balinese background. What similarities, but also, what differences!

Less gruesome were our visits to ancient historical buildings and the handicraft centre. We were impressed by the architecture of the old buildings which in a larger scale showed much resemblance with traditional Balinese architecture. Our guide explained to us that in ancient times Nepalese architects brought their art and skills to China, putting right our previous assumption that traditional Balinese architecture originated from China. We were, however, disappointed to see that—contrary to our efforts in Bali to adapt old styles to the requirements of modern times—no application of the traditional style was seen in the modern buildings in Kathmandu, which were all Western.

The R-and-R leave was of course too short to get a complete picture of the country, but we felt happy to have had this golden opportunity to acquaint ourselves—be it superficially—with a place that we had heard was so similar to Bali.

CHAPTER 62

End of Mission

It was 10 o'clock on a Friday morning, which was a holiday in Afghanistan as in other Moslem countries. I was working in our small vegetable garden, cutting fresh silverbeet leaves for dinner. Suddenly I heard Astri's voice:

"Madé, come inside, quick!"

From the open window of our dining room Astri called excitedly, "Quick, look out, come, it is dangerous out there!"

Being busy with the vegetables, I had not been aware of the noise of aeroplanes flying unusually low over our house. Alarmed by Astri's voice, I looked up in the air and saw three MIG fighter planes speeding north in the direction of the town. I imagined having seen something falling from the first plane while it lifted itself high up in the air. Before I realized what was happening, a deafening crash filled the air, then another one and immediately thereafter another one. Still, fascinated by the spectacle I had not even yet started to run for cover. Astri called again and again. Then I realized that the three aeroplanes had been bombing the town with rockets! I rushed inside.

I was wondering what they were shooting at. And who were they? For what reason? From the direction of the blasts I guessed that their target must have been the Presidential palace. More planes followed and we heard in the distance machine-gun fire and a series of explosions. Or could that be canon fire? Impossible to make out. I put the leaves on the kitchen table and quickly joined Astri inside the house. Despite the excitement, she was remarkably calm, just like she had been at similarly critical moments in Holland during World War II. We heard more gunfire and more explosions and we tried to think where would be the safest place in the house. There was no bomb shelter. We decided to stay in the corridor right in the middle of the house. There we felt safe, protected by at least two walls on all sides. However, our fears were unnecessary. The battle, or whatever it was, did not last too long. Before long we heard people walking on the street and traffic resumed as normal.

We crossed the street to the UN clubhouse where many other UN staff had already gathered. Nobody knew for sure what had happened. Some, who because of their position in UNDP were close to Government circles, told about fighting with small arms the previous day inside the President's palace. It was assumed that there had probably been a failed *coup d'etat*. Today's bombardment must have been a resumption of the fighting. In the clubhouse the atmosphere was grim and tense, with everybody waiting anxiously for news. Suddenly the Afghan cook, who had been listening to Kabul Radio, rushed into the room and broke the news: President Daud was killed in a military coup.

About five years earlier, in 1973, Daud had taken power after a bloodless coup while the king, Mohammed Zaher Shah, was abroad. His coup was facilitated by the Russians who found in the left-leaning Daud a willing vassal to put the country under Soviet rule.

The Afghan Communist Party was divided from the beginning into two camps, the "Parcham", mainly consisting of the elite in the towns, and the "Khalq", mainly based in the rural areas. Tribal and language differences partly attributed to the discord. Daud—a Parcham—was an idealist who wanted to bring his country out of its backwardness. He became more and more nationalist and less communist. His Khalq opponents succeeded in convincing the Russians that he should be removed. This occurred in April 1978, and after the coup, Mohammed Taraki, a Khalq Communist, became president.

As foreign experts with the United Nations, we were not in the least affected by the change of government. I went to the malaria office as usual. The work was not at all affected. We did not discuss politics with our counterparts, nor did they mention anything about how the change of government had come about. Perhaps because of my Asiatic nature I felt and saw a very slight change in my Afghan colleague Dr Nushin. Although he tried to conceal it, I sensed a change in his attitude towards his personnel. In contrast to the buoyant Nushin who addressed his men spontaneously and freely before, he became restrained, as if he was afraid to say something wrong. He seemed suspicious, as if he were always assessing the man to whom he talked. That apprehensive look disappeared as soon as he talked to me or to one of our WHO team. Before his own countrymen, he generally became less open. Having had my own experiences during the aftermath of the failed Communist coup in Indonesia in 1965, I fully understood the situation.

In the course of time, a number of changes in the office administration took place which made me worry about Nushin's position. There were promotions of malaria personnel to higher echelons, which to our technical assessment were not according to merit or capacity. When I enquired with Dr Nushin about it he only answered that it was in accordance with the regulations. I knew that he could not have made the proposal himself or approved of it. For that he was too good a malariologist and administrator. His deputy, however, who succeeded in keeping himself out of the limelight told me in secret that the new promoted personnel were of the Khalq faction of the Communist Party. Despite the gradual encroachment of politics into the Health Services, Dr Nushin maintained a high standard of work and discipline. This, however, deteriorated later due to the worsening political situation in the country.

As result of the introduction of educational and agrarian reform programmes, all over the country the people under the leadership of tribal and religious chiefs revolted against the Communist regime. Fighting broke out everywhere and it became difficult to do our fieldwork. The political situation became confused, because of a rift within the Khalq faction of the Communist Party, between President Taraki and his Prime Minister, Hafizullah Amin, who was also Minister of Defence. Whole garrisons of the army deserted and joined the rebellion and it appeared that the government could not contain the insurgency. In a second *coup d'etat* in September 1979, Taraki was taken prisoner and later killed by Hafizullah Amin.

In our office, Dr Nushin tried to preserve the working standard of his personnel as best as possible. We were totally dependant on our fieldworkers who fortunately for the greater part remained apolitical and did their technical work wherever possible as before. We had to contend with large gaps in our surveillance system. Nevertheless, there were no serious outbreaks of epidemics. By coincidence my assignment with WHO expired during this period, and as I had reached the pensionable age of 60, I had to leave WHO. When, in spite of my age, WHO offered me a one-year extension of service, I declined in view of the worsening situation in Afghanistan. I knew that in those circumstances nobody could save the malaria programme from deterioration. Our mission in Afghanistan terminated in September 1979.

Political Epilogue

Amin appeared to become more and more ambitious for himself than loyal to his Russian promoters. To secure his political career, he made approaches towards the Parcham faction of the Communist party, but scretly also made contacts with the Mujahedeen insurgency. Russian intelligence, knowing about these moves, found that Amin should be replaced by a more reliable ally. On Christmas Eve 1979, the Russian army invaded Afghanistan and installed a new president, the Parchamist and former KGB agent, Babrak Karmal.

CHAPTER 63

Homeward Bound

From Afghanistan to Bali

During my eleven years with WHO, we went on home leave every two years. Therefore, our final homecoming was nothing special, except that we brought with us a number of items such as clothes, kitchenware, furniture and other memorabilia that we had collected in the countries where we had lived for many years. We did not have enough money to buy a collection of Afghan carpets. The indigenous Afghan wooden settee which we had used in Kabul found its place in our living room in Denpasar under the Ramayana painting which covered the whole wall at one side. The only Afghan carpet we could afford fitted very well in front of the open fireplace in our chalet in Kintamani where our collection of copper pots and pans functioned as kitchenware as well as decoration on the kitchen wall. Other trophies found their way to Tirtagangga. Thus our cherished items were divided over our three houses, according to their particular qualities, where they still continue giving us enjoyment and delight.

Our family was happy to have us back. We were, however, not always sure now much genuine affection was shown at our reunion. We felt real affection only with my sibling elder sister who was married to our high priest. All my brothers and sisters had successively established their own families and therefore each of them had responsibilities to their own offspring. Their family units had become worlds apart, and each had little interest in each others' family lives. At religious ceremonies, however, and other occasions when all the families came together, the clan spirit in the "grand family" was evident. It was on such occasions that I felt the disturbing existence of a psychological distance between us and the others, due to our long separation but perhaps more because of our different lifestyles. While we felt the great respect they accorded us, and often became deeply involved in family matters in which our opinions were greatly appreciated, we missed the intimate personal friendship we had experienced in the West, especially in Holland. We had to accustom ourselves anew with the formalities attached to the various forms of communication, not only with people outside but also within the family. We had to accustom ourselves to the fact that people would never come by and drop in to our house just for a chat. There must always be some reason for paying a visit. In the beginning Astri had difficulty in getting used to the fact that on such visits it would take a considerable length of time, filled with standard small talk and apologies, before the essential subject would come to the fore.

Denpasar

Before our last home leave in 1978, we asked our daughter Surya, who was working in the Sari Pacific Hotel in Jakarta, to purchase a Toyota pick-up for us and to have its body converted into a comfortable Landrover station wagon. It was the first batch of the so-called Kijang pick-ups assembled in Indonesia and one of the cheapest vehicles available at that time. Being designed as working car in the field, it had a light but very strong truck engine and was provided with only the most basic of devices on the dashboard: speedometer, battery guage, temperature gauge, and fuel indicator. We arranged to have the car waiting for us in Jakarta because of our plan to make a sightseeing tour across Java on our last home leave before settling for good in Bali on retirement. When the time came though, we thought that the six-day tour over the partly still unknown and probably very bad roads at the top of Java's mountain ranges might be too strenuous for Astri, so she chose to fly from Jakarta to Denpasar. Madelief, with her husband Salmi, came over from London, and Widur arrived from Holland. They joined Merti and me in our brand-new "Kijang Landrover", while Surya followed us in her own Honda.

It was a most enjoyable and adventurous tour. The journey was very exciting especially for Merti, Madelief, Widur and Salmi, who had never been in Java. Because we chose to drive over the high mountains the temperature was always nice. It was very cold on the Tengger plateau around Mount Bromo, still a very active and smoking volcano. We had to make the visit very early in the morning to enjoy fully the magnificent sight of the rising sun over the breathtaking landscape, with the rugged mouth of the crater gaping in the centre of the vast sea of sand, the bottom of the huge caldera.

Driving into Denpasar for the first time after so many years I felt lost. The town's western outskirts were unrecognizable. Gone were the enchanting green and yellow rice-terraces on either side; they had been replaced by ramshackle shops and buildings set up in a most disorderly manner. The traffic was terrible and the overwhelming numbers of motorbikes compelled me to drive very carefully. All the time I had to fully concentrate on the traffic and before I knew it, we had already passed the Leprosy hospital where we had lived for ten years. We had to pass through the main shopping street which was even more crowded. Many of the buildings had added one or more storeys on top. I was struck by a new phenomenon which indicated that space had become very limited in Denpasar: on top of some of the big buildings people had built their *merajan* (house-temple complex), taking care of course that—in accordance with the Hindu religious concept—the complex is situated on the northeast corner of the flat concrete roof. The sight of house temples in traditional Balinese style on top of cosmopolitan structures of concrete and glass evoked feelings of disturbing disharmony.

The big market in Denpasar was still a far cry from the huge three-storey open building of concrete and cement that it is now. At that time it was a chaotic assembly of hundreds of tents and ramshackle structures of bamboo and thatch with unpaved pathways of stone and mud in between. One always had to struggle one's way through the thick crowd, thereby keeping a sharp eye on one's pocket. Although it was extremely hot and dirty, Astri always enjoyed visiting the market, because it was always full of surprises. On returning after eleven years, one of the first things we noticed was that fruits and other items one bought were no longer wrapped in banana leaves or discarded newspapers, but neatly delivered in plastic bags. I was really astonished one morning when after putting together the different items that we had bought, the shopowner's twelve-year-old daughter took out of her pocket a small calculator and told me after a few seconds what I had to pay!

During our first visits to the market we drew much public attention because of Astri's fair complexion. Because we used to talk in Dutch to each other, people thought that we were tourists and often they made funny remarks about us in Balinese. I pretended not to understand. But sometimes I could not resist reacting and would jokingly respond to their remarks in Balinese. That was of course a great surprise, causing great hilarity especially among the women, young and old. When it happened that among the frivolous crowd someone older recognized me from the 1960s as "the doctor of Balun", people became really excited. Everybody wanted to see us and asked all kinds of questions, and then it took a great effort to free ourselves. In any case, since people remembered us, we often enjoyed privileges, such as discounts without having to bargain and spontaneous help whenever needed. Sometimes we felt our homecoming among the common people with their unrestrained spontaneous behaviour a great deal more enjoyable than the reserved and formal encounters in our own grand family.

Epilogue

When Gedé Djelantik, our eldest brother, went into a coma and the doctors decided not to intervene in the fatal process of his cancer, we held an emergency meeting with the *Bagawanta* (High Priest) and the elders of the Puri in Karangasem. The *Bagawanta* suggested that for Gedé's ascension to the heavens it would be more appropriate to remove him from the hospital and have him die in the Puri. Thus we brought him to Karangasem by ambulance and laid him down in his old Balinese bed, actually the same bed that we had slept in together seventy years ago, and where on his routine evening rounds over the Puri my father used to bend himself for a few minutes over our heads, muttering affectionately his mantras to protect us from evil forces. Being with Gedé again in that same room with the unplastered red-brick floor and looking at the antique bed, a platform of bamboo and wood fixed between four poles of the house, I could not stop my tears welling up in my eyes. I arranged his sheets to make him somewhat more comfortable. Gedé woke up a little. Recognizing me he smiled and wanted to say something but he was too weak. I put a batik *kain* as a blanket over his legs. After making arrangements with the two nurses who were to take care of him, I left the room. I told the crowd of family members and curious bystanders to leave the room also, to stay outside and not to make any noise.

Driving my car to Tirtagangga where Astri was waiting, I wondered how long Gedé would last. I sensed that his smile was one of happiness and confidence and of a very quiet farewell. Indeed, he died that night very peacefully.

Early the next morning we, all the younger brothers, gathered with our High Priest and some elders outside Gedé's room on the upper front porch of the house. We consulted the Balinese calender to decide on the appropriate day of the cremation. Besides the date, a lot of considerations and problems had to be dealt with. The High Priest and most of our family were mainly concerned with the ceremonial aspects of the affair. They thought that the cremation should reflect the royal status of our family, displaying the utmost of grandeur, pomp and circumstance. From my side, knowing the limited resources of our family, the practical, financial and logistical problems were of prime importance. After a long and seemingly endless debate we came at last to a tentative course of action. We had six weeks' time for all the preparations. Being now the eldest in the family, the ultimate responsibility of all family affairs rested on my shoulders. Finally, we reached a workable compromise between the ideal and what was practically possible, and with a sigh of relief I saw my family members leave.

After the meeting, I lingered for a while on the porch, figuring out how to begin the most urgent things, and thinking about the future of the family and all the complicated social and financial obligations to be met. I looked at the dilapidated buildings in what was formerly Mekelé Trena's compound. One of those houses had been assigned to my mother. I looked at it. The small building was still there, in all its modesty, with its bamboo roof and red-brick floor and a narrow side porch, the eave of which was on the point of falling down. In that house I had been born. I found myself dwelling on the past. I saw in my fantasy the long-house bordering on the street on the west side of the compound, where we often smelled the sweet smell of opium to which one of the old women living there was addicted. Mekelé Trena's main building in the middle of the compound had been demolished long ago and in the open space that was left a few flowering trees were now languishing and wilting between untended gravel stones. Marvellously the very old frangipani tree with its capriciously contorted stem and branches stood still there as if waving at me as a faithful relic, hovering over the high verandah of the Balé Malang. It was from that elevation exactly seventy years ago that Gedé had urinated on my head as a test of loyalty. And indeed, under that frangipani the big stone on which I stood to undergo the test, was still there too. Nobody had had the courage to remove the tombstone of the mysterious black monkey!

Completely relaxed, and musing with all these old memories floating through my head, I sat down on the edge of the upper porch when I heard the nurses coming out of Gedé's room. They asked me permission to leave for a while and walked down the stairs next to where I sat. Following their steps with my eyes I realized all of a sudden that my feet were dangling exactly above the spot on the lower porch of the house, where seventy years ago I had retrieved the stray rubber ball from behind my father's back. Nostalgically, I felt again the minutes of agony when his guest, a frighteningly impressive old man, grabbed me and, holding me fast, unsuccessfully tried to draw Father's attention to his discovery: the birthmark between my collar bones.

Glossary of Balinese and Indonesian Terms

alun-alun	town square
arja	Balinese "opera", a dance-drama in which the spoken word is being sung.
balé	a building, which may be one of the buildings in a Balinese compound (but not a kitchen). Balés are named according to function. Outside a family compound, is the *balé banjar*, the community building.
balian	traditional doctor, medicine man, often believed to have magic powers.
banjar	community or clan, neighbourhood. Usually consists of 10 to 200 families.
baris	male warrior dance.
barong landung	traditional performance by a pair of giant puppets, each carried by a performer who is hidden under the puppet's skirt. The two characters represent the male and female elements in Nature, and can be interpreted as symbols of fertility.
batara	deified ancestor.
beleganjur	musical ensemble consisting of between 10 and 20 players, in which each carries only one knobbed gong, producing one tone of the tonal scale, and striking it with a wooden mallet.
blankon	common headdress for daily use usually made of batik cloth, which is already folded and stitched into the required shape.
boreh	paste or liquid (usually herbal) medicine to be applied as a linament over the skin.
Brahma	one of the Trinity, the Creator, in the Hindu religion.
Brahman	member of the highest caste among the Hindus.
Budi Utomo	first Indonesian cultural movement towards independence, which later inspired the creation of political parties.

bupati	head of government of one regency (*kabupaten*) which is part of a province.
caratan	a decanter provided with a long neck through which water is filled, and at the side of the body, a cone-shaped spout out of which the water is poured into the mouth of the drinker. By holding the decanter at its neck and tilting it from a distance while drinking, one's lips will not touch the spout, so the decanter can be passed on to the next person.
cecak	hourse lizards.
celengan	a "piggy-bank" or closed container in the shape of a pig, made of earthenware. On its back it has a slit through which a coin may be inserted (from the word *celeng* (pig).
dharma	the principle of unselfishness, kindness and goodness.
dalang	puppeteer at the shadow play.
Dalem	title for Balinese Kings.
dulang	a low, round table, usually made of wood, with one massive round leg in the middle.
gambuh	classical dance-drama, which originated from the Javanese Middle Ages and was introduced in Bali at about the turn of the century.
gambar hidup	from *gambar* (picture) and *hidup* (alive), meaning "living pictures" or the movies.
gamelan	traditional musical ensemble in Java, Sunda, Bali and other regions of Indonesia, mainly consisting of percussion instruments, drums and gongs.
gandrung	now nearly-extinct folk dance, where a young male dancer in female dress dances and invites people from the audience to dance a duet with him.
gria	compound where a Brahmana (Brahmin) family lives.
guwungan	ball-shaped bamboo basket for keeping fighting cocks.
ilut	a string and twisting pinch.
janger	a popular folk dance performed by two opposing rows of girls and boys, forming together a square, with a dance leader (the *daag*) dancing and directing the group in the middle.
kabupaten	part of a province; under the jurisdiction of a *Bupati*.
kain	loose skirt, consisting of one piece of woven cloth or batik, about 1.5 to 3 yards long.
Kawi	old form of Javanese language.
kebaya	woman's long blouse, with long sleeves, usually made of light material.
kebyar	brilliantly dynamic musical form for Balinese gamelan orchestra which arose in the 1930s.

kebyar duduk	"seated" kebyar dance, in which the dancer crouches and hops.
kechak	male member of a choir: can be part of the *kechak* dance performance or one of the boys in the *janger* ensemble.
kekawin	old Javanese song, poem (taken from the word *kawi*).
kendang	drum in the *gamelan* ensemble; in Bali held by the drummer on his lap; in the Javanese *gamelan*, it is placed on a standard.
kenong	small gong with a knob in the middle on which percussion is made with a mallet.
kepeng	old Chinese round coin of bronze, with a square hole in the middle; now used in Bali as a valuable item in offerings.
Laksmana	younger brother of Rama, in the ancient Hindu epic, the *Ramayana*.
latah	mental disease, whereby the patient cannot help him- or herself imitating another person in word or action.
leluhur	ancestry, particularly pertaining to those who have died a long time ago.
lontar	a kind of palm whose leares are used to form palm-leaf books.
lungsuran	remaining food, or left-overs, left on a plate after a meal, meant to be eaten by another person.
mebebasan	see *pepaosan*.
mepamitan	taking leave from a person of higher rank (on departure).
mepes	gesture of reverence, usually made immediately before the *sembah*. The gesture consists of both hands clasped together with all the fingers crossing each other.
merajan	house-temple.
mustika	hand gesture of meditation: the fisted right hand with its thumb upright is held in the left hand (also with the thumb in an upright position) so that both thumbs form a straight pillar in the middle.
naga	mythological snake, usually with elaborate decoration, such as a crown on its head.
ngibing	to dance at the invitation of the solo dancer in the *joged* dance (where the dancer is a female) or in the *gandrung* dance (where the dancer is a boy).
nyonyah	Indonesian (formerly Malay or Melayu) word denoting a married lady, now meaning "Mrs".
odalan	a six-month's celebration, occurring every 6 x 35 days (210 days).
Pandawas	from the epic *Mahabarata*, the five brothers, sons of Dewi Kunti: Yudistra, Bima, Arjuna, Nakula and Sahadewa.
parekan	palace servant or retainer.

pasepan	small bowl, made of earthernware or copper, used to burn incense during offerings.
pauk	kettledrum, consisting of a hollow hemisphere of brass or copper over which is stretched a skin.
pencak	originally a martial exercise, meant for self-defence. Later developed into a dance preserving the same movements.
pedanda	Brahman priest.
pelaspas	religious inauguration of a house before being occupied.
pelukatan	religious ceremony consisting of prayers and drinking *tirta* (blessed water).
penasar	actor in the Balinese dance-drama, who has the role of servant, clown, translator of the Kawi (old Javanese) into common Balinese (in order that the audience may understand what is going on).
pendopo	large building, open on all sides, used for receptions, gatherings, performances and so on.
pepaosan	a popular literary entertainment in Bali. A singer or declaimer recites before a small audience of literary amateurs, strophes from the ancient epics, and these are then translated by a *penasar*. Anybody from the audience can comment or correct the translation; the whole exercise can last for hours, or even a whole night.
perkutut	dove, loved for its song.
petu	a kind of long-armed monkey.
puri	compound, in which a noble family lives; the compound of a *Brahman* is a *gria*.
puspa	gesture of reverence, same as the *sembah*, especially in prayer.
raksasa	in general, an extraordinarily big person; in mythological stories, associated with evil (also spelled *rhaksasa*).
Rama	figure in the *Ramayana*, elder brother of Laksmana. He is believed to be the incarnation of Wishnu.
sabuk	girdle, waistband.
sanghyang	sacred dance, performed in trance; or, used before a name of a holy person or god, like "saint" in the West.
sedahan	man who functions as a caretaker of a property, usually on behalf of a landowner.
sekehe	an association formed for a specific activity.
sembah	a common gesture of greeting, also of reverence towards somebody who is older or higher in rank, or towards God or the deified ancestors in the temple. The gesture consists of both hands with the palms clasped together and raised in front up to a certain level. As a common gesture of greeting,

it is at the level of the chest; as reverence towards a higher person, it is at the level of the chin; in the temple it is with the hands raised above the head.

sumbul   act of blowing a liquid (which is prepared by chewing a herb while mixing it with enough saliva in the mouth until the mixture has the proper fluidity) over the sick parts of the body of a patient. It was common practice of traditional healers in the past.

sirih   betel, an east Indian pepper plant. The leaves are chewed as a stimulant.

Siwa   one of the Trinity in the Hindu religion, the Destroyer.

suci   unspoiled, clean; or, sacred; or, pure, sincere.

Sudra   the fourth (and lowest) caste in the Hindu caste system.

tahu   tofu (soybean curd).

teba   wild garden near a dwelling often where domestic livestock is kept.

terbana   percussion instrument, a flat drum, open at one side.

tingklik   bamboo xylophone.

tirta   holy water.

topeng   mask; mask dance; dance-drama with masked actors.

totok   genuine, pure, not of mixed race.

tuak   palm wine.

tuan   "Mr".

tumpek   denotes a day that occurs every 35 days: when Saturday (last day of the 7-day week) falls together with Kliwon (last day of the 5-day week).

udeng   common headdress, consisting of a square piece of cloth, bound around the head.

undagi   traditional architect in Bali.

waringan   banyan tree.

waru   tree hibiscus.

warung   stall, usually selling drinks (such as coffee) and some food.

wayang (kulit)   puppet shadow play.

wayang wong   traditional dance-drama, especially enacting stories from the *Ramayana*.

Wisnu   one of the Trinity in the Hindu religion, which consists of Brahma the Creator, Shiva the Destroyer and Wishnu the Maintainer or Preserver. For the Balinese. they are the manifestations of the One and Almighty God, referred to as Ida Sanghyang Widi.